Front cover photograph © George Adams Jones.

Library of Congress Cataloging-in-Publication Data

Corwin, Edward Samuel, 1878-1963.
  Corwin & Peltason's understanding the constitution.

  Bibliography: p.
  Includes index.
  1. United States — Constitution.   2. United States —
Constitutional law.   I. Peltason, J. W. (Jack Walter),
1923-   . II. Title   III. Title: Corwin and
Peltason's understanding the constitution.   IV. Title:
Understanding the constitution.
KF4528.C67   1988   342.73   88-3080
ISBN 0-03-022933-2   347.302

Request for permission to make copies of any part of the work should be mailed to:
Copyrights and Permissions Department
Holt, Rinehart and Winston, Inc.
Orlando, Florida 32887.

9 0 1   118   9 8 7 6 5 4 3

Holt, Rinehart and Winston, Inc.
The Dryden Press
Saunders College Publishing

CORWIN & PELTASON'S

Understanding the Constitution

Eleventh Edition

J. W. Peltason
University of California, Irvine

Holt, Rinehart and Winston, Inc.
Fort Worth   Chicago   San Francisco
Philadelphia   Montreal   Toronto
London   Sydney   Tokyo

CORWIN & PELTASON'S

Understanding
the
Constitution

To Suzanne

It is not enough, however, to celebrate the Constitution. We must also — or at least a considerable number of us should — cerebrate about it. We need to understand that, important as it is to see the forest, the forest is made up of trees, and unless somebody tends them, there will be no forest to be seen. That is one of the purposes of this volume: to go beyond the generalities and find out about the major constitutional issues of our time.

The Constitution of the United States, the supreme law of the land, is by no means self-explanatory. In an attempt to make it understandable, this book sets forth the main features of the Constitution and the practical significance of its most important provisions as they are construed and applied today. Attention is given also to the immediate historical origins of the Constitution and its basic principles. The central core of the Declaration of Independence and of each Article of the Constitution are discussed section by section, amplified, and interpreted in nontechnical terms. Because the constitutional system — the fundamental rules by which government power is organized and limited — includes, in addition to the documentary Constitution, basic practices and customs that we have developed during the last 200 years, those elements of our government are also discussed. In addition, there is a brief essay pointing out the hallmarks of our constitutional system: federalism, separation of powers, and judicial review.

This revision covers all relevant decisions of the Supreme Court through July 1987. An attempt has been made to avoid excessive detail and overelaborate citations. The absence of extensive documentation and the attempt to simplify may give an impression of dogmatism that I should here like to disavow. The author is well aware that there is no such thing as "the interpretation" of the Constitution; the reader is warned that others would find different meaning in the words of the Constitution and in the opinions of the judges who interpret it.

On April 29, 1963, all who revere the Constitution of the United States suffered a major loss with the death of Professor Edward S. Corwin. I think it may be said without exaggeration that "the General," as he was affectionately known by his thousands of students, knew more about the Constitution of the United States than any person who ever lived. Those of us who had the privilege of studying under him know that Chief Justice Hughes was in error when he said that the Constitution is what the judges say it is. We know that the Constitution is what Corwin said it is.

Professor Corwin combined his comprehensive knowledge about the Constitution with wisdom and powerful analytical skills so that his major works, many of which were written almost a half century ago, are still as fresh and important today as when he wrote them. This volume was among the least of his books. Although many of the views expressed and the words used are those of Professor Corwin, retained from earlier editions, the responsibility for this revision is mine. It is more than the usual cliché, however, for me to acknowledge that its merits are attributable to the teacher; its errors to his student.

I wish to thank Prentice-Hall, Inc., for permission to quote occasional sentences from previous publications.

Over the decades I have received helpful comments from many who have used or taught from *Understanding the Constitution*. For this edition, I am especially grateful to Professor Gregory Von Lehman, Georgia Southwestern College; Professor Theodore Davis, University of Mississippi, Main Campus; and Professor Gayle R. Avant, Baylor University.

To Ann Colowick, who takes editing most seriously and is most competent, I offer thanks for her insights and corrections. Paula Cousin, project editor at Holt, Rinehart, and Winston, kept the manuscript flying all over the country and still managed to get it all together in the right place and at the right time.

Kathy North, a word processor without peer, worked her magic in producing the manuscript. For this I thank her, as well as for all the other ways in which she has provided kind and capable support over the last several years.

Harriett Speegle has served as my research assistant, checking, double checking, providing materials, and going over manuscripts and books. I have come increasingly to rely on her judgments, and I wish to thank her for all of her help.

I am especially indebted to Professor Stephen Wasby of the State University of New York at Albany. He is an outstanding critic with an authoritative knowledge of our Constitution and the work of our courts. He patiently went through the manuscript during its several drafts, brought to my attention errors of fact and interpretation, and suggested many ways to make the presentation of the materials more coherent and useful.

JWP

Irvine, California
January 1988

A Note on Case Citations

The number of cases mentioned in the text has been kept to a minimum. It is more important for most people to know what the Supreme Court has said about what the Constitution means and to have some feeling for the issues involved than to know the names of the cases. Nevertheless, there are some cases of such significance that knowledge of them is part of a liberal education; still others are cited in footnotes for those who wish to inquire further.

Cases decided by the Supreme Court before 1875 are cited by the name of the court reporter. Thus, the citation *McCulloch* v *Maryland*, 4 Wheaton 315 (1819), means that this case can be located in volume 4 of *Wheaton's Reports of cases argued and adjudged in the Supreme Court of the United States*, on page 315, and that the case was decided in 1819. Cases after 1875 are cited by the volume number of *United States Reports*, a publication of the Government Printing Office that records the cases adjudged in the Supreme Court. Thus, the case *United States* v *Nixon*, cited 418 US 683 (1974), is found in volume 418 of *United States Reports*, beginning on page 683, and was decided in 1974.

For the special use of lawyers and scholars, commercial publishers make Supreme Court opinions available more quickly than does the United States Government Printing Office (GPO); now even the GPO's Preliminary Prints are not available until several years after a decision has been handed down. For this reason, cases decided in more recent years will be cited, for example, *Edwards* v *Aguillard*, 96 L Ed 2d 510 (1987), meaning that this case can be found on page 510 of volume 96 of *United States Supreme Court Reports, Lawyers' Edition*, second series, published by the Lawyers Co-operative Publishing Company, and that it was decided in 1987.

I call special attention to the comprehensive annotation of the Constitution published by the Library of Congress. A complete revision is scheduled every ten years, but a cumulative supplement to keep the volume current is available every two years. *The Constitution of the United States: Analysis and Interpretation* is available from the United States Government Printing Office in Washington, D.C. This monumental work builds on the first edition, published in 1952 under the editorship of Professor Corwin.

Contents

Background of
the Constitution

THE CONSTITUTION can best be understood within the historical situations in which it was written and has been applied. By placing the Constitution in the context of history, we learn of the conditions and conflicts that produced it and that continue to give it meaning. This book therefore begins with a brief consideration of the Declaration of Independence and the Articles of Confederation, the two most important documents affecting the background of the Constitution.

The Declaration of Independence is the first formal American state paper. It is not judicially enforceable, and it establishes no legal rights or duties. But the Declaration has had a decisive effect on the development of our governmental system. It sets forth the ideals and reflects the standards of what might be called the American creed. This creed, with its stress on the rights of people, equality under the law, limited government, and government by consent of the governed, infuses the structures and practices of the Constitution. The Declaration of Independence remains the American conscience, a constant challenge to those who would subvert our democratic processes or deny persons their inalienable rights.

THE DECLARATION OF INDEPENDENCE

In Congress, July 4, 1776 THE UNANIMOUS DECLARATION of the thirteen UNITED STATES OF AMERICA

This was the first time that "the United States of America" was officially used. Previous practice had been to refer to the "United Colonies."[1]

We celebrate our independence on the anniversary of the day it was proclaimed. The proclamation, however, had been approved by the Second Continental Congress two days before, when it adopted by a narrow vote Richard Henry Lee's resolution "to declare the United Colonies free and independent states." Thomas Jefferson, John Adams, Benjamin Franklin, Roger Sherman, and Robert R. Livingston were appointed to draft a declaration to accompany that resolution of independence, but it was Jefferson who did most of the work.

Jefferson had the task of rallying both American and world sentiment to the cause

1

of independence. As he later wrote, "Neither aiming at originality of principles or sentiments, nor yet copied from any particular and previous writing, it was intended to be an expression of the American Mind."[2] Jefferson drew on precedents that were known to all educated Englishmen and Americans, especially on John Locke's often-quoted *Second Treatise of Civil Government*, written in 1689. That volume was thought to be an authoritative pronouncement of established principles. Locke's ideas provided ready arguments for the American cause, and their use for that purpose was especially embarrassing to an English government whose own authority was based on them.

The Preamble

When in the Course of human events, it becomes necessary for one people to dissolve the political bands which have connected them with another,

---

One of the points at issue between the colonists and the English government was whether Americans and English were one people or two. Here the Americans asserted that they formed a separate entity, previously connected with the English people but not an integral part of them.

---

and to assume among the powers of the earth, the separate and equal station to which the Laws of Nature and of Nature's God entitle them,

---

Equality of sovereign nations was stated as a requirement of the law of nature; today it is part of what is called international law.

---

a decent respect to the opinions of mankind requires that they should declare the causes which impel them to the separation.

The favorable opinion of mankind was a military necessity. The demand for independence was slow in developing, and many Americans continued to hope for reconciliation with the mother country even as late as the summer of 1776. As long as the revolution remained a purely internal quarrel between England and her colonies, foreign governments were reluctant to give military assistance, and assistance was desperately needed if the Americans were to make successful their revolutionary acts. The French were especially anxious to support any move that would weaken English power, but they first wanted assurances that the Americans meant business. The Declaration of Independence notified the world that the Americans were serious, and it was both an appeal to the conscience of mankind and a call for military help.

The American Philosophy of Government

We hold these truths to be self-evident, that all men are created equal, that they are endowed by their Creator with certain unalienable Rights, that among these are Life, Liberty, and the pursuit of Happiness.

These ringing words introduced the American philosophy of self-government. About six weeks before, Virginia had adopted a constitution that contained the first American bill of rights. In it the same concepts that are found in the Declaration were stated as follows: "That all men are by nature equally free and independent, and have certain inherent rights, of which, when they enter into a state of society, they cannot by any compact deprive or divest their posterity; namely, the enjoyment of life and liberty, with the means of acquiring and possessing property, and pursuing and obtaining happiness and safety."

It did not necessarily follow that independence from England would lead to republican institutions in the United States. It is, therefore, highly significant that the Americans based their revolutionary acts on constitutional principles. The revolution was not justified so that one group of Americans could impose their will on other Americans free of English control, but so that Americans could govern themselves. The Declaration is not just a declaration of independence; it is also a defense of free government.

Many have scoffed at the assertion that all are created equal. They argue that such a statement flies in the face of the obvious facts that some have brains, talent, or virtue and others do not. The Declaration, however, does not assert that people are equal in all things. It proclaims that people are equally endowed with certain inalienable rights, among these being a right to their own lives, liberties, and pursuits of happiness. These are a person's birthrights; they are not secured by an act of governmental grace or received as a gift from others. As John Adams, a member of the drafting committee that wrote the Declaration, and a believer in equal rights but not in natural equality, wrote in 1814,

That all men are born to equal rights is true. Every being has a right to his own, as clear, as moral, as sacred, as any other being has. This is as indubitable as a moral government in the universe. But to teach that all men are born with equal powers and faculties, to equal influence in society, to equal property and advantages through life, is as gross a fraud, as glaring an imposition on the credulity of the people, as ever was practiced by the monks, by Druids, by Brahmins, by priests of the immortal Lama, or by the self-styled philosophers of the French Revolution.[3]

In 1776, people spoke of inalienable or natural rights; today, we speak of human rights, the rights that distinguish men and women from the other creatures that inhabit the earth. These truths that were self-evident to the men of 1776 underlie the culture and civilization of the free world.

How inalienable are inalienable rights? Such rights may be forfeited by wrongdoing. The government may call upon persons to sacrifice their lives and liberty in defense of the nation. But that some should be called to make the sacrifice and others favored arbitrarily, or that the innocent should be made the tools of others' happiness, is contrary to the concept of the equal right of each person to life and liberty.

How is the existence of slavery to be explained in a nation whose leaders proclaimed the doctrine of inalienable rights? The Declaration makes no distinction between black and white; in 1776 most Americans believed that slavery was an evil institution that sooner or later had to be abolished. In his original draft, Jefferson blamed the Crown for the establishment of slavery in the United States and condemned the King for waging "cruel war against human nature itself, violating its most sacred rights of life & liberty." This clause offended some of the delegates from slaveholding states. In the midst of their crisis, the Americans decided to fight one evil at a time, and Congress deleted that passage to secure united support against England. It was to be another eighty-seven years before the practices of the nation started to conform in this respect to the professions of the Declaration.

That to secure these rights, Governments are instituted among Men, deriving their just powers from the consent of the governed,

---

People create government for the purpose of securing their preexisting natural rights. That the rights come first, that government is created to protect these rights, and that government officials are subject to the natural law were not novel ideas in 1776. These ideas were based on the concepts of a state of nature, a natural law, natural rights, and the social compact. John Locke had written that before the establishment of society, people had lived in a state of nature. Thomas Hobbes, an antidemocratic philosopher, had insisted that in the state of nature, where there was no government to make and enforce laws, people made war on each other and life was "solitary, poore, nasty, brutish and short." But Locke argued that even in a state of nature there was a natural law to govern conduct. This natural law, comprising universal, unvarying principles of right and wrong, was known to people through the use of reason. For example, if an Englishman were to meet a Frenchwoman on an uninhabited and ungoverned island, he would not be free to deprive her of her life, liberty, or property. Should he attempt to do so, he would violate the natural law and could rightly be punished.

Although the state of nature was not, according to Locke, a lawless condition, it was an inconvenient one. Each person had to protect his or her own rights, and there was no agreed-upon judge to settle disputes about the application of the natural law to particular controversies. Realizing this, people decided to make a compact with one another in which each would give to the community the right to create a government equipped to enforce the natural law. Thereby each agreed to abide by the decisions made by the majority and to comply with the laws enacted by the people's representatives, provided the laws did not entrench upon the people's fundamental rights. The power of government was thus limited.

Modern social scientists and historians agree with Aristotle that people are social animals and never lived in a presocial and pregovernmental state of nature. Government, instead of being a consciously created institution, has developed as naturally as the family. But rejecting the belief that government originated through a social compact does not invalidate the belief that men and women are primary and governments are secondary and that governments derive their coercive authority from the consent of the governed. The moral primacy of the individual remains. It is on the philosophical and ethical, rather than the historical, concept of priority of men and women over governments that Americans base their insistence that governments are to be evaluated by their improvement of the well-being and protection of the rights of individuals.

That whenever any Form of Government becomes destructive of these ends, it is the Right of the People to alter or to abolish it, and to institute new Government, laying its foundation on such principles and organizing its powers in such form, as to them shall seem most likely to effect their Safety and Happiness.

In other words, the people may abolish their government whenever it ceases to protect natural rights and becomes destructive of the ends for which it was established. In a free society, where the consent of the governed is regularly expressed through open debate and free elections, it is not likely that revolutionary action will be necessary to alter the foundations of government. The colonists tried first to use constitutional devices to adjust their grievances. Finally, they felt compelled to revolt and, in the eyes of English law, to become traitors.

The doctrine of revolution pronounced in the Declaration is not a legal doctrine; there is no constitutional right to engage in revolutionary conduct. Nor should the doctrine proclaimed by the Declaration be confused with that of those who espouse change by the use of violence. Jefferson did not defend the right of a fraction of the civic community to seize the government and use it to suppress the rights of others. The conservative nature of the revolutionary right asserted is underscored by the next sentence.

Prudence, indeed, will dictate that Governments long established should not be changed for light and transient causes;

Without denying that the people have the right to change government whenever a majority of them think it destructive of their rights, the writers of the Declaration counsel caution.

---

and accordingly all experience hath shown, that mankind are more disposed to suffer, while evils are sufferable, than to right themselves by abolishing the forms to which they are accustomed. But when a long train of abuses and usurpations, pursuing invariably the same Object evinces a design to reduce them under absolute Despotism, it is their right, it is their duty, to throw off such Government, and to provide new Guards for their future security. Such has been the patient sufferance of these Colonies; and such is now the necessity which constrains them to alter their former Systems of Government. The history of the present King of Great Britain is a history of repeated injuries and usurpations, all having in direct object the establishment of an absolute Tyranny over these States.

Charges against the King

The Declaration makes no mention of Parliament. It directs its accusations at the king. The colonists were asserting the constitutional theory that their allegiances were to the Crown, not to Parliament, and that they were bound to England through the king. They were contending that Parliament had no authority over them and had no right to regulate their affairs. This colonial view of the nature of the British Empire eventually triumphed over the eighteenth-century English view that the English Parliament had authority to legislate for all the dominions. (To concentrate the attack on the king was also a good political tactic. Quite a few members of Parliament sympathized with the colonists, and there was no point in unnecessarily alienating them.)

The details of the specific charges leveled by the Declaration against the king are of less significance today than are the other parts of that document. As kings go, especially those ruling in the eighteenth century, George III was not all that bad. It is interesting to note, however, that when it came time to write the Constitution, steps were taken to guard against some of the abuses charged to the king, such steps as making sure a judge's salary and tenure of office did not depend on the will of the president, making the military dependent on and inferior to civil authorities, guaranteeing trial by jury in the jurisdiction in which a criminal offense was alleged to have taken place, and establishing fixed dates for the election of the members of the House of Representatives. The several charges against the king are listed here without additional comment.

To prove this, let Facts be submitted to a candid world.

He has refused his Assent to Laws, the most wholesome and necessary for the public good.

He has forbidden his Governors to pass Laws of immediate and pressing importance, unless suspended in their operation till his Assent should be obtained; and when so suspended, he has utterly neglected to attend to them.

He has refused to pass other Laws for the accommodation of large districts of people, unless those people would relinquish the right of Representation in the Legislature, a right inestimable to them and formidable to tyrants only.

He has called together legislative bodies at places unusual, uncomfortable, and distant from the depository of their public Records, for the sole purpose of fatiguing them into compliance with his measures.

He has dissolved Representative Houses repeatedly, for opposing with manly firmness his invasions on the rights of the people.

He has refused for a long time, after such dissolutions, to cause others to be elected; whereby the Legislative powers, incapable of Annihilation, have returned to the People at large for their exercise; the State remaining in the meantime exposed to all the dangers of invasion from without, and convulsions within.

He has endeavoured to prevent the population of these States; for that purpose obstructing the Laws for Naturalization of Foreigners; refusing to pass others to encourage their migration hither, and raising the conditions of new Appropriations of Lands.

He has obstructed the Administration of Justice, by refusing his Assent to Laws for establishing Judiciary powers.

He has made Judges dependent on his Will alone, for the tenure of their offices, and the amount and payment of their salaries.

He has erected a multitude of New Offices, and sent hither swarms of Officers to harass our people, and eat out their substance.

He has kept among us, in times of peace, Standing Armies, without the Consent of our legislatures.

He has affected to render the Military independent of and superior to the Civil power.

He has combined with others to subject us to a jurisdiction foreign to our constitution, and unacknowledged by our laws; giving his Assent to their Acts of pretended Legislation:

For quartering large bodies of armed troops among us:

For protecting them, by a mock Trial, from punishment for any Murders which they should commit on the Inhabitants of these States:

For cutting off our Trade with all parts of the world:

For imposing Taxes on us without our Consent:

For depriving us in many cases, of the benefits of Trial by Jury:

For transporting us beyond Seas to be tried for pretended offences:

For abolishing the free System of English Laws in a neighbouring Province, establishing therein an Arbitrary government, and enlarging its Boundaries so as to render it at once an example and fit instrument for introducing the same absolute rule into these Colonies:

For taking away our Charters, abolishing our most valuable Laws, and altering fundamentally the Forms of our Governments:

For suspending our own Legislatures, and declaring themselves invested with power to legislate for us in all cases whatsoever.

He has abdicated Government here, by declaring us out of his Protection and waging War against us.

He has plundered our seas, ravaged our Coasts, burnt our towns, and destroyed the lives of our people.

He is at this time transporting large Armies of foreign Mercenaries to compleat the works of death, desolation and tyranny, already begun with circumstances of Cruelty & perfidy scarcely paralleled in the most barbarous ages, and totally unworthy the Head of a civilized nation.

He has constrained our fellow Citizens taken Captive on the high Seas to bear Arms against their Country, to become the executioners of their friends and Brethren, or to fall themselves by their Hands.

He has excited domestic insurrections amongst us, and has endeavoured to bring on the inhabitants of our frontiers, the merciless Indian Savages, whose known rule of warfare, is an undistinguished destruction of all ages, sexes and conditions.

In every stage of these Oppressions We have Petitioned for Redress in the most humble terms: Our repeated Petitions have been answered only by repeated injury. A Prince, whose character is thus marked by every act which may define a Tyrant, is unfit to be the ruler of a free people.

Nor have We been wanting in attentions to our Brittish brethren. We have warned them from time to time of attempts by their legislature to extend an unwarrantable jurisdiction over us. We have reminded them of the circumstances of our emigration and settlement here. We have appealed to their native justice and magnanimity, and we have conjured them by the ties of our common kindred to disavow these usurpations, which, would inevitably interrupt our connections and correspondence. They too have been deaf to the voice of justice and of consanguinity. We must, therefore, acquiesce in the necessity, which denounces our Separation, and hold them, as we hold the rest of mankind, Enemies in War, in Peace Friends.

Conclusion

We, THEREFORE, THE REPRESENTATIVES OF THE UNITED STATES OF AMER-
ICA, in General Congress, Assembled, appealing to the Supreme Judge of the world
for the rectitude of our intentions, do, in the Name, and by Authority of the good
People of these Colonies, solemnly publish and declare, That these United Colonies
are, and of Right ought to be FREE AND INDEPENDENT STATES; that they are
Absolved from all Allegiance to the British Crown, and that all political connection
between them and the State of Great Britain, is and ought to be totally dissolved; and
that as Free and Independent States, they have full Power to levy War, conclude
Peace, contract Alliances, establish Commerce, and to do all other Acts and Things
which Independent States may of right do. And for the support of this Declaration,
with a firm reliance on the protection of Divine Providence, we mutually pledge to
each other our Lives, our Fortunes and our sacred Honor.

Did the Americans declare independence on behalf of the United States or on
behalf of each of the thirteen sovereign states? The language is ambiguous. In later
years the question became important as arguments arose about the nature of the
federal system and, especially, about the source of the national government's authority
in the field of external affairs.

The Supreme Court has taken the view that in 1776 all powers in the field of foreign
affairs passed from the English Crown to the United States and that the states never
had power to make war and peace or to deal as sovereign nations with other governments. Other Americans have insisted that the separate colonies declared their independence and that all powers of the Crown passed to each state. Those states, it is
argued, in turn created the central government, first by informal acquiescence and
then more formally in the Articles of Confederation and the Constitution. Whatever
the original intent, the first of these two views was supported by the North's victory in
the Civil War, the growth of national sentiment, and the sanction of the Supreme
Court.

The men who signed the Declaration of Independence probably gave little thought
to the matter; they had more immediate problems to solve. With full recognition of
the gravity of their acts, they pledged their lives, their fortunes, and their sacred honor.
John Hancock of Massachusetts, president of the Continental Congress, was the first
to so pledge, with his famous bold signature.

THE ARTICLES OF CONFEDERATION

Although the Second Continental Congress, which had assembled in May 1775, had
no formal governmental authority, it raised an army, appointed a commander in chief,
negotiated with foreign nations, coined money, and assumed all powers that, it
claimed, belong to an independent and sovereign nation. However, it seemed desirable to legalize those practices and place Congress's operations on a more formal
basis of authority. Accordingly, even before the Declaration had been proclaimed,
Congress appointed a committee, headed by John Dickinson of Maryland, to draft

articles of union. In 1777 Congress submitted the articles to the state legislatures, but not until March 1781 did all the states approve (Maryland, acting in behalf of the six states with no land claims, held out until the seven states with claims to western lands agreed to cede them to the Union) and our second national government begin to function.

The Articles of Confederation did not materially alter the structure or powers of the government that had been governing the United States — unofficially but effectively — since 1775. They established a league of friendship, a "perpetual Union" of states, resting expressly on state sovereignty. The state legislatures promised to treat each other's citizens without discrimination, to give full faith and credit to each other's legal acts and public proceedings, and to extradite fugitives wanted in another state.

The structure of the central government was quite simple. There was only a single-chamber Congress. There was no executive, although a congressional committee consisting of one delegate from each state managed affairs when Congress was not assembled. There was no judiciary, although Congress acted as a court to resolve disputes among the states.

Each state had one vote in the Congress, and each state legislature selected representatives to cast that vote, paid those representatives, and could recall them at any time. The only restrictions on a state's choice were that it could send no less than two nor more than seven members and that no person could be a delegate for more than three years in six or could serve at the same time as an officer of the United States.

The second article stated, "Each State retains its sovereignty, freedom and independence, and every power, jurisdiction and right, which is not by this confederation expressly delegated to the United States, in Congress assembled." In short, Congress had only those powers that were expressly delegated.

Congress could determine peace and war, send and receive ambassadors, enter into treaties (except that it could not deprive states of the right to tax imports or prohibit exports), apportion prizes taken by United States forces, coin money, fix standards of weights and measures, regulate affairs with Indians not members of any state, establish a postal system, appoint United States military officers above the rank of colonel, and decide certain disputes that might arise among the states. Any action required the approval of at least nine states, and the articles themselves could not be amended without the approval of all thirteen states.

Congress did *not* have the power to collect taxes from individuals, to regulate commerce, or to prohibit the states from coining money. To secure funds, it determined how much each state should pay, but it was up to each state to collect taxes from its citizens and turn the money over to the national treasury. If a state refused to do so, there was little that Congress could do. Likewise, Congress could negotiate treaties with foreign nations, but it had no way of making states comply with the obligation thus assumed. Resembling an international organization composed of sovereign nations rather than a national government, Congress could not impose obligations directly on individuals or enforce its legislation through its own agencies. Enforcement of congressional commands would have required sanctions against the offending states, not against individuals.

TOWARD A MORE PERFECT UNION

In retrospect, it may appear that the Americans lacked vision when they failed to establish a more tightly knit union with a strong central government. Remember, however, that they had just fought a war against centralized authority and that, with communication and transportation so slow, they had good reason to believe that there could be no self-government except through local government.

The accomplishments of the government under the Articles of Confederation should not be overlooked. It successfully concluded the war; it negotiated the Treaty of Paris of 1783, which gave the United States de jure the status of a nation; it established an enduring system for the development of western lands; and it refined the practices of interstate cooperation, which gave Americans experience in handling national problems.

And there were plenty of those. The English refused to withdraw their troops from western lands until the states lived up to their treaty obligations to indemnify British subjects for property confiscated during the war, and Congress was powerless to make either the British or the states comply. The Spanish threatened to close the mouth of the Mississippi to American trade, so foreign commerce via the Gulf of Mexico languished. The Americans, having lost the privileges of membership in the British Empire, were unable to secure their own treaty advantages from other nations, which had no desire to make agreements with a nation that could not enforce its own compliance.

Once the Revolutionary War had ended, the pressure to cooperate was reduced, and the states started to go their own ways. Some printed paper money that was worthless, and some failed to contribute their share of funds to support the central government. Trade barriers were established by some states in an attempt to give their own merchants special privileges. The seaboard states levied taxes on goods going inland. Within states, conflicts between debtors and creditors were often bitter: defaulting debtors resented the harsh laws that caused them to lose their property or go to jail; creditors resented acts that gave debtors more time to pay off debts or permitted them to pay with inflated paper currency.

Attempts were made to amend the articles to give Congress authority to collect taxes and to regulate interstate commerce. In 1781 Congress submitted an amendment to the state legislatures that would have given Congress power to collect taxes; a flaw in the articles was made apparent when the amendment failed because a single state, Rhode Island, refused to agree. Two years later New York vetoed a similar amendment. What could be done?

A relatively small group of important and articulate Americans had been agitating for a more vigorous national government, but general sentiment was against drastic changes. The nationalists had to move carefully. They needed an opportunity to present their proposals to the country. Interstate conferences to discuss navigation and commercial matters gave them such a chance. After successfully negotiating an agreement with Maryland, some nation-minded Virginians proposed that all the states send delegates to Annapolis in September 1786 to discuss the establishment of a uniform system of commerce for the entire nation. But only five states sent commissioners to the Annapolis Convention.

Although disappointed by this apparent lack of interest, Alexander Hamilton of New York and James Madison of Virginia persuaded the delegates who did come to try to salvage something. They adopted a report urging the states to send delegates to another convention to be held the following May in Philadelphia. The report further stated that such delegates should be authorized not only to discuss trade matters, but also to examine the defects of the existing system of government and "to devise such further provisions as shall appear to them necessary to render the constitution of the Federal Government adequate to the exigencies of the Union."

Even before Congress had authorized a convention, several of the state legislatures, following Virginia's lead, selected delegates. They chose distinguished men, thereby notifying the country that the approaching Philadelphia convention was to be taken seriously. Congress gave its consent, after carefully stipulating that the delegates should meet "for the sole and express purpose of revising the Articles of Confederation and reporting to Congress and the several legislatures such alterations and provisions therein as shall, when agreed to in Congress and confirmed by the states, render the federal constitution adequate to the exigencies of Government & the preservation of the Union." Ultimately, all the states except Rhode Island selected delegates.

THE CONSTITUTIONAL CONVENTION

Seventy-four persons were appointed delegates to the Philadelphia convention, and fifty-five attended, but only thirty-nine took a leading part in deliberations. This distinguished group was interested not in mere political speculation but in establishing a government that would work, and they were well equipped for the task. Seven of the delegates had served as governors of their respective states, thirty-nine had served in Congress, and eight had previous experience in constitution making within their own states. Despite this wealth of experience, the convention was composed mainly of young men. The youngest was only twenty-six, six were under thirty-one, and only twelve were over fifty-four. They were men of consequence — merchants, manufacturers, planters, bankers, lawyers. Small farmers and city mechanics were not represented, and the back-country rural areas were greatly underrepresented (but were fairly represented in several of the state ratifying conventions).

Conspicuous by their absence from the convention were Patrick Henry, Samuel Adams, John Adams, John Hancock, Tom Paine, and Thomas Jefferson — the fiery democratic leaders of the Revolution. Henry had been appointed but refused to attend; he was not in favor of revising the Articles of Confederation. "I smelt a rat," he is reported to have remarked. Jefferson and John Adams were abroad, representing the United States in a diplomatic capacity; Paine had returned to England; Hancock and Samuel Adams had not been chosen delegates. Six men stand out as leaders of the convention: George Washington, James Madison, Edmund Randolph, Benjamin Franklin, James Wilson, and Gouverneur Morris — three from Virginia, three from Pennsylvania.

Washington, first citizen of Virginia and of the United States, was unanimously selected to preside over the convention. He had been extremely reluctant to attend and had accepted only when persuaded that his prestige was needed not to ensure the success of the convention, but to insure that it would be held and taken seriously. Although he seldom spoke, his influence was potent both in informal gatherings and in the convention sessions. The universal assumption that he would become the first president under the new government inspired confidence in it.

Madison, only thirty-six at the time, was one of the most learned and informed of the delegates. He had been a member both of the federal Congress and of the Virginia Assembly. Foreseeing the future significance of the convention, Madison always sat in the front of the room, where he could hear all that was said, and he kept a detailed record of the proceedings. Even today, Madison's Notes, although he edited them in the 1820s, almost 40 years after the event, remain our major source of information concerning the convention.

Edmund Randolph, thirty-four, was governor of Virginia and a member of one of Virginia's first families. Although he declined to sign the Constitution, perhaps because he was unsure of its popularity, he later advocated its ratification.

Benjamin Franklin, at eighty-one, was the convention's oldest member. Second only to Washington in the esteem of his countrymen, Franklin had a firm faith in the people. Despite his great age, Franklin played an active role. At critical moments his sagacious and humorous remarks broke the tension and prevented bitterness.

Most of Franklin's speeches were read to the convention by his fellow Pennsylvania delegate James Wilson. This Scottish-born and Scottish-trained lawyer had signed the Declaration of Independence and represented his state in Congress. He was a strong supporter of Madison, and his work on the convention's Committee on Detail, although inconspicuous, was very important.

In sharp contrast to Franklin, Gouverneur Morris, the third Pennsylvania delegate was strongly aristocratic in his sympathies. He was an eloquent and interesting speaker and addressed the convention more often than any other member. Because of his facility with the pen, he was chosen to write the final draft of the Constitution. Years later he began a letter, "The hand that writes this letter wrote the Constitution."

In addition to these six, other prominent delegates included George Mason, Charles Pinckney, Roger Sherman, Alexander Hamilton, and Luther Martin. Hamilton, representing New York, did not play as important a role as one might expect. His influence was nullified to a great extent by his associates from New York, who opposed the Constitution. Hamilton also lost influence through his advocacy of a strong and completely centralized national government. At the opposite extreme from Hamilton was Luther Martin from Maryland, who was an ardent — and fearfully boring — champion of the small states. As soon as it was apparent that his views were in the minority, Martin left the convention and went back to Maryland.

Convention Debates and Procedures

The Virginia delegates, who were anxious to establish a strong central government, took advantage of an eleven-day delay in the opening of the convention — a delay due to the failure of a sufficient number of delegates to appear at the designated opening time — to prepare a series of proposals. They prepared a plan that imparted to the forthcoming debates a general direction that the less nationalistically inclined delegates were never able to reverse. Eventually the Virginia Plan, with modifications, became the Constitution.

Immediately after Washington was chosen to preside and rules of procedures were adopted — of which the rule of secrecy was perhaps the most significant — Randolph introduced Virginia's fifteen resolutions. The Virginia Plan contained some startling proposals. The convention's mandate from Congress, and most of the delegates' instructions from their state legislatures, restricted them to the consideration of amendments to the Articles of Confederation. The Virginians, however, proposed a completely new instrument of government differing fundamentally from those articles. They proposed that a central government be established with power to pass laws and with authority to enforce those laws through its own executive and judicial branches. They proposed that Congress be a bicameral (two-house) legislature in which states would be represented on the basis of wealth or population and that it be given all powers vested in the existing Congress plus the authority "to legislate in all cases in which the separate states are incompetent, or in which the harmony of the United States may be interrupted by the exercise of individual legislation."

For the first two weeks, the convention discussed the Virginia Plan. Delegates from the less populous states were afraid that their interests would be overlooked by a national legislature dominated by representatives from the large states. They favored a less powerful national government with more independence of action by the states. They counterattacked on June 14, when William Paterson of New Jersey introduced nine resolutions — the New Jersey Plan — as an alternative to Virginia's scheme. Except for proposing that Congress be given the power to regulate commerce and levy taxes, the plan would not have significantly altered the Articles of Confederation. All states were to have the same weight in a single-chambered national Congress, a plural executive was to administer the law, and a single national Supreme Court was to supervise the interpretation of national laws by the state courts. Although some of its provisions were incorporated into the Constitution, the New Jersey Plan was ultimately rejected, and the delegates resumed discussion of the Virginia Plan.

As deliberations continued, there were threats of withdrawal as discontent grew among delegates from the small states, and eventually the convention became deadlocked over the crucial issue of representation in the upper house of the proposed Congress. Finally, a committee of eleven, one delegate from each state (remember, Rhode Island had refused to send delegates to the Constitutional Convention, and much of the time New York was unrepresented), was appointed to work out a compromise. Three days later, on July 5, the committee presented its report, known to history as the Connecticut Compromise. The nationalists conceded that each state would have equal representation in the upper house, but only on the condition that money bills originate in the lower chamber. Furthermore, three-fifths of the slave population was to be added to the free population both for determining representation in the lower house and for apportioning direct taxes among the states according to population. Delegates from the less populous states, thus mollified, were then ready to support the establishment of a strong central government.

There remained many differences to be reconciled: questions about suffrage, the structure and authority of federal courts, and the procedures for selecting the president. Yet, on many basic issues the delegates were in general agreement. All supported the idea of a republican form of government, and all agreed that the powers of the national government should be distributed among a legislative branch, an executive branch, and a judicial branch. Without extended debate, it was decided to impose limits on the power of the states to coin money or interfere with the rights of creditors. By the end of summer the delegates had a document to present to the nation.

The framers had not prepared a mere revision of the Articles of Confederation. Instead, ignoring instructions from their state legislatures, they called for an entirely different structure of government. Moreover, contrary to their instructions from Congress and the provisions of the Articles of Confederation, they called for direct submission of their work to a special convention within each state for ratification, rather than submission through Congress to state legislatures. They also asked that the new Constitution go into effect when approved by three-fourths of the states, without the unanimity required by the Articles of Confederation. In summary, the framers called upon the nation to engage in a second American revolution.

Final Day

On September 17, 1787, after four months of debate, the delegates took their seats. General Washington called the meeting to order, and the secretary began to read the final copy of the Constitution. When that was finished, Dr. Franklin rose. Too feeble to speak for himself, the good doctor turned to his fellow delegate James Wilson and asked him to read a speech that he had prepared for the occasion. The delegates stirred in their seats. "Mr. President," said Wilson, his strong voice giving emphasis to the wisdom of one of America's sages,

> I confess that there are several parts of this constitution that I do not at present approve, but I am not sure I shall never approve of them...The older I grow, the more apt I am to doubt my own judgment, and to pay more respect to the judgment of others...On the whole, Sir, I cannot help expressing a wish that every member of the Convention who may still have objections to it, would with me, on this occasion doubt a little of his own infallibility and to make manifest our unanimity, put his name to this instrument.[4]

At the conclusion of his speech, Franklin shrewdly moved that the Constitution be signed by the members in the "following convenient form, viz., 'Done in Convention by the unanimous consent of the States present the 17th of Spr. & c...In Witness whereof we have hereunto subscribed our names.' " This ambiguous form had been drawn up by Gouverneur Morris in order to gain the support of those members who had qualms about giving their approval to the Constitution, but it was introduced by Franklin so that it might have a better chance of success.

The roll was called on Franklin's motion. The results: ten ayes, no nays, and one delegation divided. The motion was approved.

The delegates then moved forward to sign. Only three persons present at this historic meeting refused to place their names on the Constitution. Others who had opposed the general drift of the convention had already left Philadelphia. Madison's Notes tell us that Franklin, the last member to sign,

> looking towards the president's chair, at the back of which a rising sun happened to be painted, observed to a few members near him, that painters had found it difficult to distinguish, in their art, a rising from a setting sun. "I have," said he, "often and often in the course of the session, and the vicissitudes of my hopes and fears as to its issue, looked at that behind the president, without being able to tell whether it was rising or setting; but now, at length, I have the happiness to know that it is a rising, and not a setting sun."

Their work over, the delegates adjourned to the City Tavern to relax and celebrate a job well done.

Ratification Debate

Ratification of the Constitution was not without a bitter struggle within the states, especially in Virginia, Massachusetts, and New York. Both in the campaigns for the election of delegates to the ratifying conventions and in the conventions themselves, the Constitution was subjected to minute and searching debate.

By the end of June 1788, ten states had ratified — one more than was needed. But New York still had not acted, and because of its central geographic location, its approval was essential to the success of the new government. All during the previous winter and spring the debate had been intense. Hamilton, fearful of the outcome, had secured the assistance of James Madison and John Jay to write a series of articles to win over the people of New York. The influence of these articles, known as *The Federalist Papers*, on the outcome of the ratification struggle is sometimes exaggerated, but that they did help bring about the final favorable verdict is without doubt. Written under pressure and for partisan purposes, they nevertheless quickly became the most important contemporary comment on the Constitution. Their penetrating discussion of the basic problems of government and their profound analysis of our constitutional system make them even today America's most outstanding contribution to the literature of political science.

Basic Features of the Constitution

UNDERPINNING THE ENTIRE CONSTITUTION are certain basic features that establish the character of the American system of government: federalism, separation of powers, and judicial review.

FEDERALISM

A federal government is one in which a *constitution* divides governmental power between a central government and one or more subdivisional governments, giving each substantial functions. In contrast, a unitary system is one in which a constitution vests all governmental power in a central government. In a unitary system, the central government *may* delegate authority to local units, but what it gives, it has constitutional authority to take away. In a federal system, the constitution is the source of both central and subdivisional authority. Each unit has a core of power independent of the wishes of those who control the other level of government.

American federalism is only one variant of the many forms of federalism. Examples of other governments that are federal in form and practice are those of Switzerland, Australia, and Canada. In Canada a constitution reserves to the central government powers not given to the provinces. In the United States we do it the other way around, reserving to the states powers not given to the national government.

Federal systems create tension over questions about where authority resides. In the United States we have resolved that tension by tilting toward the supremacy of the national government. Other federal systems, Switzerland, for example, tilt in the other direction.

The Constitutional Basis of American Federalism

1. The Constitution grants certain legislative, executive, and judicial powers to the national government.
2. It reserves to the states powers not granted to the national government.
3. It makes the national government supreme. The Constitution, all laws passed in pursuance thereof, and treaties of the United States are the supreme law of the land. American citizens, most of whom are also state citizens, owe their

16

primary allegiance to the national government; officers of the state governments, of course, owe the same allegiance.

4. The Constitution denies some powers to both national and state governments, some only to the national government, and still others only to the state governments.

Conflicting Interpretations of American Federalism

Throughout our history, political conflicts have generated debates about the nature of nation-state relationships. Can slavery be outlawed in the territories? Does the national government have the power to regulate railroad rates or forbid racial discrimination? Who owns the oil under the seas offshore — the state or the national government? Does the national government have any responsibility to support institutions of higher education? Frequently, groups supporting particular interpretations of the nation-state relationship have switched positions, depending on the immediate issue. As issues and times have changed, so also have the details of the arguments. It is, however, a useful oversimplification to classify the arguments into two broad schools: the states' rights position and the nationalist position.

The states' rights interpretation rests on the basic premise that the Constitution is a compact among the states. The states, it is argued, created the national government and gave it certain limited powers. Any doubt whether a particular function has been given to the national government or reserved to the states should be resolved in favor of the principal parties to the constitutional contract, the states, and against their agent, the national government. Hence, the national government's powers should be construed narrowly and should not be expanded by interpretation. The clause that confers on Congress the power to legislate when "necessary and proper" to carry into execution the powers assigned to the national government (see page 74) confers the authority to legislate only if it is absolutely necessary to effect one of the national government's express powers.

According to the states' rights interpretation, the existence of the national government does not in any way curtail the full use by the states of their reserved powers. However, the existence of the reserved powers of the states does restrict the scope of the national government's granted powers. For example, because the power to regulate agriculture is reserved to the states, the national government may not use its enumerated powers in such a way as to regulate agriculture. The states' rights orientation toward our federal system is suffused with the assumption that state governments are closer to the people and therefore more accurately reflect their wishes than does the national government. The national government has to be watched carefully to make sure that it does not deprive the people of their liberties.

Nationalists, on the other hand, reject the whole idea of the Constitution as a compact among the states and deny that the national government is an agent of the states. Rather, they argue, the Constitution is a supreme law coming from "We the people of the United States." It was the people, not the state governments, who created the national government, and who gave it sufficient power to accomplish the great objectives listed in the Preamble. The national government is not a subordinate of the states. To avoid frustrating the people's intentions, the powers of the national government should be construed liberally. In addition, a liberal construction of the "necessary and proper" clause gives Congress the right to adopt any means convenient and useful to put into effect expressly delegated powers. The national government should not be denied power unless its actions clearly conflict with express constitutional limits or clearly have no constitutional basis.

Nationalists also deny that the reserved powers of the states limit the national government's use of its delegated authority. The national government, for example, may exercise to the full its power to regulate commerce among the states, whether or not such regulation touches on matters otherwise subject to the reserved powers of the states, except perhaps if it substantially interferes with functions "essential to the separate and independent existence of state governments."[1] Furthermore, states may not use their reserved powers — the power to tax, for example — in a way that interferes with programs of the national government. The national government represents all of the people; each state, only a part of the people.

In 1819 the Supreme Court had the first of many occasions to choose between these two interpretations of our federal system, when the great case of *McCulloch* v *Maryland* came before it.[2] Maryland had levied a tax against the Baltimore branch of the Bank of the United States. McCulloch, the cashier, refused to pay the tax, on the ground that a state could not tax an instrumentality of the national government. Maryland's attorneys argued that the national government did not have the power to incorporate a bank in the first place but that if it did have that power, the states had the power to tax the bank.

Chief Justice John Marshall, speaking for the Supreme Court, gave his full support to the nationalist position. Although the power to incorporate a bank is not among the powers expressly delegated, he said, it is a necessary and proper — that is to say, convenient and useful — means of carrying into effect such delegated powers as caring for the property of the United States, regulating currency, and promoting interstate commerce. Marshall wrote, in what is perhaps the most celebrated judicial statement of all time, "Let the end be legitimate, let it be within the scope of the Constitution, and all means which are appropriate, which are plainly adapted to the end, which are not prohibited, but consist with the letter and spirit of the Constitution, are constitutional." Moreover, although the states have the power to tax, they may not tax instruments created by the national government, inasmuch as "the power to tax involves the power to destroy."

The nationalist interpretation has been supported also with varying emphases, by Abraham Lincoln, Theodore Roosevelt, and Franklin Roosevelt and, throughout most of our history, by the Supreme Court. However, notwithstanding *McCulloch* v *Maryland*, many have continued to champion the states' rights interpretation. Chief Justice Roger B. Taney (Marshall's immediate successor), for example, was an advocate of *dual federalism*, the position that the national and state governments are equal sovereigns, each with its own sphere of supremacy; John C. Calhoun believed in the doctrine of concurrent majorities, a view that would effectively give states a veto over the actions of the national government. A Supreme Court majority in the 1920s espoused dual federalism. Most recently, President Ronald Reagan has espoused the view that the national government's responsibilities should be narrowly construed.

Classification of National Powers

By Constitutional Source

1. *Enumerated powers* are those that the Constitution expressly grants — for example, the power to raise and support armies and navies.

2. *Implied powers* are those that may be inferred from power expressly granted — for example, the power to operate an air force or the power to draft, from the express power to raise armies and navies.

3. *Resulting powers* are those that result when several enumerated powers are added together. For example, the authority to make paper money legal tender for the payment of debts results from adding together the enumerated powers to coin money, to regulate commerce among the several states, and to borrow money.

4. *Inherent powers* are those powers in the field of foreign affairs that, the Supreme Court has declared, do not depend on constitutional grants but grow out of the very existence of the national government. These powers — for example, to discover and occupy territory, to make treaties with other nations, to send and receive representatives — are powers that the national government would have even if the Constitution were silent, because they are powers that all nations have under international law.

By Relation to State Powers

1. *Exclusive powers* are those that only the national government may exercise — for example, the power to conduct foreign relations or to establish uniform rules of naturalization. In some cases, the Constitution explicitly gives the national government exclusive power or expressly denies states the right to act; in others, the Supreme Court has found that the nature of the national power involved rules out state actions.

2. *Concurrent powers* are those that the national government shares with the states — for example, the power to tax. Whenever action by the national government conflicts with state action, the former prevails.

3. *Expressly forbidden powers* are those the Constitution denies to the national government in relation to state governments. For example, the national government may not tax states' exports. (Remember, here we are describing the limitations on national powers in the context of nation-state relations. There are other limitations on national powers designed to protect civil liberties.)

4. *Implied limitations on national power* are limitations that grow out of the nature of the federal system — created by the Constitution — in which states are integral units. The national government may not use any of its powers — the power to tax, for example — in such a way as to destroy the states or make it impossible for them to govern.

Reserved Powers of the States

The reserved powers of the states may be classified according to the nature and subject of the power.

1. *To tax and to spend.* This power, like all powers reserved to the states, may not be used to place a burden on the national government, to frustrate its activities, or to conflict with national regulations.

2. *To regulate persons and property in order to promote the public welfare.* This power, known as the *police power,* must be exercised in a manner consistent with constitutional limitations, as must all state powers. The Supreme Court, an agency of the national government, makes the determination when a conflict is alleged between a state's exercise of its powers and a national constitutional limitation.

3. *To regulate intrastate (local) commerce* and those aspects of interstate commerce that in the opinion of Congress (or in the case of Congress's silence, in the judgment of the Supreme Court) are appropriate for state regulation.

4. *To take private property.* This power is known as the *power of eminent domain.* Under the Constitution (see page 201), the states, as well as the national government, may take property only for public purposes and must compensate the owners.

5. *To establish a republican form of state and local government.* Subject only to the constitutional requirement that each state is to have a republican form of government (see page 120), each state is free to establish whatever kind of state and local governments it wishes. Moreover, the people of each state, through their own state constitution, may impose limitations on state officials beyond those contained in the national Constitution. They cannot, however, deprive state officials of the responsibilities the Constitution gives them. To illustrate, the power to ratify or reject constitutional amendments is vested by the Constitution, under certain conditions, in state legislatures, and the people of a state cannot take that power from the legislature and vest it in the electorate.

Federalism Today

Speaking precisely and technically, Congress has no general grant of authority to do whatever it thinks necessary and proper to promote the general welfare or to preserve domestic tranquility. But as a result of the emergence of a national economy, the growth of national allegiance, and the existence of a world in which total war could destroy us in a matter of minutes, our constitutional system has evolved to the point where the national government has ample constitutional authority to deal with any national or international problem.

As recently as the Great Depression of the 1930s, constitutional scholars and Supreme Court justices seriously debated whether Congress had the constitutional power to regulate labor, business, education, housing, social security, and welfare. Only decades ago there were constitutional questions about the authority of Congress to legislate against racial discrimination. Despite an occasional "flashback" to prior, more restrictive interpretations, nowadays there are only a few subjects that the

Supreme Court might consider to be beyond the scope of national regulation — perhaps the regulation of marriage and divorce. In fact, it is accurate, even if technically incorrect, to make the generalization that Congress has the power to do whatever it believes is necessary and proper to promote the general welfare.

Today the national government is involved with the hospitals in which we are born, the families in which we grow up, the schools we attend, the places we work, the ways we travel, the places we keep our money, and the conditions under which we are buried. In fact, one is hard put to think of anything we do that is not in some way affected by a rule, regulation, or program of the national government.

The principles of federalism no longer impose serious constitutional restraints on the powers of Congress, the president, or the federal courts — most especially not on Congress. As Justice Rehnquist commented, not altogether with approval, "It is illuminating for purposes of reflection, if not for argument, to note that one of the greatest 'fictions' of our federal system is that the Congress exercises only those powers delegated to it, while the remainder are reserved to the States or to the people."[3] (See the Tenth Amendment.) There are significant restraints today on the powers of the national government, but they stem from constitutional provisions designed to protect the liberties of the people rather than from provisions designed to preserve the powers of the individual state governments.

SEPARATION OF POWERS AND CHECKS AND BALANCES

Another basic feature of the Constitution is the distribution of national powers among three departments, which are given constitutional and political independence from one another. The personnel of each branch is chosen by different procedures and holds office for terms that are independent of those of the other branches. It is the independence of the three branches, not just the distribution of functions, that is the central feature of our system of separation of powers. England also has executive, legislative, and judicial branches, but the English government is not established according to the principle of separation of powers, inasmuch as the legislature chooses the prime minister and her cabinet and the executive depends on the legislature both for retention of office and for authority. In the United States, the president's power comes not from Congress but from the Constitution.

The framers of the Constitution feared concentration of powers in a single branch. To them, separation of powers and checks and balances were desirable to prevent official tyranny and, even more important, to prevent a single segment of the population, majority or minority, from gaining complete control of the government. It was hoped that making each branch accountable to different groups would cause a variety of interests to be reflected. Hence, compromises and a balancing of interests would result.

In addition to separate functions and considerable political and constitutional independence, each branch has weapons with which to check the others. The president has a qualified veto over laws enacted by Congress, and the courts interpret the laws, but the president and the Senate select the judges; the president is commander in chief of the armed forces, but Congress provides those forces; and so on. This doctrine of separation of powers is more accurately described as "separated institutions sharing powers."[4] Each department is given a voice in the business of the others, and each is made dependent on the cooperation of the others in order to accomplish its own business. It is through this blending of powers by politically independent branches that the doctrine of checks and balances is made effective.

A blending of duties beyond that specifically authorized by the Constitution is often necessary to accomplish the business of government. This fact has resulted in a considerable straining of the constitutional doctrine that what the Constitution gives to each department, that department should not give away, and that each department should stick to its own function. For example, the Constitution vests the legislative power in Congress, and what the Constitution gives to it, Congress is not supposed to delegate to others. The Supreme Court has recognized, however, that in view of the complexity of the conditions that Congress is called upon to regulate, it is impossible for that body to make all policy decisions. As a result, the Court has approved considerable delegation of discretion. In fact, the Supreme Court has been willing to tolerate so much delegation of policy making to executive agencies that Justices Marshall and Brennan consider obsolete the doctrine against the delegation of legislative power. They have written: "The notion that the Constitution narrowly confines the Congress to delegate authority to administrative agencies, which was briefly in vogue in the 1930s, has been virtually abandoned by the Court for all practical purposes, at least in the absence of delegation creating the danger of overbroad, unauthorized, and arbitrary application of criminal sanctions in the area of constitutionally protected freedoms."[5]

Justices Marshall and Brennan are correct as far as actual declarations of unconstitutionality are concerned. Only in the 1930s and only in two cases was any legislation ever set aside for being an unconstitutional delegation of legislative power. But legislation continues to be challenged on this ground, and as recently as 1974 the Supreme Court narrowly construed an act of Congress that gave independent regulatory agencies the right to levy fees against those they regulate, in order to avoid any suggestion that Congress had given such agencies the power to levy taxes — a power presumably only Congress may exercise.[6] Despite such occasional reminders that Congress should not delegate away its essential legislative powers, the Court continues to sustain legislation delegating considerable policy-making authority to executive agencies.

Indeed, nowadays it is sufficient for Congress to set down a general policy. It may then authorize administrative officials to make rules to carry out the general policy. By so doing, Congress maintains the form of constitutional propriety: it retains its "essential" legislative duties and merely delegates what the Court has labeled "quasi-legislative" power. Thus, the Supreme Court has sustained congressional delegation of authority to the Interstate Commerce Commission to establish "fair and reasonable" interstate railroad rates, to the Federal Trade Commission to make regulations to prevent "unfair methods of competition" in interstate commerce, to the Federal Communications Commission to regulate radio and television in "the public interest, convenience, and necessity," and to the Secretary of Labor to promulgate nationwide standards governing health and safety in the workplace. Congress, however, always retains the power to rescind its delegation or to alter the policies enacted by those to whom it has given quasi-legislative discretion. Furthermore, congressional delegation of legislative authority to private associations or individuals remains unconstitutional.[7]

The doctrine of separation of powers has other corollaries beyond the one that legislative powers are not to be delegated. For example, Congress cannot interfere with executive appointive powers or with the president's responsibilities to execute faithfully the laws of the United States or with the president's power to remove executive officials. Until recent years, these corollaries were more likely to be discussed in political science classes than to be the basis of judicial decisions. But during the last decade or so, the Court has given new life to the doctrine of separation of powers. It set aside the long-established practice by Congress of delegating power subject to a legislative veto (see pages 54 — 55).[8] It warned Congress, although it sustained the practice in the particular instance considered, that Congress should not go too far in giving administrative agencies responsibility to deal with matters historically within the province of courts (see page 105).[9] It declared unconstitutional a provision of the Federal Election Campaign Act of 1974 for interfering with presidential appointing powers (see page 97).[10] The Court set aside a provision of the Gramm-Rudman Act that had assigned an executive responsibility to the comptroller general, an officer removable by Congress. The act's provisions, said the Court, by giving the comptroller general, not the president, the ultimate authority in determining how to execute the budget laws, violated the Constitution's command that Congress play no direct role in the execution of laws.[11] The doctrine of executive privilege, another corollary of the separation of powers doctrine, is discussed on page 85.

With President Nixon's resignation came litigation that resulted in an extended Supreme Court essay on the doctrine of separation of powers. Congress, acting quickly to prevent former President Nixon from taking custody of his presidential papers (as had every other president), placed the papers under the control of the administrator of the General Services Administration. Nixon challenged the law for, among other things, violating the doctrine of separation of powers. He argued that Congress had improperly delegated to a subordinate officer of the president the power to decide when and how to disclose presidential materials. Such a delegation, he contended, encroached on the president's powers over his own files and reversed the presumption of confidentiality of such materials. The Court majority, however, rejected Nixon's argument as resting on "an archaic view of separation of powers as requiring three airtight departments of government." Chief Justice Burger, in dissent, wrote, "If separation of powers principles can be so easily evaded, then the constitutional separation is a sham."[12]

The constitutional doctrine of separation of powers has been altered by two constitutional developments: the growth of national political parties and the increased legislative influence of the president. National parties, however, are such loosely organized political instruments that they are often ineffective devices for coordinating governmental action, even when the president and a majority of the Congress belong to the same party. More significant has been the president's expanding role as chief legislator. Today the president is expected to have a legislative program of his own and to use his powers and prestige to secure its adoption by Congress. The growth of presidential leadership has brought the legislative and executive branches into closer relationship than many of the Founding Fathers anticipated, and undoubtedly many of them would be surprised to discover that the president has been able to take over so many, and such important, legislative responsibilities. At the same time, the traditional independence of Congress has remained intact, as the president is frequently compelled to deal with legislators whose political security is greater than his own.

Separation of powers is of special importance in the case of the federal judiciary's independence. Both the mores of our politics and the design of the Constitution give judges a large measure of independence. The Founding Fathers took special precautions to isolate the judiciary from executive and legislative influence. They did not wish the judges to be subject to executive dominance, because they remembered how certain English kings had used judges to punish enemies and reward friends. They were also afraid that there might be times when Congress and the president might respond to political and social convulsions and act hastily and oppressively. The judges, it was hoped, with their independence and political security, would be more likely to withstand transitory gusts of popular passion and to take a more detached and long-range view. The relative independence of the judges from political influences takes on additional significance because they have the important power of judicial review.

JUDICIAL REVIEW AND JUDICIAL POWER

Judicial review is the authority of judges to interpret the Constitution and to refuse to enforce measures that, in their opinion, are in conflict with the Constitution; the ultimate authority is that of the justices of the Supreme Court. The study of the American Constitution is therefore in large measure a study of judicial decisions and opinions.

The Constitution does not specifically grant the courts the power to interpret the Constitution, but it furnishes sufficient verbal basis for the power. The first assertion of that power against an act of Congress was made in 1803 in Chief Justice John Marshall's famous opinion in the great case of *Marbury* v *Madison*.[13]

The case arose out of the following situation: The Federalists had lost the election of 1800, but before leaving office they succeeded in creating several new judicial posts. Among these were forty-two positions of justice of the peace for the District of Columbia, to which the retiring Federalist president, John Adams, appointed forty-two Federalists. The Senate confirmed the appointments and the commissions were signed and sealed, but Adams's secretary of state, John Marshall, failed to deliver certain of them. When the new president, Thomas Jefferson, assumed office, he instructed his secretary of state, James Madison, not to deliver seventeen of the commissions, including one for William Marbury.

Marbury decided to take action, and consulting the law, he found that Section 13 of the Judiciary Act of 1789 declared, "The Supreme Court shall have the power to issue writs of mandamus, in cases warranted by the principles and usages of law, to persons holding office, under the authority of the United States." (A writ of mandamus is a court order directing an officer to perform a certain ministerial duty, that is, a nondiscretionary act required by law.) Without further ado, Marbury, through his attorneys, went before the Supreme Court and asked the justices to issue a writ of mandamus to Secretary Madison ordering him to deliver the commission.

The Court, speaking through Marshall, who was now chief justice, held that Section 13 of the Judiciary Act of 1789 was repugnant to Article III, Section 2, of the Constitution, inasmuch as the Constitution itself limited the Supreme Court's original jurisdiction to cases "affecting ambassadors, other public ministers and consuls, and those to which a state is party." Since Marbury fell in none of these categories, the Court declined to take jurisdiction of his case despite the fact that Congress in Section 13 gave such power to the Court.

Where did the Supreme Court derive the authority thus to contradict Congress? Marshall reasoned that the Constitution is law, that it is the duty of courts to interpret the law in order to decide cases in accordance with it, and that therefore the Supreme Court had the authority, and indeed was duty-bound, to interpret the Constitution and of course to prefer it to any other law. He also pointed out that the Constitution enjoins the courts to enforce, as the supreme law of the land, only acts of Congress that are "in pursuance of the Constitution" (Article VI, Section 2). Therefore, the Court must first determine whether a law is in pursuance of the Constitution before it is entitled to enforce it as the "supreme law of the land."

Although the argument sounds plausible, Marshall's logic and the basic political philosophy on which his contentions rest have been continually questioned over the years. To this day, a heated debate rages about whether the consequences of judicial review are favorable or unfavorable to the maintenance of our democratic system. Critics, including several presidents, have argued that the Constitution is supreme law because it emanates from the people. Therefore, the most politically accountable and responsive agencies, Congress and the president — who, like the justices, have also sworn to uphold the Constitution — have a better claim to interpret its meaning than does the least politically accountable agency, the Supreme Court. Also questioned is Marshall's assertion that the Constitution is a law of the same kind and character as ordinary law and that the judges therefore have a superior claim to interpret it. The Constitution, it is argued, is not ordinary law but political law. The Constitution is the prime political document of the nation.

Other facets of Marshall's argument are also attacked. He assumed that Article III and Section 13 were in conflict, but this is not obvious. A perfectly reasonable construction of Article III is that it does not restrict the Supreme Court's original jurisdiction to the types of cases listed. Or the Court could have construed Section 13 as authorizing the Supreme Court to issue writs of mandamus if it had jurisdiction. Moreover, in order to rule Section 13 unconstitutional, Marshall had to ignore several canons of constitutional interpretation; for example, he decided a constitutional issue that was not necessary in order to dispose of the case. Once the Court had concluded that it lacked jurisdiction, it need not have gone on to deal with other issues, such as whether Madison had improperly failed to give Marbury his commission.

Finally, critics of judicial review have not accepted the argument that it is a necessary check on Congress and the president. They argue that Congress and the president are checked by the voters, whereas the only regular check on the judges is their own self-restraint, which seems at times to be lacking.

Most of the criticism of judicial review is directed, it should be noted, against review of acts of Congress, although it is today infrequently exercised adversely to such acts. That there must be a central review of state action by the Supreme Court is generally conceded. As Justice Holmes once put the matter: "I do not think the United States would come to an end if we lost our power to declare an Act of Congress void. I do think the Union would be imperiled if we could not make that declaration as to the laws of the several states."[14]

Restrictions on Judicial Review

John Marshall's successful assertion in *Marbury* v *Madison* that constitutional questions are justiciable — that is, appropriate for judges to decide — has meant that the Supreme Court has played the central (but not exclusive) role in constitutional interpretation. It has also meant that litigation is often as important a means for policy making as is legislation.

As important as litigation is to our policy-making processes, judges do not have a roving commission to make policy or to interpret the Constitution whenever and however they wish. Courts operate within a prescribed setting and are subject to certain limitations. First, they can only decide real legal cases and controversies. Second, individuals are not free, by filing a lawsuit, to invoke judicial power whenever they have a grievance they want the judges to decide. They must have standing and must present the judges with the proper kind of justiciable — that is, nonpolitical — question. The doctrines of standing and justiciability and other doctrines that have grown up around the limitations set on courts — a real case and controversy, mootness, ripeness, political questions — "relate in part, and in different though overlapping ways, to an idea, which is more than an intuition but less than a rigorous and explicit theory, about the constitutional and prudential limits to the powers of an unelected, unrepresentative judiciary in our kind of government."[15]

Three of the limits flowing from the doctrine of separation of powers are of special importance: the standing to sue requirement, the political doctrine limitation, and the canons of judicial interpretation.

Standing to Sue

Before a person, an organization, a corporation, or a group of persons may invoke judicial power, it must have standing, that is, be able to show past injury or immediate, concrete threat to a legal right. A speculative or abstract interest is not sufficient; a mere wish to vindicate one's preferences will not do. Nor is it enough to show a general desire to prevent Congress from acting unconstitutionally or to keep the president from exceeding presidential authority. No matter how qualified an organization may be to evaluate a problem, such qualification does not give it standing to invoke judicial power.[16] The question is "whether the party seeking relief has alleged such a personal stake in the outcome of the controversy as to assure that concrete adverseness which sharpens the presentation of issues upon which the Court so largely depends for illumination of difficult constitutional questions."[17]

In recent years, the Supreme Court and Congress have broadened and "modernized," in a variety of ways, the concept of standing, to permit a wider range of persons to resort to the courts. First, the Court has slightly lowered what was previously an absolute barrier to suits by persons whose only claim to standing is that they are taxpayers who believe a federal appropriation is unconstitutional (see page 58). In addition, "economic interests that at one time would not have conferred standing have been reexamined and found sufficient."[18] Data processing firms were permitted to challenge regulations that allowed banks to compete with them, and tenant farmers were allowed to challenge regulations of the secretary of agriculture that affected their economic status.[19]

Some noneconomic interests have also been recognized. Persons who claimed that damage to the environment limited their enjoyment of nature were granted standing to challenge some regulations of the Interstate Commerce Commission.[20] Black "testers," who were told no housing was available to them when housing was being made available to whites, had standing, even though they did not intend to move, because they were injured by being denied the statutorily created right to truthful housing information. White testers who were told that housing was available had standing, not as testers, but as persons who had been injured by being denied "the right to the important social, professional, business and economic, political and aesthetic benefits of interracial associations that arise from living in integrated communities free from discriminatory housing practices."[21]

One additional exception to the standing rule needs to be mentioned. Under what is known as the *overbreadth doctrine*, the Court has permitted persons whose own conduct may be unprotected by the First Amendment to challenge broadly written laws affecting rights under the First Amendment, most especially those relating to freedom of expression. This exception to the general rule of standing is predicated on the assumption that such a statute's very existence may cause others not before the court to refrain from constitutionally protected expression.[22]

Despite the Court's liberalization, the doctrine of standing retains its validity even in this day, when everybody seems to be rushing to court. Although a developer seeking to build in a suburb would have standing to challenge a zoning ordinance, neither low-income minority persons nor taxpayers living in a central city were allowed to challenge zoning laws that they claimed made it difficult for them to move to a suburb.[23] A person who offered no resistance after being stopped by the Los Angeles police, but who was rendered unconscious by a "choke hold," was allowed to sue for damages for that particular incident. However, because it was only speculative that he might be stopped and subjected to the same practice again, he was denied standing to challenge the constitutionality of the practice and to seek an injunction ordering the police not to use such tactics again except in life-threatening situations.[24]

The Court took a similarly restricted view of the doctrine of standing in *Allen* v *Wright*: Some black parents whose children were attending public schools in districts undergoing desegregation alleged that the IRS, by improperly allowing some private schools to retain their tax-exempt status, was making it more difficult to integrate the public schools and that this action of the IRS was thus depriving their children of their constitutional rights to attend integrated public schools.[25] Justice Brennan, who along with Stevens, Marshall, and Blackmun dissented, wrote rather angrily, "Once again, the Court 'uses' standing to slam the courthouse door against plaintiffs who are entitled to full consideration of their claims on the merits."[26]

Clearly, the Court is a long way from the view of Justice Douglas, who would have given standing to trees and other inanimate objects "about to be despoiled, defaced, or invaded by roads and bulldozers."[27] Rather, the Court is more sympathetic to the sentiments expressed by Chief Justice Burger that citizens ought to seek relief through the political process rather than always to rely on the judicial process:

Lack of standing . . . does not impair the right of (a citizen) to assert his views in the political forum or at the polls. Slow, cumbersome, and unresponsive though the traditional electoral process may be thought at times, our system provides for changing members of the political branches when dissatisfied citizens convince a sufficient number of their fellow citizens that elected representatives are delinquent in performing duties committed to them.[28]

Despite Chief Justice Burger's admonition and the Court's slight raising of some barriers to federal courthouse doors, there has been no significant slowdown in recourse to the courts for dealing with political issues. The doctrine of political questions, to which we now turn, is still alive, but the questions considered exclusively political — and thus not suitable for resolution by judges — become fewer and fewer.

The Doctrine of Political Questions

Even if persons have standing to sue, the questions they present to a court must be justiciable, not political, ones. Political questions are those the Constitution clearly directs to the Congress or the president, those that lack judicially discoverable standards for resolution, those that cannot be decided without an initial policy determination of a kind clearly appropriate for nonjudicial discretion, those that would be impossible for a court to handle without expressing lack of respect due the Congress or the president, those that involve an "unusual need" for unquestioning adherence to a policy decision already made (most of the time, if not always, such an "unusual need" arises in the area of foreign affairs), or those that could create embarrassment by leading to conflicting pronouncements by Congress, the president, and the courts.[29] For example, it is for the president to determine which foreign government is to be recognized by the United States, for Congress to determine if a sufficient number of states have ratified a constitutional amendment within a reasonable time to make the ratification effective, for Congress and the president to determine, in case of conflicting claimants, which government of a state is the legitimate one, and for Congress to determine whether states have the republican form of government required by the Constitution.[30] Since the Supreme Court decides which questions are justiciable and which are political, this limitation on the authority of the courts is a self-defined one.

In 1962 the Supreme Court significantly contracted the scope of the doctrine of political questions. Until that time, it had refused to allow federal judges to get involved in the "political thicket" — to use Justice Frankfurter's words of warning — of determining what kinds of legislative districting schemes are constitutional. State courts followed suit. Voters in urban areas who objected to arrangements that gave rural counties a disproportionate number of representatives had no judicial recourse. The only redress available was from the legislatures themselves. Since the legislatures were the product of the allegedly discriminatory district arrangements, and since the rural voters who benefited from the status quo had no desire to alter the existing pattern of representation, appeals by city voters for more equitable representation were ineffective.

In *Baker* v *Carr*, the Supreme Court ruled that schemes for determining the boundaries of legislative districts and for apportioning representatives among these districts raised justiciable questions under the equal protection clause of the Fourteenth Amendment.[31] Since then, the Supreme Court has expanded its ruling to cover the drawing by state legislatures of congressional district boundaries,[32] unit-voting schemes for choosing state officers,[33] and the drawing of districts for local governmental legislative or policy-making units such as county commissions.[34] The Court has held that not only is determining whether legislative districts are properly apportioned in terms of population a justiciable issue, but so are questions about whether electoral schemes improperly dilute the strength of racial minorities.[35] Furthermore, recently the Court has concluded that even the issue of partisan gerrymandering is justiciable.[36] It is hard to imagine a question more centrally located in the "political thicket."

Canons of Judicial Interpretation

Throughout its history, the Supreme Court has developed certain rules of interpretation to guide federal judges. Among the rules — sometimes ignored but generally followed — are these:

1. Do not decide a constitutional issue unless it is absolutely necessary in order to dispose of a case.
2. Whenever there is a choice, interpret a law in such a way as to render it constitutional.
3. If it is necessary to make a constitutional ruling, restrict it as narrowly as possible and do not anticipate or decide issues not immediately before the Court.[37]

Many critics contend that judges pay little attention to these canons, but they are part of the conventions and environment in which judges work.

As a result of the doctrine of political questions, the standing-to-sue requirements, and the restriction of judges' decisions to real cases and controversies, there are some constitutional questions for which there are no judicial answers. The nature of the president's responsibility to formulate legislative programs, the constitutional authority of the president to send arms to other nations or factions — such as the Contras in Nicaragua — without congressional authorization (or even in the face of a prohibition), and the extent of the president's power to abrogate treaties are not the kinds of questions that can readily be raised in the form of a lawsuit. Even those questions that can more readily be formulated as lawsuits are often not brought before the courts for many years, if at all. There was no authoritative judicial interpretation until 1926, for example, of the president's authority to remove executive officers,[38] or until 1969 of each congressional chamber's authority to determine the qualifications of its members,[39] or until 1974 of the prerogative of the president to withhold information,[40] or until 1981 of the question whether Congress had the authority to require a male-only registration for a possible draft.[41] We still lack authoritative Supreme Court interpretations of the extent of the presidential pocket veto.

Members of Congress, presidents, governors, legislators, school boards, sheriffs, police officers, and all public officials have a duty to act constitutionally. Often they have to measure their actions against their own reading of the Constitution, most especially if there is no Supreme Court decision that is relevant. Judges are the authoritative, but not the only, interpreters of the Constitution.

Courts in the Political Process

Courts are deliberately isolated from political battles and partisan conflicts; in a free society, however, they can never, at least not over a period of time, interpret the Constitution in a manner at variance with the desires of most of the people. Judges have the power of neither the sword nor the purse, and in order to make their decisions meaningful, they have to have the support of most of the people most of the time. Whenever judges hand down rulings that arouse the hostility of significant numbers, it is not at all certain that the rulings can be made to stick; sometimes they do not.

Judges, unlike members of Congress and even the president, are not immediately accountable to the electorate. But in time, as judges resign, retire, or die, the president, who is elected by a national majority, nominates and the Senate confirms new judges to fill vacancies. The views of the new judges will probably reflect the demands of contemporary majorities. At times, congressional majorities and the president, and the groups they represent, have been so strongly opposed to certain Supreme Court decisions that they have changed the laws to alter the structure or size or jurisdiction of courts to secure decisions more consistent with their wishes. Time after time, new judges — sometimes even the old ones — have found it necessary to reinterpret the Constitution to adjust it to changing demands. Judges interpret the Constitution, but they, like all other public officials, are servants, not masters, of the electorate.

Failure to recognize that the judges' power is limited may lead some people to believe that the Supreme Court can guarantee, for example, freedom of speech, or can ensure the preservation of our constitutional system. Judges both lead and respond to the values of the nation. But only insofar as they reflect the views of most of the people can they guarantee free speech or preserve republican government. If most of the people are strongly opposed to freedom of speech, the chances that are we shall not have it. If most desire it, the chances are that the Supreme Court will hand down decisions protecting it. In short, the Constitution ultimately is not what the judges say it is but what the people want it to be.[42]

THE POLITICAL PROCESS AND CONSTITUTIONAL DEVELOPMENT

For fifteen eventful years before the 1968 election, the Supreme Court, under Chief Justice Earl Warren, did not hesitate to participate actively in the political process. Among other things, the Supreme Court declared racial segregation in all its forms unconstitutional, enlarged the authority of Congress to legislate against racial discrimination, expanded the protection of the Bill of Rights to apply to actions by state and local officials, expanded protection for speech, limited the authority of states to regulate obscenity, raised higher the wall of separation between church and state, and insisted that legislative bodies be apportioned to reflect equal voting power among voters regardless of where they live.

The Warren Court's involvement in our political life was not unique. The Supreme Court has always been in the center of our major domestic political battles. And since interpretation of the Constitution is in the highest sense a political matter — that is, a choice among conflicting political values — the justices have frequently been attacked by those who differ with their decisions. Until the Warren Court, however, the more usual pattern was for the Supreme Court to reflect conservative views and for the criticism to come from those of liberal persuasion. The Warren Court reflected the attitudes of the less conservative members of our society. Its critics tended to be those who believe that justices should show more restraint about imposing their own values on the society. Those critics charged that the Court had moved too quickly, had opened too wide the opportunities for persons to distribute "offensive" materials, had imposed too many restraints on police and prosecutors, and had forced on the nation the justices' own ideas of how best to establish representative legislative bodies.

In recent decades, conservatives have been trying to bring the federal courts, especially the Supreme Court, "under control." In the 1968 presidential campaign, Nixon promised that if elected, he would fill judicial vacancies with persons who shared his own "strict-constructionist" constitutional views. Once in office, a somewhat unusual combination of circumstances made it possible for him to select four Supreme Court justices during his first term. To replace the retiring Earl Warren, he selected Warren Burger, a judge from the Court of Appeals for the District of Columbia. The Senate rejected his first two choices to replace the resigning Justice Fortas, but finally confirmed his third choice, Harry A. Blackmun, another federal appeals court judge and a close friend of the chief justice. In the fall of 1971 Justice Black and Justice Harlan retired. To replace them, President Nixon nominated Lewis Franklin Powell, Jr., a veteran of private practice and bar leadership from Virginia, and William Hobbs Rehnquist, an Arizonan who had served the Nixon administration in the Department of Justice. In December of 1971, the Senate finally confirmed both appointees, although Justice Rehnquist faced considerable opposition because of his conservative views, especially with respect to civil liberties and civil rights issues.

President Ford was in office too short a time to have much impact on the federal judiciary. However, in November of 1975, illness finally forced Justice Douglas — who many thought was trying to hold on until 1977, when a Democrat might be in the White House — to retire after 35 years of service, the longest of any jurist in our history. President Ford nominated John Paul Stevens, from the Court of Appeals for the Seventh Circuit. Justice Stevens has turned out to be an independent jurist, more likely to vote with the liberal justices than with the Nixon and Reagan appointees.

President Carter was the first full-term president who did not select at least one Supreme Court justice. However, soon after he took office, Congress created 117 new districts and 35 new court of appeals positions, which, along with normal vacancies created by deaths, retirements, and resignations, gave President Carter the unprecedented opportunity to appoint more than 250 federal judges. He selected substantially more blacks and women than had ever been appointed before. These Carter-selected judges — by 1986 still one-third of the appellate judges and one-third of all district court judges — reflecting in general the perspective of the administration that appointed them, have substantially slowed down the drift toward judicial conservatism of the Nixon-Reagan appointees. Until the Reagan appointees began to take over, for a brief time the lower federal courts were more liberal and activist than the Supreme Court.

The Burger Court

The differences between the Warren Court and the Burger Court, although subject to exaggeration, were significant. The Burger Court was slightly more reluctant than was the Warren Court to use judicial power to set aside legislative decisions or to interfere with administrative arrangements, and was more apprehensive about judges' participating actively and openly in the political process. It moved to a less rigorous stance on separation between church and state, was more favorable toward interpretations of the Constitution that strengthen the hands of the police, was less protective of the rights of the accused, and took a less positive stand with respect to affirmative action programs. It gave state governments more leeway in determining how justice should be administered and which movies should be considered obscene.

However, from the perspective of many conservatives, the Burger Court was a revolution that did not come off. It did not reverse outright any of the major initiatives of the Warren Court. It was the Court that issued the decision declaring most state laws against abortion unconstitutional, perhaps the greatest example in recent years of judicial intervention in the political process. In *INS* v *Chadha* (see page 54), it called into constitutional question more acts of Congress than all of its predecessors combined.[43] It approved affirmative action programs in hiring and education, especially those established by Congress.

Ronald Reagan and the Federal Courts

Ronald Reagan made it no secret that one of his highest priorities was to pack the federal courts with Reaganites. He pledged that if elected he would appoint judges who would interpret the Constitution according to the original intent of the framers; that is, he would appoint judges who would be less inclined to set aside criminal convictions, more inclined to allow states to regulate abortions, more likely to permit states greater leeway in introducing religious exercises in the public schools, and more likely to oppose affirmative action programs with race-sensitive remedies and programs.

During Reagan's first term, his only opportunity to select a member of the Supreme Court came with Justice Potter Stewart's retirement. Reagan chose Justice Sandra Day O'Connor. (The year before, perhaps anticipating her appointment, the members of the Court had decided to refer to each other no longer as Mr. Justice, but simply as Justice.) Justice O'Connor, at the time of her appointment, was a member of the Arizona Supreme Court. Although she was a lifelong Republican, the views and values she had expressed were considerably less conservative than those of many other judges nominated by President Reagan.

During his first term, President Reagan also appointed about 180 other federal judges, almost all of whom are white males who share his constitutional views.[44] Although he acted no differently from other presidents, his administration more zealously investigated to assure itself that the men and women he did recommend would, once appointed, make the kind of decisions that would meet with the approval of the president and the approval of those who had elected him.

As President Reagan finished his first term, the Burger Court was split five to four on many important decisions. Chief Justice Burger and Justice Rehnquist held down the conservative end of the Court, with Justice Rehnquist the most articulate and conservative justice. Justice O'Connor frequently voted with them. Justices White, Powell, Blackmun, and Stevens served as the swing votes. Justice White was tending more toward the conservative side, but Justice Blackmun had become more moderate. Justices Brennan and Marshall, often joined by Justice Stevens, represented the diminished liberal wing and became the Court's most frequent dissenters.

The conservatives still did not control the Supreme Court, but they were getting closer. With five of the nine justices seventy-six or older, it appeared unlikely that all of them would be able to remain active for another four years. (If the liberal justices were following the precedent of some previous justices, they were doing their best to hold off retiring or dying until there was a president in the White House congenial to their constitutional views. In the past, many justices have successfully outlived their political opponents. Oliver Wendell Holmes served until he was ninety, Roger Taney and Hugo Black until eighty-five, and another five, including Louis Brandeis, served beyond their eightieth birthdays.)

The Rehnquist Court and Beyond

In the summer of 1986, at the end of the 1985 term, Chief Justice Burger retired. President Reagan quickly nominated Justice Rehnquist to become the chief, and to replace Rehnquist he picked a member of the Court of Appeals for the District of Columbia, Antonin Scalia, a man known both for his wit and for his conservatism. The Senate Judiciary Committee rather easily recommended the confirmation of Justice Scalia but recommended the confirmation of Rehnquist as chief justice only after an exhaustive hearing. The Democratic minority members went into great detail about allegations of improper partisanship by Rehnquist prior to his service on the Court, but it was widely recognized that what was at stake was the question of constitutional views. The Senate confirmed.

The promotion of Rehnquist to the center chair and the appointment of Scalia to replace Burger did not immediately alter the constitutional balance of the Court. What had happened was the appointment of two younger conservatives to fill the posts of two older ones.

In 1986, somewhat unexpectedly, the Democrats regained control of the Senate and of the Judiciary Committee, the committee that processes Senate confirmation of presidential judicial selections. Although the rules of the game call for considerable deference to presidential discretion, the Democrats made clear that they would subject all judicial appointments to careful senatorial scrutiny. The likelihood of senatorial opposition, if any weaknesses in qualification or competence or integrity can be found, has somewhat constrained the Reagan administration to put on the federal bench only those conservative lawyers of the highest qualification.

Then, in July 1987, as the term ended, Justice Powell, who held the swing vote in many five-to-four cases, announced his retirement. President Reagan promptly nominated Judge Robert Bork, from the Court of Appeals for the District of Columbia, a former Yale law professor and a public law scholar known for his outspoken criticism of judicial activism. Bork argued that judges should declare unconstitutional only those laws and regulations that are clearly in violation of the language of the Constitution or contrary to the original intent of its framers. His nomination generated strong opposition from many quarters, most especially from black and women's groups, and led to one of the most exhaustive and divisive confirmation battles in our history. Judge Bork himself was subject to intense questioning about the constitutional views he had espoused in many articles and speeches over the years. The Bork confirmation battles also produced extensive discussions before the Senate Judiciary Committee and on the floor of the Senate about constitutional doctrines and the proper role of courts in our democracy. Finally, in October 1987, the Senate refused to confirm Judge Bork's nomination.

Following the bitter battle over Judge Bork's confirmation, President Reagan nominated another judge from the Court of Appeals of the District of Columbia, Douglas Ginsburg. Judge Ginsburg had also been a law professor but had written only a few articles. He had been on the bench so brief a time that there was less known about his constitutional views. His name was never sent to the Senate, however. He asked that it be withdrawn as the result of the publicity arising from his admission that he had in the past occasionally smoked marijuana.

On the third try President Reagan nominated Judge Anthony Kennedy from the Court of Appeals for the Ninth Circuit, a judge of conservative constitutional views but who has stated them primarily from the bench in his judicial opinions and in a much less challenging manner than had Judge Bork. Although there was rather extended discussion between the nominee and members of the Senate Judiciary Committee about his judicial orientations, a consensus quickly developed about his suitability for the Supreme Court, and he was confirmed without difficulty.

Prediction about the direction of constitutional development is always difficult. It is likely that Justice Kennedy will write opinions like Justice Powell, but how he will vote is less clear. If he votes with Chief Justice Rehnquist or stays to the middle, as did Justice Powell, he will make considerable constitutional difference, for the Supreme Court is closely divided on major constitutional issues.

What the Constitution means and will mean is decided as much by the outcome of elections as by what happens inside the Marble Palace. The process of constitution-making does not stop. Although not too many voters cast their ballots for presidential or senatorial candidates explicitly because of convictions about judicial appointments, the ballot provides the vital link between the electorate and the appointing authorities that help to ensure that what the Supreme Court decides does not vary too often, for too long, or by too much from what most of the people want it to decide.

The Constitution of the United States

THE PREAMBLE

We the People of the United States, in Order to form a more perfect Union, establish Justice, insure domestic Tranquility, provide for the common defence, promote the general Welfare, and secure the Blessings of Liberty to ourselves and our Posterity, do ordain and establish this Constitution for the United States of America.

THE PREAMBLE is the prologue of the Constitution. It proclaims the source of the Constitution's authority and the great ends to be accomplished under the Constitution. It does not, however, by its own terms create any governmental powers or vest any rights in the people.[1]

The phrase "We the People of the United States" is ambiguous. It was not the people collectively who created the Constitution, but the people of each individual state. The states established the voting requirements for delegates to the ratifying conventions, and the states administered the election machinery. It was a vote of the ratifying conventions of nine states, irrespective of the total popular vote in all states, that was essential for ratification. Whatever the historical case, there has since developed a national community of the people of the United States.

From the Preamble we learn that the Constitution claims obedience not simply because it is intrinsically excellent or because its principles have merit, but because it is ordained and established by the people. "The government of the Union," said Chief Justice Marshall, ". . . is emphatically and truly, a government of the people. In form, and in substance, it emanates from them. Its powers are granted by them, and are to be exercised directly on them, and for their benefit."[2] The people are the masters of the Constitution, not the reverse.

ARTICLE I: THE LEGISLATIVE ARTICLE

Section 1

All legislative Powers herein granted shall be vested in a Congress of the United States,

It is significant that, of the three branches of the national government, the legislative branch is mentioned first. The framers of the Constitution desired "a government of laws and not of men,"[3] and they expected Congress, except in time of war or emergency, to be the central and directing organ of the government.

With one very important exception, Congress has no legislative power except those "herein granted" by the Constitution. Powers not granted or powers that cannot reasonably be implied from the granted powers are denied to Congress and reserved to the states (see the Tenth Amendment). By way of contrast, the British Parliament has complete legislative powers over all matters. Today, however, Congress's legislative powers are so liberally construed that this contrast between the unlimited nature of Parliamentary powers and the delegated scope of Congressional powers should not be given too much significance. Nowadays, so long as Congress's actions do not violate specific constitutional rights of individuals or interfere with Constitutional powers delegated by the Constitution to the president or the federal courts, there is little that Congress wants to do that it lacks constitutional authority to do.

Moreover, in addition to those legislative powers delegated to it by the Constitution, Congress has "inherent" powers in the field of international affairs to do whatever any other legislature of any nation may do under international law.[4]

Section 1

[continued] which shall consist of a Senate and House of Representatives.

By granting legislative powers to two distinct branches of Congress, the framers created a *bicameral legislature*, as contrasted with a single chamber, or unicameral, legislature. Of the framers, only Benjamin Franklin favored a single-chamber legislature. The others felt that two chambers were needed so that in one chamber representation might be based on population while in the other representation of the states would be equal. Also, the two chambers would serve as a check on each other and prevent the passage of ill-considered legislation. Bicameralism also conformed to the framers' general belief in balanced government, a government that would represent the interests of all parts of society. The House, it was thought, would reflect the attitudes of the popular or democratic elements, and the Senate would reflect the views of the aristocratic elements.

Section 2

1. The House of Representatives shall be composed of Members chosen every second Year

---

Some of the framers favored annual terms, believing that "where annual terms end, tyranny begins." Others, including Madison, favored a three-year term. The framers compromised on a two-year term.

The bicentennial era has concentrated some attention on constitutional change. Among the proposals receiving some consideration, by a few scholars at least, is a four-year term for members of the House. The advantage, it is argued, is that we would reduce the probability that one party would win the presidential election while another dominated one or both branches of Congress. If Congress were dominated by the party of the president, the presidential election mandate could be readily implemented. Those who oppose such an amendment argue that the present midterm elections provide a desirable check on the popularity of the presidential party. They also contend that if the terms of House members coincided with a presidential election, congressional elections would become so submerged in presidential politics that representatives would be overly subject to presidential influences. The House has several times proposed an amendment to extend the terms of its members to four years; the Senate has refused to concur.

Section 2

1. [continued] by the People of the several States,

In the Great Compromise, the framers agreed that although senators were to be chosen by the state legislatures, representatives were to be elected by the people. In 1963 the Supreme Court, in *Wesberry* v *Sanders*, gave this tenet additional significance by holding that a state legislature is required to establish congressional districts consisting as nearly as practicable of an equal number of people. Said the Court, "One man's vote in congressional election is to be worth as much as another's."[5]

Since then, using this clause and the equal protection clause of the Fourteenth Amendment, the Court has laid down very stringent standards to ensure the application of what is now called "the one-person, one-vote principle": A state legislature, in drawing congressional districts, must justify any variance from precise mathematical equality by showing that it tried in good faith to come as close as possible to absolute mathematical equality. Even minor population deviations are not permissible unless a state can demonstrate that they are absolutely necessary to achieve some legitimate goal, "such as making districts compact, respecting municipal boundaries, preserving the cores of prior districts, avoiding contests between incumbent Representatives."[6] So far no state has been able to justify to the Supreme Court's satisfaction any variance from mathematical equality for congressional districts, even for those legitimate goals. The Supreme Court set aside a New Jersey reapportionment plan in which the difference between the largest district and the smallest was only 0.6984 percent of the population of the average district.[7] However, now that the Court has opened the door for judicial scrutiny to prevent excessive partisan manipulation of districts (see page 28) it may be less stringent about exact population equality.

State legislators are subject to less stringent equal population standards when apportioning their own chambers, as are city councils, county commissions, junior college districts, and other policy-making state and local government units. For such apportionment the standard is not this clause but the equal protection clause of the Fourteenth Amendment. The standard of the equal protection clause allows for the accommodation of other legitimate governmental objectives besides population equality — for example, the keeping together of neighborhoods, cities, and counties.

Section 2

1. [continued] and the Electors in each State shall have the Qualifications requisite for Electors of the most numerous Branch of the State Legislature.

The word *electors* in this paragraph means voters. The clause applies to primary as well as general elections. In the original Constitution, members of the House of Representatives were the only officials of the national government to be chosen directly by the voters. In 1787 the qualifications for voting varied widely from state to state. At the Constitutional Convention, a majority of the delegates believed that suffrage should be limited to those who possessed some kind of property; as they could not agree on the amount or kind of property to require, they finally left it to the individual states to determine the qualifications of voters for representatives.

As long as a state law does not disenfranchise in a national election anyone qualified to vote for the more numerous house of the state legislature, this clause, and its companion in the Seventeenth Amendment, do not require that the qualifications to vote in state elections be the same as those to vote in a national election. The question came up because the Republican Party of Connecticut, in conflict with state law, invited independent voters to vote in its primaries for United States representatives and senators and for statewide officers but not for state legislators. The Supreme Court said that Connecticut could not constitutionally restrict the party's right to open its primaries in this way and that the party's practice did not violate the Constitution.[8]

Although this clause gives states authority to determine qualifications for voting in congressional elections, including primaries, the right to vote in such elections is conferred by the Constitution. Accordingly, the national government may protect the voter in the exercise of this right against either private violence or state discrimination.[9] The clause should be read in conjunction with Section 4 (see page 45), which permits Congress to supersede state regulations for election of members of Congress and presidential electors.

Section 2

2. No person shall be a Representative who shall not have attained to the Age of twenty five Years, and been seven Years a Citizen of the United States, and who shall not, when elected, be an Inhabitant of that State in which he shall be chosen.

In other words, persons who are twenty-five years old or older, who have been citizens of the United States for seven years, and who are citizens of the state they represent are constitutionally eligible for membership in the House of Representatives. The House of Representatives may not add to these constitutional qualifications, nor may the Congress as a whole or any state legislature.[10]

Persons who lack the required age or duration of citizenship at the time of election may nevertheless be admitted to the House (or to the Senate) as soon as they become qualified.

Although the Constitution does not require members of Congress to reside in the districts they represent, politically it is almost essential that they be residents, since the voters normally refuse to elect a nonresident. By way of contrast, members of the British Parliament are often elected to represent districts other than those in which they live. Our insistence upon local residence reflects and supports the prevalent belief that representatives' primary obligation is to their own districts, rather than to the country as a whole.

Section 2

3. Representatives and direct Taxes shall be apportioned among the several States which may be included within the Union, according to their respective Numbers, *which shall be determined by adding to the whole Number of free Persons, including those bound to Service for a Term of Years, and excluding Indians not taxed, three fifths of all other Persons* [emphasis added]. The actual Enumeration shall be made within three Years after the first Meeting of the Congress of the United States, and within every subsequent Term of ten Years, in such Manner as they shall by Law direct. The Number of Representatives shall not exceed one for every thirty Thousand,

---

After each decennial census, Congress apportions representatives among the several states.

Direct taxes are not defined in the Constitution but are generally thought to be limited to taxes on property and a head tax, so much per person. The requirement that direct taxes be apportioned among the states according to population is of little significance today because of the Sixteenth Amendment. Other than income taxes — which the Supreme Court once ruled to be a direct tax[11] — Congress does not levy any such taxes. (See also Article I, Section 9.)

The term "other Persons" meant slaves. Because of the Thirteenth and Fourteenth Amendments, the emphasized words are obsolete.

The term "Indians not taxed" has also been rendered obsolete. States may not, generally speaking, collect income taxes from the income earned by Indians working on reservations, but Indians do pay federal income taxes, and under most circumstances they also pay state and local taxes on activities conducted outside tribal reservations. All Indians today, in one way or another, pay taxes. They are citizens and voters. They are now counted in the census and are included in determining the number of representatives to which each state is entitled in the House of Representatives.

Note that the clause does not talk about citizens, but about free people. All permanent resident aliens, legal or undocumented, are counted by the Bureau of the Census and included in the apportionment.

The restriction placed by this paragraph on the size of the House of Representatives is now meaningless. At the 1980 census, our population (excluding the District of Columbia) was 224,843,423. The constitutional limit would allow 7,495 members (224,843,423 divided by 30,000). Obviously, a chamber that size would be of little value; for many decades Congress has by law limited the number of representatives to 435, approximately one representative for every 517,000 persons counted in 1980.

Congress, after determining the number of representatives to which a state is entitled (it has used the same formula since 1929), has left it primarily up to the state legislatures to divide their respective states into congressional districts, each of which elects one representative. The party in control may carve up the state in such a way that the voters of the opposing party are concentrated in as few districts as possible or are so spread out that they can never win a district. This practice is known as *gerrymandering*. The *Wesberry* requirement (see page 37) that congressional districts be composed, as nearly as practicable, of an equal number of people made gerrymandering a little more difficult but not impossible. Since then, using the equal protection clause, the Court has imposed additional constitutional limits on gerrymandering (see page 245).

The issue of redistricting will come to the fore again after the 1990 census. Census Bureau projections suggest that, beginning with the 1992 elections, New York may lose five representatives, Pennsylvania three, and Illinois, Michigan, and Ohio two each. Florida and Texas will probably gain four new House members, California three, Arizona two, and Georgia, Arkansas, Colorado, Utah, Washington, and Oregon one each.[12] Experts do not agree about these predictions, but whether a state receives new seats, loses some, or keeps the same number, the state legislature will have to redistrict to ensure compliance with the requirement that the districts represent equal populations.

Section 2

3. [continued] but each State shall have at Least one Representative;

After the 1980 census, three states — Alaska, Wyoming, and Vermont — had fewer than 517,000 inhabitants; each, however, was given its constitutional minimum. Delaware, North Dakota, and South Dakota, even though their populations are above the national average for one representative, also have only one representative, since their numbers are not sufficient to win them an additional seat. The situation after the 1990 census is not likely to be different. Because of this requirement, not even the House of Representatives can provide that every person in the United States has equally weighted voting power with every other person; one person in the least populous state has more voting power than a person in a more populous state.

Section 2

3. [continued] and until such enumerations shall be made, the State of New Hampshire shall be entitled to chuse three, Massachusetts eight, Rhode-Island and Providence Plantations one, Connecticut five, New-York six, New Jersey four, Pennsylvania eight, Delaware one, Maryland six, Virginia ten, North Carolina five, South Carolina five, and Georgia three.

This was a temporary provision until a census could be taken to determine the basis of representation. It has no significance today.

Section 2

4. When vacancies happen in the Representation from any State, the Executive Authority thereof shall issue Writs of Election to fill such Vacancies.

The chief significance of this clause is that vacancies in the House of Representatives are not filled by gubernatorial appointment, as are vacancies in the Senate. In many instances, when the next election is less than a year away, governors do not call special elections.

Section 2

5. The House of Representatives shall chuse their speaker and other Officers;

In principle, the Speaker of the House is chosen by the House of Representatives; in fact, the speaker is chosen by the majority party — or, more precisely, by a majority of the majority party. The duties and powers of the speaker and of the other officers are determined by the rules and practices of the House. Curiously enough, the Constitution does not specify that the speaker must be a member of the House. The framers simply assumed that the examples of the British House of Commons and of the state assemblies would be followed.

Section 2

5. [the House] shall have the sole Power of Impeachment.

It is a common error to think that the power to impeach means the power to remove a person from office; in fact, impeachment is only the first step toward removal. The power of impeachment is the power to accuse and to initiate formal charges. The House ordinarily exercises its authority in a two-step process: After an investigation and a report from its Judiciary Committee, the House first considers a resolution of impeachment; if the resolution carries, the House then votes on detailed articles of impeachment. The House has adopted impeachment resolutions against fourteen persons, one of whom then immediately resigned, so articles of impeachment have actually been prepared and voted on only thirteen times. Those involved included one senator, one president, and one Supreme Court justice; the rest were judges in the lower federal courts. Impeachment charges against two other federal judges are pending.

The most celebrated impeachment deliberations were against President Nixon. Although the House Judiciary Committee recommended to the House that it impeach the president, he resigned before the matter was brought to the floor of the House. The House then dropped the matter. It need not have done so, since resignation does not necessarily prevent the House from acting, or the Senate from trying a person impeached by the House, but in every such case resignation has terminated the matter.

Section 3

1. The Senate of the United States shall be composed of two Senators from each state, *chosen by the Legislature thereof*, for six Years; and each Senator shall have one Vote [emphasis added].

The emphasized portion of this paragraph has been superseded by the Seventeenth Amendment. The framers adopted equal representation of all states in the Senate at the insistence of the smaller states, which made it their price for accepting the Constitution. As a result, the 400,000 inhabitants of Alaska have the same number of representatives in the Senate as the 24 million inhabitants of California. On the one hand, the New England states, with 5 percent of the total population, have 12 percent of the

Senate seats, and the mountain states, with only 5 percent of the total population, have 16 percent. On the other hand, the Middle Atlantic states, with 16 percent of the total population, have only 6 percent of the Senate seats; the east north-central states, with 18 percent of the total population, have only 10 percent. These figures account for the disproportionate influence that mining and agricultural interests — especially mining — have sometimes exerted on legislation in the Senate.

Section 3

2. Immediately after they shall be assembled in Consequence of the first Election, they shall be divided as equally as may be into three Classes. The Seats of the Senators of the first Class shall be vacated at the Expiration of the second Year, of the second Class at the Expiration of the fourth Year, and of the third Class at the Expiration of the sixth Year, so that one third may be chosen every second Year;

As a result of this original division of senators into three classes, the Senate is a continuous body. Only one-third of the senators' terms expire at the same time; hence, at least two-thirds of its members at any time have been members of the preceding Congress.

That the Senate is a continuing body, whereas the House is not, sometimes has constitutional significance. The Supreme Court, for example, has pointed out that although a Senate subpoena issued five years earlier is still clearly valid, a subpoena issued by the House at the same time may not be valid, because "the House is not a continuing body" and the subpoena thus comes from a prior Congress.[13]

A contentious question, answered differently by different vice presidents and by different sessions of the Senate, is whether in each new Congress two-thirds of the senators are bound by the Senate rules of the prior Congress, including the rule that an extraordinary majority of the Senate is required to terminate debate. If the Senate is bound, a minority may filibuster (see page 57) attempts by a majority of the senators to alter the rules to make it easier to terminate debate. If the Senate is not so bound, a simple majority of the senators may at the beginning of a new session alter the previous session's rules.

Section 3

2. [continued] and if Vacancies happen by Resignation, or otherwise, during the Recess of the Legislature of any State, the Executive thereof may make temporary Appointments *until the next Meeting of the Legislature, which shall then fill such Vacancies* [emphasis added].

This clause was modified by the Seventeenth Amendment, which provides for the direct election of senators.

Section 3

3. No Person shall be a Senator who shall not have attained to the Age of thirty Years, and been nine Years a Citizen of the United States, and who shall not, when elected, be an Inhabitant of that State for which he shall be chosen.

You have to be a little older (but not necessarily wiser) and have lived in the United States a little longer to be eligible to serve as a senator than to be a member of the House of Representatives.

Section 3

4. The Vice President of the United States shall be President of the Senate, but shall have no Vote, unless they be equally divided.

The vice president has much less control over the Senate than the speaker has over the House. In fact, the vice president seldom presides over the Senate. He is more inclined to do so when the issue before the Senate is controversial and a close vote is expected. The first vice president, John Adams, exercised his casting vote at least twenty times, a record that still stands.

Section 3

5. The Senate shall chuse their other Officers, and also a President *pro tempore*, in the Absence of the Vice President, or when he shall exercise the Office of President of the United States.

The president pro tempore of the Senate is chosen by the majority party. This officer is normally the member of the majority party with the longest continuous service in the Senate. Unlike the vice president, the president pro tempore can, being a senator, vote on any matter before the Senate.

Section 3

6. The Senate shall have the sole Power to try all Impeachments. When sitting for that Purpose, they shall be on Oath or Affirmation.

When the House of Representatives impeaches a federal officer, the officer is tried before the Senate. In 1987, when the Senate tried and convicted Judge Harry Claiborne, Judge Claiborne was allowed to speak to the whole Senate for an hour, but the actual taking of testimony and hearing of witnesses was done by the Senate Judiciary Committee.

Section 3

6. [continued] When the President of the United States is tried, the Chief Justice shall preside: And no Person shall be convicted without the Concurrence of two thirds of the Members Present.

This provision disqualifies the vice president, who might be personally involved because he or she is in the line of presidential succession, from presiding over a trial of the president.

Of those impeached by the House, the Senate has convicted five, all judges of the lower federal courts. Others have resigned before Senate trial. The most celebrated Senate impeachment trials were those of Supreme Court Justice Samuel Chase in 1802 and President Andrew Johnson in 1868. In neither case did the Senate sustain the impeachment charges, although in Johnson's case the vote was only one shy. The recent impeachment hearings of Judge Claiborne before the Senate Judiciary Committee were given wide attention on cable television.

Section 3

7. Judgment in Cases of Impeachment shall not extend further than to removal from Office, and disqualification to hold and enjoy any Office of honor, Trust or Profit under the United States: but the Party convicted shall nevertheless be liable and subject to Indictment, Trial, Judgment and Punishment according to Law.

Despite its ambiguous language, the Constitution has always been construed to make removal from office automatic upon conviction by a two-thirds vote of the Senate. Disqualification, however, is not mandatory. Of its five convictions, the Senate voted for disqualification in only two. In those two cases, disqualification required a simple majority vote. In the most recent instance, in which the Senate voted guilty on the impeachment of Judge Harry Claiborne, they did not vote to disqualify him from any "Office of honor, Trust or Profit under the United States," but his chances of being appointed to such an office do not seem very good. He was sentenced to a prison term for income tax evasion.

This provision clearly says that it is not double jeopardy to subject an officer of the United States both to trial before the Senate on impeachment charges and to trial before the courts on criminal charges.

What of a related issue: May an officer of the United States be brought to trial before being removed from office through impeachment? In the case of judges, the answer is yes. In the case of the vice president, the answer is probably also yes. Vice President Spiro T. Agnew resigned and pleaded no contest to certain criminal charges. In the case of the president, the answer is probably no. The difference is that, whereas the business of government is not seriously jeopardized if one judge is brought to trial or even if the vice president is forced to be on the defense in a criminal court, the entire business of government could be endangered if the president were prosecuted for a crime. Fortunately, only once has the issue involving a president been a serious one. The grand jury investigating the coverup of the Watergate scandals named President Nixon as an unindicted coconspirator. The jury did not indict him, largely in order to avoid the thorny question of whether or not he could be forced to trial while still serving as president.

President Ford's pardon of President Nixon was predicated on the assumption that after leaving the White House, a president may be tried criminally for actions undertaken while he or she was serving as president. No one may sue the president, however, either in or out of office, for damages for any injury the president might have caused. This "absolute presidential immunity from damage liability extends to all acts within the outer perimeter of the President's official responsibility." The Court has suggested very strongly that presidential immunity stems from the Constitution itself. "We consider this immunity," wrote Justice Powell for the Court, "a functionally mandated incident of the President's unique office, rooted in the constitutional tradition of separation of powers and supported by our history."[14] Justice White, speaking for three dissenting justices, responded, "Attaching absolute immunity to the office of the President, rather than to particular activities that the President might perform, places the President above the law. It is a reversion to the old notion that the King can do no wrong." (Judges and prosecutors have this same absolute immunity from civil suits for damages, but judges may be liable for payment of attorneys' fees for persons who have secured injunctions to prevent the judges from depriving persons of their constitutional rights.[15] Cabinet members and presidential assistants have only a qualified or good faith immunity from civil suits for damages.[16])

Section 4

1. The Times, Places and Manner of holding Elections for Senators and Representatives, shall be prescribed in each State by the Legislature thereof;

Subject to congressional revision (see the continuation of this paragraph), this clause confers on the legislature in each state "authority to provide a complete code for congressional elections, not only as to times and places, but in relation to notices, registration, supervision of voting, protection of voters, prevention of fraud and corrupt practices, counting of votes, duties of inspectors and canvassers, and making and publication of election returns; in short, to enact the numerous requirements as to procedure and safeguards which experience shows are necessary in order to enforce the fundamental rights involved."[17]

Section 4

1. [continued] but the Congress may at any time by Law make or alter such Regulations, *except as to the Places of chusing Senators* [emphasis added].

The emphasized portion has been modified by the Seventeenth Amendment.

The paragraph covers primaries and preprimaries in which candidates for the Senate and the House are nominated, if such primaries effectively control the choice or are state-required.[18] Congressional power as to times, places, and manner consequently extends to such primaries.

Congress has established the first Tuesday after the first Monday in November in even-numbered years as the date for the election of representatives, except where other times are prescribed by state constitutions. All states hold these elections on the same day, and all states now elect senators on that same date.

Congress requires that the district rather than the at-large system be used for the election of representatives and that elections be by secret ballot. Also, Congress has placed a limit on contributions to congressional candidates and has adopted extensive regulations to prevent corrupt and fraudulent practices in connection with these elections.

In *Oregon* v *Mitchell* the Supreme Court, by five-to-four vote, ruled that this section authorizes Congress to set aside state age requirements for voting for Congress and for presidential electors, but not for state and local officials.[19] So far as the eighteen-year-old vote is concerned, the Twenty-sixth Amendment settled the issue.

Section 4

2. The Congress shall assemble at least once in every Year, and such Meeting shall be on the first Monday in December, unless they shall by Law appoint a different Day.

The Twentieth Amendment has superseded this paragraph. Congress now convenes in January.

Section 5

1. Each House shall be the Judge of the Elections, Returns and Qualifications of its own Members,

Does this section authorize each chamber to add to the stipulated constitutional qualifications, or does it merely authorize each house to determine if a particular member has those qualifications? Until 1969 both the House and the Senate had adopted the former construction, and on occasion each chamber had denied duly elected persons their seats because they were morally or politically objectionable to a majority of the chamber. For example, in 1900, the House had refused to admit Brigham H. Roberts from Utah because he was a polygamist. That and other precedents, which sprang in the first instance from the practice of the British Parliament and of the early state legislatures, were relied on by the House of Representatives in 1967 when it excluded Adam Clayton Powell, Jr., for alleged misconduct and for being held in contempt by a court for refusing to pay a judgment against him for slander. The speaker ruled that since the question was whether Powell should be excluded rather than whether he should be expelled (see paragraph 2), only a majority was necessary, although in fact the vote on exclusion was passed by more than two-thirds.

Powell and thirteen voters from his district asked the District Court for the District of Columbia for a declaratory judgment that the House had acted unconstitutionally and for an order requiring House officers to pay Powell his salary. Both the District Court and the Court of Appeals dismissed Powell's complaint, stating that the question was a political one and that it would violate the doctrine of separation of powers if judges got involved.

By the time the case was before the Supreme Court, Powell had been reelected and admitted to Congress. Many observers felt that the Court would avoid handling such a politically ticklish issue by holding the question moot or that if it did accept the case, it would rule either that the issue was a political question or that the long historical practice of Congress had settled the construction in favor of allowing each chamber to add to constitutional qualifications. However, the Court ruled that Section 5 merely authorizes the House to determine if its members meet the qualifications prescribed in the Constitution.[20] Since Powell met those qualifications, the House had no power to refuse to admit him to its membership.

Subject only to the limitation that it may not add to the qualifications stipulated by the Constitution, each chamber determines finally which person is entitled to be seated, for example, when there is a challenge to the validity of an election (as on grounds of vote fraud).[21] Each chamber may, if it wishes, refer a disputed matter to the courts, and a state may recount votes in a senatorial or congressional race in the event of a challenge. But neither chamber is bound by a state's verification of the accuracy of returns or a court's decision in an election contest.

Section 5

1. [continued] and a Majority of each [house] shall constitute a Quorum to do business; but a smaller Number may adjourn from day to day, and may be authorized to compel the Attendance of absent Members, in such Manner, and under such Penalties as each House may provide.

2. Each House may determine the Rules of its Proceedings, punish its Members for disorderly Behaviour, and, with the Concurrence of two thirds, expel a Member.

Although it takes only a majority — that is, the majority of a quorum — to prevent a member-elect from being seated, it takes two-thirds of a quorum to expel a member once he or she has been admitted to membership. Since members of Congress are not subject to impeachment, expulsion by their respective chambers is the only way they may be unseated, except, of course, by defeat at the polls.

Section 5

3. Each House shall keep a Journal of its Proceedings, and from time to time publish the same, excepting such Parts as may in their Judgment require Secrecy; and the yeas and Nays of the Members of either House on any question shall, at the Desire of one fifth of those Present, be entered on the Journal.

This requirement is consistent with the belief that in a republic the proceedings of the legislature should be published, except in unusual circumstances.

The journals should not be confused with the *Congressional Record*. The journals are the official record of congressional acts, resolutions, and votes, whereas the *Record* purports to be a report of what is said in each house. In fact, because of the practice of freely allowing members to "revise and extend their remarks," as well as to print articles, speeches, poems, and so on by nonmembers, much appears in the *Congressional Record* that was never said on the floors of Congress.

By the parliamentary device of resolving itself into a Committee of the Whole, the House of Representatives avoids the constitutional necessity of a roll-call vote on the demand of one-fifth of those present.

Section 5

4. Neither House, during the Session of Congress, shall, without the Consent of the other, adjourn for more than three days, nor to any other place than that in which the two Houses shall be sitting.

This clause has little significance. Nowadays, although the two chambers take "recesses," they do not "adjourn," but remain in continuous session. They do this in part to avoid a presidential pocket veto (see page 52). Moreover, there is never any question about holding meetings of the entire House or Senate in any place except the Capitol in Washington, D.C.

Section 6

1. The Senators and Representatives shall receive a Compensation for their Services, to be ascertained by Law, and paid out of the Treasury of the United States.

Although elected by the people of the states, members of Congress must look to the national treasury for their compensation. During the struggle for ratification of the Constitution, many persons objected to this provision because it permits members of Congress to determine their own salaries. In practice, members of Congress have been somewhat reluctant to increase their salaries for fear of public displeasure. When in 1815 Congress abandoned a $6 per diem stipend and voted itself a raise to $1,500 per year, the outcry was so great that nine members resigned and many others were defeated at the polls. In recent decades, Congress has tried without success to decrease the political liability of members of Congress for increasing their own salaries. Congress has provided for a quadrennial review by a top-level commission (the Commission on Executive, Legislative, and Judicial Salaries) of the salaries of cabinet officers, members of Congress, and federal judges. The commission's recommendations are submitted to the president for recommendations which are subsequently submitted to Congress with the report. Each house of Congress must vote on the president's proposal within sixty days, and if both houses approve, the adjustment takes effect with the first pay period after thirty days have elapsed. (*INS* v *Chadha* may call for some alteration in such practices, although the Court, prior to its decision in *Chadha* but as recently as 1980, treated congressional vetoes of salary recommendations as effective.)

Out of fear of giving challengers an issue at the next congressional election, Congress has set aside most proposed increases, not only for itself but for top-level federal civil servants, cabinet officers, and federal judges.

Section 6

1. [continued] They shall in all Cases, except Treason, Felony and Breach of the Peace, be privilege from Arrest, during their Attendance at the Session of their respective Houses, and in going to and returning from the same;

The words "breach of the peace" are construed, not as a particularly defined crime, but as a term covering all criminal offenses. The exemption extends, therefore, only to arrest for civil offenses while engaged in congressional business. With the abolition of imprisonment for civil offenses, this clause lost its significance. As the Supreme Court has emphasized by quoting approvingly from Jefferson, "legislators ought not to stand above the law they create but ought generally to be bound by it as are ordinary persons."[22]

Section 6

1. [continued] and for any Speech or Debate in either House, they shall not be questioned in any other Place.

The protections of the speech and debate clause extend, not only to members, but also to those who are acting as their authorized agents. State legislators obtain no protection from this provision.[23] They may have equivalent protection under their respective state constitutions, before their state courts. Still undecided is whether or not members of Congress can waive their rights under this clause, or even if the Congress could do so.[24]

The speech and debate clause exempts members of Congress from arrest, prosecution, or suit for anything they say on the floor of Congress, in committee, or in committee reports. What they say with respect to these legislative matters cannot be introduced as evidence in any criminal prosecution, nor may there be a judicial inquiry into motives for making a speech related to the legislative process or into why a member has cast a particular vote.[25] The protection extends, however, only to a legislative act that has been performed. A promise to deliver a speech, to vote or solicit others to vote, or to introduce a bill at some future date is not "speech or debate," and matters relating to such conversations may be introduced in trials of members of Congress for bribery or conspiracy to commit bribery.[26]

Nonlegislative functions — issuing news releases, making speeches outside Congress, performing errands for constituents, and keeping voters informed, for example — are not protected by congressional immunity. Thus, although a senator and his assistants could not be compelled to respond to any questions about the senator's introduction in a Senate subcommittee of the famed but classified "Pentagon Papers," the senator had no such immunity from questioning about arrangements he had made for the subsequent publication of those papers by a private publisher or about the way the papers had come into his possession. Introducing materials in a committee is a legislative function; having the materials published by a private publisher is not.[27] Nor did the speech and debate clause protect Senator Proxmire from the threat of standing trial for libel when his staff issued press releases and made telephone calls about his accusations that a scientist had wasted public funds on a project for which the senator granted his famous — or, some would say, infamous — "Golden Fleece Award."[28] (The senator made a settlement.)

House members and their staffs were immune from suit for publishing and distributing to other members of Congress a report that allegedly violated rights of privacy (the report told of the grades and disciplinary problems of named students). But no such immunity protected the superintendent of documents, who distributed the same report to the general public, even though he acted in response to a congressional request. Distribution of a committee report inside Congress is a legislative function; distribution of the same report outside Congress is not.[29]

The speech and debate clause protects a congressman only from being questioned in "any other Place" about speeches and debates, making it quite clear that the clause does not limit the power of each chamber to discipline its own members, for example, for defaming others under a cloak of congressional immunity. This is a power that the chambers understandably have been reluctant to exercise.

Although this clause extends only to members of Congress, the separation of powers principle, as we have noted, confers upon presidents absolute immunity for anything they say or do that has any remote connection with their official responsibilities. In fact, presidents have greater immunity from lawsuits for what they have said and done than do members of Congress. Judges, both federal and state, when acting in their judicial capacities, share this absolute immunity with the president.

Section 6

2. No Senator or Representative shall, during the Time for which he was elected, be appointed to any civil Office under the Authority of the United States, which shall have been created, or the Emoluments whereof shall have been encreased during such time;

The ineligibility clause has resulted in little litigation. A taxpayer tried to challenge Justice Black's appointment to the Supreme Court on the grounds that as a senator he had voted for legislation improving the retirement benefits of members of the federal judiciary. The Court ruled that the taxpayer lacked standing to raise the issue.[30] Justice Black, who served for thirty-four years, died eight days after retiring and never received any benefits of the Retirement Act.

The issue was raised again after President Carter nominated Representative Abner Mikva, a liberal Democrat from Illinois, to the Court of Appeals for the District of Columbia. Some senators challenged Mikva's nomination as a violation of this clause because a judicial pay raise had gone into effect during his term, though after he had resigned his House seat. Shortly after his nomination was confirmed, Congress passed a law granting members of Congress standing to contest such judicial appointments on eligibility grounds. Senator McClure, a conservative Republican from Idaho, raised the challenge in a suit financed by the National Rifle Association. A three-judge district court ruled, however, that despite the law, a senator lacked standing to challenge a nomination confirmed by the entire Senate. The Supreme Court affirmed that ruling without comment.[31]

Section 6

2. [continued] and no person holding any Office under the United States, shall be a Member of either House during his Continuance in Office.

The incompatibility clause, which stems from the doctrine of separation of powers, contrasts sharply with the British system, in which most high executive ministers are also members of Parliament. It makes members ineligible to serve in the executive branch while retaining membership in Congress. It does not, however, prevent the appointment of members of Congress as temporary representatives of the United States at international conferences. Senators have sometimes served temporarily as members of the United States delegation to the United Nations General Assembly.

Does the clause prevent members of Congress from serving in the military reserve forces? Some reservists who opposed our involvement in Vietnam thought so, and as taxpayers and citizens they sought a judicial order to require the Secretary of Defense to strike congressional members from the reserve lists and to declare that service by members of Congress in the reserves is prohibited by the incompatibility clause. The Supreme Court dodged the issue by holding that those who raised the question lacked standing to sue.[32]

Section 7

1. All Bills for raising Revenue shall originate in the House of Representatives; but the Senate may propose or concur with Amendments as on other Bills.

This provision, based on the theory that the House is more directly responsive to the will of the people than is the Senate, was inserted at the insistence of the more populous states, to relate taxation to representation. It has not, however, kept the Senate from originating revenue measures under the pretense of amending House bills, by striking out an entire measure except the title and the enacting clause. This paragraph, moreover, does not have the same significance that it had in 1787, when senators were chosen by state legislatures.

Although not constitutionally required, there has been a tradition, often breached, that appropriation bills, as well as those raising revenues, ought to originate in the House.

Section 7

2. Every Bill which shall have passed the House of Representatives and the Senate, shall, before it becomes a Law, be presented to the President of the United States; if he approve he shall sign it, but if not he shall return it, with his Objections to that House in which it shall have originated, who shall enter the Objections at large on their Journal, and proceed to reconsider it. If after such Reconsideration two thirds of that House shall agree to pass the Bill, it shall be sent, together with the Objections, to the other House, by which it shall likewise be reconsidered, and if approved by two thirds of that House, it shall become a Law. But in all such Cases the Votes of both Houses shall be determined by yeas and Nays, and the Names of the Persons voting for and against the Bill shall be entered on the Journal of each House respectively. If any Bill shall not be returned by the President within ten Days (Sundays excepted) after it shall have been presented to him, the Same shall be a Law, in like Manner as if he had signed it, unless the Congress by their Adjournment prevent its Return, in which Case it shall not be a Law.

The framers expected Congress to be the dominant branch of the government, but they did not wish it to be in a position to arrogate to itself all powers. So they gave the president a qualified veto, both to prevent Congress from overstepping its boundaries and to enable the president to influence the actual course of legislation.

After a bill has been passed in *identical* form by both houses of Congress, it is presented to the president, who can do one of three things:

First, the president can sign the bill; it then becomes the law of the land.

Second, the president can return it to the house in which it originated, stating the reasons for disapproval. If the bill is then repassed by a two-thirds vote of *both* houses, which means two-thirds of a quorum of the members thereof, it becomes law despite the president's veto. On the other hand, if the bill does not secure the approval of two-thirds of a quorum of the members of both houses, the veto is sustained, and the bill does not become law.

Third, the president can refuse to sign the bill but retain possession of it. It then becomes law at the end of ten days (excluding Sundays) after its receipt "unless," as the Constitution says, "Congress by their Adjournment prevent its [a bill's] Return, in which Case it shall not be a Law." The bill is thus subject to what is called the "pocket veto." The pocket veto applies differently to the three different kinds of adjournments. It probably does not apply to the first, there is a dispute about the second, and it clearly applies to the third.

The first, to which it probably does not apply, is the intrasession recesses that Congress frequently takes for short periods, for example, over Christmas and other holidays. In 1970 President Nixon tried to pocket veto a health bill during such an intrasession recess. Senator Kennedy argued that the pocket veto could not be used for such adjournments and took the question to federal court. The Court of Appeals for the District of Columbia agreed with him. The Department of Justice decided not to take the matter to the Supreme Court.

Second, there are the intersession congressional adjournments. These days Congress does not end its first session until November or December, and then it starts the second session the following January. (In the early days of the Republic, Congress used to go home during the summer and not start its second session until the following December.) There continues to be a debate between Congress and the president whether the pocket veto can be used between sessions. In 1976 President Ford, in response to another suit by Senator Kennedy, agreed that as long as the House and Senate designated officers to receive veto messages during such between-session recesses, he would not use a pocket veto. President Reagan, however, abandoned that policy and pocket vetoed measures during intersession adjournments, including one that tied aid for El Salvador to its compliance with certain human rights conditions. Thirty-three House Democrats and the Senate filed a suit charging that such pocket vetoes are unconstitutional. A federal district judge sided with the president, and the Court of Appeals sided with the members of Congress, but the Supreme Court "punted." It held that since the El Salvador aid statute had expired, there was no longer a live case or controversy.[33]

The third type of adjournment, called adjournment *sine die*, comes at the end of the second session, when a particular Congress adjourns never to return again (although in one sense the Senate, as a continuing body, has never adjourned). Everyone agrees that the pocket veto applies to such adjournments.

Unlike many state governors, the president cannot approve parts of a bill and veto other parts; approval or disapproval must be given to the bill as a unit. Because the president does not have an *item veto*, Congress has been able to get measures past the president by using *riders*, provisions that are not germane to the main purpose of a bill. Riders are most effective when tacked on to appropriation bills, thus forcing the president to accept them in order to secure funds for the operations of the government. President Reagan is only the most recent of many presidents who have urged Congress either to grant the president an item veto or to propose a constitutional amendment that would do so. Congress, so far, has shown little enthusiasm for this enhancement of presidential powers.

Not only has Congress been unwilling to give the president such authority, but in the Budget and Impoundment Control Act of 1974, as a reaction to President Nixon's refusal to permit the spending of funds that Congress had appropriated, it imposed a "legislative veto" (see pages 54 — 55) over presidential "rescissions" and "impoundments." However, in the aftermath of the *Chadha* case (see next page), and in the face of major budget deficits in recent years, Congress has been considering, as a substitute for a presidential item veto, the easing of restrictions it has imposed on presidential control over spending.

Section 7

3. Every Order, Resolution, or Vote to which the Concurrence of the Senate and House of Representatives may be necessary (except on a question of Adjournment) shall be presented to the President of the United States; and before the Same shall take Effect, shall be approved by him, or being disapproved by him, shall be repassed by two thirds of the Senate and House of Representatives, according to the Rules and Limitations prescribed in the Case of a Bill.

Despite the inclusive language of what has come to be known as the *presentment clause*, there are certain orders, resolutions, and votes, in addition to questions of adjournment, that require the concurrence of both houses but are not presented to the president for action.

For example, when a constitutional amendment is proposed by a two-thirds vote in both houses of Congress, it is submitted immediately for ratification without being sent to the president. Congress does not exercise ordinary legislative powers when it proposes constitutional amendments. It operates under the powers given it in Article V. Article V is a self-contained, complete statement of methods for amending the Constitution, and it omits the president from the procedure.

A second exception to the requirements of the presentment clause used to be the legislative veto. Congress started to use the legislative veto in a small way in the 1930s and in a big way beginning in the 1970s, until the Supreme Court in *INS* v *Chadha* (1983) called the practice to a halt.

In 1932 Congress started to condition some of its more general delegations of powers to the president, and to executive departments, on the approval by Congress, or by one house, of a particular exercise of that power. (Sometimes it even gave veto power to a legislative committee.) The resolutions of approval or disapproval were not submitted to the president.

The legislative veto came in many forms. In some laws, Congress stipulated that what the president did was to be effective unless disapproved by either or both chambers within a certain number of days. In others, Congress provided that what the president did would be effective only if approved by both houses of Congress within a certain time period. For example, under the 1973 War Powers Act, unless Congress adopts a concurrent resolution of approval within sixty days, troops sent into combat by the president are to be withdrawn. Under the Budget and Impoundment Control Act of 1974, if the president withholds funds temporarily, thus making a *deferral*, it must be reported to Congress, and the action is effective unless overturned by a resolution of either chamber. If the president wishes to impound funds permanently, an act called *rescission*, the rescission of the appropriation is ineffective unless both the House and the Senate approve within forty-five days.

The use of the congressional veto sparked criticism of it as an evasion of the presentment clause and of the one-house veto as a violation of the bicameralism provisions of Article I. Most scholars, however, supported the practice, at least in the form that called for action by both chambers.

Presidents of both parties felt otherwise. Often when presented with legislation delegating powers to them and their agents, but subjecting such delegation to a legislative veto, presidents complained that the provisions were an unconstitutional invasion of presidential powers. Nonetheless, they had little choice. Congress looked upon the legislative veto as an essential means of exercising oversight of the executive departments to ensure that they were carrying out the intent of Congress. Without the legislative veto, Congress could overturn the actions of the president and executive officials only by enacting overriding legislation, which would have to be presented to the president for approval or veto. Congress was not about to give up the practice.

The Supreme Court kept out of the battle for half a century but in a sweeping decision, *INS* v *Chadha*,[34] ruled the legislative veto unconstitutional. The particular provision in question granted the attorney general authority to suspend the deportation of certain aliens, but all such suspensions had to be reported to Congress. Either chamber could veto the suspension of deportation by passing a resolution of disapproval in the current session or in the next. If Congress did nothing, the alien's status became that of a lawful resident.

The Court could have worded its opinion so that it applied only to this particular use of the legislative veto, or only to one-house vetoes, but the language of the Court was so broad that it sounded "the death knell for nearly 200 other statutory provisions,"[35] more laws than the Supreme Court has declared unconstitutional in our entire history. But despite the sweep of its language and the predictions of disaster by the judicial dissenters and other supporters of the legislative veto, so far the *Chadha* decision seems to have had little consequence.

Congress has not rushed to review laws containing a legislative veto, preferring to leave the matter to the courts. The substantive provisions of most laws containing a legislative veto are likely to be sustained, even though the legislative veto is no longer enforceable. The test is whether the veto was critical to Congress's decision to pass the law in the first place. Not unless the delegations of power "to the executive or to an independent agency have been so controversial or so broad that judges believe Congress would have been unwilling to make the delegation without a strong oversight mechanism" is the entire law to be considered unconstitutional. Moreover, "it is not only appropriate to evaluate the importance of the veto in the original legislative bargain, but also to consider the nature of the delegated authority that Congress made subject to a veto."[36]

The *Chadha* decision left intact the constitutionality of "report and wait" provisions: Congress may specify in the original act that no final rule or regulation may be issued until so many legislative days — usually 30 — after the proposed regulation has been submitted to specified committees of both chambers. "This interval gives Congress an opportunity to review the regulations and either to attempt to influence the agency's decision, or to enact legislation preventing the regulations from taking effect."[37] "The value of the reservation of the power to examine proposed rules. . .

before they become effective is well understood by Congress."[38] Congress is aware that most federal executives, although perhaps no longer subject to a legislative veto, nonetheless are unlikely to act contrary to the express wishes of Congress or its leaders. Federal executives are sensitive to the fact that year after year they must return to Congress for funds. Other congressional options are to be more precise in congressional delegations and to delegate only for brief periods, thereby alerting the executive officials that if they act in a fashion that annoys many members of Congress, the law delegating authority to them is not likely to be reenacted.

Congressional Organization and Procedure: The Unwritten Constitution

The Constitution provides the barest outline of congressional organization and gives only a partial description of how Congress operates. Basic practices have developed over the past two hundred years. Of special importance are the role of political parties, the selection of committee leaders, and the rules governing debate.

Political Parties in Congress

The nature of the party system is as significant as a formal constitution in determining how a governmental institution operates. The Soviet one-party system, for example, makes meaningless the formal constitutional discretion of the Soviet legislature. The constitutional structure of the English and French parliaments is much the same, yet the French multiparty system leads to a kind of legislature very different from that produced by the English two-party system.

If political parties are so important, why is our Constitution silent about their organization and operation? The Founding Fathers considered parties divisive and baleful influences. Although they knew that "factions," as they called parties, might develop, they hoped that the constitutional arrangements would curtail party influences and make it difficult for parties to operate. To a considerable extent they were successful. While parties have always played a significant role in the operation of Congress, they have not always been decisive factors in determining the outcome of legislative struggles, nor have they served as important agencies in coordinating the executive and legislative branches. They have, however, always played a role of some significance in the operation of Congress.

Congressional candidates are nominated by parties, they run in elections as representatives of those parties, and the majority party in each house "organizes" that chamber. Prior to the opening of a Congress, each party in each chamber holds an organizing meeting.[39] (The Republicans call their meetings a *conference*, the term also used by Senate Democrats; House Democrats keep the older name, *caucus*.) At those meetings the parties choose their officers and nominate their candidates for the various congressional offices, the most important being (in the case of the representatives) the Speaker of the House and (in the case of the senators), the majority leader. The party conferences also confirm the assignment of party members to the standing committees of the Congress (the formal appointments are made subsequently by the chamber), elect the floor leaders and their assistants (the assistants are known as *whips*), and select policy committees to mold strategy during the coming sessions.

Each party may also hold conferences during the course of the sessions, but only the recommendations of the organizing conferences receive the united support of party members. All Democratic House members, for example, support their party's candidate for speaker; all Republicans support their conference's candidate. Thus, the party with the most members selects the speaker and other House officers. The vice president, who presides over the Senate, may belong to the minority party in the Senate, but the president pro tempore who presides in his absence is always a member of the majority party in the Senate.

Selection of Committee Chairpersons

The standing committees and subcommittees process bills, hold investigations, and recommend legislative action. They are composed of members of both parties, each party being represented in a ratio approximately equal to its strength in the entire chamber.

The chairpersons of committees and subcommittees are influential leaders. For decades they were picked by strict seniority: the member of the majority party who had the longest continuous service on the committee became chairperson. No matter how much he or she might differ with party colleagues, no matter how much his or her ideas might be out of tune with those of the president (even if both belonged to the same party), the senior member became chairperson. But, beginning in 1971, Democrats and Republicans in both the House and the Senate began to make changes in their procedures. The custom of seniority still prevails, but there is now merely a presumption that the senior member will be chosen as chairperson, no longer an automatic guarantee. The chairpersons of all committees and subcommittees now know that if they displease a majority of their fellow party members, they may be voted out of their posts.

Rules and Debate

With so many members and so many issues, the time of the House is carefully controlled. The House Rules Committee, except for certain privileged matters, normally stipulates the amount of time and the conditions under which the House may debate legislation (the Rules Committee merely recommends, but its recommendations are almost always accepted by the House). Representatives may be ruled out of order if their remarks are not pertinent to the topic at hand, and their speech is subject to rigorously enforced time limits.

In the Senate, however, debate is practically unlimited. Once senators gain the privilege of the floor, they may talk on any subject for as long as they wish. This rule of unlimited debate and the right to talk about anything even if it has no connection to the subject at hand permits a few determined senators to tie up the business of the Senate by *filibustering* — talking to delay or to prevent the Senate from voting. Senators who strongly object to a measure seldom have to engage in a filibuster. By merely threatening to do so, they are normally able to deter the Senate leaders from attempting to bring the objectionable measure before the Senate for consideration.

Once a filibuster is begun, it is difficult to stop. It takes a vote of three-fifths of the senators duly chosen and sworn in — in most instances sixty senators — to apply *clo-*

ture (or *closure*, as it is sometimes called), that is, to end debate. (It requires two-thirds of those present and voting to close debate on a motion to amend Senate rules.) Although the Senate in recent years has been more inclined than in the past to invoke cloture, the power to talk and talk and talk remains a significant weapon of Senate minorities.

Enumeration of Congressional Powers

Section 8 enumerates the legislative powers granted to Congress. In interpreting these powers, we should, as Chief Justice Marshall put it, never forget that it is a Constitution we are reading, a Constitution "intended to endure for ages to come, and consequently to be adapted to the various crises of human affairs."[40] Furthermore, each separately enumerated grant should be read as if the necessary-and-proper clause (see page 74) were part of it.

Section 8

1. The Congress shall have Power To lay and collect Taxes, Duties, Imposts and Excises, to pay the Debts and provide for the Common Defence and general Welfare of the United States;

This paragraph grants to Congress the important powers of the purse: the power to collect taxes, pay debts, and spend money for the common defense and general welfare.

The power to pay debts is not restricted to the payment of the legal obligations of the national government. On the contrary, Congress may pay off obligations that are merely moral or honorary, and when this power is tied to the power to spend for the general welfare, it results in the power of Congress to decide who shall receive dollars from the federal treasury.

A word of caution: the general welfare clause is tied to the power to tax and to spend; no general power is granted to Congress to legislate for the general welfare. But, as noted in the discussion of federalism, liberal construction of congressional powers and the demands of our times have removed any serious constitutional limits stemming from this clause.

James Madison argued that Congress could tax and spend only to carry out one of its other granted powers — that is, Congress could tax and spend to establish post offices and post roads (Section 8, paragraph 7), to regulate commerce with foreign nations (Section 8, paragraph 3), and so on. From the first, nevertheless, the power of Congress under this clause has been interpreted as being *in addition to* its other powers and, hence, exercisable in its own right without reference to them. (Justice O'Connor appears to be a modern-day convert to the Madisonian position. She argued in dissent that Congress's use of the spending power to regulate the drinking age for liquor was an unconstitutional attempt to regulate what had been given to the states.)[41]

Congress raises and spends billions of dollars every year to aid agriculture, education, and business, to alleviate conditions of unemployment, and to take care of the poor, the aged, and the disabled, although not one of these activities is specifically within its other delegated powers. About one out of every five dollars that state and local governments spend comes from the federal government. Some of the money comes with relatively few strings, as with block grants for such purposes as education or manpower training, in which the state and local units have considerable flexibility in using the dollars. Some federal dollars come through "categorical grants," in which there are rather specific conditions that state and local governments must follow if they wish to receive the federal funds, sometimes including the requirement that the state use its own resources to match the federal grant. By tying conditions to the funds it makes available, Congress has been able to regulate vast areas — how highways are built, how the National Guard is trained, even how universities and colleges post student grades and assign faculty members to do research.

The four constitutional limits on the congressional power to spend are not very constraining. First, the expenditure must be for the general welfare, but "the level of deference to the congressional decision is such that the Court has more recently questioned whether 'general welfare' is a judicially enforceable restriction at all."[42] Second, if Congress restricts the way states spend federal monies, it must do so unambiguously.[43] Third, the restraints must be reasonably related to the purpose of the expenditure. But the Court is also deferential to congressional conclusions about what is related; for example, the right of a state to use federal funds otherwise available to it to build highways may be conditioned upon the state's agreeing not to allow persons under 21 to buy alcoholic drinks in the state.[44] Fourth, the Congress may not, via conditions on expenditures, violate other clauses of the Constitution.

It is difficult, almost impossible, to secure a judicial hearing on the constitutionality of a federal grant.[45] In rare instances, a state may raise the issue: South Dakota was allowed to do so in connection with federal highway funds. Taxpayers lack standing to challenge federal expenditures merely because they dislike them or believe them to be unconstitutional. They must show that there is a logical link between their status as taxpayers and the challenged legislative enactment, and that there is a "nexus" between this status and a specific constitutional limit, such as the limitations on the taxing and spending power imposed by the establishment of religion clause of the First Amendment.[46] In fact, in our entire two-hundred-year history, the Court has allowed only one taxpayer suit against a federal grant. That suit challenged, as a violation of the establishment clause, a federal grant of funds for instructional materials to schools, including religious schools.[47]

Not only can Congress spend for regulatory purposes, it can also tax for such purposes. Congress can heavily tax activities — for example, the manufacturer of dangerous white phosphorus matches or the issuing of bank notes by state-chartered banks; the fact that the impact of the tax makes the activity uneconomic raises no constitutional problems. Of course, Congress may not use its authority to tax in a fashion that deprives persons of specific rights secured by the Constitution. For example, Congress has attempted to regulate gamblers and gambling, the sale of narcotics, and traffic in dangerous weapons through some rather elaborate tax laws. To the extent that, to comply with such laws, gamblers, narcotics peddlers, and sellers of dangerous weapons are, in effect, required to produce evidence that they are engaging in illegal activities, the measures unconstitutionally violate the guarantees against compelling persons to testify against themselves.[48]

The power to tax and to spend has become one of the two major sources — the other is the power to regulate commerce among the states — of the so-called national police power, the power to regulate persons and property for the safety, health, and welfare of society. Congress has no general grant of police power, but it may and does use its delegated powers for police-power purposes.

Section 8

1. [continued] but all Duties, Imposts and Excises shall be uniform throughout the United States;

The uniformity clause keeps Congress neither from levying taxes that fall unequally on the people in various states nor from defining a tax in geographic terms. Congress may make *reasonable* geographic classifications. Thus a unanimous Court upheld the Crude Oil Windfall Profit Tax Act of 1980, which levied a higher tax on all oil except from wells located in a northerly section of Alaska. The exemption was not drawn on state political lines. Rather, it reflected a congressional judgment that unique climatic and geographic conditions make drilling wells in that region so much more costly than elsewhere that they justified exempting that oil from the windfall profit tax in order to encourage further exploration in that area.[49]

Section 8

[In all subsequent paragraphs of Section 8 the words "The Congress shall have Power" are understood.]

2. To borrow Money on the Credit of the United States;

Congress borrows money by authorizing the sale of government securities to banks, businesses, and private individuals. The most important forms of government securities are bonds, treasury certificates, and treasury notes.

3. To regulate Commerce with foreign Nations,

Prior to 1937, Congress's power over foreign commerce was greater than its power over commerce among the states. Nowadays, Congress's power over commerce among the states is so expansive that the distinction between the two kinds of commerce is of little significance. Still of some importance is that state taxation of foreign commerce is subject to closer scrutiny than taxation of interstate commerce. In addition to the tests used to determine whether a state tax violates the "dormant commerce clause" (see page 64), a state tax on foreign commerce is unconstitutional if it "prevents the Federal Government from speaking with one voice when regulating commercial relations with foreign governments."[50] Property owned by a foreign corporation is especially protected. For example, a state can tax a domestic airplane or railroad car if the airplane or railroad car is in the state for a certain number of days, if the tax is proportioned to the time in the state, if the tax rate does not discriminate against interstate commerce, and if the tax is related in some way to services provided by the state. But such a test will not justify a state tax on the ship of a foreign nation when the ship is docked in a port in that state.[51]

The Supreme Court's bold language against state taxation of foreign commerce should not be taken too seriously. The Court takes its cue on these matters from the president and Congress. The Court, for example, sustained a Florida tax on fuel purchased in the state by foreign air carriers, whether the fuel was used to fly within or without the state and regardless whether the airline engaged in any business in the state. Although federal authorities had not specifically authorized such action, by implications arising out of more than 70 agreements with other nations, the federal government had made it clear that it did not object to such state taxation.[52]

Section 8

3. [continued] and among the several States,

The commerce clause is another important basis on which Congress has developed a national police power. It is also an excellent demonstration that the vague words and phrases of certain sections of the Constitution have enabled a document written in 1787 in the days of the oxcart to be adapted to the needs of modern industrial society.

Commerce, in the sense of this clause, includes not only buying and selling (traffic), but all forms of commercial intercourse, of transportation, and of communication. Congress's power extends to commerce if it is carried on with foreign nations or "concerns more states than one." The power of Congress over such commerce is the power to govern it. In the words of Chief Justice Marshall in *Gibbons* v *Ogden*, that power "is complete in itself, may be exercised to its utmost extent, and acknowledges no limitations other than are prescribed in the Constitution."[53]

Congress is not obliged, when regulating "commerce among the several states," to consider the effect of its measures on matters that generally have been regulated by the states. Indeed, it may regulate intrastate activities (those within a state) when they substantially affect interstate or foreign commerce. And although Congress's measures are usually intended to benefit commerce, they are not required to do so. Congress may even prohibit or greatly restrict commerce in order to promote the national health, safety, and welfare, or for humanitarian purposes. From 1808 it proscribed the African slave trade. Many years later it prohibited the transportation of lottery tickets between the states and, still later, the transportation of liquor into states having "dry laws." Congress has made it a federal crime to use the channels of interstate commerce for the shipment of stolen automobiles or impure foods, in the traffic of "white slavery," in the business of "loan sharks," or for travel to commit certain specified crimes. Congress has also closed the channels of interstate commerce to goods of enterprises engaged in commerce or in production for commerce that do not pay all employees minimum wages and overtime pay as prescribed by federal law. To make this law effective, Congress not only has banned the interstate transportation of goods so produced, but has also made it a federal offense to produce goods under such conditions when the goods are "intended" for sale in interstate commerce (Fair Labor Standards Act). To safeguard interstate commerce from interruption by strikes, Congress may regulate employer-employee relations in businesses and industries that "affect" such commerce, and has in fact done so (the Wagner and Taft-Hartley Acts).[54] Congress has also used the commerce clause to justify comprehensive federal regulations in many areas.[55]

The commerce clause is also the constitutional peg for the 1964 Civil Rights Act, which forbids discrimination because of race, religion, or national origin in places of public accommodation and because of race, religion, national origin, or sex in employment. "Congress' action in removing the disruptive effect which it found racial discrimination has on interstate travel is not invalidated because Congress was also legislating against what it considers to be moral wrongs."[56] Congress may also extend its laws to remote places of public accommodation, since its power over interstate commerce extends to the regulation of local incidents that might have a substantial and harmful effect on that commerce. Congress has authority to enact such laws because discrimination restricts the flow of interstate commerce and because interstate commerce is being used to support the discrimination. Thus, the Supreme Court sustained the application of the Civil Rights Act to what Justice Black in dissent characterized as "this country people's recreation center, lying in what may be, so far as we know, a little 'sleepy hollow' between Arkansas hills, miles away from any interstate highway" because the park leased its paddle boats from an Oklahoma company, its jukebox was made outside of Arkansas, and it played records manufactured outside the state. Ingredients served in the snack bar were obtained from out-of-state sources, and as the Court majority speaking through Justice Brennan wrote, "it would be unrealistic to assume that none of the 100,000 patrons actually served by the Club each season was an interstate traveler." Justice Black contended that the commerce clause should not be stretched "so as to give the Federal Government complete control over every little remote country place of recreation in every nook and cranny of each precinct and county in every one of the 50 states."[57] But he dissented alone.

Although Justice Rehnquist and Chief Justice Burger have warned "it would be a mistake to conclude that Congress' power to regulate pursuant to the Commerce Clause is unlimited,"[58] the fact is "the task of a court in reviewing congressional commerce clause regulations is exceedingly narrow." A court may invalidate legislation enacted under the commerce clause only if it is clear that there is no rational basis for a congressional finding that the regulated activity affects interstate commerce, or that there is "no reasonable connection between the regulatory means selected and the asserted ends."[59]

Occasionally a member of the Supreme Court raises some questions about congressional use of commerce clause powers, especially if there are also some Tenth Amendment concerns because of the impact on state governments, but in reality the Court has turned over to Congress the interpretation of the scope of its powers under the commerce clause. Congressional regulations, when based on the commerce clause, are seldom challenged. When challenged, the Court, with a cohesion that is rare, has no difficulty in concluding that Congress may regulate such purely local transactions as fees charged by real estate brokers and lawyers, or mining, or the preservation of farm land.[60]

From the commerce clause, Congress also derives its full powers over the "navigable waters of the United States," including waters that may be made navigable by "reasonable improvements." Those waters are subject to national planning and control; the authority of Congress over them "is as broad as the needs of commerce," including flood protection, watershed development, and the recovery of the cost of improvements through utilization of power.[61]

The commerce clause is important, moreover, not only as a grant of power to

Congress but also as a limit on the power of the states. In giving this power to the national government, the Constitution took it away from the states, at least in large part. Therefore, whenever a state, in professed exercise of its taxing power or police power, passes a law materially affecting interstate or foreign commerce, the question necessarily arises whether the law is not really an unconstitutional regulation of foreign or interstate commerce. Of course, if the state law conflicts with a federal regulation, the federal regulation supersedes it.

Not only does a congressional regulation supersede a conflicting state regulation, but an act of Congress conferring power on states under the commerce clause also preempts judicial judgments. ". . . When Congress has struck the balance it deems appropriate, the courts are no longer needed to prevent states from burdening commerce, and it matters not that the courts would have invalidated the state tax or regulation under the Commerce Clause in the absence of congressional action."[62] If Congress ordains that the states may regulate an aspect of interstate commerce, as it has done, for example, with respect to insurance, any action taken by a state within the scope of the congressional authorization is rendered invulnerable to commerce clause challenge.[63] (The state action, however, may violate other provisions of the Constitution, the equal protection clause, for example.)

When, Congress is silent, however, the Supreme Court finally determines whether a state regulation that affects commerce is permissible. In the exercise of this great power, the Court has handed down hundreds of decisions, some of which involved vast commercial interests. It has laid down scores of rules about which volumes have been written. There is not space to discuss all those rules in a book like this, but in essence, the Court weighs the local interest against the general commercial interest and then gives the right-of-way to the interest it deems, all things considered, the more important one.

The Court has adopted a two-tiered approach to analyzing whether state economic regulations violate the commerce clause. First, when a state statute directly discriminates against state commerce or when its effect is to favor in-state economic interests, the law is likely, without much inspection, to be struck down.[64] Discriminating laws may be struck down either for a discriminatory purpose against out-of-state commerce or for a discriminatory effect on such commerce.[65] "Where simple economic protectionism" is found, "a virtual per se rule of invalidity has been erected."[66] If the purpose is not protectionist but the law does have a discriminatory effect, the law is subject to strict scrutiny, and the burden falls on the state to demonstrate that (1) the statute serves a legitimate local purpose and (2) the purpose cannot be served as well by available nondiscriminatory means.[67]

There is a less demanding test when a state statute has only an indirect effect on interstate commerce and when it regulates evenhandedly. In such an instance, the Court examines whether the state's interest is legitimate and whether the burden on interstate commerce clearly exceeds the local benefits.

In hundreds of cases the Supreme Court, when Congress was silent, performed this balancing role with respect to state police-power laws (those passed to promote the public health, welfare, and safety). Here are a few examples: Arizona was not allowed to impose a fourteen-passenger-car or seventy-freight-car limit on interstate trains, nor could it require interstate trains to carry a "full crew" as defined by the state legislature.[68] Illinois could not require interstate trucks to be equipped with specific kinds of contoured mudguards.[69] Wisconsin and Iowa could not ban trucks longer than fifty-five feet, because such a ban placed a substantial burden on interstate commerce and the evidence did not support the states' contentions that such regulations made the highways safer.[70] Washington could not ban supertankers from Puget Sound.[71] New Jersey could not prohibit the importation of solid or liquid waste that originated or was collected outside the state, since the prohibition imposed on out-of-state commercial interests the full burden of conserving the state's remaining landfill space and was a freeze on the flow of commerce for protectionist reasons.[72]

Here are a few "coulds": Arkansas could regulate the wholesale electric rates charged by rural power cooperatives to their member retail distributors.[73] Maine could prohibit the importation of bait fish because the state proved to the satisfaction of the judges that its purpose was to protect its own wild fish and that there was no other available means to do so.[74] (If procedures are developed that make sampling of fish and inspection for disease feasible, Maine may no longer be able to justify its import ban.)

In recent years, the Court has distinguished between the role of state and local governments as participants in the market and their role as regulators of commerce. When they are acting as participants in the market, they are not subject to the restraints of the commerce clause. South Dakota could give preference to in-state buyers for the cement it produced, and Maryland could favor in-state processors in getting rid of abandoned automobiles.[75] However, what a state may do without violating the commerce clause may violate the privileges and immunities clause — the one in Article IV, not the one in the Fourteenth Amendment — by limiting the ability of out-of-state residents or businesses to participate in that particular business (see page 116).

As difficult as the issues are when it comes to deciding whether or not a state law enacted to promote the public well-being should be applied to interstate commerce, questions relating to the application of state taxes to interstate commerce are even more complicated. (These questions also get combined with Fourteenth Amendment considerations: Under the due process clause, a state may not tax that which is not within its jurisdiction, over which it has no control, and on which it confers no benefits; according to equal protection considerations, the tax must be for a legitimate purpose and have a rational relation to that purpose.)

The Supreme Court, in *Complete Auto Transit, Inc.* v *Brady*, attempted to clarify the apparently conflicting precedents it has spawned. The Court adopted the following four-pronged test to measure the constitutionality of state taxes as they relate to interstate commerce: (1) Is the tax applied to an activity that has a substantial nexus with the taxing state? (2) Is it fairly apportioned? (3) Does it not discriminate against interstate commerce? (4) Is it fairly related to the services provided by the state? If the answer to all four questions is yes, the tax is constitutional.[76] Then in 1987 the Court added an "internal consistency" test. Under this test a state tax must be of a kind that, if applied by every jurisdiction, would cause no impermissible interference with free trade. As a result, a "flat tax" — a tax at a single rate upon trucks, for example, that imposes the same rate on out-of-state trucks as on in-state trucks even though out-of-state trucks may use a state's highways much less — is unconstitutional unless a state can show that administrative difficulties make collection of more finely calibrated user charges impracticable.[77] Justice Scalia, who along with Chief Justice Rehnquist dissented from the Court's adoption of the internal consistency test, stated that the Court should be content to outlaw evident discrimination and leave "finer tuning" to Congress. The results of the Court's application of the negative commerce clause doctrines to review state taxation of interstate commerce have, he argued, "not to put too fine a point on the matter, made no sense."[78]

There has been considerable controversy in recent years over the adoption by more than twenty states of the unitary business principle, under which they tax the income of corporations that do business around the world. The Supreme Court has said this unitary tax does not violate either the commerce clause or the due process clause. It has given its approval as well to a formula used by the states that in some instances permits the taxation of the same income by more than one state. The Court's action means that in some instances two states will tax the same income. The justices have told Congress that if it wishes to place limits on state taxation beyond those required by the Constitution, it should do so, because making rules regarding the apportionment of taxes to an interstate business is "essentially a legislative task."[79]

There is certainly no field in which the Court's reviewing power has been more valuable than its review of state regulations and taxation under the commerce clause. Although we have fifty state legislatures, we have one national economic and industrial system — one prosperity. Nor is there any field in which the Court has, on the whole, done better work in maintaining the national authority "in full scope without unnecessary loss of local efficiency."[80] In interpreting the due process clause of the Fourteenth Amendment, the Court has frequently been lured into questionable positions by that will-o'-the-wisp word *liberty*, but commerce clause cases are generally down-to-earth cases, well seasoned with facts and figures.

Section 8

3. [continued] and with the Indian Tribes;

This clause confers on Congress plenary and exclusive power to deal with the Indian tribes.[81] Since 1871, when Congress declared that henceforth there would be no more treaties negotiated with Indian tribes, this clause has been the primary source of federal authority over Indians. It also "singles Indians out as a proper subject for separate legislation."[82] Treaties, however, remain a basis of many Supreme Court rulings. Nowadays, current doctrine is that treaties and statutes are to be interpreted to benefit Indians.

Because of the power conferred on Congress by this clause and because of the special historical relationship between the national government and the Indian tribes, the Supreme Court sustained an act of Congress giving Indians belonging to federally recognized tribes a preference in employment by the Bureau of Indian Affairs. "The preference . . . is granted to Indians not as a discrete racial group, but, rather, as members of quasisovereign tribal entities whose lives and activities are governed by the BIA in a unique fashion. . . . The legal status of the BIA is truly sui generis. . . . As long as the special treatment can be tied rationally to the fulfillment of Congress's unique obligation toward the Indians, such legislative judgments will not be disturbed."[83]

The national government, acting through the Bureau of Indian Affairs in the Department of the Interior, counts 280 Indian tribes, pueblos, and groups within the continental United States. There are also slightly more than 200 Native Alaskan communities served by the Bureau. Of the 1,418,195 people who designated themselves as Indians in the 1980 census, about 680,000 live on or near reservations (this number includes all Native Americans in Alaska and those in Oklahoma who live on or near the former reservations in that state). Non-reservation Indians — any Indian is free to move anywhere he or she wishes — are entitled to be treated like any other citizen.

To be eligible for most benefits provided by the Bureau of Indian Affairs, one must live on or near a reservation. Reservation Indians, like those living off the reservation, are American citizens by act of Congress. Today, by act of the states in which the reservations are located, reservation Indians have the right to vote.

The tribes have inherent powers to govern themselves and their own people. They are "domestic, dependent nations."[84] In governing themselves, the tribes are unconstrained by the Bill of Rights or the Fourteenth Amendment. Although, by the Indian Civil Rights Act of 1968, Congress imposed restraints on tribal governments similar, but not identical, to those contained in the Bill of Rights and the Fourteenth Amendment, federal courts have only limited power to review tribal actions for conformity with this law. When a female member of the Santa Clara pueblo, and her daughter, challenged as illegal and unconstitutional a tribal regulation denying membership to children of women who marry outside the tribe, but not to children of men who do so, the Supreme Court refused to permit federal courts to consider the claim.[85]

The clause conferring authority on Congress to regulate commerce with Indian tribes also places limits on the power of the states to do so. State laws of a general nature may be applied on reservations only if their application does not impair a right granted or reserved by federal law and does not interfere with the self-government Congress has reserved for the tribes.

State regulation of the commercial activities of Indian tribes is allowed only if the state overcomes two independent but related barriers: a state may not act if its authority has been preempted by federal law or if its actions interfere with a tribes' ability to exercise its sovereign functions.[86] For example, a state may not apply its general rules on hunting and fishing to either Indians or non-Indians on reservations, even if there is no specific federal preemption, since such state regulations are "incompatible with federal and tribal interests reflected in federal law and there is no state interest at stake sufficient to justify overriding tribal regulations."[87]

Congress has also stipulated that only federal and tribal criminal laws are to apply on reservations, except where Congress has specified to the contrary. Congress has delegated to the states the right to exercise jurisdiction over some crimes committed on reservations, and most states have elected to exercise that jurisdiction. In recent years, some Indian tribes have operated high-stakes bingo games on their reservations for the benefit of non-Indians, even though such games are against the laws of the states in which they are located. So far the Supreme Court has sided with the Indian tribes. These state laws, the Court has concluded, are "regulatory" and not "prohibitory" and thus not within the grant of criminal jurisdiction given by Congress to the states.[88]

Over other persons living on reservations, Indian tribes have only the jurisdiction conferred on them by Congress, but with Congress's approval they may exclude non-members from reservations.[89] Congress has excluded tribal courts from criminal jurisdiction to try and punish non-Indians for offenses committed on reservations. The

Supreme Court has left open whether tribal courts have power to exercise civil subject-matter jurisdiction over persons not of that tribe in cases between Indians and non-Indians over issues arising in or related to reservations.[90]

"States may tax Indians only when Congress has manifested clearly its consent to such taxation." Moreover, statutes are to be construed liberally in favor of the Indians, with "ambiguous provisions interpreted to their benefit."[91] The Indian commerce clause, however, does not of its own force bar all state taxation of matters that indirectly affect the economic interests of the tribes. It prevents only undue discrimination against or burden on Indian commerce. Thus, the state of Washington was allowed to collect a sales tax on sales of cigarettes to nonmembers of a tribe, including nontribe Indians, in stores operated by the tribes on reservations.[92] (Tribes also collected their own taxes on those same transactions.) On the other hand, states may not levy taxes that fall, even indirectly, on reservation Indians or tribal activities unless Congress, by express authority, has conferred such powers on them. A state may not, for example, collect taxes on income earned by Indians on reservations, collect a fuel tax from a non-Indian firm that cuts trees on a reservation and transports them to a tribal sawmill, or collect a sales tax on tractors delivered to an Indian tribe.[93] New Mexico was told that federal law preempted its collecting a tax on the receipts that a non-Indian construction company received from a tribal school board for building a school on the reservation. [94] (New Mexico could collect the same tax from the contractor for work he did for the federal government.)

These limitations on the power of states to tax Indian activities on reservations do not extend to off-reservation activity. New Mexico was allowed to collect a sales tax on a ski resort operated by the Mescalero Apache tribe off the reservation, although it could not tax the property the tribe owned and used in operating the resort.[95]

Section 8

4. To establish a uniform Rule of Naturalization,

Naturalization is the legal process by which a foreigner is admitted to citizenship. In view of the inherent power of any sovereign nation to determine its own membership, the naturalization clause must today be reckoned superfluous.

By virtue of this same inherent power, Congress has the right to determine which foreigners may enter the United States, for what purposes, and on what conditions. "Over no conceivable subject is the legislative power of Congress more complete than the admission of aliens."[96] This power extends even to granting the attorney general discretion to determine which, if any, aliens who advocate "the economic, international and governmental doctrine of world communism" should be admitted to the United States.[97]

Although aliens are in the United States at the sufferance of the national government and may be removed through administrative procedures, while they are here this grant of authority does not permit Congress to deprive aliens, any more than it may citizens, of freedom of worship, freedom of speech, fair trials for criminal prosecutions, or other fundamental rights protected by the Constitution. Furthermore, congressional power to regulate the admission of aliens includes authority to preempt conflicting state laws. For example, "Congress has broadly declared as federal policy that lawfully admitted resident aliens who become public charges for causes arising after their entry are not subject to deportation; and that as long as they are here they are entitled to the full and equal benefit of all state laws for the security of persons and property."[98]

Section 8

4. [continued] and uniform Laws on the subject of Bankruptcies throughout the United States;

Bankruptcy laws enable debtors to obtain release from their obligations upon surrender of their property to their creditors. Thus are the "wholly broke made whole again." Congressional enactments take priority over conflicting state laws.

Congress's power under this clause is wide, but not unlimited. It is subject to the Fifth Amendment's prohibition of taking private property without just compensation. For example, there is substantial doubt that Congress could, by bankruptcy legislation, retroactively destroy a creditor's ownership in property sold to a debtor.

In 1973, when Congress designed a special law to deal with the bankruptcy of eight northwestern and midwestern railroads, the act was challenged for violating the uniformity requirement of the bankruptcy clause. The contention was that this highly complicated act applied only to some parts of the country and dealt with those subject to its provisions differently from bankrupt railroads in other parts of the nation. The Court responded that the uniformity requirement does not call for geographic uniformity. It requires only uniform treatment for all creditors and debtors covered by the law. Furthermore, during the time the act was in effect, the only bankrupt railroads were those covered by it.[99]

A decade later, however, the Supreme Court seemed to give the uniformity provision a somewhat different interpretation. When the Rock Island Railroad was in the midst of bankruptcy proceedings, Congress enacted a law ordering the trustee to provide up to $75,000,000 as a priority item to pay the unemployment benefits of workers who might not find jobs with the successor organization. The bankruptcy court refused to implement this act because it amounted to an unconstitutional taking of the railroad's property without just compensation. Congress then reenacted the law with the additional provision that if the railroad's property were taken to pay for the unemployment benefits to its workers, the railroad had a right to bring an action against the federal government for compensation. On review, the Supreme Court, ignoring the taking of property issue, held that because the act applied only to one railroad, it was not uniform and therefore exceeded the authority of Congress.[100]

Section 8

5. To coin Money, regulate the Value thereof, and of foreign Coin, and fix the Standard of Weights and Measures;

This power, in conjunction with the power to borrow money on the credit of the United States, gives Congress the authority to issue paper money and to make it legal tender for the payment of all debts.

Section 8

6. To provide for the Punishment of counterfeiting the Securities and current Coin of the United States;

It would seem that Congress has this power, even without this clause, as a result of the necessary-and-proper clause.

Pursuant to this authority, Congress has enacted two statutes designed to make it more difficult to counterfeit money, by restricting photographic reproductions of currency. The first, enacted during the Civil War to combat the surge in counterfeiting caused by the great increase in government obligations, makes it a criminal offense for any person to print or in any manner publish a likeness of currency. The second, adopted in a 1958 law codifying Treasury practice, permits the printing or publishing of the likeness of any security for certain purposes and for those purposes only, namely, "for philatelic, numismatic, educational, historical or newsworthy purposes." In addition, publication must be in articles, books, journals, newspapers, or albums, the illustrations must be in black and white, the reproduction must be undersized by at least three-fourths or oversized by at least one and one-half, and the negatives used in making the illustrations must be destroyed after their final use.

The Supreme Court (1984) declared the purpose requirement an unconstitutional violation of the First Amendment because it was not a content-neutral regulation of time, place, and manner and would require the government to determine whether the message being conveyed was newsworthy or educational (see page 149). The Court assumed that the requirement that the illustration must be in a publication was unconstitutional, but it left that issue open for final determination for another day. (Time, Inc., was the party to the suit and since the publication requirement caused it no problems, the Court ruled that Time lacked standing to raise the issue.) The Court upheld the constitutionality of the size and color requirement and said nothing about the one requiring the negatives to be destroyed.[101]

Section 8

7. To establish Post Offices and post Roads;

This clause, combined with the power to regulate interstate commerce and to spend for the general welfare, permits Congress to subsidize airlines, railroads, and shipping companies, and to grant money to the states for road building and maintenance. But the fact is that, through its powers to tax and to spend for the general welfare, Congress could perform those same functions even in the absence of this grant. Today, this provision is superfluous, but when the framers wrote it they resolved any doubts about the ability of the national government to establish a postal system. Of course, the Founding Fathers could not have anticipated the liberal interpretation of the necessary-and-proper clause (see page 74).

Section 8

8. To promote the Progress of Science and useful Arts, by securing for limited Times to Authors and Inventors exclusive Right to their respective Writings and Discoveries;

Because of this clause, Congress may grant exclusive rights to authors and inventors only for limited times. Copyright protection is afforded to "original works," including books, plays, musical works, pantomimes, sculptural works, motion pictures, and sound recordings. The owner of a copyright is given certain exclusive rights with respect to such works, including the right to reproduce the copyrighted work and to license its sale. The copyright law does not protect ideas or principles, but rather the particular manner in which they are expressed or described.

Works are protected from the moment of creation, whether published or unpublished, and do not need to be registered or identified with a copyright notice. Registration with the Register of Copyrights is, however, a prerequisite for bringing suit for infringement; registration must occur within five years of publication or copyright protection is lost. The protection extends through the life of the author plus fifty years. For anonymous works and works prepared by an employee at the request of an employer, the protection is for seventy-five years from the date of first publication or one hundred years from the year of creation, whichever expires first.

Notwithstanding the exclusive right of copyright owners, there are certain circumstances under which it is permissible to reproduce or display copyrighted works without the permission of the copyright owner. Traditionally, the courts have considered copying for such purposes as criticism, comment, news reporting, teaching, scholarship, and research to be fair use. The standards of fair use described in the current statute include (1) the purpose and character of the use, including whether it is for commercial or educational purposes, (2) the nature of the copyrighted material (e.g., periodical, film, book, videotape), (3) the amount of the work used in relation to the whole, and (4) the effect of the use on the potential market for or value of the copyrighted work.

Penalties for copyright infringement include injunctions against infringing actions, the impoundment and destruction of infringing copies, awards of actual or statutory damages, and the assessment of costs and attorneys' fees. Statutory damages may range from $250 to $10,000 per infringement. If the infringement is found to be willful, a court may increase the statutory damages to $50,000. There are also criminal penalties for willful infringements undertaken for personal or commercial advantage or for financial gain. On the other hand, an innocent infringer, who is defined as one who was not aware and had no reason to believe that his acts constituted an infringement, is protected by a provision that allows the court in its discretion to reduce statutory damages to $100.

The Supreme Court, five to four, has decided that manufacturers of videotape recorders do not infringe the rights of owners of copyrighted television programs. The evidence indicated that the largest use of videotapes was for "time-shifting purposes," to allow the viewer to see the material at a time different from that in which it was telecast, and thus there was little evidence that copyright owners suffered financial harm.[102] Congress could override this decision, but in view of the millions of people with videotape machines in their homes, such action seems unlikely.

Persons who invent or discover any new and useful art, machine, manufacture, or composition of matter, certain types of plants — including man-made microorganisms[103] — and so on may secure a patent from the Patent Office, part of the Department of Commerce. A patent gives its holder the exclusive right to the invention or discovery for seventeen years and, like a copyright, may be sold, assigned, or willed. Litigation growing out of conflicting patents may be appealed to a special court, the U.S. Court of Appeals for the Federal Circuit in Washington, D.C.

Although the copyright power is governed by the same introductory and limiting phrase as the patent power, the Supreme Court has not insisted on the same standards for copyrights as for patents. To secure a copyright, originality is sufficient. To secure a patent, it is necessary to establish that the materials are useful, innovative, and beyond the state of the art. Congress, in exercising the patent power, may not "enlarge the patent monopoly without regard to the innovation, advancement or social benefit gained thereby. . . . Innovation, advancement, and things which add to the sum of useful knowledge are inherent requisites . . . in a patent system which by constitutional command must 'promote the Progress of . . . useful Arts.' This is the *standard* expressed in the Constitution, and it may not be ignored."[104]

Congress's power to protect trademarks — words, letters, or symbols used in connection with merchandise to point out the ownership and origin of the product — stems not from this clause but from the commerce clause. For a trademark to be registered with the Patent Office, it need not be original, merely distinctive. Registration of a trademark grants the right to its exclusive use in interstate commerce for twenty years with unlimited rights of renewal. Obviously, no state can adopt any regulation that conflicts with federal patent or copyright laws, but the Constitution does not exclude states from providing copyright protection for records and tapes not covered by federal law.[105] A state may even enforce its trade secrets acts to protect processes that are unpatented or even unpatentable.[106]

Section 8

9. To constitute Tribunals inferior to the supreme Court;

All federal courts except the Supreme Court rest exclusively on acts of Congress. Any court, except the Supreme Court, can be abolished by act of Congress. It is not clear whether Congress must provide for the judges of the courts it abolishes. In 1802, when Congress first exercised its power to abolish a federal court, no provision was made for the displaced judges. But the only other time Congress has exercised this power, when the commerce court was abolished in 1913, Congress redistributed the commerce court judges among the circuit courts.

Section 8

10. To define and punish Piracies and Felonies committed on the high Seas, and Offences against the Law of Nations;

Congress can make any crime under international law a crime under national law. In the past, this has not been important because international law has dealt chiefly with governments rather than individuals. Developments since the end of World War II, placing individuals under the obligations of international law, could give this paragraph unexpected importance.

Section 8

11. To declare War, grant Letters of Marque and Reprisal, and make rules concerning Captures on Land and Water;

The purpose of this clause was to transfer to Congress a power that in Great Britain belonged to the king, the executive branch. This purpose has not been realized. The president has been primarily responsible for our participation in all our wars, although the role of Congress has recently been enhanced (see page 92).

Letters of marque and reprisal formerly authorized private individuals to prey upon the shipping and property of enemy nations without being considered pirates. The Pact of Paris of 1856 bans this practice.

Section 8

12. To raise and support Armies,

Inasmuch as the framers did not foresee the development of air power, the 1947 act of Congress creating the air force as an independent element of national military power rests on the general *inherent* power of the national government in the fields of foreign relations and national defense. Thus, Congress has the power to raise and support modern military forces of all kinds.

Under conditions of total war, this and the following clause, plus the inherent powers of the national government in the field of foreign relations, confer greater powers than the entire remainder of the Constitution. These include the power to draft people and materials; to requisition property; to allocate and ration materials; to direct the production, marketing, and consumption of all products; and to do whatever is "necessary and proper" to further the successful prosecution of a war. In the words of Chief Justice Hughes, "The power to wage war is the power to wage war successfully."[107] One must have a wide-ranging imagination to comprehend the full scope of these powers.

Congress used its war powers in 1946 when it passed a law giving the federal government control of materials, plants, and information dealing with atomic energy, a statute that has been termed "the most remarkable exercise of governmental power" in the entire history of the country.

The power to raise and support armies, along with the companion clause "To provide and maintain a Navy" and the necessary-and-proper clause, gives Congress the power to register and conscript people during war or peacetime. Does it permit Congress to draft men while not drafting women? When the question was presented to the Supreme Court in 1981, the majority concluded that, since women as a group are not eligible for combat, Congress could choose, if it wished, to order only men to register. The dissenting justices did not challenge the power of Congress to exclude women from combat positions but argued that their exclusion from registration contravened the "equal protection component of the Due Process Clause of the Fifth Amendment" (see page 243).[108]

Section 8

12.   [continued] but no Appropriation of Money to that Use [the raising and supporting of armies] shall be for a longer Term than two Years;

This limitation is to ensure the dependence of the army on Congress and is a reflection of the framers' belief in civilian supremacy and their fear of standing armies.

Section 8

13.   To provide and maintain a Navy;

The navy was not thought to be a threat to liberty, and no limitations were placed on appropriations for it. Moreover, a two-year limitation would not be feasible, as the construction of naval vessels often takes longer than two years and appropriations have to be pledged in advance.

Section 8

14.   To make rules for the Government and Regulation of the land and naval Forces;

The power here conferred is shared, especially under combat conditions, by the president in the capacity of commander in chief. Congress's power under this section, like all its powers, is subject to specific constitutional limitations. However, "judicial deference . . . is at its apogee when legislative action under the congressional authority to raise and support armies and make rules and regulations for their governance is challenged."[109]

Persons in the land and naval forces do not have the same constitutional freedoms as do those not subject to military jurisdiction, but the Supreme Court has narrowed the definition of persons subject to the rules for the regulation of the armed forces to include only those currently having military status (see page 182).

Congress may legislate for those in the armed forces with more flexibility than is allowed for civilians. Thus, the Court has upheld against the charges of vagueness and overbreadth Article 133 of the Military Code, which punishes "conduct unbecoming an officer and a gentleman," and Article 134, which proscribes "all disorders and neglects to the prejudice of the good order and discipline in the armed forces."[110]

Section 8

15.   To provide for calling forth the Militia to execute the Laws of the Union, suppress Insurrections and repel Invasions;

From an early date, the president has been authorized by Congress to employ not only the state militias but also the armed forces of the United States against "combinations of persons too powerful to be dealt with" by ordinary judicial processes. Presidents have used their authority under these statutes to dispatch troops to break up combinations of persons interfering or threatening to interfere with the execution of federal court orders. Presidents have even "federalized" a state's militia, now known as the National Guard, just to take it away from the command of a governor. When the president calls the National Guard into federal service, the president exercises the same control over it as over any unit of the armed forces of the United States.

In the exercise of these powers, the president may, in case of "necessity," declare *martial law*. Of this there are various degrees and kinds, the most extreme being that in which military courts temporarily take over the government of a region.

Section 8

16. To provide for organizing, arming, and disciplining the Militia, and for governing such Part of them as may be employed in the Service of the United States, reserving to the States, respectively, the Appointment of the Officers, and the Authority of training the Militia according to the discipline prescribed by Congress;

Congress and the states cooperate in the maintenance of the National Guard. Normally, it operates under the direction of the states, subject to provisions made by Congress. When called into the service of the United States, the National Guard becomes a part of the United States military forces and is subject to government by Congress and the president. When the National Guard is not in federal service, Congress can still exercise a considerable degree of control through conditions attached to grants of money to the states for the National Guard. In 1986 — 1987 several governors objected to the training of their state militias in Honduras, contending that this assignment of military forces was an improper use designed to put pressure on the government of Nicaragua. Their objections, however, lacked constitutional status.

Section 8

17. To exercise exclusive Legislation in all Cases whatsoever, over such District (not exceeding ten Miles square), as may, by Cession of particular States, and the Acceptance of Congress, become the Seat of the Government of the United States, and to exercise like Authority over all Places purchased by the Consent of the Legislature of the State in which the Same shall be for the Erection of Forts, Magazines, Arsenals, dock-Yards, and other needful Buildings;

After many years in which Congress exercised direct authority over the District of Columbia, with the district having only appointed officials, the District of Columbia Self-Government Act of 1973 finally brought a considerable measure of home rule to the district. The citizens of the district elect their own mayor, city council, and school board; the council has limited authority to legislate and to levy taxes, but Congress still retains ultimate legislative authority. A National Capital Service Area consisting of the principal federal buildings provides a federal enclave within the district.

This clause probably requires Congress, if it should ever vote to admit the District of Columbia as a state (see page 118), to retain exclusive jurisdiction over a small part of it as "the Seat of the Government of the United States."

Section 8

18.   —— And To make all Laws which shall be necessary and proper for carrying into Execution the foregoing Powers, and all other Powers vested by this Constitution in the Government of the United States, or in any Department or Officer thereof.

As is the case with the general welfare clause, this clause (variously known as the *necessary-and-proper clause*, the *elastic clause*, and the *coefficient clause*) is subject to misunderstanding. Congress is not here granted the power to make all laws that shall be necessary and proper for any purpose whatsoever, but only to make laws necessary and proper to execute its enumerated powers or to execute powers vested by the Constitution in the president, the Senate, or the courts. However, because of the expansive interpretation given to the several enumerated powers and the generous interpretation of the necessary-and-proper clause, nowadays there is hardly any subject that Congress cannot deal with. Thus, to be precise and technically accurate in noting that this clause is not a general grant of power is to convey the wrong impression. This may be one of those rare instances when those who are technically wrong are more accurate than those who are precisely right, and a classic example of how a little learning can be a dangerous thing.

As we have noted, in the famous case of *McCulloch* v *Maryland*, Chief Justice Marshall construed the word *necessary* to mean "convenient" or "useful" and rejected the narrow interpretation "indispensable." As an example, the authority to establish a Federal Reserve banking system is not among the enumerated powers of Congress, but Congress can so act because establishing such a system is a necessary and proper (that is, *convenient*) way of executing its powers to lay and collect taxes, to borrow money on the credit of the United States, and to regulate interstate commerce.

"Inherited" Powers: The Power to Investigate

In addition to specifically vested powers, each house of Congress enjoys important powers by inheritance, as it were, from the English Parliament and the early state legislatures. One important inherited power is that of conducting investigations to gather information needed to legislate, to propose constitutional amendments, or to perform other constitutional functions.[111] As a necessary adjunct to its investigating power, each house may subpoena witnesses and punish those who refuse to produce documents or answer questions. Each chamber may itself determine a witness's guilt and have that witness held in custody for as long as the chamber is in session. The more common practice is to turn the recalcitrant witness over to the federal prosecutor for action under a federal law making it a crime to refuse to answer pertinent questions or produce pertinent testimony when ordered to do so by a congressional committee.

Are there constitutional limits to Congress's investigating authority? Or to be more precise, what are the limits of the authority of Congress to compel persons to furnish materials or to answer questions? Congress is not supposed to use its investigatory powers, any more than its legislative powers, to abridge the freedoms protected by the First Amendment. The Supreme Court has warned Congress that the First Amendment sets boundaries on its investigatory authority. But a majority of the justices has never been mustered to sustain an actual claim that testimony compelled by Congress, even about political beliefs and activities, has in fact abridged rights secured by the First Amendment.

The doctrine of separation of powers also limits Congress's investigatory power. As the Supreme Court has stated it, "The power to investigate must not be confused with any of the powers of law enforcement; those powers are assigned under our Constitution to the Executive and Judiciary." Congress "has no power to expose for the sake of exposure."[112] It may compel answers only if the information sought is needed by Congress in the pursuit of its legitimate business. However, few limits have been placed on what constitutes such pursuit. For example, legislative investigations need not be justified by the development of proposals for new legislation; investigations to determine whether and how government programs are functioning are appropriate.

Since witnesses before congressional committees are not on trial in a formal sense, the committees are not required to give witnesses the same rights they would have in a court of law. Committees, however, must comply with whatever procedural rules they choose to adopt.[113] In addition, witnesses have a right, under the Fifth Amendment, to refuse to answer questions if the answers would expose them to the risk of criminal prosecution. (Congress, by granting limited immunity from prosecution, may impose legal obligations upon persons to testify, see page 187.)

By far the most important restraint on congressional investigations has been the Supreme Court's insistence on a strict construction of the federal law defining the offense of contempt of Congress. Contempt of Congress, as defined by the law, is the refusal to answer *pertinent* questions. Before the Supreme Court will permit a conviction, (1) the parent chamber must have clearly authorized the committee to make the particular investigation (in the case of investigations by committees of the House of Representatives, since neither the House nor its committees are continuing bodies, the authorization must occur during the term of Congress in which the investigation takes place); (2) the committee must have authorized the investigation; (3) the committee must have made clear to the witness the subject under investigation, the pertinence of the question to the subject, and the reason the committee insisted that it be answered; (4) the grand jury indictment must have specified the subject under committee investigation and the pertinent questions the defendant is charged with refusing to answer.[114]

Limitations on Congressional Powers

Whereas Section 8 enumerates the legislative powers of the national government, Section 9 limits them. Section 9 — and Section 10, which restricts the powers of the state governments — were originally looked on as a kind of bill of rights.

Section 9

1. The Migration or Importation of such Persons as any of the States now existing shall think proper to admit, shall not be prohibited by the Congress prior to the Year one thousand eight hundred and eight, but a Tax or duty may be imposed on such Importation, not exceeding ten dollars for each person.

This paragraph refers to the importation of slaves into the United States and is of historical interest only.

Section 9

2. The Privilege of the Writ of Habeas Corpus shall not be suspended, unless when in Cases of Rebellion or Invasion the public Safety may require it.

The writ of habeas corpus — known in the eighteenth century as the Great Writ — was primarily a remedy against executive detention. By this writ a judge could inquire of an arresting officer or jailer why a particular person was in custody. If no proper explanation could be given, the judge could order the prisoner's release. But once it was determined that a person was being held as the result of a sentence imposed by a court with proper jurisdiction, that ended the matter. Since then, Congress has expanded the use of the writ to permit federal courts to review the actions of officials to determine not merely whether a person is being detained as the result of a judicial sentence, but also whether that sentence was obtained as the result of a constitutionally proper trial.[115]

Congress is the authority to order the suspension of the privilege, although in situations in which the president can validly declare martial law, the president can also suspend the writ. The greater power includes the lesser.

State courts may not inquire why persons are held under the authority of the United States; federal courts, on the other hand, do have jurisdiction to determine if persons are being improperly held by federal or state authorities.

In recent decades, the habeas corpus business of federal district judges has grown tremendously, causing considerable resentment among state judges; partly in response to that criticism, the Supreme Court has started to limit somewhat the scope of federal district judges' habeas corpus jurisdiction. Prior to seeking a federal habeas corpus writ to review the actions of state courts, a person must first exhaust state remedies, including a petition for review by the Supreme Court. The Supreme Court has also ruled that if defendants fail to raise constitutional claims in state proceedings, they are not to be given any relief by means of a writ of habeas corpus in federal court unless they "demonstrate cause and actual prejudice." The mere proof that state courts committed an error will not suffice.[116] In *Stone* v *Powell* the Court decided that when a person has had a hearing in a state court on the allegation that the evidence used against that person was extracted in violation of Fourth Amendment rights, the matter can no longer be looked into by federal courts upon a habeas corpus petition.[117] So far the Court has not extended this rule to other constitutional claims but has restricted it to those relating to searches and seizures. For example, the Court has refused to extend *Stone* v *Powell* to cover the Sixth Amendment claim of denial of effective assistance of counsel.[118]

Section 9

3. No Bill of Attainder [shall be passed]

A bill of attainder is the infliction of punishment by the legislature. At common law, a bill of attainder was a death sentence, but early in our history we departed from that restrictive definition. Imprisonment, banishment, confiscation of property, denial of jobs, and other kinds of punishment are now recognized as attainders forbidden by this clause.

Congress, by general law, may determine what conduct will be considered a crime, but it may not impose punishment; this must be done by a court of law.

In the last four decades, the Court has entertained four serious challenges under this clause, twice holding that Congress had violated it. The first time, a provision of an appropriations bill named three federal employees and declared that they should receive no compensation from the federal treasury, other than for military or jury services, unless reappointed to office by the president with the consent of the Senate.[119] The second challenge was to a provision that no member of the Communist Party should be allowed to serve as a trade union officer.[120] In both instances Congress was found to have passed a bill of attainder in that it had inflicted punishment — that is, loss of job — without trial on named individuals or on members of a specific political group.

The third serious challenge was by former President Nixon, who argued that the Presidential Recordings and Materials Preservation Act of 1974, which took control of his presidential papers away from him and vested it in the administrator of general services, was a bill of attainder. As Justice Stevens said: "The statute before the Court . . . singles out one, by name, for special treatment. Unlike all other former Presidents in our history (and subsequent ones), he is denied custody of his own presidential papers. The statute implicitly condemns him as an unreliable custodian of his papers. Legislation which subjects a named individual to this humiliating treatment must raise serious questions under the Bill of Attainder Clause." But seven members of the Court ruled that this was not a bill of attainder. Nixon, they argued, was a legitimate "class of one"; Congress was motivated, not by a desire to punish, but rather by a desire to provide an appropriate process for disposing of presidential papers. Justice Stevens, in concurrence, stated that the decisive fact was that Nixon had made himself a class different from all other presidents by resigning under unique circumstances and accepting a pardon. But it was precisely because of those facts, the dissenters contended, that Congress had "punished" Nixon and passed a bill of attainder.[121]

The fourth modern bill-of-attainder challenge was presented by some male students who charged that Congress had imposed a bill of attainder when, by what has come to be known as the Solomon Amendment, it required all men who wished to apply for federal student financial aid to indicate that they had complied with the registration requirements of the Military Selective Service Act. Although a federal district judge agreed with the students, the Supreme Court did not. Chief Justice Burger, speaking for the Court, pointed out that any student who wished to apply for aid could become eligible for it at any time by registration. In addition to not singling out an identifiable group as is characteristic of a bill of attainder, the Solomon Amendment was also said not to impose punishment, because the sanction was a mere denial of a noncontractual governmental benefit. "It imposed no affirmative disability approaching the kinds of disabilities historically associated with punishment."[122]

Section 9

3. [continued] or ex post facto Law shall be passed.

An ex post facto law is a retroactive criminal law that works to the disadvantage of an individual — for example, by making a particular act a crime that was not a crime when committed or by retroactively reducing the proof necessary to convict or by increasing punishment retroactively.[123] "To fall within the *ex post facto* prohibition, two critical elements must be present: first, the law must be retrospective, that is, it must 'apply to events occurring before its enactment'; and second, it must disadvantage the offender affected by it. . . . No violation occurs if a change does not alter 'substantial personal rights,' but merely 'changes modes of procedure which do not affect matters of substance.' "[124] The prohibition does not prevent passage of retroactive penal laws that work to the benefit of an accused — a law decreasing punishment, for instance.[125]

Although the due process clause imposes some barriers to retroactive civil laws, the ex post facto clause imposes none, not even to civil laws that work against individuals — say, an increase in income taxes applied to income previously earned.[126]

"So much importance did the Convention attach (to the ex post facto prohibition) that it is found twice in the Constitution"[127] — here as a limitation on the national government and in Section 10 as a limitation on the states.

Section 9

4. No Capitation, or other direct, Tax shall be laid, unless in Proportion to the Census or Enumeration herein before directed to be taken.

A capitation tax is a poll or head tax. The precise meaning of the term *direct tax* is today uncertain (see page 39).

Section 9

5. No Tax or Duty shall be laid on Articles exported from any State.

Although Congress cannot tax articles exported from states, it can, under its power to regulate commerce with foreign nations, prohibit those exports by such means as embargoes.

Section 9

6. No Preference shall be given by any Regulation of Commerce or Revenue to the Ports of one State over those of another: nor shall Vessels bound to, or from, one State, be obliged to enter, clear, or pay Duties in another.

By giving Congress the power to regulate interstate and foreign commerce, the states were prevented from discriminating against the commerce of other states. This section prevents Congress, in regulating such commerce, from discriminating against the trade of a single state or of a group of states.

Section 9

7. No money shall be drawn from the Treasury, but in Consequence of Appropriations made by Law; and a regular Statement and Account of the Receipts and Expenditures of all public Money shall be published from time to time.

It is this clause, more than any other, that gives Congress control over the acts of the other branches of government — the president, the courts, the military, and so on — since all depend on Congress for money to carry out their functions. Congress, and not the courts, determines with what specificity executive agencies are to account for their expenditures. Taxpayer suits cannot be maintained to force Congress or a federal agency to comply with this clause. Thus, a taxpayer was denied the right to challenge before the courts the constitutionality of an act of Congress that permits the Central Intelligence Agency to account for its expenditures "solely on the certificate of the Director."[128]

Section 9

8. No Title of Nobility shall be granted by the United States:

Section 10 imposes the same limitation on the states. One wonders how our lives might have been enriched if the Constitution had not prohibited the national government and the states from granting titles of nobility: Babe Ruth might have become not just the Sultan of Swat but the Duke of Swat, and Lindbergh the Earl of Flight. Elvis Presley might have become the Prince of Memphis, and who knows who might have become the Archduke of Albany or the Duke of Dupont Circle or the Marquis of Irvine. But then again, titles might have been passed out by the national government and the states, not in recognition of outstanding public service, but for patronage purposes.

Section 9

8. [continued] And no Person holding any Office of Profit or Trust under them, shall, without the Consent of the Congress, accept of any present, Emolument, Office, or Title, of any kind whatever, from any King, Prince, or foreign State.

Acquainted with the history of previous republican governments, and aware of the ability of foreign sovereigns to bribe and corrupt republican officials, the framers took precautions to prevent any foreign state from securing undue influence within the executive agencies of the national government.

Limitations on States

Section 10

1. No State shall enter into any Treaty, Alliance, or Confederation;

When the government of the United States was formed, the individual states lost their international personalities, if, in fact, they ever possessed them. Constitutionally, the states can neither negotiate with foreign states nor have any direct relations with them. The national government possesses a monopoly over the foreign affairs of the United States. States may not exercise their reserved powers in such a way as to intrude on the national government's exclusive right to deal with international affairs. For example, states traditionally regulate the distribution of estates, but those regulations must give way if they impair the effective exercise of the nation's foreign policy by conflicting with agreements between the United States and other nations.[129]

Section 10

1. [continued] [No state shall] grant Letters of Marque and Reprisal;

This power was given to Congress in Section 8, paragraph 11 (see page 71), and this section makes clear that states are not to have any authority over such matters.

Section 10

1. [continued] [No state shall] coin Money; emit Bills of Credit; make any Thing but gold and silver Coin a Tender in Payment of Debts;

This provision makes quite clear that the national government is in charge of our currency system. The practice of states issuing their own currencies made commercial life difficult under the Articles of Confederation. That there is but one currency system for the entire United States is a major factor binding the Union together.

Section 10

1. [continued] [No state shall] pass any Bill of Attainder, ex post facto Law,

These limitations imposed on the national government are herein also imposed on the states.

Section 10

1. [continued] [No state shall pass] or Law impairing the Obligation of Contracts, or grant any Title of Nobility.

After the Revolution, the thirteen states, operating under the weak and ineffective

Articles of Confederation, passed through a difficult period of readjustment as a result of the economic and political dislocations of the war's aftermath. Many citizens were in debt; the farmers who had speculated freely in land while prices were rising were especially burdened. Property and debtor laws were extremely harsh. Defaulting debtors were thrown into jail and deprived of all their holdings. In many states, the legislatures, responsive to farmers' pressure, passed laws to alleviate the lot of debtors. Paper money was made legal tender for the payment of debts, bankruptcy laws were passed, and sometimes the courts were closed to creditors. These laws, in turn, aroused the creditor classes, who, feeling that their rights had been infringed, demanded action to put a stop to such "abuses" of power by the state legislatures. Creditors, in fact, were foremost among the groups that brought the Constitutional Convention about; the prevention of such interferences with private rights by state legislatures was one of the major purposes of the convention. As James Madison put the matter in a speech to his fellow delegates, intrusions in private rights by state legislatures "were evils which had, more perhaps than anything else, produced this Convention." This paragraph of the Constitution was the principal result of this concern.

When the framers spoke of "contracts" whose obligations could not be impaired by state law, they had in mind the ordinary contracts between individuals, especially contracts of debt. The meaning of the word, however, was early expanded by judicial interpretation to include contracts made by the states themselves, including franchises granted to corporations. As a result, the "obligation of contracts" clause became, prior to the Civil War, the most important defense of the rights of property in the Constitution. States were prevented from passing any law, whether in the interest of the public welfare or not, that might materially disturb rights secured by contract.[130] In the late 1830s, however, the Supreme Court began to restrict the application of the contracts clause. By the 1890s [131] it had been established that all franchises should be narrowly construed in favor of the states and that all contracts implicitly recognized the general police power of the states to regulate property (including contract rights) for the public welfare.

By the 1930s the contract clause had ceased to be a serious limitation upon state powers. It came to mean no more than that a state could impair the obligation of contracts, provided it did so to promote the general welfare and not "in a spirit of oppression" and "without reasonable justification." Then, after more than forty years, in 1977 and — to show that it was not a fluke — again in 1978, in the words of the dissenters, the Court "dusted off" the contract clause and declared a state law unconstitutional. In 1977 the Court declared that New Jersey had violated the Contract Clause when it set aside a provision of an earlier law enacted to protect bondholders. Justice Blackmun wrote for the Court, "Whether or not the protection of contract rights comports with current views of wise public policy, the Contract Clause remains a part of our written Constitution."[132] In the 1978 decision, Justice Stevens reiterated, "The Contract Clause remains part of the Constitution. It is not a dead letter." The Court declared unconstitutional the application of a Minnesota law that imposed additional pension obligations on employers beyond those they had previously undertaken by contract with their employees.[133]

Despite these two holdings, more recent decisions make it clear that the contract clause is not likely to become once again a major limitation on the power of the states to regulate property. A unanimous Court upheld the application of an Alabama law prohibiting oil producers from passing on to purchasers any increase in severance taxes, despite preexisting contracts stipulating that purchasers were to absorb such increases. The Court pointed out that the Alabama law, unlike those involved in the 1977 and 1978 decisions, did not "prescribe a rule limited to contractual obligations or remedies, but imposed a generally applicable rule of conduct designed to advance a broad societal interest." Alabama was attempting to shield consumers from the burdens of tax increases, and its prohibition applied to all oil and gas producers, regardless of whether they happened to be parties to contracts providing for tax increases to be passed on to purchasers.[134] The Court also ruled that Kansas could regulate natural gas prices, even if it slightly impaired the contractual rights of an energy company, because the company was operating in a highly regulated industry, and the state's interest in protecting consumers is a significant and legitimate one.[135] And the Court did not find it difficult to conclude that Pennsylvania could prohibit mine owners from holding surface owners to their contractual waiver of liability for surface damages.[136] In short, if states avoid singling out contracts, laws passed to promote the general welfare are not likely to run afoul of this clause even if they do incidentally impair the obligations of a contract.

Section 10

2. No State shall, without the Consent of the Congress, lay any Imposts or Duties on Imports or Exports, except what may be absolutely necessary for executing its inspection Laws: and the net Produce of all Duties and Imposts, laid by any State on Imports or Exports, shall be for the Use of the Treasury of the United States; and all such Laws shall be subject to the Revision and Controul of the Congress.

Without the express consent of Congress, but subject to its revision, states may levy an inspection tax on imports and exports. (Inspection laws are concerned with quantity and quality.) Congress, not the courts, decides whether or not the inspection tax is more than "what may be absolutely necessary for executing [the state's] inspection laws."

The ban on duties and imposts on imports and exports used to be construed to forbid taxation of imports until removed from their original package and of exports after they had begun to move to a foreign country. The Court has now removed such rigid limitations on state taxation. The clause is designed to prevent (1) state exactions that interfere with the exclusive power of the federal government to regulate foreign commercial relations, (2) exactions by seaboard states, taxing goods that flow through their ports, that might disturb the harmony among the states, and (3) in the case of state duties on imports (Congress cannot tax exports either), state exactions that interfere with the exclusive power of the federal government to raise revenues from tariffs. Short of these limitations, a state may collect nondiscriminatory taxes — for example, a general property tax applied to imported tires, even though in their original package,[137] or a tax on imported goods, such as tobacco, stored under bond in a customs warehouse and destined for domestic manufacture or sale,[138] or a tax on the gross income from stevedoring activities for loading and unloading cargo ships.[139]

Section 10

3. No State shall, without the Consent of Congress, lay any Duty of Tonnage, keep Troops, or Ships of War in time of Peace, enter into any Agreement or Compact with another State,

---

A duty of tonnage is a charge on a vessel, according to its cargo capacity, for entering or leaving a port or navigating public waters.

A state has the constitutional right, without the consent of Congress, to provide for and maintain a militia; it may not keep a standing army or maintain its own navy.

"Read literally, the Compact Clause would require the states to obtain congressional approval before entering into any agreement themselves. . . . But it has never been so interpreted. Congressional assent is required only for agreements that enhance the political power of states in relation to the national government" or those that might offend the sovereignty of other states.[140] An agreement between New Hampshire and Maine "locating an ancient" boundary did not require congressional assent.[141] Nor was congressional approval required for the agreement among twenty-one states to establish an administrative headquarters to audit multistate taxpayers and to facilitate the collection of state taxes from such taxpayers.[142]

When congressional consent is required, Congress may give it in advance, as it has done many times, for example, when it authorizes states to make civil defense compacts to be effective sixty days after such agreements have been transmitted to Congress, unless Congress disapproves by concurrent resolution. Sometimes congressional consent is granted in more general terms, as when Congress gave approval for two or more states to enter into agreements for the cooperative enforcement of their respective criminal laws.

Congressional approval of an interstate compact makes such compact federal law, subject to construction by federal rules rather than the rules of a state.[143] Disputes over the interpretation of such compacts are disputes between states and thus are subject to the original jurisdiction of the Supreme Court.[144]

Section 10

3. [continued] [No State shall, without the Consent of Congress, . . . enter into any Agreement or Compact with another State], or with a foreign Power, or engage in War, unless actually invaded, or in such imminent Danger as will not admit of delay.

This clause reflects conditions in the eighteenth century, when it was possible that a state government might have to assume some responsibility for repelling a foreign invasion until the forces of the national government could be alerted and mobilized to do so.

The framers made it very clear, in every way possible, that the states have no right to negotiate with foreign countries. States have no power whatsoever to declare war. That power belongs to Congress alone. As to engaging in hostilities, any invasion of any state is an invasion of the United States.

ARTICLE II: THE EXECUTIVE ARTICLE

Section 1

1. The executive Power shall be vested in a President of the United States of America.

What is the significance of the fact that the words "herein granted," which appear in the legislative article, are omitted in the executive article? Does Section 1 confer the executive power on the president, or does it merely designate the title of the person who is given certain specified duties by the rest of the article? The more general view, and the one that conforms to presidential practices, is that this section gives the president a power that has never been defined or enumerated and, in fact, cannot be defined since its scope depends largely on circumstances. Although not so broad, this executive power is akin to the prerogative formerly claimed by the English Crown to act for the public good "without the prescription of the law" and "sometimes even against it."[1] The president can issue proclamations of neutrality, remove executive officials from office, make executive agreements with foreign nations, and take emergency action to preserve the nation, although such powers are not specifically granted to the president by the Constitution.

When the President acts pursuant to an express or implied authorization from Congress, it is an exercise not only of presidential powers but also those delegated by Congress. "In such a case the executive action would be supported by the strongest of presumptions and the widest latitude of judicial interpretation, and the burden of persuasion would rest heavily upon any who might attack it. . . . When the President acts in the absence of congressional authorization he may enter a zone of twilight in which he and Congress may have concurrent authority, or in which its distribution is uncertain. . . . In such a case the . . . validity of the President's action, at least so far as separation of powers principles are concerned, hinges on a consideration of all the circumstances which might shed light on the views of the Legislative Branch toward such action, including congressional inertia, indifference, or quiescence. . . ." Finally, when the President acts in contravention of the will of Congress, "his power is at its lowest ebb," and the Court can sustain these actions "only by disabling the Congress from acting upon the subject."[2]

During the Korean War, President Truman ordered the secretary of commerce to take temporary possession of the steel mills to avoid a strike that would disrupt production of steel desperately needed to produce the weapons of war. No law authorized this action. The Taft-Hartley Act, passed over his veto, gave the president the authority to seek an eighty-day court injunction against strikes that jeopardized the national safety, but the president refused to do so because the union had previously agreed to postpone the strike for a much longer period and because it would have been politically unwise for him to use it.

Where did the president secure his authority to order this seizure? From his power as chief executive and commander in chief, argued the attorneys for the president. The steel companies challenged this contention, and the Supreme Court agreed with them that the president had acted unconstitutionally.[3] Although Justice Black announced the opinion of the Court, only he clearly denied that the president had any general executive powers. Five other justices joined with him to reject the president's claim to act in this particular instance, but did so because Congress had indicated by the Taft-Hartley Act that the president should not seize property to avert strikes. In the absence of that legislation, a different question would have been presented. Moreover, it is possible that if the justices had been convinced the emergency action was necessary, they would not have interfered, even in the face of the Taft-Hartley Act. When it is remembered that three justices agreed with the president and four carefully limited their concurrence to the particulars of the immediate case, the steel seizure decision does not appear to undermine the general position that the president has authority to act without prescription of law — and perhaps, in desperate situations, even against the law — to preserve the national safety. Such actions are subject, however, to the peril of subsequent judicial reversal, of impeachment, or of political defeat.

Since the steel seizure case, the Supreme Court has four times specifically acknowledged that the president has inherent executive authority, although in each instance it rejected the assertion that inherent presidential power applied in that particular case. In the first, a majority of the Court ruled that because of the presumption against prior restraint of publications (see page 147), the executive authority of the president did not justify a court's acceding to the president's request to restrain a newspaper from publishing secret documents (the Pentagon Papers) that had fallen into its hands.[4] In the second case, a unanimous Court, one justice not participating, held that the executive authority of the president does not extend to authorizing electronic surveillance of conversations of persons suspected of engaging in domestic subversion.[5]

The third instance was the celebrated case of *United States* v *Nixon* (1974).[6] The Supreme Court rejected President Nixon's claim that he had an inherent power, growing out of the doctrine of separation of powers, to have an absolute say about what information he would withhold and what he would release to a court. There is no such absolute executive privilege. The responsibility to decide what information should be released and under what conditions is a judicial one, not an executive one. The president, like other persons, is subject to a subpoena of materials needed for criminal prosecutions. In this particular case, the Supreme Court, holding that the tapes in President Nixon's possession were needed for a criminal prosecution, thus sustained the order of the trial judge that the president release the materials to the court.

The Supreme Court also ruled, however, that the president does have a *limited executive privilege*, stemming both from the doctrine of separation of powers and from powers granted by Article II. Executive privilege is something that most presidents have long insisted vests in their office, but this was the first time the Supreme Court had acknowledged that it existed, albeit in a limited fashion. The president does have the right to claim confidentiality of executive communications, especially if claiming that their disclosure would reveal military or diplomatic secrets. Faced with such assertions, the courts are to show "utmost deference." And even outside those areas, the president's "singularly unique role" requires that great efforts be made to ensure that presidential communications be kept confidential. To that end, the trial judge was instructed to inspect the subpoenaed materials *in camera* (in secret) and to release only the information that he thought related to the trial. Other material was to be returned to the president and "restored to its privileged status." In short, the president has the right to claim executive privilege for materials under his control, subject only to the limitation that if they are needed for a criminal trial and do not reveal military or diplomatic secrets, a trial judge may have limited access to them.

Left unanswered by the Supreme Court, since the issue was not before it, was the right of the president to withhold information from Congress. The principles of *United States v Nixon* would seem to suggest that under certain circumstances — for example, when the House of Representatives or one of its committees is carrying out its responsibilities under the impeachment clause — the doctrine of executive privilege would not justify the president's refusal to submit materials in response to a congressional subpoena. When President Nixon refused to release materials in connection with the House Judiciary Committee's investigation of activities that might warrant his impeachment, the House chose not to take the issue to the courts; rather, the president's failure to respond to the congressional subpoena became one of the grounds for impeachment charged against him by the committee.

The fourth case relating to the inherent executive powers of the president grew out of negotiations with the Iranian government, conducted by President Carter and confirmed by President Reagan — negotiations that led to the release of American hostages. The president signed an executive agreement with Iran under which the United States agreed to terminate all legal proceedings in the United States by our nationals against the Iranian government and to transfer such claims to a specially created Iran — United States Claims Tribunal for binding arbitration. In addition, one billion dollars of the assets of Iran held by U.S. banks were transferred to English and Algerian banks to be held to cover the settlement of claims by American nationals. The rest of the Iranian assets held by American banks were returned to Iranian control. A unanimous Court upheld the president's power to act, even though it entrenched on judicial power. The Court stressed the long-standing exercise by the president of the power to enter into executive agreements to settle claims, the long-standing acquiescence by Congress in the exercise of such presidential power, and, in this specific instance, the fact that Congress had taken no action to disapprove of what the president did. The Court cautiously decided, "While it is not concluded that the President has plenary power to settle claims, even against foreign governmental entities, nevertheless where, as here, the settlement of claims has been determined to be a necessary incident to the resolution of a major foreign policy dispute between this country and another, and Congress has acquiesced to the President's action, it cannot be said that the President lacks the power to settle such claims."[7]

Section 1

1.   [continued] He shall hold his Office during the Term of four Years, and, together with the Vice President, chosen for the same term, be elected, as follows

See also the Twenty-second Amendment, which limits the president's tenure, and the Twenty-fifth Amendment, which provides for replacement of the vice president, whenever the office becomes empty.

Section 1

2.   Each State shall appoint, in such Manner as the Legislature thereof may direct, a Number of Electors, equal to the whole Number of Senators and Representatives to which the State may be entitled in the Congress: but no Senator or Representative, or Person holding an Office of Trust or Profit under the United States, shall be appointed an Elector.

At various times, some state legislatures have directed the selection of electors by the legislature itself, some by voters in districts, some by voters of the entire state, and some by a combination of these methods. At present — except for Maine, which elects two of its four electors by congressional districts — all electors in all states and in the District of Columbia are elected by voters on a statewide ticket.

In exercising this power, state legislatures are subject to all constitutional commands. In addition to the obviously applicable Fifteenth and Nineteenth Amendments, other clauses that particularly apply are the First Amendment and the equal protection clause of the Fourteenth, which together, among other things, protect the rights of association as applied to minor parties. In addition to the clearly unconstitutional denial of the right to vote because of race or sex, a legislature cannot enforce a scheme that would give the voters in one part of a state more electoral votes than voters in another district. A state may not use procedures for nominating electors that make it too difficult for minor parties to get their presidential electoral candidates on the ballot,[8] that impose greater demands on city folks than on country people in order to get the candidates they favor on a ballot,[9] or that set too early a deadline for filing and make it too difficult for independent candidates to run for president.[10]

Section 1

3. [This entire paragraph has been superseded by the Twelfth Amendment.] The Electors shall meet in their respective States, and vote by Ballot for two Persons, of whom one at least shall not be an Inhabitant of the same State with themselves. And they shall make a List of all the Persons voted for, and of the Number of Votes for each; which List they shall sign and certify, and transmit sealed to the Seat of the Government of the United States, directed to the President of the Senate. The President of the Senate shall, in the Presence of the Senate and House of Representatives, open all the Certificates, and the Votes shall then be counted. The Person having the greatest Number of Votes shall be the President, if such Number be a Majority of the whole Number of Electors appointed; and if there be more than one who have such Majority, and have an equal Number of Votes, then the House of Representatives shall immediately chuse by Ballot one of them for President: and if no Person have a Majority, then from the five highest on the List the said House shall in like Manner chuse the President. But in chusing the President, the Votes shall be taken by States, the Representation from each State having one Vote; A quorum for this Purpose shall consist of a Member or Members from two thirds of the States, and a Majority of all the States shall be necessary to a Choice. In every Case, after the Choice of the President,the Person having the greatest Number of Votes of the Electors shall be the Vice President. But if there should remain two or more who have equal Votes, the Senate shall chuse from them by Ballot the Vice President.

The framers of the Constitution had difficulty in working out the procedures for selecting the President and the Vice President. Selection by Congress was rejected because it would make the president dependent on Congress and would violate the doctrine of separation of powers. Election by the state legislatures was rejected because of lack of confidence in those bodies, which "had betrayed a strong propensity to a variety of pernicious measures."[11] Direct popular election was rejected because the less populous states felt that the more populous states would always elect the president, and because most of the delegates thought that the expanse of the country rendered "it impossible that the people can have the requisite capacity to judge of the respective pretensions of the Candidates."[12] So, for lack of something better, the framers devised the system set forth in Section 1, paragraph 3, which they expected would work in somewhat the following fashion: The several state legislatures would prescribe procedures to select the most eminent persons in the states — electors — who would then cast their electoral ballots for the two persons they considered the best qualified to serve as president. When the votes of the electors of the various states were collected, the person with the most votes, provided those votes were a majority of those cast by the whole number of electors, was to be declared president; the person with the second highest number of votes was to be vice president. It was expected that almost every elector would cast one vote for a candidate from his own state and that the votes would be so dispersed that often no person would have a majority. In that case, the House of Representatives, voting by states, would make the final selection from the five candidates receiving the most electoral votes.

But the framers reckoned without political parties. Parties, by presenting a single slate for president and vice president, completely changed the operation of the electoral system and thus made the original provision for it unworkable. The failure became apparent in the election of 1800, when Jefferson and Burr tied for first place in the electoral college. It was the first major breakdown of the constitutional system, and the Twelfth Amendment was needed to repair the breach.

Section 1

4. The Congress may determine the Time of chusing the Electors, and the Day on which they shall give their Votes; which Day shall be the same throughout the United States.

Congress designated the first Tuesday after the first Monday in November in presidential election years as the day for the selection of electors. The electors do not give their votes, however, until the first Monday after the second Wednesday in December. On that date the electors of each state assemble at such place as their state legislature directs (normally the state capitol), give their votes, and certify six lists, which are distributed as follows: one is sent by registered mail to the president of the Senate, two are delivered to the secretary of state of their state, two are sent by registered mail to the administrator of general services, and one is delivered to the federal district judge of the district in which the electors have assembled. No chances are taken of losing these precious documents, which usually record a foregone conclusion. Then in January (see the Twentieth Amendment) the president of the Senate, in the presence of the Senate and the House of Representatives (see the Twelfth Amendment), opens the certificates and the electoral vote is counted; the winners are formally proclaimed elected.

Electors remain constitutionally free to cast their ballots for any person they wish. There have been maverick electors, who ignored the wishes of the voters who had chosen them, but in no case have they affected the outcome of an election. States may authorize political parties to require electors to pledge in advance that they will vote for the party candidate,[13] but what could be done to enforce such a pledge remains unsettled.

The states choose the electors, and the legislature of each state determines how electors will be selected, but Congress counts the electoral votes. Most of the time the counting is routine, but in 1876 Congress found that Rutherford B. Hayes, the Republican candidate, had 165 uncontested electoral votes, Samuel J. Tilden, the Democrat, had 184 clear votes, one less than necessary, and there were disputes about which was the right slate of electors from Florida, South Carolina, and Louisiana and about one electoral vote in Oregon. How those disputes would be resolved would determine who would become president. The House was controlled by the Democrats, the Senate by the Republicans. The practice up to that time had been that the consent of both houses was required to validate the electoral count.

To break the deadlock, Congress, by an act approved by the president, created an electoral commission consisting of five House members chosen by the House, five senators chosen by the Senate, and five justices of the Supreme Court, four of whom were designated in the act, with the fifth to be chosen by those four. The electoral commission ended up with eight Republicans and seven Democrats, and by a vote of eight to seven the commission resolved the disputes in favor of Hayes.

As a result of that disputed election, Congress enacted a provision that if the vote of a state is not certified by the governor, it shall not be counted unless both houses of Congress concur.

Section 1

5. No Person except a natural born Citizen, or a Citizen of the United States, at the time of the Adoption of this Constitution, shall be eligible to the Office of President; neither shall any Person be eligible to that Office who shall not have attained to the Age of thirty five Years, and been fourteen Years a Resident within the United States.

This clause contains the only constitutional distinction between naturalized and natural-born citizens. Whether a person born abroad of American parents is a natural-born citizen within the meaning of this section has not yet been decided. There is a considerable body of opinion that such a person is "natural-born" even if perhaps not native-born. The issue is likely to be resolved only if a political party nominates a person born outside the United States to American citizens and he or she is elected. The answer will come from the electorate.

The Twelfth Amendment states explicitly that the same qualifications are required for eligibility for the vice presidency.

Before the election of President Hoover, there was some question whether the fourteen-year residence requirement meant any fourteen years or fourteen consecutive years immediately prior to election. Although a legal resident, Hoover had been abroad a good part of the fourteen years immediately preceding his nomination. His election settled any doubts; the interpretation of this requirement came from the most authentic source — the same source that created the Constitution — the people.

Section 1

6. In Case of the Removal of the President from Office, or of his Death, Resignation, or Inability to discharge the Powers and Duties of the said Office, the Same shall devolve on the Vice President, and the Congress may by Law provide for the Case

of Removal, Death, Resignation or Inability, both of the President and Vice President, declaring what Officer shall then act as President, and such Officer shall act accordingly, until the Disability be removed, or a President shall be elected.

This clause is supplemented by the Twenty-fifth Amendment. The Twenty-fifth Amendment confirms the precedent established by John Tyler when he succeeded to the presidency on William Henry Harrison's death. He signed all state papers "John Tyler, President of the United States" and established that on the death or resignation of the president, the vice president becomes president, not merely acting president. In the event of the president's disability, the "powers and duties" of the presidency devolve on the vice president who serves only as acting president.

If there is no vice president (a contingency less likely to occur since the adoption of the Twenty-fifth Amendment), by act of Congress the first in the line of succession is the Speaker of the House, followed by the president *pro tempore* of the Senate, the secretary of state, and the other cabinet officers in the order in which their departments were created. No one, however, may act as president without possessing the constitutional qualifications of a president. Cabinet members would serve only until either a speaker or a president pro tempore became qualified.

The Twenty-fifth Amendment provides procedures for judging whether the president is unable to discharge the duties of the office.

Section 1

7. The President shall, at stated Times, receive for his Services, a Compensation, which shall neither be encreased nor diminished during the Period for which he shall have been elected,

To preserve the president's independence, Congress is prohibited from increasing or diminishing the president's salary during the period for which elected. Of course, today presidents are likely to have considerable income from assets acquired prior to moving to the White House.

Section 1

7. [continued] and he shall not receive within that Period any other Emolument from the United States, or any of them.

This provision was inserted to prevent the president's own state from paying compensation and to ensure the president's independence from any state. The president is totally dependent on the federal government for salary, which is now $200,000 a year. Also received are the use of the White House, free secretarial and executive assistance, and generous travel and official allowances.

8. Before he enter on the Execution of his Office, he shall take the following Oath or Affirmation: "I do solemnly swear (or affirm) that I will faithfully execute the Office of President of the United States, and will to the best of my Ability, preserve, protect and defend the Constitution of the United States."

The chief justice of the United States normally administers this oath or affirmation, but any judicial officer may do so. Calvin Coolidge's father, a justice of the peace, administered the oath to his son.

Section 2

1. The President shall be Commander in Chief of the Army and Navy of the United States, and of the Militia of the several States, when called into the actual Service of the United States;

This is another provision to ensure civilian supremacy over the military. A civilian, the president, is commander in chief of our armed forces. (Although the Air Force is not mentioned in the Constitution, the president's status as commander in chief of that branch of the armed forces is not in question.) The president appoints all military officers with the consent of the Senate, governs hostile territories subjugated by our armed forces until their disposition is determined by Congress or by treaty, and as commander in chief, makes the ultimate decisions on all matters of strategy.

The president's war powers are vastly more than purely military ones. During the Civil War, President Lincoln, as a war measure and without congressional authorization, in the Proclamation of Emancipation, declared that all slaves in areas in rebellion were free. Moreover, the president's powers as commander in chief are augmented by the executive powers and by such powers as Congress may delegate. Under conditions of total war, when the distinction between soldier and civilian may be blurred, the resulting "aggregate of powers" may be very great, although not unlimited. Outside the theater of war, the courts will review presidential acts.

During World War II, President Roosevelt authorized the army to create "defense zones" on the West Coast; under his order, supported by an act of Congress, 112,000 persons of Japanese ancestry (two-thirds of whom were citizens of the United States) were first compelled to obey a curfew and then forced out of their homes and put into relocation camps. Those measures were sustained by the Supreme Court on the general ground of military necessity, although the Court ruled that the executive order did not justify the continued detention of such persons after their loyalty had been established.[14] (The Court also made it clear that it would have not sustained such an executive order if it had authorized continued detention.) Nowadays, there is a growing consensus that this was no justification for these measures and that they were, in fact, largely motivated by prejudice. The matter of appropriate reparations remains before the courts and Congress.

The Court does not always go along with the president. In *Ex parte Milligan* (1866), martial law had been declared in Indiana because of a threatened invasion. The Court set aside the declaration, ruling that martial law can never be applied to citizens in states where the courts are open and their processes unobstructed.[15] President Roosevelt's order establishing martial law in Hawaii after the attack on Pearl Harbor was held illegal by the Court because it lacked such justification and was contrary to statute.[16] It should be noted that both of those cases were decided *after* the conclusion of hostilities.

Congress shares with the president authority over the armed forces: it supplies the money and makes regulations for their governance. Although Congress has the power to "declare war," the president is able to give orders to the military forces that may lead to hostilities and is able to direct our foreign relations to that end. President Polk, by sending troops into disputed territory, deliberately precipitated the Mexican War. President Truman ordered American forces to resist communist aggression in Korea; President Johnson used military power to intervene in the Dominican Republic; Presidents Eisenhower, Kennedy, and Johnson ordered American forces into Vietnam, although before the major escalation of our military effort in Vietnam, President Johnson secured from Congress a resolution to support his action. President Reagan sent troops to invade Grenada and told Congress about it afterwards. He also ordered troops into Beirut and the Persian Gulf.

An example of the president's power over the armed forces that had amusing rather than serious consequences occurred when President Theodore Roosevelt sent the navy halfway around the world after Congress had threatened to withhold appropriations for a global tour. Congress was then presented with the choice of appropriating money to bring the fleet home or leaving it where it was.

Throughout our history, Congress has resisted, but only recently with some success, the president's predominant role in controlling our military forces. Whenever it chooses to do so, Congress clearly has the constitutional authority to refuse to grant funds for military uses or to place conditions on the use of the funds it does grant. As a practical political fact, however, it has been difficult for Congress to resist the president or to limit the way in which the authority of the commander in chief of the armed forces is exercised. The Vietnam War, however, caused Congress, near the end of that war, to become increasingly assertive of its authority. In 1970 Congress stipulated that no funds should be used to send ground troops into Cambodia or Laos, an unprecedented restraint on presidential discretion to send armed forces wherever the president thinks necessary.

Then, in the War Powers Act of 1973, Congress stipulated that thenceforth, in every possible instance, before the president committed the armed forces of the United States, Congress should be consulted and that forces should be committed only (1) pursuant to a declaration of war by Congress, (2) by specific statutory authorization, or (3) in a national emergency. After committing the armed forces under the third condition, the president is to report within forty-eight hours to Congress, and the troop commitment is to be terminated within sixty days unless Congress concurs with the presidential action. Another thirty days are allowed if the president certifies to Congress that unavoidable military necessity, involving the safety of United States forces, requires continued use of the troops. The president is to end any deployment of troops at any time if so directed by Congress by a concurrent resolution, which is not subject to a presidential veto.

There has been a constant debate between presidents and congressional leaders over the application of the War Powers Act. Presidents have not been inclined to adhere strictly to the reporting requirements and it is not always obvious whether or not our forces are in situations where imminent involvement in hostilities is clearly indicated. For example, when President Reagan sent forces into Lebanon, there was considerable debate between the president and Congress about whether the act should come into play. President Reagan insisted that the American military forces had not been committed to engage in hostile actions and that therefore the War Powers Act did not apply. Congress insisted that it did. Congress adopted a resolution, and the president signed it. The resolution superseded the War Powers Act and set a time limit for the involvement of our troops in Lebanon. When President Reagan ordered the bombing of Libya, he called a bipartisan group of congressional leaders to the White House, after he had given final approval for the raid and after the bombers had taken off. After the raid, Reagan filed a report but, like his predecessors, did so " 'in accordance with my desire that the Congress be informed on this matter, and consistent with the War Powers Resolution,' thereby again refusing to acknowledge that he was reporting *under* the War Powers Resolution."[17] The lesson of those instances, including the rescue of the *SS Mayaguez* and the invasion of Grenada, is that "in low-intensity and low-risk conflict situations that produce quick and seemingly favorable military outcomes, the political power of Congress to limit the chief executive through strict enforcement of the War Powers Resolution is very feeble if it is not dead altogether."[18]

Perhaps as significant as the new congressional limits on presidential discretion to deploy the armed forces are the growing political restraints. As recent history in Korea and Vietnam illustrates, presidents and their parties run a serious risk of defeat in the next presidential election if the armed forces are used, with or without congressional approval, as an instrument of foreign policy and the result is a substantial number of American casualties over an extended period of time.

Section 2

1. [continued] he [the President] may require the Opinion, in writing, of the principal Officer in each of the executive Departments, upon any Subject relating to the Duties of their respective Offices,

---

Although there is no mention of the cabinet in the original Constitution, that body came into existence as early as 1793; from the beginning, the president's power over the heads of the major executive departments has extended beyond merely requiring written reports upon subjects relating to the duties of their respective offices. Cabinet members serve at the president's pleasure, and presidential control over their official acts is complete. The executive departments, however, and usually their duties, are created by law, and the money needed for their operation comes from Congress.

The cabinet has never been a prominent feature of American government, and its collective advice is seldom significant. With the adoption of the Twenty-fifth Amendment, the cabinet has been given a constitutional role of importance (in deciding whether the president is disabled.

Section 2

1. [continued] and he shall have Power to grant Reprieves and Pardons for Offenses against the United States, except in Cases of Impeachment.

A reprieve postpones punishment. There have not been many requests for reprieves since the federal death penalty was struck down by the Supreme Court because of procedures by which it was imposed. (It has not been restored except for very few offenses.) A full pardon restores persons to all civil rights and revises their legal status in all respects. In most instances, however, the president merely grants a limited pardon and restores some civil rights. The president can pardon persons before they are formally charged or have been brought to trial, during the trial, or after conviction. (The president cannot pardon people before they commit an offense, for no one can be excused from obeying the law.) The power extends only to offenses against the United States, not to those against the laws of a state.

The president's power to pardon extends to persons held in criminal (but not civil) contempt of court by a federal judge. "The power flows from the Constitution alone ... and ... it cannot be modified, abridged, or diminished by the Congress."[19] The president may reduce or commute sentences and may impose conditions even though the conditions are not provided by statute. The president may not, however, set conditions that offend the Constitution or that make the sentence more severe, rather than less.

The most celebrated presidential pardon was President Ford's pardon of former President Richard M. Nixon. Nixon had not been charged with any crime, but President Ford pardoned him for any crimes that he might have committed while president.

President Carter used the power when he first came into office to grant "full, complete and unconditional pardon" to all persons, whether or not they had been formally convicted, who had violated the draft laws during the Vietnam era, except military deserters, employees of the selective service system, and persons who had violated the draft laws through force or violence. Americans who had left the United States to avoid the draft and had become citizens of another country were permitted to return freely and apply for their citizenship. Congress reacted angrily to this use of the presidential pardon, by barring the use of certain supplemental appropriations for the administration of the amnesty program, but since expenses were minimal and other funds were available, the congressional protest was symbolic.

Most of the time presidential pardoning power is exercised routinely. Each year about 400 people petition the president for executive clemency, asking for a reduced prison term or a pardon. The requests are processed by a pardon attorney according to guidelines established by the president. President Reagan adopted stringent guidelines, for example, a longer wait before persons become eligible to be considered for a pardon. "Executive clemency is a very personal thing. Each president handles it differently."[20]

Section 2

2. He shall have Power, by and with the Advice and Consent of the Senate, to make Treaties, provided two thirds of the Senators present concur;

The Senate as a body has provided the president with very little formal advice beyond votes approving or disapproving of treaties. The president nevertheless seeks advice from senatorial leaders from time to time, especially members of the Senate Committee on Foreign Relations. In general, the president negotiates a treaty and then presents it to the Senate for approval. The final step in the making of a treaty is its ratification, which precisely speaking is the president's act.

There are several explanations for the two-thirds vote requirement. The southern states were afraid the northern states, which were in a majority, would negotiate treaties disadvantageous to them. They remembered that John Jay of New York, secretary of foreign affairs for the Confederation, had proposed a treaty with Spain conceding the right to close the mouth of the Mississippi at New Orleans in return for concessions to northern merchants. The two-thirds rule gives sectional groups the power to veto such treaties.

In addition to being international compacts, treaties are the "supreme law of the land," and their self-executing provisions are, therefore, enforced by courts, just as any other laws; this fact, too, is sometimes urged in favor of the two-thirds requirement.

Now that the United States is continuously involved in international negotiations, the process of treaty making has achieved considerable significance. At the same time, the two-thirds rule makes it possible for a few senators representing perhaps a minority of the electorate to block treaties desired by the majority, and many have suggested that ratification be by a simple majority of *both* houses of Congress. There are, however, some senators who think that the treaty-making procedures should be made more difficult. Adherents to this view have proposed that, in addition to the two-thirds requirement, the approval of both houses be required before a treaty shall operate as law. In point of fact, since the House of Representatives must approve any appropriations or any legislation necessary to carry out the terms of the treaty, it already enjoys considerable power in this area.

Securing a two-thirds vote of the Senate for treaty ratification has at various times imposed obstacles to the ratification, and it is not surprising that various ways have been devised to get around those obstacles. One is the joint resolution of Congress, an ordinary legislative procedure. Texas was annexed in this fashion after the Senate refused to do so by treaty. Another device is the executive agreement, of which there are two types: (1) Inasmuch as Congress and the president have cognate powers in the field of foreign affairs, it is constitutionally permissible for Congress to delegate to the president larger powers than would be allowable in domestic affairs. Thus, the president is often empowered by Congress to make executive agreements, for example, reciprocal tariff agreements. (2) As part of undefined executive powers, growing out of the authority to appoint and receive diplomatic officials, and as the nation's official spokesman, the president has the power to negotiate with foreign nations agreements that do not require the consent of Congress. As long as the agreements are not countermanded by Congress, they, like treaties, become the "law of the land."

It was once thought that executive agreements differed from treaties in that they were concerned with affairs of less importance; in fact, executive agreements have sometimes dealt with highly important matters. For example, in September 1940 President Roosevelt handed over to Great Britain fifty naval vessels in exchange for certain leases of military bases. The Atlantic Charter in 1941, the Yalta Agreement of 1944, and the Potsdam Agreement of 1945 are other examples of executive agreements. In 1970 President Nixon signed an "Agreement of Friendship and Cooperation" with Spain that constitutes a significant security guarantee. And in most years there are about five times more executive agreements implemented than formal treaties ratified.

As part of its reassertion of congressional authority in the field of foreign affairs, Congress, in the Case Act of 1972, required the secretary of state to notify Congress within sixty days of any executive agreement. If the agreement has national security considerations, notification may be made on a classified basis, with only members of the House and Senate Foreign Affairs Committees being told of the agreement.

Since the adoption of the Case Act, there has been considerable conflict between the president and the Department of State on one side and congressional leaders on the other over the definition of an executive agreement. The president and the Department of State define executive agreements as those reached with another nation under the president's constitutional powers to conduct foreign relations or to act as commander in chief, or under authority granted to the president by Congress. Administration spokespersons maintain that a mere exchange of understandings between the president and the head of another nation is not covered by the Case Act, not even the European Declaration signed in Helsinki in 1975, in which the heads of many nations indicated their agreement not to interfere with the existing boundaries in Europe. Some members of Congress take issue with this narrow definition of an executive agreement and have pressed, so far unsuccessfully, for legislation that would require the president to submit executive agreements for congressional review and possible veto.

Once a treaty has been ratified or an executive agreement implemented, courts have authority to construe the agreement.[21] But who has the power to abrogate treaties? The Constitution is silent. After President Carter terminated a mutual defense treaty with Taiwan as part of the agreements leading to recognition of the Peoples' Republic of China, several senators filed a suit asking a federal judge to set aside the presidential action. They charged that the president could not abrogate a defense treaty without the consent of the Senate or Congress. The Supreme Court dismissed the case: four justices balked on the grounds that the issues were political — a dispute between Congress and the president in which courts should not intervene; the fifth, Justice Powell, balked on the grounds that the issue was not ready for judicial disposition, since neither the Senate nor the House had chosen to confront the president on the matter. Only Justice Brennan went to the merits, and he was of the view that abrogation of the defense treaty with Taiwan was a necessary incident to executive recognition of the Peking government and was part of the presidential power to recognize and withdraw recognition from foreign governments.[22]

Section 2

2. [continued] and he [the President] shall nominate, and by and with the Advice and Consent of the Senate, shall appoint Ambassadors, other public Ministers and Consuls, Judges of the supreme Court, and all other Officers of the United States, whose Appointments are not herein otherwise provided for, and which shall be established by Law: but the Congress may by Law vest the Appointment of such inferior Officers, as they think proper, in the President alone, in the Courts of Law, or in the Heads of Departments.

Officers who are appointed by the president with the advice and consent of the Senate (only a majority vote is required) are known as *superior,* or *senatorial*, officers. Officers who can, if Congress permits, be appointed by the president alone, by the courts, or by heads of departments, are known as *inferior* officers.

Congress violated the appointments clause and the principle of separation of powers when it provided in the 1974 amendments to the Federal Election Campaign Act of 1971 for the appointment of two members of the Federal Election Commission by the president, two by the Senate, and two by the House, with confirmation of all six members by both the House and the Senate. It would have been different if the commission had been merely an advisory body like the Civil Rights Commission, some of whose members are selected by the speaker, some by the president pro tempore of the Senate, and some by the president. But the only way "officers of the United States," who exercise significant authority to administer government programs and enforce the law, may be appointed is in the manner prescribed by the appointments clause.

The 1974 procedures for the selection of members of the Federal Election Commission violated the Constitution also by calling for the confirmation of the officers by the House and the Senate. The Constitution permits confirmation only by the Senate, not by the Senate and the House.[23]

An appointments clause issue was also raised by the events of Watergate. After President Nixon fired a special prosecutor who had been appointed by the attorney general to look into the Watergate charges, Congress decided that we needed a process for appointing a prosecutor to look into allegations of misbehavior by the president and members of the presidential staff — a prosecutor who would be independent of the president and the attorney general. In 1978 Congress passed a law that set up a special three-judge federal court to appoint and supervise independent counsel to look into allegations of executive branch misconduct. Almost a dozen such counsel have been appointed. President Reagan's Department of Justice has argued that the special prosecutor system violates "the constitutional imperative that all federal prosecutors must be accountable to the president . . . and makes such a prosecutor subject to the direction and control of a court rather than the executive." The matter is now before the courts.[24]

An appointments clause issue was also raised by the Bankruptcy Amendments and Federal Judgeship Act of 1984, which provided for the continuation of the terms of all bankruptcy judges, whose terms had expired a short time before because of Congress's delay in enacting a new bankruptcy statute, and then for their reappointment or the appointment of their successors by the courts of appeals. The provision raised several constitutional issues. The most obvious issue was the charge that by this act Congress, which has no power to appoint federal officers, in effect appointed 242. When President Reagan signed the new law, he expressed his constitutional concerns. The lower courts have ruled there was no constitutional violation.

The Senate has normally refused to accept federal appointments over the objection of a senator from the state in which the office is located, provided the senator is of the same party as the president. This practice, known as *senatorial courtesy,* permits a senator to veto presidential appointments and gives each senator extensive control over federal patronage in his or her state. Because of this custom, senators from the state in which the appointment is to be made are usually consulted by the president before the appointment is sent to the Senate for confirmation.

The "consent of the Senate" part of this clause is subject to increasing attention these days. Until recently the rules of the game were that, beyond the patronage considerations flowing from senatorial courtesy, the Senate should give its consent to the presidential appointment of a federal judge, especially to the Supreme Court, once it was assured of the candidate's integrity, fairness, and legal competence. Often such concerns masked issues of constitutional orientation, but the conventions required that there be a rather subdued discussion of constitutional issues and only a veiled reference to expected judicial policy choices. Nowadays, with a more sophisticated understanding that the Supreme Court justices are involved in the great issues of our times and that they must make choices among competing political values, there is a more open concern about such matters.

It is still considered improper for judicial candidates to respond to senatorial probes of how they will vote in specific cases. The rules still call for considerable deference to presidential choices, since, as we have noted, the president's power to nominate judges is the major link between the electorate and federal courts. Nonetheless, the Senate takes its consent role very seriously, especially when the Senate is of a different party from the White House. There is a growing tendency to probe the constitutional values of the future judges and justices.

Section 2

3. The President shall have Power to fill up all Vacancies that may happen during the Recess of the Senate, by granting Commissions which shall expire at the End of their next Session.

The word *happen* here has come to mean "happen to exist." The clause allows the president to fill temporarily *any* vacancies while the Senate is recessed, no matter how or when they occurred.

This clause provides an interesting example of the questions that remain, after two hundred years, about the meaning of what appears to be uncomplicated constitutional language. From 1789 to 1980 many federal judges were appointed by presidents under this clause. Although there were doubts about the wisdom of such appointments, and although in recent years few interim appointments were made, there was no constitutional challenge to the practice. Then, in December of 1980, President Carter, after he had lost the election and while the Senate was in recess, made an interim appointment to the federal district court. The man thus appointed had previously been nominated for approval by the Senate, but the Senate had recessed without having confirmed him and sixteen other Carter nominees. The judge sat for 50 weeks before his nomination was withdrawn by President Reagan. His actions as a judge were challenged, and a panel of the Court of Appeals for the Ninth Circuit held the appointment unconstitutional. The decision was reversed by the appellate court en banc (the entire court).[25] We still lack a judicial ruling whether this clause permits a president to make a recess appointment of a person the Senate has rejected, a different question from a recess appointment of a person whom the Senate has failed to confirm.

Section 3

He shall from time to time give to the Congress Information of the State of the Union, and recommend to their Consideration such Measures as he shall judge necessary and expedient;

The opening address of the president at each session of Congress is known as the state-of-the-union message. George Washington and John Adams gave their addresses in person, but Jefferson sent his in writing. President Wilson revived the practice of personally delivering the speech.

At the beginning of each session, the president is now also required by law to send Congress a budget message and an economic report. From time to time the president sends messages, addresses Congress on specific subjects, and makes recommendations for legislation. In this manner the president is able to focus national attention on national problems. As an extension of this practice, the executive branch develops many legislative proposals, which are then formally introduced by members of Congress.

Section 3

[continued] he may, on extraordinary Occasions, convene both Houses, or either of them,

Whenever it is thought necessary, the president can call a special session of Congress. Once in session, Congress has full powers. In contrast, most state legislatures, when called into special session, are limited to discussion and action on the particular matters laid before them by the governor.

Nowadays Congress is in session almost all the time, and there is no need for special sessions. In the past, in addition to special sessions of Congress, the Senate was occasionally called into special session by itself to ratify treaties and appointments, which it does without the concurrence of the House.

Section 3

[continued] and in Case of Disagreement between them, with Respect to the Time of Adjournment, he may adjourn them to such Time as he shall think proper;

The president has never been called upon to exercise this duty.

Section 3

[continued] he shall receive Ambassadors and other public Ministers;

The president is the only officer who can speak officially for the United States to foreign governments. Foreign governments may speak to the United States only through the president, or the president's agent, usually the secretary of state. The president's power to receive ambassadors includes the power to recognize new states or governments.

The increasing importance of foreign relations during the last several decades accounts in no small part for the increasing power of the president in all fields. The nature of the problems of foreign policy requires that the initiative and general direction be in the president's hands.

Section 3

[continued] he shall take Care that the Laws be faithfully executed,

The president's duty to see that the laws are enforced is supported by his powers as commander in chief. As already pointed out, Congress very early authorized the president to use the armed forces when necessary to overcome combinations too powerful to be dealt with by judges, federal marshals, and the regular federal police forces.

The president is constitutionally obliged by this clause to enforce all the laws of the United States, whether or not the president approves of them, including all federal court decisions and all regulations of federal agencies, as they apply to all the people all the time. But there are so many laws and regulations that the president of course has great discretion in deciding which laws and regulations will take priority. The Reagan administration, for example, has been less vigorous than the Carter administration, in enforcing the many laws and regulations relating to the civil rights of minorities, women, and the disabled, but has given more attention to laws and regulations relating to the civil rights of children and fetuses.

Does this clause require the president to comply with all laws? This question was raised when Congress, by what has come to be known as the Boland Amendment, prohibited any agency of the United States involved in intelligence activities, directly or indirectly, from using any funds to support any groups operating in Nicaragua. When it was discovered that federal funds from the sale of arms to Iran had been diverted to help the Contras, a group working to overthrow the communist government of Nicaragua, President Reagan at first denied knowledge of such activities. Subsequently he argued that such a law was only advisory to him and the National Security Agency, since that agency was not engaged in intelligence. Moreover, the president argued that, because of his own constitutional status as commander in chief and as the chief spokesperson for the United States, the Boland Amendment could not constitutionally be applied to him or his direct agents in dealing with foreign affairs. His critics, including many members of Congress from both parties, contended that Congress intended the law to apply and that the president had a responsibility under this clause to see to it that he and those who reported to him complied with it.[26]

In addition to being a grant of power to the president, this clause limits congressional power. Under the separation of powers doctrine, the president, not the Congress, executes the laws. Thus, the Court declared unconstitutional a provision of the Gramm-Rudman-Hollings Act that gave the comptroller general, an officer removable by Congress, a responsibility under certain circumstances to put into effect budget reductions. "The Constitution does not," said the Court majority, contemplate an active role for Congress in the supervision of officers charged with the execution of the laws it enacts. . . . To permit an officer controlled by Congress to execute the laws would be, in essence, to permit a congressional veto. Congress could simply remove, or threaten to remove, an officer for executing the laws in any fashion found to be unsatisfactory to Congress.[27]

Section 3

[continued], and shall Commission all the Officers of the United States.

This clause and the one before, plus the undefined executive power clause, give the president unrestricted power to remove all *executive* officers. The president is charged with the duty of faithfully executing the laws and therefore must have control over those through whom enforcement takes place. Congress may not restrict the presidential power to remove such officers. This unlimitable removal power, however, does not extend to officers who have quasi-legislative or quasi-judicial functions conferred upon them by act of Congress, such as members of the Federal Trade Commission, the Interstate Commerce Commission, or the Federal Communications Commission. The president has no authority to remove those officers except as given by Congress.[28]

What makes an officer quasi-legislative or quasi-judicial, and what are the distinctions between executive and legislative powers, are not questions to which there are easy answers or "bright-line rules."

Section 4

The President, Vice President and all civil Officers of the United States, shall be removed from Office on Impeachment for, and Conviction of, Treason, Bribery, or other High Crimes and Misdemeanors.

The first person to be impeached was Senator Blount from Tennessee in 1797, but the Senate dismissed the proceedings against him after deciding that members of Congress are not civil officers of the United States subject to impeachment. The Senate did, however, expel Senator Blount.

What are impeachable offenses? Throughout our history there have been three constructions:

1. A *loose construction*, that incompetent or politically objectionable officers, especially if they be judicial officers, are liable to impeachment and removal from office. This view appears to have been the position of Thomas Jefferson. If it had been adopted by Congress, it could have made our governmental system similar to the British system, in which government officials may be turned out of office because of lack of confidence in them, without any suggestion of wrongdoing on their part.

2. A *strict construction*, that the only impeachable offenses are those that break criminal laws. This position was the view of President Nixon and the lawyers who defended him. It appears to have been the view also of many of those who voted not to sustain the impeachment charges against Justice Chase and President Andrew Johnson.

   Although an impeachment charge by the House and a trial by the Senate may flow from conduct that leads to criminal charges, impeachment proceedings are independent proceedings. Judge Harry Claiborne, after a full jury trial, was convicted by a federal court of tax evasion. He refused to resign. The House brought in four articles of impeachment, three stating that the Senate should remove Judge Claiborne from office upon an independent finding by the Senate that he had willfully filed false tax returns. The fourth article was based on the view that conviction by a federal court of a serious crime is by itself sufficient grounds for the Senate to act. The Senate, by two-thirds, voted guilty on the three impeachment articles based on independent findings. Although a majority of those present and voting voted guilty on the fourth article, the vote was less than two-thirds, so Judge Claiborne was not found guilty as charged in that particular article.

3. The prevailing *moderate construction* that impeachable offenses need not be criminal in character but must reflect a serious dereliction of duty, a substantial violation of constitutional and legal responsibilities, or a sustained failure to meet one's obligations. This construction was the view of those on the House Judiciary Committee who voted to impeach President Nixon. It was also the view of those who voted to impeach and then convict Judge Robert W. Archbald (1912—1913) and Judge Halsted L. Ritter (1933—1936), each of whom was convicted on charges of misconduct in office and judicial improprieties, although in neither instance were the offenses criminal.

The Judicial Conference, which supervises judicial conduct takes the same position. It recommended to the House that it impeach a judge, despite his acquittal on federal charges, on the grounds that what he did nonetheless constitutes impeachable conduct. The matter is still pending.

May a person be impeached and removed from office for misconduct performed before assuming office? We have no precedents. Vice president Agnew's resignation and pleading no contest to certain offenses, some of which took place while he was governor of Maryland, made it unnecessary for Congress to face that issue.

The interpretation of the impeachment provisions is primarily the responsibility of the House and the Senate. Fortunately, only a few precedents are available to give us guidance as to their meaning.

ARTICLE III: THE JUDICIAL ARTICLE

Section 1

The judicial Power of the United States shall be vested in one supreme Court, and in such inferior Courts as the Congress may from time to time ordain and establish.

The Supreme Court is the only federal court required by the Constitution. The Founding Fathers were purposely vague about the nature of the federal court system because they were unable to agree on the need for inferior (the term refers to the jurisdiction of these courts, not their quality) federal courts. Some thought that since the supremacy clause (see page 54) imposes on state courts a responsibility, whenever appropriate, to apply the Constitution and federal laws, there was no need for lower federal courts. But the First Congress created such courts, and they have always been part of our federal court system.

Under present legislation there are ninety-four district courts, including territorial courts. There are specialized trial courts, such as the Claims Court and the Court of International Trade. There is a Foreign Intelligence Surveillance Court, consisting of seven district judges who serve part-time reviewing applications by the government for electronic surveillance of foreign agents.

At the appellate level there are twelve courts of appeals with general jurisdiction. The United States Court of Appeals for the Federal Circuit, has special jurisdiction to hear appeals from all federal courts of cases relating to patents, trademarks, and copyrights, appeals from district courts of cases in contract and internal revenue in which the United States is the defendant, and appeals from a variety of other specialized courts and agencies, such as the Patent Office, the Claims Court, and the Court of International Trade. There are specialized appellate courts consisting of judges from other courts, such as the Foreign Intelligence Surveillance Court of Review, consisting of three judges, which reviews applications denied by the Foreign Intelligence Surveillance Court, and the Temporary Emergency Court of Appeals, consisting of judges designated by the Chief Justice to sit in panels of three to hear appeals from district courts in cases arising under economic stabilization laws. All these courts are inferior to the Supreme Court, but all exercise the judicial power of the United States.

Federal district judges have authority to appoint federal magistrates. Magistrates appointed to full-time positions have eight-year terms; those serving only part-time, in less populated areas, serve four-year terms. Full-time magistrates have authority over a wide range of matters. Among their duties are disposition of initial motions, including making recommendations to the district judge whether or not evidence in a criminal case should be suppressed (see Fourth Amendment). The magistrate's authority to take these initial actions, subject to final approval by the district judge, has been upheld against claims that it violates the due process requirement that persons have their cases heard from the beginning to end by judges appointed by the procedures of Article II and for the terms set forth in Article III.[1] Magistrates also have jurisdiction to preside over civil trials with the consent of both parties, and over nonjury trials for petty offenses with the consent of the defendant. Bankruptcy judges, appointed by the courts of appeals for fourteen-year terms, also operate under the supervision of district judges and dispose of matters rising under federal bankruptcy laws. The decisions of bankruptcy judges may be appealed to the district judge or to a special appellate panel of bankruptcy judges established by the judicial council of each federal court of appeals.

In recent years there has been continuing discussion about the possibility of creating some kind of national court of appeals to take from the Supreme Court some of its work. Despite endorsement by several blue-ribbon commissions, including Chief Justices Burger and Rehnquist and some of the other members of the Court, there has not been a consensus about the need for such a court, the jurisdiction it should be given, or the way its judges should be chosen.

In addition to courts created under Article III to exercise the judicial power of the United States, Congress has created other courts under its Article I authority to establish whatever is necessary and proper to carry into execution powers granted to the national government. These so-called legislative, or Article I, courts are district courts in Guam, Northern Mariannas, and the Virgin Islands, the Court of Military Appeals, the U.S. Claims Court, and the Tax Court. Magistrates and bankruptcy judges, referred to earlier, are Article I judges. Judges of Article I courts may be selected by other procedures and serve for other terms than those prescribed by the Constitution for judges of Article III courts, which exercise the judicial power of the United States. Article I courts could be given nonjudicial duties, which might be inappropriate to vest in an Article III court, although at the moment no such duties are assigned to any Article I court.

Occasionally it is difficult to know whether a court has been created to exercise the judicial power of the United States under Article III or the legislative power of Congress under Article I. In practice, Congress indicates whether it considers a court to be an Article I or an Article III court by specifying in the case of Article I judges that they are to serve for a fixed number of years or, in the case of Article III judges, that they are to serve "for good behavior," although there is nothing to prevent Congress from giving Article I judges lifetime tenure if it wishes to do so, and it has done so in the past.

Distinguishing the conditions that make it appropriate for Congress to delegate adjudication to officers who do not enjoy the tenure and salary protections of Article III judges is "one of the most confusing and controversial areas of constitutional law."[2] In 1982 the Supreme Court declared unconstitutional the system of bankruptcy courts established by the Bankruptcy Reform Act of 1978. That act created bankruptcy courts whose judges were appointed for fourteen-year terms, were removable for non-impeachable offenses, and, unlike Article III judges, were not given constitutional guarantees that their salaries would not be reduced. These courts were given jurisdiction over all civil proceedings relating to bankruptcy matters. The Supreme Court declared the act unconstitutional because it authorized bankruptcy judges to resolve cases normally within the purview of state courts. Justice Brennan, speaking for a plurality, stated that the Constitution allows legislative courts to be used in only three situations: (1) to establish territorial courts, (2) to establish courts-martial, and (3) to enforce public rights — matters that arise between the government and one of its citizens. He argued that only Article III courts could decide disputes between two individuals.[3]

Four years later (this time Justice Brennan was in the minority), the Court explained that the distinction between public rights and private rights is not controlling. Rather, it is merely an understanding that when public rights are involved, the danger of encroaching on judicial power is less than when private rights are relegated initially to administrative adjudication. Article III, said Justice O'Connor for the Court, serves two functions: (1) to protect the role of the independent judiciary and (2) to safeguard litigants' right to have their claims tried before judges who are free from potential domination by other branches of government. Litigants may waive their personal rights and consent to have their claims heard elsewhere, but they may not cure by consent the things that undermine the independence of the judiciary. The Court warned Congress not to take too much business from Article III judges. In this particular instance, however, the majority held that Congress could confer on the Commodity Futures Trading Commission jurisdiction to settle disputes between traders and their brokers, including state law counterclaims. Here Congress had created a limited scheme to provide an inexpensive and expeditious alternative forum for a class of questions of fact that are peculiarly suited to resolution by administrative agencies.[4]

Judicial power, the only kind of power that Article III courts may exercise, is the power to pronounce a judgment and carry it into effect between parties engaged in a real and substantial controversy over a legal question. Unlike the International Court of Justice and some state courts, federal courts have no authority to give advisory opinions. Nevertheless, they may render "declaratory judgments." Such judgments, binding on both parties, define their respective legal rights. They may be used to free one or both parties from uncertainty regarding their rights, say, under an ambiguous contract. However, they are most likely to be sought by persons who believe that governmental officials are threatening action that, if taken, will deprive them of their constitutional and legal rights.

Section 1

[continued] The Judges, both of the supreme and inferior Courts, shall hold their Offices during good Behavior,

---

The Constitution provides for the appointment of judges by the president with the consent of the Senate, but it is silent about the number and size of the courts and the qualification of the judges. Today there are nine members of the Supreme Court; at various times there have been six, seven, and ten. The number of judges serving on a district court or a court of appeals varies with the number and nature of the cases to be handled. Usually one judge hears a case in a district court, and three circuit judges hear cases in a court of appeals, although such courts of appeal at times hold hearings en banc (with all their judges participating).

Although the Constitution here refers to members of both the Supreme Court and the inferior federal courts as judges, in Article I, Section 3, paragraph 6, it refers to the "Chief Justice." Since the Judiciary Act of 1789, members of the Supreme Court have always been referred to as "Justice" and, until November of 1980, more formally as "Mr. Justice." In November 1980, anticipating the arrival of the first woman justice, the title "Mr. Justice" was dropped. The chief justice is properly designated as the chief justice of the United States, not of the Supreme Court, but is known informally to fellow justices as "the chief."

The phrase "during good behavior," which means virtually for life, has been interpreted by some to mean that Congress has the constitutional power to create procedures to terminate judges for "bad behavior," even if the behavior in question falls short of impeachable offenses. Congress has refused to go that far. However, in 1980, following the example of the states, Congress authorized the judicial council of each circuit, consisting of some circuit judges and some district judges from the circuit, to investigate complaints against judges. If the judicial council finds that a complaint is justified, it may request judges to retire, it may censure or reprimand them, it may order that no cases be assigned to them, or it may take "other appropriate actions" short of removal. If the council thinks that impeachment may be warranted, it refers the matter, through the Judicial Conference (which consists of the chief justice, the chief judges of the twelve courts of appeals, and a number of district judges elected by their peers), to the House of Representatives, the procedure followed in the case of Judge Alcee Hastings, a federal district judge in Florida. Appeals from the decision of a council may be taken to the Judicial Conference.

Some argue that the good behavior language means that impeachable offenses for federal judges differ from those for other officers, such as the president, who is elected for a fixed term. In other words, in addition to "Treason, Bribery, or other High Crimes and Misdemeanors," for which the president, the vice president, and other civil officers may be impeached, it is argued that federal judges may be impeached on the charges of willful misconduct in office, failure to perform their duties, habitual intemperance, or other conduct that brings the judicial office into disrepute. Whatever the merits of this contention, the House has been more inclined to bring impeachment charges (ten times) and the Senate to sustain them (five times — one judge resigned) against federal judges than against other civil officers, and some of those impeached were charged with misbehavior that fell short of treason, bribery, or other crimes and misdemeanors.

Section 1

[continued] and shall, at stated Times, receive for their Services, a Compensation, which shall not be diminished during their Continuance in Office.

To ensure judicial independence, Congress is prohibited from decreasing judicial salaries during the term of any particular judge, but unlike the president's salary, judicial salaries may be increased.

Congress has established a complex scheme calling for adjustments in the salaries of federal employees, including federal judges, to keep up with the cost of living. However, almost every year Congress either sets aside the proposed adjustments or modifies the formulas for members of Congress, cabinet officers, federal judges, and top-level civil servants. But unless Congress acts promptly, the compensation clause preserves raises proposed for judges. The issue is "when . . . does the Compensation Clause prohibit the Congress from repealing salary increases that otherwise take effect automatically pursuant to a formula previously enacted? Is the protection of the Clause first invoked when the formula is enacted or when increases take effect?" The answer is, when they take effect. Thus, in the years when Congress repeals the proposed raises prior to the effective date, the judges are not entitled to the increases. But when Congress does not get around to repealing or postponing the previously authorized increases until after the date the raises were due to go into effect, Congress is not allowed to diminish the salaries of federal judges. In one of the years for which the repeal of salary increases was struck down, the president had signed the repealing statute on October 1, the very day the salary increases became effective.[5]

Section 2

1. The judicial Power shall extend to all Cases, in Law and Equity, arising under this Constitution, the Laws of the United States, and Treaties made, or which shall be made, under their Authority;

This clause and those that immediately follow outline the scope of federal judicial power. The distinction between cases in law and cases in equity is inherited from England. In law, the party bringing the case usually asks for damages; in equity, an injunction is usually requested. The common law compensates for injury already done, whereas equity prevents or stops the injury from occurring. Nowadays the same federal judges can hear both types of cases and can hear both types of matters in a single case.

The Constitution merely prescribes the boundaries of the judicial power of the United States. Except for the original jurisdiction of the Supreme Court (see page 110), no federal court has jurisdiction over any case unless Congress exercises its power under this clause. Federal courts, however, have generously interpreted Congress's authority to confer jurisdiction on them: it extends to giving federal courts the power to construe "every law that the Legislature may constitutionally make."[6] For example, Congress, by reason of its authority over foreign commerce and foreign relations, may even give federal courts jurisdiction to hear civil suits brought by a foreign plaintiff against a foreign state.[7]

What Congress gives to federal courts under this clause, may it take away? Could Congress, if it wished, deprive federal judges of the authority to hear certain kinds of cases? Could Congress go so far as to strip federal courts of jurisdiction to hear any cases? Periodically members of Congress, disgruntled by the decisions of federal judges, especially those on the Supreme Court, have introduced bills to take certain kinds of cases from the federal courts. Most recently bills have been introduced either to take from all federal courts their jurisdiction to deal with cases relating to abortion, school prayer, and school busing or to eliminate the appellate jurisdiction of the Supreme Court over such matters. Adoption of those bills would raise difficult constitutional issues and would profoundly affect the nature of our constitutional system.

If a *federal question* is involved, a case that starts out in a state court may be taken to the Supreme Court from the highest state court to which an appeal can be made. For example, if X is tried and convicted of murder under state law in a state court and exhausts his state appeals, he may then ask the United States Supreme Court to pass on his contention that his trial was not a fair one under the due process clause of the Fourteenth Amendment.

Section 2

1. [continued] to all Cases affecting Ambassadors, other public Ministers and Consuls;

Since the national government is responsible for good relations between the United States and foreign governments, it was reasoned that cases affecting foreign public ministers should be within the judicial power of the United States. For the federal courts to assume jurisdiction, such officials must be materially affected by the case without necessarily being parties to it.

Section 2

1. [continued] to all Cases of admiralty and maritime Jurisdiction;

This jurisdiction is concerned with ships and shipping. Under the English rule, it extended only to the high seas and those rivers in which the tide ebbed and flowed. Under the Constitution, however, such jurisdiction reaches all "navigable waters of the United States, whether or not subject to the ebb and flow of the tide" and "all causes of damage or injury, to person or property, caused by a vessel on navigable water, notwithstanding that such damage or injury be done or consummated on land."[8] A collision between two boats, whether small pleasure craft or large commercial ones, on the navigable waters of the United States, even in a very small river inside a state, is within the admiralty jurisdiction of the United States.[9]

This grant of jurisdiction to federal courts is exclusive. States may not extend their laws, such as workers' compensation, to areas covered by maritime law. The rough dividing line between state and maritime jurisdictions is the gangplank, with some confusion and legal difficulties over the jurisdiction of the seaward side of the pier.[10]

Airplanes are not ships for purposes of admiralty jurisdiction. Congress can exercise its power to regulate foreign and interstate commerce to provide rules for airplane crashes and to bring them under federal jurisdiction, as it has done by providing for wrongful death and tort suits for airplane accidents on the high seas.

Section 2

1. [continued] to Controversies to which the United States shall be a Party; — to Controversies between two or more States; *between a State and Citizens of another State* [emphasis added]; — between Citizens of different States;

The Eleventh Amendment modified the emphasized portion of the section.

Article III authorizes Congress to extend federal jurisdiction to any case involving conflicts between citizens of different states. Corporations nowadays are considered citizens of the state of their incorporation and of their principal place of business. Congress has legislated that diversity cases — those founded on conflicts between citizens of different states — involving amounts of less than $10,000 shall not be entertained by federal courts. Thus, if the only ground for federal jurisdiction is that the case is between citizens of different states and if the amount in controversy is less than $10,000, the case is not to be heard in a federal court; it must be resolved in a state court. A diversity case that originates in a state court may, if the amount in controversy exceeds $10,000, be removed by the defendant to the federal district court.

The $10,000 requirement does not deter many suits, and many people are urging Congress to raise it, as it has done in the past, or to eliminate all diversity jurisdiction of federal courts. They argue that the reasons to fear that state courts would favor their own citizens no longer persist and that the elimination of diversity jurisdiction would free federal courts to deal with federal issues.

Section 2

1. [continued] between Citizens of the same State claiming Lands under Grants of different States, and between a State, or the Citizens thereof, and foreign States, Citizens or Subjects.

At the time of the adoption of the Constitution, many states had conflicting claims to western lands. Today this clause is unimportant. This clause was also modified by the Eleventh Amendment.

In summary, the judicial power of the United States extends to the following cases in law and equity:

1. Cases in which jurisdiction is based on the *nature of the dispute*:
   a. cases arising under the Constitution, under a federal law, or under a federal treaty
   b. cases arising under admiralty and maritime jurisdiction
   c. cases involving title to land that is claimed under grants by two or more states

2. Cases in which jurisdiction is based on the *parties to the dispute*:
   a. cases in which the United States is a party
   b. cases in which a state is a party
   c. cases in which the parties are citizens of different states
   d. cases that affect foreign ambassadors, ministers, and consuls

The power of the federal courts over certain types of cases does not in itself exclude state courts from exercising concurrent jurisdiction. But Congress is free to make the federal jurisdiction exclusive and has done so in the following kinds of cases, among others: crimes against the United States, civil cases of admiralty and maritime jurisdiction, prize cases (cases arising out of the capture of enemy or abandoned property on the high seas), cases to which a state is party (except cases between a state and its citizens or a state and citizens of another state or foreign country), and cases involving foreign ambassadors and other public ministers.

Within any state, there are two court systems, the state court system and the federal court system, neither of which is superior to the other. Over some matters both systems have jurisdiction, over others only the state courts have jurisdiction, and over still others only the federal courts have jurisdiction. A dispute between two citizens of New York over the terms of a contract signed in New York would be within the exclusive jurisdiction of the New York courts. A suit involving more than $10,000 between citizens of different states would be within the jurisdiction of both the federal courts and the courts of the state in which the defendant is located. (Where a defendant is located, especially a corporate one, is not a simple thing to determine.) A suit arising under the Sherman Antitrust Act would be within the exclusive jurisdiction of the federal courts.

Section 2

2. In all Cases affecting Ambassadors, other public Ministers and Consuls, and those in which a State shall be Party, the supreme Court shall have original Jurisdiction.

"The original jurisdiction of the Supreme Court is conferred by the Constitution, is self-executing and needs no legislative implementation."[11] However, the original jurisdiction of the Supreme Court is not constitutionally exclusive. Congress can give concurrent jurisdiction to other courts, and it has done so, except for suits between states. Suits between a state and the United States or between a state and a political subdivision of another state or a corporation or a private citizen are within the Supreme Court's original, but not its exclusive, jurisdiction. The Supreme Court ordinarily refers such suits to lower federal courts for first hearing.

The Supreme Court is reluctant to take cases involving its original jurisdiction since, as an appellate tribunal, it is "ill-equipped for the task of fact finding."[12] (When it hears a boundary dispute between states, the Court ordinarily appoints a special master to hear the evidence and make recommendations to the Court.) It will not accept original jurisdiction if a "state is only nominally a party and in reality is standing in to vindicate grievances of individuals."[13] But like so many judicial generalizations, there is a contrary one. Although a state may not invoke the original jurisdiction of the Supreme Court to forward the claims of individual citizens, it may act as a representative of its citizens, as *parens patriae*, as the lawyers call it, when the injury alleged affects the general population of a state in a substantial way. Thus, the Supreme Court permitted Maryland and a number of other states to challenge a Louisiana tax on natural gas taken from the continental shelf and brought into the state for processing prior to being shipped out of state. The tax fell not on just a few of the states' citizens, but on a great many of them. In addition, the states, as purchasers of natural gas for governmental purposes, had a substantial interest in the matter.[14]

The Supreme Court's role in resolving disputes between states is limited to deciding a legal dispute, and it will not allow itself to become an arbitrator between conflicting states about nonlegal matters.[15] For that purpose, the states must resort to an interstate compact to resolve their differences or go to Congress to seek a settlement.

Section 2

2. [continued] In all the other Cases before mentioned, the supreme Court shall have appellate Jurisdiction, both as to Law and Fact, with such Exceptions, and under such Regulations as the Congress shall make.

Appellate jurisdiction is the power to hear and decide appeals of decisions of lower courts. In all cases except those mentioned on page 110, the Supreme Court has only appellate jurisdiction and, furthermore, only the appellate jurisdiction specifically granted it by Congress. The completeness of congressional control of the Supreme Court's appellate jurisdiction is illustrated by the 1869 decision in *Ex parte McCardle*. In 1868 the Supreme Court announced that it would hear the appeal of a newspaper editor who had challenged the constitutionality of one of the Reconstruction acts. When the Court had heard arguments on the merits of the case and was considering the decision, Congress, anticipating that the Court might declare the act unconstitutional, repealed the habeas corpus provision that had allowed the issue to be appealed to the Supreme Court. The Court thereupon held that it had no power to decide the case.[16]

Members of Congress proposing to restrict the Supreme Court's appellate jurisdiction, as well as the original jurisdiction of the lower federal courts, on such subjects as abortion, busing, and school prayer, point to *Ex parte McCardle* as evidence that Congress may do so (see page 107). Some scholars, however, have pointed out that McCardle had another route to the Supreme Court. They argue that the McCardle case stands only for the principle that Congress may abolish the habeas corpus way to the Supreme Court, not that it may cut off all appeals to the Court on constitutional matters.

Despite the great and increasing volume of federal litigation, the Supreme Court has been able to keep up with its work, more or less, because Congress has given it the authority to select for review only the most important cases within its appellate jurisdiction. There are certain types of cases, however, that the Supreme Court is under statutory obligation to review when asked to do so by the proper party. The Court is the one, however, that decides whether a case falls within the obligatory review requirement. Under the terms of the law, the Court is to review

1. final judgments by the highest state court to which a case could be carried against the validity of a treaty or statute of the United States;

2. final judgments by the highest state court to which a case could be carried in favor of the validity of a state statute that had been challenged on the ground of being repugnant to the Constitution, treaties, or laws of the United States, except those applicable only in the District of Columbia;[17]

3. decisions of a United States court of appeals in which a state statute was held invalid as repugnant to the Constitution, treaties, or laws of the United States;

4. decisions of federal district courts in which an act of Congress was held unconstitutional in any civil action to which the United States or one of its agencies or officers was a party; and

5. certain other district court decisions that require a three-judge district court.

With the exception of these kinds of cases, which are said to go to the Supreme Court *on appeal,* the Supreme Court has discretion whether to accept a case. It accepts, by granting a *writ of certiorari,* only cases that it considers to be of sufficient public importance to merit its attention. The formal distinction between the discretionary certiorari and the mandatory appeal procedures should not be given too much weight. The Supreme Court also dismisses many appeals "for want of a substantial federal question." In short, the Supreme Court has wide discretion in determining which cases it will accept, whether the cases are presented to it for certiorari or on appeal.

A distinction needs to be made, however, between the consequence of the Supreme Court's dismissing a case "for want of a substantial federal question" and the consequence its denial of a writ of certiorari. The denial of a writ of certiorari has no value as precedent. All it means is that, for whatever reason, four or more justices could not agree that the Supreme Court should accept the case for review. But when a case reaches the Supreme Court on appeal and the Court then dismisses it "for want of a substantial federal question," the dismissal does have precedential value; the Supreme Court has performed its reviewing function, even though it has rendered no formal opinion. For example, if the Supreme Court dismisses, "for want of a substantial federal question," an appeal in which a state law is challenged as violating the Constitution, lower-court judges should take note that the Supreme Court has reviewed the law and concluded that it does not violate the Constitution. "Votes to affirm summarily and to dismiss for want of substantial federal questions are votes on the merits of the case."[18] However, a dismissal "for want of jurisdiction" means that the Court had no occasion to adjudicate the merits of the constitutional questions presented, and such a dismissal, like a denial of certiorari, has no precedential effect.[19]

Section 2

3. The Trial of all Crimes, except in Cases of Impeachment, shall be by Jury; and such Trial shall be held in the State where the said Crimes shall have been committed; but when not committed within any State, the Trial shall be at such Place or Places as the Congress may by Law have directed.

This section guarantees the right to a trial by jury to persons accused of crimes by the national government. (See also the Sixth Amendment.) It also responds to one of the charges brought against George III in the Declaration of Independence, "For transporting us beyond the Seas to be tried for pretended offences," and requires that the trial be held in the state where the crime was committed. It is not always clear, however, where some crimes were committed: For example, federal statutes permit trial in any state from, through, and to which obscene materials are mailed. The statutes have been applied without effective constitutional challenge on this point.

Section 3

1. Treason against the United States, shall consist only in levying War against them, or in adhering to their Enemies, giving them Aid and Comfort. No person shall be convicted of Treason unless on the Testimony of two Witnesses to the same overt Act, or on Confession in open Court.

There are two separate grounds for treason: (1) levying war against the United States and (2) giving aid and comfort to the enemy. Levying war is being part of a group of armed persons actually moving against the government. Giving aid and comfort means deliberately promoting the cause of a declared enemy of the United States. Since Congress never formally declared war against North Vietnam, it is doubtful that any person could have been convicted of treason for adhering to its cause and giving it aid and comfort, but there is no precise court holding on the matter. Those who take up arms against the United States as part of a hostile force, however, probably risk prosecution for treason even without a congressional declaration of war.

No person may be convicted of treason on circumstantial evidence alone. The accused must make a confession in open court, or there must be two witnesses to an overt act that, either by itself or with other evidence, convinces the jury of the defendant's guilt.

This section does not prevent Congress from making it a federal crime to use force and violence against the government or to conspire to do so. It may be possible for aliens to commit treason against the United States, because while within the boundaries of the United States they owe our government temporary allegiance.

Section 3

2. The Congress shall have Power to declare the Punishment of Treason, but no Attainder of Treason shall work Corruption of Blood, or Forfeiture except during the Life of the Person attainted.

In sixteenth- and seventeenth-century England, "attainders of treason" worked "corruption of blood," making it impossible for the traitor's family to inherit from him. Having been traitors themselves in rebelling against King George, the framers may have felt a certain tenderness for such unfortunates.

ARTICLE IV: STATES' RELATIONS

Section 1

Full Faith and Credit shall be given in each State to the public Acts, Records, and judicial Proceedings of every other State. And the Congress may by general Laws prescribe the Manner in which such Acts, Records and Proceedings shall be proved, and the Effect thereof.

Note that it is the acts of a state, not its laws, that get full faith and credit.

Congress has supplemented the full-faith-and-credit clause by providing that "acts, records, and judicial proceedings or copies thereof, so authenticated, shall have the same full faith and credit in every court within the United States and its territories and possessions as they have by law or usage in the courts of such State, Territory, or Possession from which they are taken." This provision includes federal as well as state courts.

This clause applies especially to judicial decisions. Suppose that a Pennsylvania court awards X a $50,000 judgment against Y, also a Pennsylvanian; after moving to New York, Y refuses to pay. Thanks to the full-faith-and-credit clause, X does not have to prove her case all over again and secure a new judgment against Y in a New York court. The New York courts will give full faith and credit to the Pennsylvania judgment and will enforce the judgment even if it is not one that the New York courts would have granted originally.

Or suppose that X, a New Yorker, while driving his car in New Jersey, injures Y or his property and then returns to New York without doing anything about it. Following a certain procedure, Y may sue X in the New Jersey courts; if they decide in Y's favor, the New York courts must aid Y in collecting the judgment, whether X appeared in the case or not.

How much faith and credit must a state give to a divorce decree granted by another state? The material question raised is that of *domicile*. Each state has the power to regulate the marriages and divorces of its own residents. Clearly, a divorce granted by a state to two bona fide residents must be given full faith and credit by all the other states, although they might not themselves have granted the divorce for the grounds alleged. However, if one North Carolinian, for example, goes to Nevada and obtains a divorce after the six weeks necessary under Nevada law, the Constitution does not require the North Carolina courts to recognize the divorce. The Supreme Court has ruled that under such circumstances the North Carolina courts could refuse to recognize the Nevada decree on the ground that Nevada courts lacked jurisdiction to grant the divorce because the plaintiff, in the eyes of North Carolina, had not acquired a bona fide domicile in Nevada.[1] If, however, both parties to the divorce make their appearance in the divorce-granting state and the issue of domicile is raised and decided, neither they nor their heirs can, in any other court, challenge the validity of the divorce on the ground that the state lacked jurisdiction. By a rule of American jurisprudence, *res judicata*, once a person has had a "day in court," that person may not raise the same issue again in a separate proceeding.[2]

According to the *divisible divorce* concept, although a state may have to recognize a divorce decree of another state when domicile has been acquired in that state, it may have greater discretion in recognizing decisions on alimony, property, and custody of children. Some interesting legal problems stem from this concept. This is not the place to get involved in such highly technical matters, other than to note that situations have occurred in which the woman who had been the legal wife was not the legal widow. The dissolution of a marriage can create all kinds of legal tangles.

The full-faith-and-credit clause is involved in the *conflict-of-laws* (choice of law) questions that arise so frequently in a federal system. Which laws should be applied to decide particular disputes?

Take, for example, a case in which a widow sued an insurance company to recover for her husband's death. Ralph Hague had been killed in Wisconsin when the motorcycle on which he was a passenger was struck from behind by an automobile. Although the drivers of both vehicles were Wisconsin residents, as was Hague, and the accident took place in Wisconsin, his wife brought suit in a Minnesota court — she had moved to Minnesota after her husband's death.

Which law should the Minnesota courts apply, that of Wisconsin or that of Minnesota? It made a difference, since the law of Minnesota allowed three times the damages allowed by the law of Wisconsin. The Minnesota courts chose to apply their own laws. The Supreme Court upheld Minnesota's action against a challenge that it violated both the full-faith-and-credit clause and the due process clause. (The tests under both clauses are in effect the same; but, as Justice Stevens in concurrence pointed out, the question was whether the full-faith-and-credit clause required Minnesota to apply Wisconsin laws or whether the due process clause prevented Minnesota from applying its own laws.) Since Hague had worked in Minnesota, the insurance company did business in Minnesota, and Hague's wife had become a citizen of Minnesota before instituting the litigation, the Supreme Court ruled that Minnesota had significant enough contact with the accident for it to apply its own laws if it chose.[3]

In a fascinating decision with many implications for interstate relations, in 1979 the Supreme Court, for the first time, got to the issue whether a state could be sued against its wishes in the courts of another state. The Court ruled that it could. Nevada was being sued because of an accident in California that had involved a Nevada vehicle and a Nevada employee. The Court ruled that it could. The Court ruled that the full-faith-and-credit clause did not require California courts to enforce a Nevada law requiring that such suits take place only in Nevada courts and limiting the amount of money that could be recovered.[4] It is the acts, not the laws of other states, that are entitled to full faith and credit.

The trend in recent years has been to read the full-faith-and-credit clause as giving state courts more latitude in deciding whether to use laws of their own state, rather than those of a sister state, in dealing with issues brought before them. Nonetheless, the Court decided that Kansas had violated both the due process clause and the full-faith-and-credit clause when it applied its law to all claims in a class action suit brought in behalf of oil royalty owners. Most of the royalty owners lived outside Kansas, the defendant was a Delaware corporation whose principal place of business was Oklahoma, and almost all the oil leases were for land outside Kansas. Said the Court, "We conclude that application of Kansas law to every claim in this case is sufficiently arbitrary and unfair as to exceed constitutional limits."[5]

Section 2

1. The Citizens of each State shall be entitled to all Privileges and Immunities of Citizens in the several States.

"This clause was intended to 'fuse into one Nation a collection of independent, sovereign states.' "[6] It is not, however, a clause whose "contours . . . have been precisely shaped by the process and wear of constant litigation and judicial interpretation. . . . Historically, it has been overshadowed by the appearance in 1868 of similar language in Paragraph 1 of the Fourteenth Amendment, and by the continuing controversy and consequent litigation that attended the Amendment's enactment and its meaning and application."[7]

The clause is also, along with the privileges and immunities and equal protection clauses of the Fourteenth Amendment, the Ninth Amendment, and the interstate commerce clause, the source of the right to travel throughout the United States, a right whose "textual source . . . has proved elusive."[8] The right to travel throughout the United States is a fundamental right (see page 233), subject to careful court scrutiny to ensure that citizens who migrate from one state to another are not disadvantaged simply because of the timing of their migration.

The clause does not wipe out all differences between the citizens of a state and those of other states. "It is discrimination against out-of-state residents on matters of fundamental concern which triggers [this clause.]"[9] If the discrimination affects fundamental rights, the state must show that (1) there is a "substantial reason" for the difference in treatment and (2) the difference in treatment bears a close or substantial relation to that reason.[10]

A state may exclude nonstate citizens from voting in its elections or serving as elective officers. It does not have to permit out-of-state citizens to attend its tax-supported institutions, such as schools, or to hunt its game or fish, for the same fees as charged its own citizens. On the other side of the constitutional divide, it may not ordinarily tax citizens of other states at discriminatory rates, deprive them of a means of livelihood, or deny them access to any part of the state.

New Hampshire fell afoul of this clause when it imposed a tax on the income of citizens of other states but not on its own citizens, even though the nonresidents were exempt from the New Hampshire tax if they paid such a tax to their own state.[11] Nor could New Hampshire limit admission to its bar to its own residents.[12] And South Carolina was told it could not require nonresident commercial shrimp boats to pay a substantially higher fee than its own residents paid.[13] Nor could Alaska attempt to alleviate its unemployment problem by requiring private employers in the oil and gas exploration and transportation business to give preference to Alaska residents.[14] (The Court has, however, sustained similar laws giving employment preference to citizens of a particular city.[15]

On the other hand, Montana was permitted to charge nonresident elk hunters a higher fee than its own residents. The higher fee did not interfere with out-of-state hunters' livelihoods, only their sport and amusement. "Whatever right or activities may be fundamental under the Privileges and Immunities Clause," wrote the Court, "we are persuaded, and hold, that elk hunting by nonresidents in Montana is not one of them."[16]

In short, the privileges and immunities clause "does not preclude disparity of treatment in the many situations where there are perfectly valid independent reasons for it"; it does preclude a state from discriminating against nonresidents "seeking to ply their trade, practice their occupation, or pursue a common calling within the State."[17]

American citizens become citizens of a state the moment they move to a state with the intent to remain. May a state distinguish among its residents by establishing length-of-residency requirements for certain purposes? Recently the Supreme Court has set aside a variety of such *durational residency* requirements. In reviewing such requirements, the Court sometimes uses this clause, sometimes uses the equal protection clause, and sometimes bases its decisions on the right to travel.

A state must show a compelling interest before it will be permitted to deny newly arrived residents the rights accorded all other citizens. To illustrate: A state may not make newly arrived citizens wait a year before becoming eligible for welfare payments, medical care, or voting rights. A day seems to be as long a wait as the Court will tolerate for welfare payments or medical care,[18] fifty days or so for the right to vote.[19] On the other hand, states may impose a one-year durational residency requirement on those seeking divorces, because that constraint is not considered such a burden on the right to travel as those declared unconstitutional.[20]

What about a durational requirement to attend public colleges and universities without paying out-of-state fees? A one-year requirement is constitutionally permissible. A state may not, however, create an irrefutable presumption that any person who comes into the state to attend a college is not a resident of the state, and a state cannot disqualify such a person from acquiring residency while attending school.[21] But those who move into the state just before enrolling in a state-supported university or college may be required to give evidence of their intention to remain after they finish their schooling, by such things as driver's licenses, car registration, voter registration, and continuous, year-round residence. Moreover, if students wish to establish their own residence, they may be required to provide evidence of their financial independence from their parents.

Section 2

2.   A Person charged in any State with Treason, Felony, or other Crime, who shall flee from Justice, and be found in another State, shall on Demand of the executive Authority of the State from which he fled, be delivered up, to be removed to the State having jurisdiction of the Crime.

This paragraph provides for what is known as *interstate rendition*, or — more commonly — *extradition*. Although it is a self-executing provision, Congress has implemented it by making the governor of the asylum state responsible for returning a fugitive, on the request of the governor or chief magistrate of the state from which the person fled.

Despite the positive language of this clause, in 1861 the Supreme Court held in *Kentucky* v *Dennison* that although governors are constitutionally obligated to return fugitives on receiving a properly certified request, federal courts lack authority to order them to do so.[22] Until 1987 that decision, based on an obsolete view of the relations between the national government and the states, was left undisturbed.[23]

Under that doctrine governors occasionally exercised their discretion and refused to honor extradition requests. For example, in 1976 Governor Jerry Brown of California refused to extradite Dennis Banks, an American Indian activist, to South Dakota, from which he had fled after being convicted of "felony riot." In 1984 Governor Scott M. Matheson of Utah rejected an extradition request from Illinois for a business official wanted for trial for murder because of an industrial accident in one of his company's plants.[24]

In 1987 the Court, noting the *Kentucky* v *Dennison* concept that the states and federal government must be viewed in all circumstances as coequal sovereigns is not representative of the law today, reversed that decision and made it clear that federal courts do have the power to order governors to fulfill a state's obligation under the extradition clause.

Once the governor of the asylum state has issued the warrant of arrest and rendition, the courts of that state have only four issues to consider before delivering up the fugitive: whether the extradition documents are in order, whether the petitioner has been charged with a crime in the demanding state, whether the petitioner is the person named in the request, and whether the petitioner is a fugitive. They have no authority to inquire whether the demanding state had probable cause for an arrest, whether the charges are substantial, or whether the prison conditions of the demanding state violate the Eighth Amendment prohibition against cruel and unusual punishment. Those matters are to be heard in the courts of the demanding state.[25]

Congress has made a federal crime of interstate or foreign travel with the intent to avoid prosecution or confinement by a state for certain felonies. Those who violate this law are to be brought back to the federal judicial district in which the original crime is alleged to have been committed, making it possible for federal officers to turn the fugitive over to state officials for prosecution or confinement.

Section 2

3. No Person held to Service or Labour in one State, under the Laws thereof, escaping into another, shall, in Consequence of any Law or Regulation therein, be discharged from such Service or Labour, but shall be delivered up on Claim of the Party to whom such Service or Labour may be due.

The Thirteenth Amendment, abolishing slavery, nullified the fugitive slave clause.

Section 3

1. New States may be admitted by the Congress into this Union;

The normal procedure is as follows: (1) the inhabitants of a territory file a petition for admission to the Union; (2) the president approves a congressional resolution authorizing the inhabitants of the territory to draw up a constitution; (3) a majority of both houses of Congress and then the president approve the proposed constitution; (4) the territory is admitted to the Union.

Although Congress and the president may withhold their approval of admission until the territory complies with or agrees to certain conditions, once a state is admitted, it possesses the same political powers as the other states. For example, in 1910 President Taft vetoed legislation admitting Arizona to the Union, because its proposed constitution permitted the voters to recall state judges. After deleting that clause, Arizona was admitted (in 1912) and promptly proceeded to restore the objectionable provision. Since the right to determine the method of selection, tenure, and removal of its own judges is a political power enjoyed by each state, Arizona's power in this respect could not be less than that of other states; Taft's condition was unenforceable.

Conditions on admission, such as those relating to public lands in the state, may be enforced as contracts that do not detract from the state's political power. When admitted to the Union, Minnesota agreed, in return for certain public lands it received from the national government, not to tax land still owned by the national government within the state. This agreement the Court enforced.[26]

When it became apparent that a proposed constitutional amendment to extend additional representation to the District of Columbia would fail to be ratified, its proponents turned to advocating that the District of Columbia be admitted as a state. Under their plan a small part of the District of Columbia would be retained as the seat of government of the United States, as required by the Constitution, but the rest of it could be admitted as a state. Such action would give the people of the district everything the proposed amendment would have — and more — and could be done with only the vote of a majority of both houses of Congress and the approval of the president.

The district, in fact, has held a constitutional convention, adopted a proposed constitution and petitioned Congress for admission of "New Columbia" under the terms of Article IV, Section 3. The prospects are not promising as long as the Republicans control the White House since admission of the district as a state would undoubtedly add two Democratic Senators and one Democratic member of the House.

The Civil War conclusively settled the question whether or not a state can constitutionally secede from the Union. In the words of the Supreme Court, ours is "an indestructible Union composed of indestructible States."[27]

Section 3

1. [continued] but no new State shall be formed or erected within the Jurisdiction of any other State; nor any State be formed by the Junction of two or more States, or Parts of States, without the Consent of the Legislatures of the States concerned as well as of the Congress.

Five states have been formed within the jurisdiction of other states with the consent of the legislatures concerned and of Congress: Vermont from New York in 1791, Kentucky from Virginia in 1792, Tennessee from North Carolina in 1796, Maine from Massachusetts in 1820, and West Virginia from Virginia (by a rump legislature during the Civil War) in 1863. When Texas was admitted to the Union, Congress consented to the division of the state into five states if the Texas legislature should ever so wish and thereby increase the number of senators from Texas to ten!

Section 3

2. The Congress shall have Power to dispose of and make all needful Rules and Regulations respecting the Territory or other Property belonging to the United States; and nothing in this Constitution shall be so construed as to Prejudice any Claims of the United States, or of any particular State.

When Puerto Rico, the Philippines, and Hawaii were annexed, the question arose whether or not "the Constitution followed the flag." The Supreme Court met the problem by distinguishing between "fundamental" and "formal" parts of the Constitution. The fundamental provisions are those that provide for fair trials, freedom of speech, and those rights necessary to an ordered scheme of liberty. The formal provisions are those, such as trial by jury, which at that time were considered forms appropriate for Americans but not essential for freedom and not the only way to secure justice.[28] The Court ruled in the Insular Cases that unless Congress provides otherwise, in unincorporated territories — those Congress has neither explicitly nor implicitly made an integral part of the Union — only the fundamental provisions apply.

Today all territories — Puerto Rico, Guam, the Northern Marianas, American Samoa, and the Virgin Islands — are unincorporated. The Insular Cases have never been specifically overruled, but their continuing validity has been questioned and it was assumed that as far as the constitutional protections for individuals were concerned, all provisions of the Constitution were applicable to the territories. Then in 1982 the Court seemed to give the Insular Cases continuing vitality. It upheld the Commonwealth of Puerto Rico's authority to vest the right to fill vacancies in its legislature in the voters of the party in which the former legislator was a member. Citing the Insular Cases, the Court wrote, "It is not disputed that the fundamental protections of the United States Constitution extend to the inhabitants of Puerto Rico."[29] Does the Court's use of the words "fundamental protections" suggest that the nonfundamental parts of the Constitution do not apply? And in a modern context what are the nonfundamental parts?

Congress may treat territories differently from states "so long as there is a rational basis for its action."[30] Thus, Congress was allowed to make lower social security payments to dependent children in Puerto Rico than to those in the states. The right to receive financial aid from the federal government is not a constitutionally protected right. Moreover, the distinction between the payments is rational, said the Court, because (1) Puerto Rican citizens (who are, by the way, American citizens; see page 224) do not pay federal taxes, (2) the cost of treating Puerto Rico as a state would be very high, and (3) the payment of the greater benefits might disrupt the Puerto Rican economy.

Section 4

The United States shall guarantee to every State in this Union a Republican Form of Government,

---

The Constitution does not define "a republican form of government." John Adams observed, "The word *republic* as it is used, may signify anything, everything, or nothing."[31] The framers undoubtedly meant a form that, as distinguished from aristocracy, monarchy, or direct democracy, rests on the consent of the people and operates through representative institutions. In the landmark case of *Luther* v *Borden*, the Supreme Court held that what "a republican form of government" means is a political question, a responsibility of the Congress, not of the courts, to answer.[32] Whenever Congress permits the senators and representatives of a particular state to take their seats in Congress, that state must be deemed to have "a republican form of government" within the meaning of the Constitution.

Because the Court firmly holds to the view that interpretation of the guarantee clause is a political question and not a justiciable one, the clause is seldom raised in litigation. But in 1902, after Oregon adopted the *initiative,* whereby its citizens are able to legislate directly without the intervention of the legislature,[33] a company that had been taxed under a law passed by the initiative procedure argued that such action transgressed the clause requiring states to have republican forms of government. The Court again refused to intervene, holding that "violation of the . . . guaranty of a republican form of government . . . cannot be challenged in the courts."[34]

Long ago Charles Sumner pointed out that the guarantee clause is "a sleeping giant." No other part of the Constitution gives "Congress such supreme power over the states." And there are those who today argue that the clause imposes on Congress the responsibility to supervise state activities directly to ensure that they meet the test of a republican form of government.[35] But the primary restraint on congressional intervention into state matters remains, as it has always been, more political in nature than constitutional. Whenever Congress, responding to national majorities, feels the need to intervene in state matters, this clause is not the only one available to justify its intervention.

Section 4

[continued] and shall protect each of them against Invasion; and on Application of the Legislature, or of the Executive (when the Legislature cannot be convened) against domestic Violence.

Invasion of a state by a foreign power would also be an invasion of the United States.

Congress has delegated to the president the authority to send troops into a state to protect it from domestic violence, on the request of the appropriate state authority. In 1842 there were two governments in Rhode Island, each of which claimed to be the legitimate one. When President Tyler indicated that he was prepared to send troops to defend one of these against domestic violence from the other, he was at the same time determining which government was the legitimate one. The Supreme Court, refusing to intervene, called the question political.[36]

When necessary to enforce federal laws or federal judicial decrees or to preserve the property or "the peace of the United States," the president may send federal law enforcement agents or even troops to the scene of resistance. Under such circumstances, the president does not act at the request of state officials and may act even against their wishes. Under such circumstances, the president is not "ordering troops into a state" but enforcing the laws of the United States, which cover the length and breadth of the land.[37]

ARTICLE V: THE AMENDING POWER

The Congress, whenever two thirds of both Houses shall deem it necessary, shall propose Amendments to this Constitution, or, on the Application of the Legislatures of two thirds of the several States, shall call a Convention for proposing Amendments, which, in either Case, shall be valid to all Intents and Purposes, as Part of this Constitution, when ratified by the Legislatures of three fourths of the several States, or by Conventions in three fourths thereof, as the one or the other Mode of Ratification may be proposed by the Congress;

Amendments to the Constitution must be both proposed and ratified. The Constitution provides two ways to propose and two ways to ratify. So far, all amendments have been proposed by Congress, and all but one, the Twenty-first, have been ratified by the state legislatures.

The formal amendatory procedures have been criticized as undemocratic. One-fourth of the states plus one, which could reflect the wishes of much less than one-fourth of the people, could block amendments desired by a large majority. It is also possible for amendments to be adopted without a direct expression of popular opinion. The latter criticism would be largely met were Congress to require ratification by state conventions called for that purpose, rather than by state legislatures chosen to deal with other issues.

Of the many attempts to get Congress to call a constitutional convention, so far the closest to success came in the spring of 1967, when thirty-three state legislatures, only one short of the number required, petitioned Congress to call a convention to propose an amendment to reverse Supreme Court rulings requiring both chambers of state legislatures to be apportioned on the basis of population. Suddenly, the many unanswered questions about how such a convention might operate ceased to be only of academic interest. But the thirty-fourth state legislature never acted, pressures for a reapportionment amendment abated as many states were reapportioned, and interest in a constitutional convention temporarily died down.

Concerns about a constitutional convention have revived because there are two active campaigns for the calling of such a convention. A number of state legislatures have petitioned Congress to call a convention to propose an amendment permitting states to ban abortions. But the most active campaign is by the National Taxpayers Union. By the beginning of 1988, thirty-two of the required thirty-four legislatures had passed resolutions calling for a national convention to write an amendment requiring the federal budget to be balanced each year, except during times of war or other emergencies declared by an extraordinary majority of Congress. Although the president has no formal role to play in the amendatory process, President Reagan endorsed such an amendment. The National Taxpayers Union is mounting a major campaign in the hope of adding the two more convention calls it needs for success. At the same time, opponents of such an amendment, including Common Cause, organized labor, and many constitutional scholars, are trying to get states (such as Maryland and Iowa) that had previously adopted a resolution calling for a convention to repeal their call.[1]

There are many questions relating to a constitutional convention for which there are no clear answers. How would a convention be run? How would delegates be apportioned? How would they be chosen? Could members of Congress become delegates? Are the petitions from the several states sufficiently identical to reflect support for a particular amendment? Have they been presented within a period to indicate there is a "contemporaneous national wish" for such an amendment? Congress, not the courts, would decide such questions.

Of greatest concern is the issue whether Congress could call for a limited convention, restricting what the convention could consider. Scholars are divided on whether a convention could constitutionally ignore such a congressional limit. Once in session, a convention might, as did the Convention of 1787, "run away" and propose an entirely new constitution. Because of such concerns, many observers believe that if thirty-four legislatures ever petition Congress to call a convention, do so in language that makes it clear they all want a particular amendment, and do it within the proper time, Congress is more likely to propose the amendment itself than to run the risk of calling a national convention.

Proposed amendments must be ratified. Congress decides which of the two methods of ratification will be used — approval by the legislatures of three-fourths of the states or approval by special state conventions in three-fourths of the states. Governors have no role in the ratification process. When Congress proposed the Twenty-first Amendment, repealing the Eighteenth Amendment (prohibition), it left to each state the determination of the manner in which delegates to its ratifying convention would be chosen.

Many questions arising out of Article V, especially those that relate to ratification, are political questions; indeed, it is probable that the Court would, if occasion arose, accept Justice Black's statement, made in 1939, "Congress, possessing exclusive power over the amending process, cannot be bound by and is under no duty to accept the pronouncements upon that exclusive power by this Court."[2]

May a state legislature, having rejected an amendment, change its mind and ratify? After it has ratified, may it change its mind and rescind its ratification? If a state constitution requires ratification to be by a two-thirds vote of each chamber of the state legislature, may a majority of that legislature subsequently rescind ratification? When are ratifications untimely? The lack of an absolutely clear and agreed-upon answer to these questions points to a danger spot in our Constitution, for the one thing that we should know for sure is what is and what is not required to amend the Constitution.[3]

The predominant opinion, based on post — Civil War congressional practices, is that after voting against an amendment, a state legislature may reconsider and ratify but that once a legislature has ratified an amendment, its ratification cannot be rescinded and will be counted. On July 20, 1868, Secretary of State Seward certified to Congress that the required twenty-eight states (there were then thirty-seven states) had approved the Fourteenth Amendment; however, Ohio and New Jersey had, prior to that date, "withdrawn their earlier assent." The next day, Congress declared the amendment a part of the Constitution and directed the secretary of state to promulgate it. On July 28 the secretary so certified. In the interim two other states had added their ratification. (Authority to make the initial certification of amendments, subject to ultimate congressional approval, has since been transferred to the administrator of general services.)

This Fourteenth Amendment precedent was frequently cited during the battles over the ratification of the Equal Rights Amendment (ERA). In the fall of 1978, when

Congress extended the period for ratification of the ERA, some members argued that, since the time was being extended, it was only fair that rescissions be counted (four states had already voted to rescind), but Congress refused to authorize rescissions. If the appropriate number of states had ratified, the issue of rescissions would have arisen again when Congress decided whether to certify the amendment.

Ratification of an amendment must take place within a "reasonable time." Congress determines what constitutes a reasonable time. Beginning with the Eighteenth Amendment, submitted in 1917, Congress placed a seven-year limit in the body of most proposed amendments. However, when it submitted the Child Labor Amendment in 1924, it failed to set a time limit. Only twenty-eight state legislatures ratified it, the last in 1937. A reasonable time has long since passed, although Congress has never said so. (Moreover, Supreme Court decisions since 1937 have provided Congress with other means of outlawing child labor, so the amendment is unnecessary.) Beginning with the Twenty-third Amendment, proposed in 1960, Congress adopted the practice of setting a seven-year limit in the submission resolution rather than making it a formal part of the amendment. Thus, when it appeared that the ERA would not be ratified within the seven-year limit, advocates of extending the time limit successfully argued that since the time limit was not part of the text of the proposed amendment but was contained only in the resolution submitting it to the states, the time for ratification could be extended by a majority vote of both houses, instead of the two-thirds required to propose an amendment. When, in August of 1978, Congress proposed an amendment to give a greater voice in national affairs to the people of the District of Columbia, it pointedly reverted to previous practice and put the seven-year limit right in the body of the proposed amendment.

More than five thousand amendments have been introduced in Congress, but only thirty-three have been proposed. Twenty-six of those have been ratified. Two of the rejected amendments were proposed along with the ten that were finally ratified as the Bill of Rights. Another that was not ratified (1810) would have withdrawn citizenship from any person who accepted a title of nobility or who received, without the consent of Congress, an office or emolument from a foreign power. On the eve of the Civil War, Congress proposed an amendment that would have prohibited any amendment to the Constitution that interfered with slavery in any of the states. The rejections of the Child Labor Amendment, the Equal Rights Amendment, and the second District of Columbia Amendment are somewhat unusual. During most of our history, if a coalition of political forces has been strong enough to get two-thirds of both houses of Congress to propose an amendment, it has ordinarily reflected a consensus strong enough to make ratification probable.

[continued] Provided that no Amendment which may be made prior to the Year One thousand eight hundred and eight shall in any Manner affect the first and fourth Clauses in the Ninth Section of the first Article;

This provision referred to the importation of slaves and possesses only historical interest today.

[continued] and [provided] that no State, without its Consent, shall be deprived of its equal Suffrage in the Senate.

Some consider this provision unamendable, and others contend that there are ways in which even it can be changed. It could be repealed, they say, by amendment, and then another amendment could be adopted that would permit unequal representation in the Senate.

Other Methods of Constitutional Development

The Constitution, written before the industrial and democratic revolutions had made their imprint on the nation, continues to be a living, fundamental law for our powerful industrial democracy. Obviously, the Constitution has had to change as the nation changed. Although the framework is the same, fundamental alterations have been made in the operation of the government within that framework. The formal amending process has been relatively unimportant in this development; less formal, more subtle methods have been employed.

Congressional Elaboration

The framers were wise and humble men who doubted that they had either the moral right or the necessary wisdom to prescribe the details of governing the nation for future generations. They knew that a rigid, detailed, and restrictive constitution would have little chance of enduring. They painted in broad strokes, made their grants of power general, and left it to Congress to develop the structure of government by ordinary legislation. Examples of congressional elaboration appear in such legislation as the Judiciary Act of 1789, which laid the foundation of our national judicial system, in the laws establishing the organization and functions of all federal executive officials subordinate to the president, in Congress's application and interpretation of its powers under the impeachment clauses, and in its rules of procedure, internal organization, and practices.

Presidential Practices

The president has great discretion in developing the nature and role of the office. There has been no change in the formal constitutional position of the president, but nowadays the president participates in the making of legislative policy to an extent not anticipated by the Founding Fathers; if they had anticipated it, they would probably have disapproved. With the growth of political parties, the president became a national party leader and an active participant in party battles. In response to crises, the presidency has grown into the pivotal office of our national government, and the president has become a key legislator as well as the nation's chief executive.

Judicial Interpretation

As we have already seen, the courts are the authoritative interpreters of the Constitution. The words of the Constitution are sufficiently broad to accommodate divergent interpretations. As conditions have changed, so have judicial interpretations of the Constitution. In the words of Woodrow Wilson, "The Supreme Court is a constitutional convention in continuous session." At one time, the Supreme Court ruled that the national government could not regulate child labor.[4] Today the national government does so with the approval of the Supreme Court. The Supreme Court's response to a persistent public demand made formal amendment unnecessary.[5] Perhaps the best illustration of how judicial interpretation has altered our constitutional system is that the power of the courts to interpret the Constitution is itself the result of judicial interpretation. It should be noted that although the Supreme Court has the final judicial say about the meaning of our Constitution, the Constitution is also interpreted daily by the hundreds of federal judges and by thousands of state judges.

Customs and Usage

The president's cabinet and the local residence requirement for congressional members are examples of constitutional customs. A more significant example is the custom of presidential electors' pledging themselves to support the candidates of their party, a practice that has transformed the electoral college into an automatic transmitter of the electorate's choice.

The "Unwritten Constitution": Summary

Surrounding the formal document are customs and usage, congressional statutes, judicial decisions, and presidential practices that supplement the written Constitution. These rules are sometimes called the "unwritten Constitution." It has been primarily through the use of informal methods of development and alteration in this unwritten Constitution that our governmental system has grown. The Constitution was democratized by the extension of the suffrage within the states and by the extraconstitutional development of national political parties. The national government has been strengthened to meet the emergencies of a national economy and an interdependent world without fundamentally changing the written Constitution. In short, our Constitution provides for a living, organic, and growing governmental system.

ARTICLE VI: THE SUPREMACY ARTICLE

1. All Debts contracted and Engagements entered into, before the Adoption of this Constitution, shall be as valid against the United States under this Constitution, as under the Confederation.

At the time of the Constitutional Convention, the securities and currency issued by the Confederation and the several states had depreciated in value. Later, Alexander Hamilton, Washington's brilliant secretary of the treasury, proposed that the national government assume the debts of the several states and pay in full the debts of the Confederation. Adoption of this proposal did much to strengthen the new Union, at a handsome profit to speculators in Confederation securities.

---

2. This Constitution, and the Laws of the United States which shall be made in Pursuance thereof; and all Treaties made, or which shall be made, under the Authority of the United States, shall be the supreme Law of the Land; and the Judges in every State shall be bound thereby, any Thing in the Constitution or Laws of any State to the Contrary notwithstanding.

This clause lays down one of the key principles of the Constitution, a principle that makes federalism work: *The powers of the national government are limited, but within the field of its powers it is supreme, and the state courts are bound to uphold this supremacy.* Any provision of a state constitution or any state law is null and void if it conflicts with the Constitution, with a federal law passed in pursuance of the Constitution, or with a treaty made under the authority of the United States. To take a single example, a Pennsylvania law punishing advocacy of sedition against the United States is unenforceable because it conflicts with a similar federal law.[1] (However, a state can pass a law directed at subversion of the state itself.)

A considerable portion of our judges' time is taken trying to determine whether the federal government has preempted a state's action. Preemption may be either expressed or implied. "Absent explicit preemptive language, Congress's intent to supersede a state law may be inferred because the scheme of federal regulation may be so pervasive as to make reasonable the inference that Congress left no room for the States to supplement it, because the Act of Congress may touch a field in which the federal interest is so dominant that the federal system will be assumed to preclude enforcement of state laws on the same subject, or because the object sought to be obtained by federal law and the character of obligations imposed by it may reveal the same purpose."[2] "Even where Congress has not completely displaced state regulation . . . state law is nullified to the extent that it conflicts with federal law," as when compliance with both federal and state regulations is impossible.[3]

Discerning the will of Congress with respect to preemption is no more precise than discerning the meaning of the Constitution. Take the problems of deciding whether Congress has preempted the regulation of nuclear energy. There is perhaps no field in which the federal government has exercised more pervasive authority than in regulating nuclear plants to ensure their safety. Yet a unanimous Court decided California could impose a moratorium on any new nuclear plants until the state energy commission was satisfied that there was a feasible way to dispose of nuclear waste. California acted, so its legislature declared, not for reasons of safety but to prevent excessive costs to its citizens. "The legal reality remains," concluded the Supreme Court, "that Congress has left sufficient authority in the states to allow the development of nuclear power to be slowed or even stopped for economic reasons. Given this statutory scheme, it is for Congress to rethink the division of regulatory authority in light of its possible exercise by the states to undercut a federal objective. The courts should not assume the role which our system assigns to Congress."[4]

Federal regulations issued by executive agencies with authority from Congress have no less preemptive effect than federal statutes.[5]

The Existence of the States and the Supremacy Clause

Although the powers of Congress are granted by the Constitution without any reference to the states, Congress is not to exercise its powers in a fashion that impairs the states' integrity or ability to function effectively. This prohibition is made explicit by the Tenth Amendment. Yet it is easier to make this generalization than to cite cases in which the existence of the states has constrained the exercise of congressional powers. The only case in modern times was *National League of Cities* v *Usery*, and it was overruled nine years later in *Garcia* v *San Antonio Metro*.[6] In *National League of Cities* the Supreme Court, by a sharply divided vote, held that federal wage and hour regulations could not be applied to the employees of state governments. Here Congress, said the Court, had interfered with the states' "freedom to structure integral operations in areas of traditional governmental functions" . . . "functions essential to separate and independent existence."[7]

Following *National League of Cities* the Court went out of its way to make it clear that the reach of that decision was exceedingly limited.[8] The Court started to distinguish between traditional state activities that are integral parts of state governments — generally immune from federal regulation — and all other state activities, such as a state-owned railroad, which are not immune from federal regulation.[9] The decisions following *National League of Cities* were hard to reconcile with it. Justice Stevens, one of the dissenters, called for its reversal. He said, "*National League of Cities* not only was incorrectly decided, but also is inconsistent with the central purpose of the Constitution itself, that it is not entitled to the deference that the doctrine of *stare decisis* ordinarily commands for this Court's precedents. . . . I believe that the law would be well served by a prompt rejection of *National League of Cities*' modern embodiment of the spirit of the Articles of Confederation."[10]

Then in *Garcia* Justice Blackmun, who had provided the fifth vote in *National League of Cities*, switched and wrote the opinion for the Court overruling it. There is no principled way, he argued, to distinguish between traditional and non-traditional state governmental functions. Although agreeing that "the States occupy a special and specific position in our constitutional system and that the scope of Congress' authority under the Commerce Clause must reflect that position," he clearly rejected the view that the Supreme Court is the primary agency to prevent Congress from extending its powers in such a way as to intrude into the province of the states. Rather, he argued, "the Framers chose to rely on a federal system in which special restraints on federal power over the States inhered principally in the workings of the National Government itself. . . . State sovereign interests, then, are more properly protected by procedural safeguards inherent in the structure of the federal system than by judicially created limitations on federal power."[11]

Justice Powell, in what for him was an unusually strong opinion, accused the majority of rejecting almost 200 years of the understanding of the constitutional status of federalism, "of ignoring the Tenth Amendment," of propounding "a view of federalism that pays only lip service to the role of the States," of reflecting an "unprecedented view that Congress is free under the Commerce Clause to assume a State's traditional sovereign power, and to do so without judicial review of its action." Justices Rehnquist and O'Connor, perhaps anticipating the views of justices likely to be nominated by President Reagan, predicted that the principles of *National League of Cities* would "in time again command the support of a majority of the Court" and that "this Court will in time again assume its constitutional responsibility."[12]

If the principles of federalism are not much of a barrier to congressional exercise of the commerce power, they are even less of one when Congress acts to enforce the Fourteenth and Fifteenth Amendments. That congressional actions to enforce those amendments may interfere with essential state functions is of no constitutional consequence.[13]

Modern constitutional interpretation has been generous in its construction of the scope and reach of congressional powers. Still, the debate over *National League of Cities* and *Garcia* and the division of opinion among the justices should give Congress a mild warning that the existence of the states does set some limits on its exercise of the powers granted to it.

United States Treaty Power

Treaties are of two types: self-executing and non-self-executing. Self-executing treaties require no implementation by Congress to have internal application as supreme law of the land. If the president, with the consent of two-thirds of the Senate, makes a self-executing treaty giving foreign nationals certain rights in return for reciprocal concessions for American nationals, such a treaty is valid as internal law. It takes precedence over any conflicting state constitutions or laws. Non-self-executing treaties, although establishing a binding international obligation, must be implemented in this country by Congress; the implementing legislation becomes supreme law of the land, enforceable in the courts.

Treaties, like national laws, must conform to the national Constitution. A treaty, or a law implementing a treaty, that abridged First Amendment freedoms would be just as unconstitutional as a law that did the same thing. "This Court has regularly and uniformly recognized the supremacy of the Constitution over a treaty."[14] Nonetheless, the limitations of federalism, such as they are, do not appear to limit the scope of the national government's treaty-making power as they do its law-making powers.

Note that whereas the supremacy clause makes only those "laws of the United States made in pursuance" of the Constitution the supreme law of the land, it makes "all treaties made, or which shall be made, under the authority of the United States" supreme law. Does this difference in constitutional language have any significance? The question came to the Supreme Court in the famous case of *Missouri v Holland* (1920). After Congress, in 1913, had passed a law regulating the hunting of migratory birds, several district judges ruled that the law was unconstitutional because regulation of wild game is not among the powers delegated to the national government. Three years later, the United States became party to a treaty with Canada (through Great Britain) in which the national government promised to protect the birds migrating between Canada and this country in return for a promise by Canada to do the same. To fulfill our obligations under this treaty, Congress passed a law even more stringent than its 1913 enactment. This time the case went to the Supreme Court. Justice Holmes, speaking for a unanimous Court, said,

> Acts of Congress are the supreme law of the land only when made in pursuance of the Constitution, while treaties are declared to be so when made under the authority of the United States. . . . We do not mean to imply that there are no qualifications to the treaty-making power; but they must be ascertained in a different way. . . . The only question is whether it is forbidden by some invisible radiation from the general terms of the Tenth

Amendment. . . . We see nothing in the Constitution that compels the Government to sit by while a food supply is cut off and the protectors of our forest and our crops are destroyed.[15]

Today discussions of whether the treaty power is broader than the national law-making power have lost much of their significance. With the liberal construction of the national government's legislative powers, there are few subjects of national importance that Congress cannot directly regulate.

---

3. The Senators and Representatives before mentioned, and the Members of the several State Legislatures, and all executive and judicial Officers, both of the United States and of the several States, shall be bound by Oath or Affirmation, to support this Constitution;

This clause makes it clear that the first allegiance of all Americans, including state officials, is to the national Constitution. If a state governor, for example, is ordered by the state constitution or legislature to perform an act contrary to the national Constitution, the governor's duty is nonetheless to comply with the national Constitution.

---

3. [continued] but no religious Test shall ever be required as a Qualification to any Office of public Trust under the United States.

This provision applies only to the national government, but as a result of the adoption of the First and Fourteenth Amendments, the same prohibition applies to state and local governments.[16]

Note that Article I, Section 3, paragraph 6, and Article II, Section 1, paragraph 8, on pages 43 and 91, are additional evidence of the framers' concern for religious freedom. Whenever the Constitution calls for an oath to God to tell the truth or to perform responsibilities, an alternative is provided for those who may have religious convictions against the swearing of such oaths. They, or anyone, may choose merely to affirm that they will tell the truth or carry out their duties.

ARTICLE VII: RATIFICATION OF THE CONSTITUTION

The Ratification of the Conventions of nine States, shall be sufficient for the Establishment of this Constitution between the States so ratifying the Same.

The Constitutional Convention was a revolutionary body. The delegates were representatives of the states acting in response to a call by the Congress of the Confederation. Since the Articles of Confederation could be amended only with the consent of all thirteen state legislatures, and since they created a "perpetual Union," Congress, when it called the convention, had explicitly stated that no recommendations should be effective until approved by Congress and ratified in accordance with the terms of the Articles that is, by all thirteen state legislatures. Nevertheless, the delegates to the convention boldly assumed power to exceed their mandate and proposed an entirely new government, which was to go into effect upon ratification by specially chosen conventions of only nine of the thirteen states.

Done in Convention by the Unanimous Consent of the States present the Seventeenth Day of September in the Year of our Lord one thousand seven hundred and Eighty seven and of the Independence of the United States of America the Twelfth. *In Witness whereof We have hereunto subscribed our Names,*

(For a discussion of the signing of the Constitution, see pages 14 — 15.)

Amendments to the Constitution

THE BILL OF RIGHTS

Much of the opposition to ratification of the Constitution stemmed from its lack of specific guarantees of certain fundamental rights. The Constitutional Convention failed to adopt such guarantees because they were thought to be unnecessary and dangerous — unnecessary because the Constitution itself prohibits bills of attainder, ex post facto laws, and suspension of the writ of habeas corpus except in times of public danger, and requires trial by jury in federal criminal cases; dangerous because prohibitions might furnish an argument for claiming powers not granted the new government. For example, to forbid the national government to *abridge* freedom of the press might be thought to imply that it had the power to *regulate* the press if it could do so without abridging it. It was also urged that the protection of fundamental rights ultimately rested not on paper guarantees but in the hearts and minds of the nation's citizens.[1]

Despite those arguments, there was a general demand for a bill of rights; the Constitution was adopted with the understanding that the first business of the first Congress would be the consideration of amendments suitable for the purpose. Congress proposed twelve such amendments on September 25, 1789, ten of which were ratified and became part of the Constitution on December 15, 1791. One that was not ratified prescribed the ratio of representation to population in the House of Representatives; the other prohibited any increase in compensation to members of Congress until an election for representatives had intervened.

THE BILL OF RIGHTS AND THE STATES

By 1787 most state constitutions contained a bill of rights. In general, people were confident that they had sufficient political power to prevent abuse of authority by state and local officials. But the national government was new, distant, and threatening; the Bill of Rights was added to the Constitution to restrict its powers. In *Barron* v *Baltimore*, John Marshall confirmed the obvious: The Bill of Rights applies only to the national government; it imposes no restraints on state and local authorities.[2]

The national government, however, responsive to a broad-based political community, proved less a threat to civil liberties and civil rights than did state and local governments. Furthermore, the primary responsibility for the administration of justice vests in the states; the failure of the national Constitution to restrain state and local authorities left large segments of governmental activity without federal constitutional limitation. True, state constitutions contain most of the same guarantees as the Bill of Rights; however, state judges, who alone have jurisdiction to construe their respective state constitutions, until very recently seldom applied their state bills of rights so as to restrain state or local officials (see page 134).

After the adoption of the Fourteenth Amendment, which does apply to state (and local) governments, the Supreme Court was urged to construe the amendment, especially its due process clause, as applying the same limitations to the states that the Bill of Rights applies to the national government. Although in 1895 the Supreme Court brought within the scope of the due process clause a provision of the Bill of Rights forbidding the taking of private property without just compensation,[3] for decades it refused to go further.

Then in 1925, in *Gitlow* v *New York*, the Supreme Court took the momentous step of holding that the word *liberty* in the due process clause of the Fourteenth Amendment includes liberty of speech.[4] By the early 1940s, the Supreme Court had *incorporated* within the due process clause all the provisions of the First Amendment. In short, by construction of the Fourteenth Amendment, the substantive restrictions that the Bill of Rights places on the national government in order to protect freedom of religion, of speech, of the press, of petition, and of assembly are given national constitutional protection against abridgment by state and local authorities.

What of the other parts of the Bill of Rights? If the due process clause of the Fourteenth Amendment imposes on state governments the same limitations that the First Amendment places on the national government, does the rest of the Bill of Rights also come within the scope of the Fourteenth Amendment? For some time, a persistent minority of Supreme Court justices argued that it did; they would have construed the due process clause of the Fourteenth Amendment to mean that the states should follow precisely the same procedures that the Bill of Rights requires of the national government. What national authorities cannot do because of the Bill of Rights, these justices contended, state authorities could not do because of the due process clause of the Fourteenth Amendment. Ultimately, their arguments have almost carried the day: the Supreme Court has not gone quite so far as to incorporate into the Fourteenth Amendment all the applicable provisions of the Bill of Rights, but it has come very close to doing so.

The Court applies the *doctrine of selective incorporation*, also known as the *doctrine of selective absorption* or, because it was explained by Justice Cardozo in *Palko* v *Connecticut*, as the *Palko test*.[5] According to this view, the Fourteenth Amendment's due process clause does not prescribe any specific procedures for the administration of justice or the execution of governmental affairs. Rather, it forbids states to adopt a procedure that "offends some principle of justice so rooted in the traditions and conscience of our people as to be ranked as fundamental," or to deprive people of rights "implicit in the concept of ordered liberty." The application of this general standard of fundamental fairness has resulted in the selective incorporation or absorption into the due process clause of almost all the provisions of the Bill of Rights. Those few not incorporated, such as the Fifth Amendment requirement of indictment by grand jury, merely provide certain procedures that will secure justice but that are not the only procedures that will do so. States indict persons other than by grand jury and still do justice.

Beginning in the 1930s and accelerating after 1964, the Supreme Court selectively incorporated provision after provision of the Bill of Rights into the requirements of the due process clause of the Fourteenth Amendment. In 1968 a Court majority revised the Palko test to permit the easier incorporation of additional provisions: the Supreme Court now asks if a particular procedure is considered fundamental to an American system of ordered liberty. Using this standard, the Supreme Court ruled that trial by jury for serious offenses is essential for due process. The Court conceded that in some societies justice is secured without using juries (in England most criminal trials take place before judges without juries), but "in the American states, as in the federal judicial system . . . a general grant of jury trial for serious offenses is a fundamental right, essential for preventing miscarriages of justice and for assuring that fair trials are provided for all defendants."[6]

By 1970, the Bill of Rights had been, for all practical purposes, incorporated into the Fourteenth Amendment. Today, except for the Second, Third, and Tenth Amendments, which are not applicable, the Fourteenth Amendment imposes on states all the requirements the Bill of Rights imposes on the national government, *except* indictment for serious crimes by a grand jury and trial by jury in all civil cases involving more than $20.

What does it mean to say that the Bill of Rights, or at least most of it, has been absorbed into the Fourteenth Amendment? The absorption has three major consequences: (1) the Supreme Court has jurisdiction to review cases involving the application of these provisions and to establish standards to guide the behavior of state and local, as well as national, authorities; (2) the federal district judges, through habeas corpus petitions, have greater jurisdiction to hear complaints by persons alleging that they are being held contrary to the commands of the Constitution; (3) Congress has the power to pass whatever laws are necessary and proper to implement constitutional guarantees in the states.

The "nationalization" of the Bill of Rights has not, however, ended constitutional debate, nor is each provision of the Bill of Rights treated in the same fashion. The old battles are being fought in new ways. For example, the Supreme Court now distinguishes between "constitutional rights so basic to a fair trial that their infraction can never be treated as a harmless error" and "constitutional errors which in the setting of a particular case are so unimportant and insignificant that they may, consistent with the Federal Constitution, be deemed harmless, not requiring the automatic reversal of the conviction."[7] Examples of the former are the use of coerced confessions, denial of the right to counsel, lack of an impartial judge, conviction by a jury that acted on an indictment by a grand jury from which persons were excluded because of their race, or conviction and death sentence by a jury from which a juror was improperly dismissed because of opposition to the death penalty.[8]

An example of a possibly harmless error might be a passing comment by a prosecutor about a defendant's failure to take the stand. Such a comment violates the right against self-incrimination, but if the state reviewing courts find that it was "harmless beyond a reasonable doubt," the Supreme Court might not insist on reversal.[9] Similarly, admitting into evidence a codefendant's confession when the codefendant refused to take the stand, and was therefore not subject to confrontation, violates the confrontation clause of the Sixth Amendment, but in view of the defendant's own minutely detailed and consistent confession, the Court ruled the violation a harmless error.[10] Violation of the right to confront witnesses (see page 207) does not require reversal if the reviewing court "may confidently say, on the whole record, that the constitutional error was harmless beyond a reasonable doubt."[11]

The Supreme Court has also distinguished between provisions whose incorporation is to be applied retroactively and those whose application is only prospective. When the Court announces a new constitutional rule for the conduct of criminal prosecutions, that rule is to be applied retroactively to all cases not yet final — state or federal.[12] In cases that were final but are being challenged again under habeas corpus petitions, some rules are applied retroactively, and some are not. For example, persons prosecuted by a state are now entitled under the Fourteenth Amendment to a jury trial (since May 20, 1968), but if a person convicted *before* May 20, 1968, was denied a jury trial and later, by a habeas corpus petition, challenges the conviction, that person need not be retried. At the time of the original trials, states were following the then-authoritative construction of the Constitution, and it cannot be said that all convictions made in the absence of jury are so inherently unfair that they should be upset years after they were imposed. The court has ruled otherwise, however, with respect to other "incorporations"; for example, after bringing the Sixth Amendment guarantee of the right to the assistance of counsel into the Fourteenth Amendment, the Supreme Court held that any person under sentence who was without the assistance of counsel at trial is entitled to a retrial, even if at the time of the original trial the state was following the then-authoritative construction of the Constitution. No trial held without the assistance of counsel can be considered fair.[13]

On the grounds that there are no superfluous parts of the Constitution, the Court has held that the due process requirements of the Fifth and Fourteenth Amendments are additional limitations on national and state governments beyond those enumerated in the other provisions of the Bill of Rights, and that they protect other fundamental rights, such as the right of privacy.

After the Supreme Court had incorporated most of the provisions of the Bill of Rights into the Fourteenth Amendment, little attention was paid by state judges or anybody else to the bills of rights in their respective state constitutions. "The Supreme Court took such complete control of the field that state judges could sit back in the conviction that their part was simply to await the next landmark decisions."[14] Then, after the United States Supreme Court had begun in the mid-1970s to retreat from an expansive interpretation of some provisions of the Bill of Rights, especially those relating to the rights of persons accused of crimes, some observers, including Justices Brennan and Stevens, began to urge state supreme courts to step into the breach.[15] Justice Stanley Mosk of the California Supreme Court has pointed out that by using their state constitutions, "state supreme courts — once thought to be mere bus stops en route to the U.S. Supreme Court — can have the final word."[16]

A few state supreme courts have taken up the challenge, particularly in the arena of rights of criminal defendants and protection of the press. The trend toward a greater state court role in protecting civil liberties has become stronger in recent years, especially in Oregon, California, New Jersey, Wisconsin, Massachusetts, and Washington. Examples are the decision of the Minnesota Supreme Court barring newsroom searches allowed by the U.S. Supreme Court in *Zurcher* v *Stanford* (see page 156); decisions in California and other states requiring an equalization of funding among school districts — an equalization not required by the Supreme Court's interpretation of the U.S. Constitution in *San Antonio School District* v *Rodriguez* (see page 251); and decisions of some state courts requiring exclusion of unconstitutionally seized evidence, which will keep such evidence out of those state courts despite the Supreme Court's limited good faith exception, announced in *United States* v *Leon* (see page 180).

Although the trend toward state courts' staking out a different line of interpretation from the U.S. Supreme Court could become strong if the Supreme Court moves more toward the views of its most conservative justices, for the moment few lawyers are familiar with state constitutional law. Despite somewhat more adventurous stands on the part of state courts in relying on their own state constitutions, the United States Supreme Court and the United States Constitution remain the dominant protections for civil liberties and civil rights. Finally, and perhaps most importantly, most of the state judges who might step into the breach, giving more protection for some rights under their state constitutions than the Supreme Court is giving to the same rights under the national Constitution, lack the protection of lifetime tenure. They may make themselves targets for electoral reprisal if they anger significant portions of the electorate. In a California judicial retention election in 1987, Chief Justice Rose Bird and two of her colleagues were defeated for, among other things, interpreting the California constitution to provide more protection from death sentences than the U.S. Constitution requires.

AMENDMENT I: RELIGION, SPEECH, ASSEMBLY, AND PETITION

Congress shall make no law respecting an establishment of religion,

The First Amendment is directed specifically to Congress. The Fourteenth Amendment, as now interpreted, imposes the same restrictions on the states.

God is not mentioned in the Constitution, and the word religion occurs in only one other place: in the prohibition of any religious test as a qualification for office. The framers of the Constitution were not irreligious. Several of them came from states with established religions, but all probably agreed that religious matters should not fall to the jurisdiction of the national government.

There are two religion clauses — this one, forbidding the establishment of religion, and the next, prohibiting governments from interfering with the free exercise of religion — but they provide no definition of *religion*. The Supreme Court has been reluctant, understandably, to get into this question. Clearly, "far-out" religions are entitled to the same constitutional protections as are the more traditional ones, and establishment questions are raised by governmental interactions with other than traditional churches. However, as Chief Justice Burger has written, "Only beliefs rooted in religion are protected by the Free Exercise Clause. . . . One can, of course, imagine an asserted claim so bizarre, so clearly nonreligious in motivation, as not to be entitled to protection under the [Constitution]."[1] But, as he has also written, "religious beliefs need not be acceptable, logical, consistent, or comprehensible to others in order to merit First Amendment protection."[2] As difficult as the cases involving the two religion clauses have been, they promise to become even more complicated as the pervasiveness of governmental actions continue and as the number of less orthodox religious groups expands.

Establishment clause cases are not easy. They stir deep feelings, and the justices, reflecting differences in the nation, are often divided among themselves. Jefferson's "wall of separation between church and state" has become "as winding as the famous serpentine wall" he designed for the University of Virginia.[3] "The Establishment Clause . . . erects a blurred, indistinct, and variable barrier depending on all the circumstances of a particular relationship."[4]

Especially troublesome questions arise when a dispute breaks out between factions within a congregation or between a congregation and its own external church authorities. Obviously, civil judges should not decide in such a dispute which side is orthodox and which heretical. But if the dispute involves questions about who owns church property, the Supreme Court has given judges permission to decide such issues by using rules previously established by the church.[5]

Some have argued that the establishment clause does not forbid governmental support for religion but merely governmental favoritism toward a particular religion. The Supreme Court has rejected this construction,[6] although this *no-preference doctrine* has been vigorously espoused by Chief Justice Rehnquist. And Justice White has made it clear that he would "support a basic reconsideration of our precedents," along the lines espoused by Chief Justice Rehnquist.[7]

As presently construed, all levels of government must be completely neutral, aiding neither a particular religion nor all religions. "A given law might not *establish* a state religion but nevertheless be one 'respecting' that end in the sense of being a step that could lead to such establishment and hence offend the First Amendment."[8] Indeed, in *Lemon* v *Kurtzman* the Court established a three-part test a statute must pass to survive an establishment challenge, especially if it sends out a warning signal by engendering political divisiveness along religious lines: (1) The statute must have a secular purpose. "While the Court is normally deferential to a State's articulation of a secular purpose, it is required that the statement of such purpose be sincere and not a sham."[9] (2) Its primary effect must neither advance nor inhibit religion. (3) "Excessive entanglement" with religion must be avoided by the government.

Sometimes the Court gives an *accommodationist* interpretation to the establishment clause. It has emphasized, in *Lynch* v *Donnelly* (see page 139), that the Constitution does not "require complete separation of church and state; it affirmatively mandates accommodation, not merely tolerance of all religions, and forbids hostility toward any."[10] The Court's accommodationist view does not reject the test announced in *Lemon* v *Kurtzman*, but has given a new twist to it. For a statute to survive a challenge that it violates the establishment clause, the statute's "secular legislative purpose" need not be an *exclusively* secular one. The statute must still have a "primary effect that neither advances nor inhibits religion," but a "law is not unconstitutional simply because it *allows* churches to advance religion."[11] It is okay if the benefit to religion is only slight or incidental or if the law happens to coincide or harmonize with the tenets of some religions. And, although the statute and its administration must still avoid "excessive government entanglement with religion," divisiveness along religious lines is not by itself sufficient to invalidate government conduct.[12]

Applying these generalities, we find that the establishment clause forbids states to introduce devotional exercises of any variety into the public school curriculum, including denominationally neutral prayers, devotional reading of the Bible, recitation of the Lord's Prayer, or the posting of the Ten Commandments on the walls of public classrooms.[13]

The Court has not, as is often said, made it unconstitutional for students to pray in the public schools. Any student may pray silently anytime he or she wishes to do so. What the Constitution forbids is the sponsorship or encouragement of prayer, directly or indirectly, by public school authorities. On its way to the Supreme Court is the question of the constitutionality of the laws of twenty-three states authorizing an official moment of silence at the opening of each school day, during which time students may engage in voluntary prayer or meditation. The lower federal courts have declared some of these laws unconstitutional, and in 1984 the Senate voted against proposing a constitutional amendment on silent prayer. The Court has already declared unconstitutional an Alabama statute authorizing public school teachers to hold a one-minute period of silence for "meditation or voluntary prayer," because the state rather clumsily made it clear that the purpose of the statute was to return voluntary prayer to the schools.[14] In its opinion the Court rather strongly hinted that if a state law providing for a moment of silence had a more neutrally phrased purpose, it would pass muster.

In 1984 Congress made it unlawful for any public high school receiving federal funds (almost all of them do) to keep student groups from using school facilities for religious worship if the school opens its facilities for other student meetings. What Congress did was to make it unlawful for such high schools "to deny equal access to, or discriminate against, any student who wishes to conduct a meeting within that limited open forum on the basis of the religious, political, philosophical, or other content of the speech at such meetings." (Although adopted to provide equal access for worship, this law also provides federal protection for unpopular and unfashionable student groups to hold meetings in high schools during noninstructional times.) Congress made it clear that it was not authorizing any public official to influence the form or content of any prayer or religious activity, to require any person to participate in religious activities, or to authorize any school to expend public funds, beyond the incidental cost of providing the space for student-initiated meetings. This law has yet to be tested before the Supreme Court.

The Supreme Court has already decided that a university that makes its facilities generally available for student activities does not violate the establishment clause if it allows some student groups to use its facilities for religious worship. On the contrary, if the university were to ban religious activities while allowing other kinds of programs, it would violate the constitutional provision against "prohibiting the free exercise" of religion (see page 141). However, in sustaining this practice, the Court pointedly noted, "University students are, of course, young adults. They are less impressionable than younger students and should be able to appreciate that the University's policy is one of neutrality toward religion."[15] Moreover, the Court has refused to set aside lower court rulings forbidding the use of public school facilities by religious groups and by students who wish to conduct prayer meetings before the start of classes. These actions suggest that what the establishment clause permits at the college level it may forbid in precollegiate public schools. Now that Congress has acted to provide equal access for religious worship in public high schools, that question is likely to come back to the Supreme Court for full-dress review.

A state may not ban from the teaching in its schools of Darwin's theory of evolution because of "its supposed conflict with the biblical account, literally read."[16] Nor may a state forbid the teaching of evolution unless accompanied by instruction in the theory of "creation science."[17] School authorities may not permit religious instructors to come into the public school building during the school day to provide religious instruction, even on a voluntary basis.[18] On the other hand, the Constitution does not prevent the study of the Bible or religion in public schools when presented as part of a secular program of education.[19] Schools may release students from part of the compulsory school day so that the students can receive religious instruction, provided it does not take place in public school buildings.[20]

An especially troublesome and controversial area is government aid to church-operated schools. The principles are easy to formulate, but application is difficult. A state may provide aid to promote the well-being and education of students; it may not give aid to religion. At the college level, the problems are relatively simple. The students are presumed to be mature, and there is less pervasiveness of religion in the curriculum. Tax funds may be used to build buildings and operate programs at church-operated schools, provided tax funds are not used to support sectarian education. Such grants to colleges require no elaborate intervention by government authority to ensure that they will be used only for secular purposes.[21] Unanimous decisions are rare in establishment clause cases, but the Court held unanimously (although it was not unanimous in its reasons) that state rehabilitation aid payments to a blind student for education could be used by that student to study at a Christian college to become a pastor. Although it is well settled, Justice Marshall said for the Court, that a state may not grant aid to a religious school, it is equally well settled "that the Establishment Clause is not violated every time money previously in the possession of a State is conveyed to a religious institution."[22] The law was designed to help the visually handicapped and had a secular purpose. That the funds ultimately had the effect of helping a religious school was not a constitutional vice, since the money was paid to the student and it was his independent and private choice which kind of education he would seek.

"The Court has been particularly vigilant in monitoring compliance with the Establishment Clause in elementary and secondary schools."[23] The secular and religious parts of the institution are more closely interwoven. The students are younger and more susceptible to indoctrination, and the chances are that aid given to church-operated schools will seep over to aid religion.[24] Therefore, the Supreme Court has looked at tax assistance to church-operated elementary and secondary schools with much greater skepticism than such aid at the college level.

Tax funds may be used to provide school children, including those in church-operated schools (except those that deny admission to pupils because of race or religion),[25] with textbooks,[26] lunches, and transportation to and from school.[27] Also approved has been the use of public funds to provide and score standardized tests in church-operated schools, to provide diagnostic services for speech and hearing in church-operated schools, and to provide guidance and remedial services outside church-operated schools.[28] A state may reimburse sectarian schools for the costs of administering state-required and state-prepared tests, and for costs of complying with state attendance and data-collection requirements.[29] The Court, in *Mueller* v *Allen*, one of the accommodationist cases, has also approved a tax deduction for public and private school expenses, including tuition payments, even though the bulk of the deductions are claimed by parents sending children to sectarian schools.[30] These uses of tax dollars are viewed as promoting the health, safety, and secular education of students, not as aiding religion.

On the other side, tax funds may *not* be used directly to maintain facilities, provide instructional equipment such as maps, charts, records, or laboratory equipment,[31] provide auxiliary services such as counseling to students inside church-operated schools, produce teacher-prepared tests, or transport students on field trips.[32] States may not send public school teachers to teach even secular subjects in sectarian schools, even after school hours, even in classrooms leased by the public schools.[33] Similarly, states may not use public funds to provide remedial instruction and guidance services to parochial school students in parochial schools, even if the schools are subject to supervision to ensure that there are no religious influences in these services.[34] A state may not directly reimburse parents for tuition paid to send children to parochial schools.[35] (It may do so indirectly, as we have noted, by providing a tax exemption for expenses of sending children to either public or private schools.)

If taxes can be used for textbooks, why not for teachers? If for standardized tests, why not for teacher-prepared tests? If for transportation to school, why not for transportation on field trips? If for books, why not for maps? If for counseling outside a parochial school, why not inside? "A textbook is ascertainable," but a teacher's handling of a subject is not.[36] A standardized test is not prepared by church schools, but teacher-prepared tests are an "integral part of the teaching process."[37] Transportation to and from school is a routine round trip every student makes every day and is unrelated to any aspect of the curriculum; field trips are controlled by teachers and are an aid to instructional programs. Counseling outside a school is less likely to involve religious matters than is counseling within the "pervasively sectarian atmosphere of the school."[38] As for its approval of tax-purchased books but disapproval of tax-purchased records, maps, and other kinds of instructional materials, the Court has recognized there is a "tension" between its holdings. Nonetheless, the judges argue, when a standardized textbook is used both in public and church-operated schools, it provides assurance that the books will not be sectarian or used for sectarian purposes, whereas there is much greater danger that other kinds of teaching materials may be diverted to religious purposes.[39]

Laws requiring business establishments to close on Sunday have passed the Supreme Court's tests. Whatever their original purpose, they now have the secular purpose and effect of promoting family living by providing a common day of rest and recreation.[40] Tax exemptions for church property as well as for property of other nonprofit institutions have also been allowed. A tax exemption neither advances nor inhibits religion, is neither sponsorship nor hostility, and, unlike a direct subsidy, does not involve excessive entanglement. It perhaps involves even less entanglement than there would be if churches were not included within the nonprofit exemption. There would then be need to get into such matters as liens, foreclosures, and assessments of church properties.[41] On the other side, the Court set aside a Massachusetts law giving churches the right to veto liquor licenses for taverns located within a 500-foot radius of the church. "The mere appearance of a joint exercise of legislative authority by Church and State," said the Court, "provides a significant symbolic benefit to religion."[42]

Lynch v *Donnelly* (1984) most clearly establishes a new accommodationist orientation by some members of the Court. The Court held that the city of Pawtucket, Rhode Island, could pay for and display a Nativity scene in the heart of its shopping district, along with Santa's house and sleigh, Christmas trees, lights, and other symbols of the

Christmas season. The Court concluded that the city fathers had commercial — not religious — purposes in mind, that the effect provided little or no benefit to religion in general or to the Christian faith in particular, and that there was no excessive entanglement between religion and government. The City, said the Court, "has principally taken note of a significant historical religious event long celebrated in the Western World. . . . The crèche in the display depicts the historical origins of this traditional event long recognized as a National Holiday."[43]

In *Marsh* v *Chambers* (1983) the Court simply ignored the three-part test to sustain the centuries-old practice of paying chaplains to open sessions of state legislatures and Congress. It merely noted that the nation from its very beginning had opened its legislative sessions in this fashion and that legislators, unlike school children, are adults "presumably not readily susceptible to . . . peer pressure."[44] The dissenting justices contended that, "if any group of law students were asked to apply [the three-part test of the Lemon decision] to the question of legislative prayer, they would nearly unanimously find the practice to be unconstitutional," suggesting that the dissenters, if professors, would flunk their colleagues in a constitutional law test. The case may also demonstrate that judges believe legislators need the help of prayers more than do students.

When Congress exempted religious organizations' nonprofit activities, religious and secular, from the Civil Rights Act's ban on religious discrimination in employment, was the exemption favoritism toward religion contrary to the establishment clause? The Court upheld the exemption on accommodationist grounds, with the majority making a distinction between exemptions and regulations. For exemptions, said the Court, there are less rigorous establishment clause standards. Laws discriminating *among religions* are subject to strict scrutiny, whereas laws affording a uniform benefit *to all religions* are to be analyzed according to the *Lemon* test, and they concluded that exempting religious organizations so that they may hire only members of their own religion for nonreligious but nonprofit activities did not violate that test.[45] (The Court left open the question of the application of this exemption to secular employment by religious organizations in profit-making ventures.)

---

or prohibiting the free exercise thereof;

"The Court has struggled to find a neutral course between the two Religion Clauses, both of which are cast in absolute terms, and either of which, if expanded to a logical extreme, would tend to clash with the other."[46] To illustrate: It violates the establishment clause for a state to give employees an absolute right to be absent from work on their chosen Sabbath and keep their jobs,[47] but it violates the free exercise clause for a state to deny unemployment compensation to Sabbatarians who refuse to accept positions requiring them to work on Saturday.[48] Exempting religious organizations from some of the requirements of the federal civil rights acts raises, as we have seen, establishment clause questions. On the other hand, to apply the civil rights laws to such organizations could raise free exercise clause questions. If Congress drafts those who have religious scruples against participation in war, it might violate the free exercise clause, but if it exempts them, it might violate the establishment clause. So far, Congress and the Court have avoided this particular issue. Congress's modern practice is to exempt from military conscription persons who, by reason of religious belief, are conscientiously opposed to participation in war, but not those who are opposed on "political, sociological, or philosophical grounds." The Supreme Court, in part to avoid a clash between the two clauses, has construed the word *religious* so broadly that any deeply held humanistic opposition to participation in any and all wars in any form is included within the congressionally granted exemption.[49]

Another example of the tension between the two clauses is the issue whether public schools and universities may provide or must provide religious groups with opportunities to engage in religious activities on school premises. If schools do so, questions are raised under the establishment clause; if schools do not do so, questions are raised under the free exercise clause. As noted, the Supreme Court has already decided that if a university opens its facilities to groups, it may not deny the facilities to those who wish to use them to engage in worship.[50] And as noted, Congress has stipulated by law that any school district receiving federal funds and making its facilities open to outside groups may not deny them to such groups because they are to be used for religious purposes. The Supreme Court has sidestepped the issue, although Chief Justice Burger, and Justices White, Rehnquist, and Powell have made clear their convictions that high school students would be deprived of their rights under the freedom of religion clause if a school district were to deny students the right to use for religious purposes facilities otherwise available.[51]

Because there can be no compulsion by law of any form of worship and because the government recognizes neither orthodoxy nor heresy, everyone has an *absolute right to believe* whatever he or she wishes. A state may not compel a religious belief nor deny any person any right or privilege because of beliefs or lack of them. Such things as a religious oath — for example, an oath that one believes in the existence of God — as a condition of public employment or of eligibility for an elected position are unconstitutional (see Article VI, Section 3, page 129). [52] So also is disqualification of clergy from serving in public offices. "However widely that view [that clergy would promote the interests of one sect] may have been in the 18th century by many, including enlightened statesmen of that day, the American experience provides no persuasive support for the fear that clergymen in public office will be less careful of antiestablishment interests or less faithful to their oaths of civil office than their unordained counterparts."[53]

Although carefully protected, the *right to act* in accordance with one's belief is not, and cannot be, absolute. Religion may not be used to justify action, or refusal to act, contrary to a nondiscriminatory law properly enacted to promote the public safety, morals, health, or general welfare of the community. No one has a right to refuse to bear arms, to refuse to pay taxes, including social security taxes, to practice polygamy, or to invade the rights of others because of religious convictions. However, when governments entrench on religious activities, the Supreme Court will look closely to ensure that there has been no violation of the free exercise clause. "Laws and governmental regulations infringing on religious practices by criminalizing religiously inspired activity or by compelling conduct that some find objectionable for religious reasons may be applied to such persons only if the government demonstrates an especially important governmental interest and that it is pursuing this interest by narrowly tailored means."[54] Chief Justice Burger, in an opinion for the Court — an opinion accepted in whole by only two other members — would have applied a less stringent test to governmental actions conferring benefits, such as food stamps: "Absent proof of an intent to discriminate against particular religious beliefs or against religion in general, the Government meets the burden when it demonstrates that a challenged regulation for governmental benefits, neutral and uniform in its application, is a reasonable means of promoting a legitimate public interest."[55] Most of the justices, however, reject this notion that the free exercise clause applies differently to laws conferring governmental benefits than to laws imposing a prohibition.[56] Wrote Justice O'Connor, "The welfare state was not the fall of the Free Exercise Clause."[57]

Applying strict standards of scrutiny to laws affecting religious freedoms, the Court over the years has made the following decisions: Persons may be required to comply with Sunday closing laws in the interest of providing a common day of rest and recreation, even if Sunday is not their sabbath.[58] Parents may be compelled to have their children vaccinated as a condition of attending public schools, whether or not vaccination violates their religious beliefs.[59] The Society for Krishna Consciousness could be confined to selling and distributing their literature at a state fairgrounds to a fixed location, even though the distribution and selling of religious literature is a ritual for them.[60] (Members of the group were free to wander the fairgrounds and talk with patrons.) The Amish can be required to collect and pay social security taxes for their employees, even though both payment and receipt of social security benefits is forbidden by their faith.[61] (Congress exempts from such taxes self-employed persons who have religious scruples, but not employers or employees.) An orthodox Jew was not entitled to an exemption from an air force regulation prohibiting the wearing of headgear indoors, even though the wearing of a yarmulke was akin to a silent prayer and prescribed by his religion.[62] A native American could be required, as a condition of securing food stamps, to obtain a social security number for his child, even though such an action would violate the parent's religious beliefs.[63] If a church-affiliated school engages in racially discriminatory practices, it may be denied the benefit of having its donors receive a tax deduction for their contributions to it.[64] (Whether a church could be denied such benefit because of its discriminatory practices has not been decided, but the answer is probably not.)

On the other side, a state's interest in promoting patriotism does not justify its compelling Jehovah's Witnesses (or anyone else) to salute the flag, which to them is a symbol of the Evil One, as a condition of attending public schools, or forcing people to display on license plates a state motto — in the case decided, New Hampshire's motto, Live free or die.[65] Along the same lines, in face of three centuries of established religious practices, a state may not compel the Amish to send their children to schools beyond the eighth grade (compelling schooling up to the eighth grade is constitutional).[66] States may not require parents to send children to public schools if parents wish to educate them in religious ones.[67] Nor would the Supreme Court permit states to deny unemployment compensation to Sabbatarians who refused to accept or who quit positions requiring them to work on Saturday or to Jehovah's Witnesses who quit jobs for religious reasons.[68] In neither case did the state show a substantial countervailing interest to justify the burden on the free exercise of religion. But what of the state's contention that it would violate the ban on establishing a religion to provide unemployment benefits to those who quit jobs for religious reasons, while denying such benefits to those who quit for personal but nonreligious reasons? The payment of unemployment benefits to those unemployed for religious reasons "reflects nothing more than a governmental neutrality in the face of religious differences," a conclusion prompting Justice Rehnquist in dissent to charge that the Court's opinion added "mud to the already muddied waters of First Amendment jurisprudence."[69]

---

or abridging the freedom of speech,

The right of freedom of speech is essential to the preservation and operation of democracy. "Nevertheless, there are categories of communication and certain special utterances to which the majestic protection of the First Amendment does not extend because 'they are no essential part of any exposition of ideas, and are of such slight social value as a step to the truth that any benefit that may be derived from them is clearly outweighed by the social interest in order and morality.' "[70] Libelous speech is such a category. Anyone (except, under most circumstances, a member of Congress, a judge, or the president) who slanders or libels another may be penalized. Obscene speech is another kind not entitled to constitutional protection, nor is child pornography protected. Fighting words which by their very utterance injure and provoke others to imminent attack, are outside the pale of protection. So are incitements of others to immediate acts of violence. Constitutional problems are involved, however, in the definition and determination of libelous speech, obscene speech, seditious incitement, or fighting words. The Supreme Court is very suspicious of definitions that cast their nets too wide.

Fighting Words

Fighting words must be limited to those that "have a direct tendency to cause acts of violence by the person to whom, individually, the remarks are addressed"; words that are merely abusive, harsh, or insulting are not sufficient.[71] In fact, one close student of the subject, David O'Brien, has concluded that the Court has so narrowly applied the category as to virtually eliminate it. O'Brien quotes John Hart Ely: "Fighting words are no longer to be understood as a euphemism for either controversial or dirty talk but require instead an unambiguous invitation to a brawl."[72] Moreover, it has been suggested that the fighting-words exception "might require a narrower application in cases involving words addressed to a police officer, because a properly trained officer may reasonably be expected to exercise a higher degree of restraint 'than the average citizen, and thus be less likely to respond belligerently to fighting words.' "[73] Nonetheless, the Supreme Court has reaffirmed that fighting words — those that provoke immediate violence — are not protected by the First Amendment. In fact, the Court has emphasized that "words that create an immediate panic" are not entitled to constitutional protection.[74] Such words, however, are apparently not a new category of speech outside the scope of the First Amendment, but just another way to talk about fighting words.

Libel

Libel prosecutions (libel refers to the written word, slander to the spoken one, although nowadays libel is used as the generic term to refer to both) used to be a favorite means of suppressing criticism of government officials and preventing discussion of public issues. In seventeenth-century England seditious libel was defined to include criticism of the king or his ministers, whether true or false, and the stirring up of public discontent. Under the Constitution, however, persons cannot be made to pay damages for defaming *public officials* or *public figures* merely because they have issued false statements. As established by the Court in the leading case of *New York Times* v *Sullivan*, there must also be clear and convincing evidence — a greater burden than the usual one in a civil case, which is a preponderance of evidence — that the false comment was made "with knowledge that it was false or with reckless disregard of whether it was false or not."[75] (In establishing the fact that a publication was made with knowledge of its falsity or with reckless disregard for its truth, public officials and figures may inquire into the state of mind of editors and publishers: the First Amendment does not protect conversations among news people from judicial scrutiny.)[76]

Public figures subject to the difficult burden of proof to show that they have been libeled are of two kinds: famous persons who are public figures for all purposes and in all contexts, and those who are not so famous but who have allowed themselves to be so injected into a particular public controversy that they are public figures for a limited range of issues. (Persons do not lose their status as private individuals merely because their names get into the papers for having been robbed or having gotten a divorce that received a great deal of publicity or being a scientist supported by a federal grant whose work a United States senator thinks a waste of public funds.)

A different libel rule prevails for comments made about private individuals. A state may permit a private individual to recover actual damages upon a showing of negligence on the part of those responsible for the defamatory falsehood, for example, by showing that they issued a false statement without taking responsible precautions to check it.[77] Note that, even private individuals must show not only negligence, or fault, but, at least in the case of a media defendant, also falsity — that the statements made were not true. States may constitutionally leave on defendants the common law burden of proving truth only when private individuals claim defamation in matters "of exclusively private concern."[78]

The amount of damages that may be collected by private individuals is an issue for which there is no coherent and consistent Court majority. Apparently, to secure punitive damages, in contrast to actual ones, a private defendant in a matter relating to public concern must meet the stringent *New York Times* v *Sullivan* test of proving the defendant published a falsehood knowing that it was false.[79] However, in the case of private individuals bringing suit about *private* matters, the less stringent requirement of proving that what was published was false and that the publisher of it was negligent is sufficient for punitive damages. An example of a private matter would be the publication by a credit firm of a credit rating: such firms are liable for punitive damages if they negligently publish a false statement.[80]

The reasons to permit easier libel actions by private persons than public ones are that private persons have less effective means of responding to defaming statements, they have not voluntarily exposed themselves to the risk of injury from falsehoods, the public's interest in knowing about them is less compelling, and they are entitled to some protection of their right to privacy.

First Amendment and due process concerns do not keep a person who has been libeled from bringing an action in any state in which the magazine or newspaper regularly circulates, even if it causes inconvenience for the defendant to go there to defend.[81] On the other hand, First Amendment considerations do require appellate courts to set aside the normal rule that the findings of trial courts are to be reversed only when they are clearly erroneous. In reviewing libel judgments, appellate courts are to make an independent judgment to "determine whether the record establishes actual malice with convincing clarity."[82]

Obscenity

What of obscenity? Production, sale, mailing, or transportion of obscene matter is not entitled to constitutional protection, although its mere possession for private use cannot be made a crime.[83] The Supreme Court, however, has had the same difficulty as has everybody else who has tried to define obscenity. As Justice Brennan has written, "No other aspect of the First Amendment has, in recent years, commanded so substantial a commitment of our time, generated such disharmony of views, and remained so resistant to the formulation of stable and manageable standards."[84] Since the Supreme Court entered the field in 1957, more than ninety separate opinions have been written by the justices.

In *Miller* v *California* (1973) Chief Justice Burger, speaking for five members of the Court, once again tried to clarify the constitutional standards. A work — a book, a film, a play — may be considered obscene provided (1) the average person, applying contemporary standards of the community in which the court sits, finds that the work, taken as a whole, appeals to a prurient interest in sex; (2) the work depicts in a patently offensive way sexual conduct specifically defined by the law or by decisions of the courts;[85] and (3) the work, taken as a whole, lacks serious literary, artistic, political, or scientific value.[86] The Chief Justice explicitly rejected part of the previous test, the so-called *Memoirs* v *Massachusetts* formula, namely, that no work should be judged obscene unless it was "utterly without redeeming social value." He argued that such a test made it impossible for a state to outlaw hard-core pornography. He also stipulated, and the Court has since reaffirmed, that the standards of offensiveness are to be those of the community from which the jury comes, rather than what the jury might believe to be the standards of the nation.[87] The jury is to use its common sense and general knowledge about local community standards. Because of the variability of community standards, it is possible for a book or a movie to be legally obscene in one state or city but not in another. A jury may not, however, take into account the effect of the materials on children in determining community standards, otherwise, it would reduce the adult population to reading or seeing only that which is fit for children.[88]

A *prurient* interest is a morbid one. The Court has never made clear what makes an interest in sex prurient, but it has made clear that a work that appeals to a normal interest in sex or that merely promotes "lust" cannot be declared obscene. "Material that, taken as a whole, does no more than arouse a good, old-fashioned, healthy interest in sex may not be included in the definition."[89]

For the third prong of the Miller test, "whether the work, taken as a whole, lacks serious literary, artistic, political, or scientific value," unlike the first two, community standards are not the measure. Rather, the measure is whether "a reasonable person would find such value in the material, taken as a whole."[90] In other words, a jury is not to find materials obscene merely because most of the people in their community believe the materials to be "trash," but only if a "reasonable person" would find no value in it. What this means, in practical fact, is that defendants may bring forward "experts" to testify on the literary merits of materials alleged to be obscene, and juries are to consider their views.

In determining whether materials are obscene, a jury may consider the motives of sellers to see if they are engaging in commercial exploitation of sexually offensive materials: the circumstances of distribution are relevant in determining whether the materials are being forced on people, and the motives of sellers are relevant in determining whether social importance claimed for materials is a pretense or a reality.[91]

When persons are criminally prosecuted for selling obscene materials, the state must establish its case beyond a reasonable doubt, proving not merely the fact of the sale but also the obscenity of the materials. There is a less burdensome standard of proof in civil actions, for example, an attempt by a government to close a theater as a public nuisance by proving it routinely shows only obscene movies. The Supreme Court has not made clear, however, whether the less stringent standard of a preponderance of the evidence will do in judging matter obscene in a civil proceeding or whether states have to use the more demanding "clear and convincing" standard or one of its variants.[92]

Some members of the Supreme Court, instead of trying to refine the definition of obscenity, would abandon the effort. Justices Brennan, Marshall, and Stevens, after struggling for years to develop a constitutional definition, have come to the conclusion that it is impossible to do so without endangering protected speech and miring the Court in "case-by-case determination of obscenity." These justices would let adults see or read whatever they wish and would permit only narrowly drawn statutes designed to prevent pornography from being forced on persons or made available to minors.[93] Justice Stevens, however, would provide some latitude for civil regulations that treat panderers of obscenity as public nuisances, and he finds acceptable time, place, and manner regulations for the sale and distribution of pornography.[94]

Nonobscene but erotic literature and movies, as well as vulgar, offensive, and lewd speech, although constitutionally protected, nonetheless are entitled to less protection than political speech. Cities may regulate by zoning ordinance where "adult motion pictures" may be commercially shown. "The state may legitimately use the contents of these materials as a basis for placing them in a different classification from other motion pictures."[95] School authorities may punish students for using "indecent" or "lewd" or "suggestive" speech in school rooms and school assemblies.[96]

There are limits, however, to the regulation of offensive but nonobscene speech. "When a zoning ordinance infringes upon a protected liberty, it must be narrowly drawn and must further a sufficiently substantial governmental interest." So said the Court when it struck down a zoning ordinance of the Borough of Mount Ephraim in New Jersey that prevented "non-obscene nude dancing" in an adult book store by excluding from a small shopping district all live entertainment. Chief Justice Burger in dissent chided his colleagues for trivializing and demeaning "that great Amendment."[97]

When it comes to children, less is required in order to restrict materials. Sexually explicit materials either about minors or aimed at minors are not protected by the First Amendment. State and local governments, provided they act under narrowly drawn statutes, can, for example, ban the knowing sale of "girlie" magazines to minors, even if such materials would not be considered legally obscene if sold to adults. States may make it a crime to depict sexual conduct by children visually, even if the depicted behavior would not be considered obscene if done by adults. Even those members of the Court who would allow adults to read and see anything about adults agree that when it comes to children, the states may step in to make criminal the production or sale of pornographic materials about children or aimed at them.[98]

Seditious Speech

What of seditious speech, that is, speech advocating the use of force as a political tactic or as a means to overthrow the government? Since World War I the Supreme Court has considered issues relating to seditious speech a number of times in a variety of contexts. In 1951, in *Dennis* v *United States*, the Court sustained the application of the Smith Act, a federal statute making it illegal to advocate the violent overthrow of the government, to the leaders of the Communist Party of the United States, even though there was no evidence that they actually urged people to commit specific acts of violence.[99] However, that decision, although never specifically overruled, has been undermined by later rulings. The Supreme Court has made it clear that the Smith Act can be applied only to those who incite imminent lawless action.

The net result is that seditious incitement, if narrowly defined by statute and narrowly applied by the courts, is another exception to the protection of the First Amendment. Or perhaps it is better to state it positively: The First Amendment protects the abstract advocacy of violence and forbids a government to make it a crime or to punish persons for what they advocate, except "where such advocacy is directed to inciting or producing imminent lawless action and is likely to incite or produce such action."[100]

Rules for Protected Speech

Outside the areas of fighting words, libel, obscenity, and seditious incitement, the Supreme Court has elaborated a whole series of doctrines to measure the constitutionality of laws that appear to restrict freedom of expression.

Prior Restraint

The Court is especially suspicious of laws that impose restraints prior to publication, including licensing schemes that require permission before a speech can be made, a motion picture shown, or a newspaper published or that in any way try to interpose the authority of government between someone trying to communicate something and the audience. The Supreme Court has not gone so far as to declare all forms of prior censorship unconstitutional, but "a prior restraint on expression comes to this Court with a 'heavy presumption' against its constitutionality."[101] In the celebrated case *New York Times Company* v *United States* (1971), the Supreme Court held that the government had not met this burden when the attorney general tried to secure a court injunction against publication, by the *New York Times*, the *Washington Post*, and other newspapers, of the so-called Pentagon Papers, a classified study of some of the decisions leading to our involvement in the Vietnam War. Three concurring justices — Black, Douglas, and Brennan — made it clear that, in their view, the First Amendment forbids a court to impose, however briefly and for whatever reasons, any prior restraint on a newspaper. (Justice Brennan might make an exception for publication of troop movements during time of war.) The dominant view, however, was more limited: in this particular instance, the government had failed to show that the publication of these particular documents would cause immediate and specific damage to the nation's security.[102]

In the Pentagon Papers case, the government attempted to assert its right to act without any specific congressional authorization. But in 1979, when the government learned that *The Progressive* was about to publish an article entitled "The H-Bomb Secret: How We Got It, Why We're Telling It," federal prosecutors sought an injunction pursuant to the Atomic Energy Act. The act authorizes the government to enjoin the dissemination of restricted data concerning the design, manufacture, or utilization of atomic weapons. The district judge could "find no plausible reason why the public needs to know the technical details about hydrogen bomb construction" and issued a preliminary restraining order. The courts refused to expedite the case and it never reached the Supreme Court's docket because the government abandoned the effort to enjoin publication after the information in the article was published in other places.[103]

Today, other than for motion pictures and then only for obscenity, one of the few examples of prior censorship that has passed Supreme Court muster has been requirements that literature not be distributed on a military base without prior approval of post headquarters. The Supreme Court acknowledged special military interests in keeping military activities free of partisan political entanglements and noted that military bases are not ordinary forums of public discussion.[104] The Court held that the First Amendment does not preclude the CIA from enforcing employment agreements requiring agents to submit all their writings about the CIA for prepublication review, even those that contain no classified material.[105] The Court has also permitted judges to restrain newspapers from publishing information the newspapers obtained by using pretrial discovery procedures to compel their legal adversaries to produce materials. Said the Court, "An order prohibiting dissemination of discovered information before trial is not the kind of classic prior restraint that requires exacting First Amendment scrutiny."

Vagueness

Laws touching First Amendment freedoms must not be so vague that people are afraid to exercise protected freedoms. Such vague laws have a "chilling effect" on freedom of speech. For example, New York's attempt to ban "sacrilegious movies" and publications of "criminal deeds of bloodshed or lust . . . so massed as to become vehicles for inciting violent and depraved crimes" was declared unconstitutional because the definitions used were so vague that no one could know what was or was not allowed.[106]

Overbreadth

Closely related to vagueness and sometimes shading into it is the overbreadth doctrine. Overbroad statutes, whatever their purpose, that have a "chilling effect upon First Amendment rights" are especially suspect. "Because First Amendment freedoms need breathing space to survive, government may regulate in the area only with narrow specificity."[107] In fact, if an overbroad statute significantly affects freedom of speech, the Court may hold not merely that the law as applied to a particular person is unconstitutional, but that the law on its face is unconstitutional. In such instances, even if the defendant's language might have been punished under a more narrowly drawn statute, the defendant has standing to challenge the law.[108]

Since the application of the overbreadth doctrine to striking down a statute is "strong medicine," there must be a "realistic danger that the statute compromises First Amendment protections of parties not before the Court." For example, the Court struck down a regulation forbidding all First Amendment activities within the Los Angeles International Airport. The airport commissioners, by declaring that LAX was not a public forum, were trying to avoid the accusation that they were allowing some but not others to pass out handbills and approach travelers. Their sweeping ban, however, made it possible to find "virtually every individual who enters LAX" to violate the resolution by engaging in some "First Amendment activity."[109] Another example of the use of the overbreadth doctrine is the Court's holding unconstitutional, on its face, a Houston ordinance making it unlawful to assault, strike, or in any manner oppose, molest, abuse, or interrupt any policeman in the execution of his duty. This ordinance was so broad that it prohibited speech that in any manner interrupts an officer. The Constitution does not, wrote Justice Brennan for the Court, "allow such speech to be made a crime."[110] A similar fate befell a Columbus, Ohio, ordinance that made it a crime for a person "to abuse another by using menacing, insulting, slanderous, or profane language."[111] Schaumburg, Illinois, was not allowed to forbid direct solicitation of funds by organizations that did not use at least 75 percent of the money they collected for direct charitable purposes. Such an ordinance was overbroad and unconstitutional on its face. It effectively prevented solicitation by "advocacy organizations," organizations that use funds to advocate such causes as cleaning the air and banning the bomb.[112]

Least Drastic Means

Even for an important purpose, a legislature may not choose a law that impinges on First Amendment freedoms if there are other ways to handle the problem. To illustrate, a state may protect the public from unscrupulous lawyers, but it may not do so by forbidding organizations to make legal services available to their members or by forbidding attorneys from advertising.

Content Neutrality

Content-neutral laws are much less likely to be struck down than those that restrict speech based on content. For example, a law forbidding the posting of any signs on telephone poles would be more likely to pass constitutional muster than one forbidding all posters advocating racism.

Centrality of Political Speech

Even among protected speech, the amount of constitutional protection varies with the kind and character of the speech. "Not all speech is of equal First Amendment concern." Political speech about matters of public concern is "at the heart of the First Amendment's protection."[113] The following examples show the Court's concern for speech relating to political matters: The University of Missouri was told that it lacked constitutional authority to expel a student for distributing an underground campus publication containing indecent materials.[114] The Georgia legislature violated the Constitution when it denied a seat to a duly-elected member because of critical comments he had made about American participation in the Vietnam War.[115] Virginia could not punish a newspaper for publishing confidential proceedings of a judicial review commission, even though the legislature thought such publications presented a clear and present danger to the orderly administration of justice.[116]

Commercial Speech

Commercial speech is now entitled to constitutional protection, but because there are common-sense differences between it and other kinds of speech, it is subject to more regulation than are other varieties. Decisions of the Supreme Court dealing with "more traditional First Amendment problems do not extend automatically to this as yet uncharted area."[117] For example, overbreadth analysis is not applicable, and perhaps not the prohibitions against prior restraint.

Commercial speech is subject to a four-part analysis: "(1) For commercial speech to come within [the First Amendment], it at least must concern lawful activity and not be misleading. (2) Next, we ask whether the asserted governmental interest is substantial. If both inquiries yield positive answers, we must determine (3) whether the regulation directly advances the governmental interest asserted, and (4) whether it is more extensive than is necessary to serve that interest."[118]

The Court is more likely to sustain disclosure requirements for commercial speech than for noncommercial speech. Outside of commercial speech, as much scrutiny is applied to laws compelling people to say things they do not wish to say as to laws keeping them from speaking — perhaps more.[119] In the case of commercial speech, although "unjustified or unduly burdensome disclosure requirements might offend the First Amendment . . . an advertiser's rights are adequately protected as long as disclosure requirements are reasonably related to the State's interest in preventing deception of consumers."[120]

A law forbidding "false and misleading" political speech would be clearly unconstitutional. Who is to say, in the realm of political matters, what is false and misleading? But a law forbidding false and misleading advertising is constitutional. What is false and misleading advertising can be established. Moreover, advertisers' access to the truth about their products and prices "substantially eliminates any danger that governmental regulation of false or misleading advertising will chill accurate and non-deceptive commercial expression."[121]

What a state has made illegal (prostitution, discrimination, or gambling, for example), it may forbid commercial advertising to promote. It may not, however, forbid the political advocacy of the same activities, that is, advertisements urging that gambling be made legal, that discrimination be practiced in general, or that prostitution be legalized.

What about commercial speech that is neither false and misleading nor designed to promote anything but perfectly legal activities? Where the underlying conduct, although legal, is of such a nature that a government could make it illegal, advertising about it may be regulated, even forbidden. Thus, Puerto Rico could prohibit advertising by legal gambling casinos aimed directly at island residents, even though Puerto Rico allowed advertising directed to tourists.[122]

The Court recently sustained the right of Congress to give the U.S. Olympic Committee, a congressionally chartered private corporation, exclusive control of the use of the word *Olympics*. The committee had denied to another group the right to promote the "Gay Olympics." The Court treated this federal law as an appropriately aimed trademark regulation of commercial speech, with whatever incidental limit on expressive speech was justified as necessary to further a substantial governmental interest.[123]

When it comes to advertising by professionals — doctors, lawyers, pharmacists — misleading advertising may be forbidden; truthful advertising may not. That which *might* be misleading may be regulated by narrowly drawn restrictions if the state demonstrates that a particular regulation furthers its substantial interest.[124] Professional advertising on radio and television merits special consideration and is subject to greater restraint than print advertising.

Here are some specific examples applying the guidelines about state regulation of commercial speech: A state may forbid the practicing of optometry under a trade name.[125] Since it is illegal to discriminate in employment on the basis of sex, a city may make it illegal for newspapers to publish want ads under the headings "Male Help Wanted" and "Female Help Wanted," just as it could forbid advertisements for prostitution or for illegal drugs. Governments may not, however, forbid newspapers to publish advertisements advocating "sexism or other controversial subjects."[126] A state may not forbid pharmacists to advertise the prices of prescription drugs or lawyers to advertise their charges or to list their fields of specialization.[127] A city may not ban For Sale signs in front of homes, even if the purpose of the ban is to prevent panic selling by whites in neighborhoods becoming racially integrated.[128] Nor may governments ban advertising of contraceptives.[129]

Corporate Speech

Corporations are entitled to freedom of speech. A state may not prohibit corporations from spending money to influence votes on referendum proposals, nor may it ban promotional advertising by an electric utility or prohibit a utility from including pronuclear statements in its bills.[130] Justices Brennan and Marshall, two stalwart champions of freedom of expression, dissented from these decisions, contending that corporations, as artificial persons spending stockholders' funds, could reasonably be subject to limitations not permissible for natural persons.

Time, Place, and Manner Regulations

The Supreme Court has come very close to the view that, except for the narrowly defined categories of libel, obscenity, fighting words, and seditious incitement to violence, *pure speech* — that is, speech unconnected with action — including commercial speech and that of corporations, is constitutionally protected from any except reasonable time, place, and manner regulations. Regulations designed to regulate the time, place, or manner of speech are subject to a three-part test. (The Supreme Court seems partial to three-part tests.) The regulation must be neutral with respect to the content of the expression and must be applied even-handedly, it must leave open ample alternative channels for communication of the information, and it must be "narrowly tailored" to serve a significant governmental interest. (Justice Stevens is of the view that this generalization is of little help. He quipped, "Any student of history who has been reprimanded for talking about the World Series during a class discussion of the First Amendment knows that it is incorrect to state that a time, place, or manner restriction may not be based upon either the content or subject matter of the speech."[131])

A relatively recent example of congressional time, place, and manner regulations is a federal law, stemming from World War II concerns, requiring all foreign agents in the United States to register and to notify the Department of Justice of any materials they intend to distribute in the United States. If the Department of Justice declares that the materials come within the statutory definition, the distributor must see that they are properly labeled as "political propaganda." The Supreme Court sustained the law as an appropriate exercise of congressional authority. The Court concluded that the statute merely gives people additional information about the source of the materials. The dissenting justices contended that even if Congress used the "propaganda" designation with a completely neutral purpose, Congress has burdened political discourse and has given no persuasive justification of the burden. Such a burden, they argued, is contrary to consistent Supreme Court holdings that limitations on First Amendment freedoms can be justified only by a compelling governmental interest.[132] (As a side issue, it is a mark of how far we have gone into modern federalism that we now assume that Congress has authority to act unless a specific constitutional provision forbids it to do so. In this case, there was no discussion by any justice about the precise constitutional authority under which Congress was acting. The statute appears to be based on congressional authority over the mails and over commerce among the states.)

Symbolic Speech

When speech becomes enmeshed with conduct it loses its character as pure speech. Even so the "Court has repeatedly warned States and government units that they cannot regulate conduct connected with [First Amendment freedoms] through the use of sweeping, dragnet statutes that may, because of vagueness, jeopardize these freedoms." Of course, almost every law may have an effect on speech activities, but the only laws subject to First Amendment scrutiny are those that regulate symbolic speech, conduct with "a significant expressive element," or those that have the "inevitable effect of singling out" expressive activity.[133]

"The Constitution does not bar enactment of laws regulating conduct, even though connected with speech, press, assembly, and petition, if such laws specifically bar only the conduct deemed obnoxious and are carefully and narrowly aimed at that forbidden conduct."[134] Moreover, "We cannot accept the view," wrote Chief Justice Warren, "that an apparently limitless variety of conduct can be labeled speech whenever the person engaged in the conduct intends thereby to express an idea."[135] Or, as Chief Justice Burger has written, "Conduct that the State police power can prohibit on a public street does not become automatically protected by the Constitution merely because the conduct is moved to a bar or a 'live theatre' stage, any more than 'live' performance of a man and woman locked in a sexual embrace at high noon in Times Square is protected by the Constitution because they simultaneously engage in a . . . political dialogue."[136]

The line between speech and conduct is, of course, not easy to draw. A majority of the justices held that school authorities had violated the Constitution when they suspended two students who had defied their principal by quietly and passively wearing black armbands to school to protest the Vietnam War.[137] The Supreme Court had less difficulty in unanimously sustaining the constitutionality of the 1965 amendment to the Selective Service Act that made it a crime knowingly to destroy or mutilate draft cards.[138]

Campaign Finances

Concerned about corruption and about the unfair advantage that people and interests of wealth have in the political process, especially elections, Congress has regulated campaign financing. Restrictions on what people may *give* to candidates are constitutionally permissible. Restrictions on what they may *spend* in behalf of candidates without consulting them are not. Limitations on contributions only marginally restrict a contributor's ability to express political views; limitations on expenditures directly affect what people can say and where, when, and how they can say it.[139] Moreover, only contributions to candidates can be limited, not those to groups that advocate causes or work for or against ballot measures.[140]

Congress tried to close an obvious loophole by forbidding any independent political campaign committee from spending more than $1,000 to further the election of a presidential candidate. But the Supreme Court declared the limit unconstitutional. As long as a committee maintains no obvious ties to the presidential candidate, it may spend whatever its members wish to further the candidate's political fortunes. Congress may, however, condition the funds it provides to finance presidential campaigns on an agreement by candidates and their political parties to limit the amount that will be spent by the candidate and the party committee that receives them.[141]

Congress may subject trade union and commercial corporation political action committees to more regulation than is permissible for other kinds of political action committees. Trade unions and commercial corporations can be forbidden to spend any union or corporate funds to elect candidates — but they cannot be limited with respect to advocating causes.

As difficult as the line-drawing is for regulation of political expenditures, it is simple compared with the Court's struggles over the question whether and how the First Amendment restricts the ability of a public school board to decide which books may be kept in a public school library. In *Board of Education* v *Pic*, the justices wrote seven different opinions and seventy-four pages, but they were unable to get a majority behind any of the opinions. Apparently, what it comes down to is that the First Amendment does apply, actions of school boards are subject to federal court review, and although school boards have wide discretion in deciding which books are suitable for the library, they may not remove books from library shelves simply because they dislike the ideas contained in those books. The dissenting justices felt that the choice of books for a school library should be left to school boards.[142]

---

or of the press;

Until recently little attention has been paid to the question whether the press has freedoms beyond those of other persons. It was assumed that freedom of speech was used as a synonym for freedom of the press. One explanation of the Constitution's speaking of the two freedoms separately is that freedom of speech was thought to protect oral communications, and freedom of the press, written ones. Another explanation is that the framers added the phrase "of the press" because "dissemination" had more often been the object of official restraint than had mere personal expression. Although Justice Stewart wrote, "That the First Amendment speaks separately of freedom of speech and freedom of the press is no constitutional accident, but an acknowledgment of the critical role played by the press in American society,"[143] the prevailing view is that of Chief Justice Burger: "The First Amendment does not 'belong' to any definable category of persons or entities; it belongs to all who exercise its freedoms."[144] In 1985 Justice Brennan went out of his way to point out that, at least within the context of defamation law, "at least six Members of this Court . . . agree today that . . . the rights of the institutional media are no greater and no less than those enjoyed by other individuals or organizations engaged in the same activities." A year later, Justice O'Connor, in an opinion joined on this point only by Justices Marshall and Powell, carefully established a rule for libel suits by private individuals against *media defendants* (see page 144), reserving for another day the question of whether the same standard would apply against a nonmedia defendant.[145] If the view ever prevails that some privileges belong only to the press, the Court will have to determine who qualifies for those benefits.

Although the Court has never defined the press, it has been especially solicitous of protecting publications from any kind of taxation that could possibly have an intimidating effect on them. General taxes, along with such economic regulations as fair labor standards acts, antitrust laws, and so on, can be applied to the press. But when Huey Long, as governor of Louisiana, persuaded the legislature to impose a tax on some newspapers that had been critical of him, the Supreme Court, in *Grosjean* v *American Press Co.*, declared the taxation unconstitutional. The Court perceived that the tax had been imposed to punish a select group of newspapers.[146]

So careful is the Court to protect the press from possible government threats that in *Minneapolis Star* v *Minnesota Comm. of Revenue* it declared a Minnesota tax unconstitutional, even though it had been adopted with no evil intent and in amount less than the sales taxes on other enterprises. Rather than collect a sales tax on every newspaper or magazine sold, Minnesota imposed a tax on ink and paper used by publications, exempting the first $100,000 worth of ink and paper consumed in each calendar year so that the tax would fall most heavily on the largest newspaper in the state. "Whatever the motive of the legislature in this case," said Justice O'Connor for the Court, "we think that recognizing a power in the State not only to single out the press but also to tailor the tax so that it singles out a few members of the press presents such a potential for abuse that no interest suggested by Minnesota can justify the scheme."[147] In a similar vein, the Court struck down an Arkansas sales tax that applied to general-interest magazines and exempted newspapers and magazines published within Arkansas, and religious, professional, trade, and sports magazines. Selective taxation of the press is unconstitutional, even where there is no evidence of any improper censorial motive, most especially where, as here, the exemption depends on the content of the magazines. Arkansas could have collected a tax on the sales of all magazines and newspapers, but not some of them.[148]

The Court has also acknowledged the press exemption from the Federal Campaign Act's limitation on corporations' expenditures in behalf of political candidates: it is quite clear that such a limitation on a press corporation would be unconstitutional.[149]

The only limitation the Supreme Court has ever permitted (see page 144) on a newspaper's right to the truthful publication of materials, whether they have obtained such materials lawfully or unlawfully, is on the use of information gained through the discovery process of a court when a newspaper is a party to a suit.

Some news people claim not only the right to be free from governmental interference to publish what they wish, but also the right of access to all news sources. However, there is no general constitutional right of access that allows news people, or anybody else, to go wherever they wish to interview whomever they desire or to see whatever documents they claim are of general public interest. Neither the First nor the Fourteenth Amendment guarantees to the news media a right of access to government information not available to the public generally.

Although there is no general constitutional right of access, in *Richmond Newspapers, Inc.* v *Virginia*, in what Justice Stevens called a "watershed case," the Supreme Court did rule "that the acquisition of newsworthy matter is entitled to some constitutional protection." The Court held that a trial judge could not, even with the consent of the prosecutor and defendant, close a trial to the press and public without a specific finding by the judge that there is some "overriding interest" that would justify such a closure. Said Chief Justice Burger, "It is not crucial whether we describe this right to attend criminal trials to hear, see, and communicate observations as a right to access, or a right to gather information." Whatever it is called, the Court did find that the right of access to trials is protected by a combination of the First, Ninth, and Fourteenth Amendments. Moreover, Chief Justice Burger even seemed to concede some special role for the press. Although pointedly saying that media representatives enjoy only the same right of access as the public, he did recognize that the media often function as "surrogates for the public" and are "accorded special seating and priority of entry so that they may report what people in attendance have seen and heard."[150] Clearly, if this right of public access is extended to other governmental proceedings beyond trials, the decision will deserve Justice Stevens's accolade.

Since *Richmond*, the Court has talked more enthusiastically about the value of open trials.[151] The Court has extended this First Amendment right of access to preliminary hearings as well as to trials, but not, at least not yet, to grand jury proceedings.[152] The Court set aside a Massachusetts statute requiring the exclusion of the press and public during the testimony of a minor victim in a sex offense trial.[153] It also refused to allow a trial judge in a rape and murder case to close the jury selection process to protect the privacy of potential jurors, who were subject to questioning about their past sexual experiences and attitudes. The presumption that trials must be kept open, including questioning of jurors, can be overcome "only by an overriding interest based on findings that closure is essential to preserve higher values and is narrowly tailored to serve that interest."[154] Moreover, the judge must make a finding that there is a "substantial probability" — not merely a "reasonable likelihood" — that a right to a fair trial or hearing will be undermined by the opening of a proceeding.[155] In other words, a trial judge who closes any portion of a trial had better have very persuasive reasons, and must put those reasons in writing. Note, however, that the press does not have a general constitutional right to take pictures in courtrooms or to televise the proceedings. There the courts have had to balance rights to fair trial under the Sixth Amendment (see page 204) with rights under the First Amendment.

Although the Constitution does not require that it do so, Congress has taken significant steps to provide access to government files. The Freedom of Information Act of 1965, as amended in 1974, requires federal agencies to make information available on request, with certain exceptions, such as defense secrets, criminal investigation files, and interoffice memorandums relating to pending decisions.

Does the First Amendment confer on news people an immunity from being compelled by a grand jury or another government agency to divulge the sources of their information? Although some states have conferred a qualified privilege on news people so that they may more readily gather the news, the First Amendment provides no such immunity. A reporter has no less an obligation than any other citizen to respond to a grand jury subpoena and answer relevant questions.[156] Nor does the First Amendment protect the files of news people from being searched by the police with a valid search warrant. It does not make any constitutional difference that the news people may themselves be innocent of any suspected wrongdoing.[157] Congress has, however, provided news people special protection from such searches. Congress has prohibited courts from issuing warrants to federal, state, and local police officers that would authorize those officers to search "the products of news organizations and others engaged in First Amendment activities," except when the news people are themselves suspected of a crime related to the materials they are holding or when there is reason to believe that the immediate seizure of the materials is necessary to prevent death or serious bodily injury. (Materials in news people's files are still subject to subpoena.)

The freedom of access of the public can also be inhibited by the news media themselves. In some cities there may be only a single newspaper, and it may also own the local television station. The Court has been hostile to government imposition of access regulations on the printed media and to laws giving persons a right to reply to media attacks on them. A unanimous Court declared unconstitutional a Florida law giving political candidates a right to reply in a newspaper's columns to its critical editorial comments. As the Court declared, "A responsible press is an undoubtedly desirable goal, but press responsibility is not mandated by the Constitution and like many other virtues, it cannot be legislated."[158] The Court has been more tolerant of access requirements for the broadcast media: Congress does have the power to confer upon "legally qualified candidates for Federal office" a right to demand that broadcasters sell them time.[159]

Other Media

The Constitution protects communications by mail, radio, television, motion pictures, billboards, handbills, and picketing. For each of these media, there are special problems that result in different degrees of protection. "Each method of communicating ideas is 'a law unto itself' and that law must reflect the 'differing natures, values, abuses, and dangers of each method.' "[160]

Mail

"The United States may give up the Post Office when it sees fit, but while it carries it on the use of the mails is almost as much a part of free speech as the right to use our tongues."[161] In striking down the first act of Congress ever to be held in conflict with the First Amendment, an act that required the postmaster general to detain unsealed foreign mailings of "communist political propaganda," Justice Douglas said for the Court, "The Act sets administrative officials astride the flow of mail to inspect it, appraise it, write the addressee about it, and await a response before dispatching the mail. . . . The regimen of this Act is at war with the 'uninhibited, robust, and wide-open' debate and discussion that are contemplated by the First Amendment."[162] Six years later the Court extended this decision to void laws authorizing postal authorities to make administrative determinations of obscenity, exclude it from the mails, and cut off mail delivery to persons sending it.[163]

Whereas administrative censorship of the mails is unconstitutional, householder censorship is not. "The mailer's right to communicate must stop at the mailbox of an unreceptive addressee."[164] The Supreme Court upheld a law giving householders the absolute right to ask the postmaster to order mailers to delete their names from all mailing lists and to refrain from sending any advertising materials those householders in their sole discretion believe to be "erotically arousing or sexually provocative." It makes no constitutional difference if the householder includes in such a category a "dry-goods catalogue." This is not governmental censorship.[165] Moreover, Congress may forbid the deposit into any authorized mailbox of any material on which no postage has been paid. Mailboxes are part of the national postal system and do not have public forum status as a street does.[166]

Customs officials, in contrast to postal authorities, may seize obscene materials. But this administrative action must be reviewed promptly by the courts. Judicial proceedings must be commenced within fourteen days of the seizure and concluded within sixty days.[167] Although it may not authorize administrative interference with the mails, Congress may make it a crime knowingly to send obscene material through the mails, even if it is sent to adults who have requested it.[168] Congress may even make it a crime, as it has done, to transport such material, even if it is carried in a briefcase and is designed only for private use.[169]

Broadcasting

"Of all forms of communications, broadcasting has received the most limited First Amendment protection."[170] "The broadcast media pose unique and special problems not present in traditional free speech cases."[171] "There is no 'unabridgeable' First

Amendment right to broadcast comparable to the right of every individual to speak, write, or publish. . . . This is not to say that the First Amendment is irrelevant . . . to broadcasting . . . but it is the right of viewers and listeners, not the right of the broadcasters, which is paramount."[172]

The First Amendment prevents governmental censorship of broadcasters. And although no one has a right to a license, the Federal Communications Commission (FCC), which regulates and licenses broadcasting, may not censor in advance what is broadcast. It does have authority to forbid the use of indecent language, even though such language may not be obscene; to rebuke a station for broadcasting such language; and to take into account, in subsequent determinations of license renewals, that a station has broadcast such language. Broadcasting, unlike the printed media, "confronts the citizen, not only in public, but in the privacy of the home" and "is uniquely accessible to children, even those too young to read."[173]

The Supreme Court, in *FCC v League of Women Voters of California*, in a five-to-four watershed decision, declared unconstitutional a federal statute regulating broadcasters. That statute stated, "No noncommercial educational broadcasting station which receives a grant from the Corporation for Public Broadcasting [all public television stations and most public radio stations] may engage in editorializing." Justice Brennan, writing for the majority, distinguished this ban from the previously sustained *fairness doctrine* — a requirement that all licensees must provide balanced presentation of all points of view and take positive steps to invite controversial views — on the ground that the ban on editorializing strikes at "the heart" of the First Amendment. It "singles out noncommercial broadcasters and denies them the right to address their chosen audience on matters of public importance." The restriction was not "narrowly tailored to further a substantial government interest."[174] The dissenting justices felt that those who take government dollars could be subject to what the justices considered reasonable limitations designed to protect stations from being unduly influenced by federal authorities, to keep the stations from becoming privileged outlets, and to prevent government subsidies of editorials to which many taxpayers might object.

Perhaps the most important consequences of *FCC v League of Women Voters of California* will be reactions to the footnotes in the majority opinion, noting that the "prevailing rationale for broadcast regulation has come under increasing criticism in recent years" because technological changes such as cable, direct beam broadcast, and videotapes might be undermining the theory that the scarcity of channels justifies substantial government regulation of television. "We are not prepared, however," said Justice Brennan, "to reconsider our long-standing approach without some signal from Congress or the FCC that technological developments have advanced so far that some revision of the system of broadcast regulation may be required."

In another footnote the Court said that if the FCC demonstrated that the fairness doctrine reduces, rather than enhances, free speech, the Court "would then be forced to reconsider the constitutional basis" of its earlier rulings upholding the doctrine.

Congress, the president, and the FCC have responded to this invitation, but they are giving the Supreme Court conflicting signals. Congress, aware that the Reagan administration and its FCC appointees would like to repeal the 38-year-old FCC fairness regulations, attempted to make those regulations into law. President Reagan vetoed the bill and the Senate decided not to attempt to override the veto. Then the FCC repealed its fairness doctrine regulations, contending that the doctrine is unconstitutional and contrary to the public interest. Congressional leaders threatened to reimpose the doctrine by legislation attached as a rider to an appropriations bill that would be veto-proof. President Reagan responded that he knew of no bill that he would not veto if it contained a fairness doctrine requirement. If Congress and the president or the FCC reimposes fairness requirements, then the Supreme Court will probably be asked to decide once again if such regulations are constitutional.

The Court has yet to determine "whether the characteristics of cable television make it sufficiently analogous to another medium to warrant application of an already existing standard or whether those characteristics require a new analysis."[175] It has decided, however, that cable partakes "of some of the aspects of speech and the communication of ideas as do the traditional enterprises of newspaper and book publishers, public speakers and pamphleteers,"[176] and that when cities regulate cable television they are subject to appropriate First Amendment constraints. What this generalization means will be worked out through case-by-case application.

Motion Pictures and Plays

The Constitution tolerates more regulation of motion pictures than of printed media. A state or city may require motion pictures to be licensed before being shown to the public, whereas such prior censorship is not permitted in the case of printed media.[177] However, even with respect to motion pictures, the Supreme Court is suspicious of prior restraint; it insists on procedures to ensure prompt judicial determination whether a particular picture is unfit to be shown.[178] And the only permissible grounds on which a license may be withheld is obscenity, as constitutionally defined.[179]

Live performances such as plays and revues are, along with motion pictures, entitled to some constitutional protection.[180] Yet live theater is subject to greater regulation than either the printed page or the motion picture. The First Amendment, especially in view of the Twenty-first, does not protect liquor licensees from state regulations forbidding sexually suggestive performances in places where liquor is sold.[181]

Picketing

The right to picket, when picketing is unaccompanied by threats or violence, is protected by the Constitution, but since picketing involves "elements of both speech and conduct . . . picketing can be subjected to controls that would not be constitutionally permissible in case of pure speech."[182] Even peaceful picketing can be restricted if it is conducted for an illegal purpose, that is, designed to pressure someone to do something that the law forbids them to do.[183]

However, the Constitution forbids statutes aimed at picketing that are not narrowly drawn. At the same time the Constitution, by the equal protection clause of the Fourteenth Amendment as well as the First Amendment, forbids a state to choose by subject matter the kinds of peaceful picketing it will allow. Illinois, for example, found itself in constitutional difficulty when, to draw its ban on picketing of residences as narrowly as possible, it exempted peaceful labor picketing of places of employment.[184] The statute, the Court said, made an impermissible distinction between labor picketing and other peaceful picketing, although dissenting Justice Rehnquist complained that a state's constitutional ability to protect residential privacy was being made almost impossible to enforce.[185] Note that the Constitution is not the only restraint on a state's ability to regulate picketing. A state may not interfere with picketing protected by federal legislation.

Handbills, Sound Trucks, and Billboards

Reasonable content-neutral restraints can be imposed on the time, place, and manner in which handbills may be sold or distributed. A general ban on handbills is unreasonable as is a ban on handbills that do not carry the name and address of the author.[186] Regulation with any aspect of prior restraint is likely to be struck down.[187] On the other side, the federal government may forbid the use of mailboxes for distribution of leaflets;[188] a government may ban sound trucks that give out loud and raucous noises;[189] a city may ban the posting of signs on public property.[190]

Billboards on private property are entitled to constitutional protection, and a San Diego ordinance banning off-site billboards was declared unconstitutional, but the decision was "a virtual Tower of Babel from which no definitive principles can be clearly drawn." A plurality of the justices found that San Diego had erred in allowing on-site commercial billboards but not on-site noncommercial messages. Two other justices felt the vice of San Diego's action was its failure to prove that such action was necessary to promote traffic safety or to improve the beauty of the city.[191]

---

or the right of the people peaceably to assemble, and to petition the Government for a redress of grievances.

The Constitution protects the right to assemble peaceably in *public places*, but those who wish to protest or otherwise express their views have no constitutional right to do so "whenever and however and wherever they please."[192] No one has a right to take over a school, to seize and hold the office of a mayor, or, most especially, to take over a university chancellor's office. State and local governments have the power to make reasonable regulations to preserve order.

Time, place, and manner regulations designed to preserve the public peace must be precisely drawn and fairly administered. The courts will look carefully at regulations or police actions that entrench on this right, especially in circumstances that raise suspicion that the law is not being applied evenhandedly. Not constitutional are regulations permitting authorities to determine which groups will be allowed to hold public meetings or giving police wide discretion to determine whom to arrest and courts latitude to determine whom to convict. For example, the Court struck down a Louisiana law defining "disturbing the peace" so broadly that it would permit arrest merely for holding a meeting on a public street or public highway.[193]

The extent of government's power to regulate forums depends on the kind of forum. The Court has recognized three: the traditional public forum, such as a street or a park, the public forum created by government designation, and the nonpublic forum.[194]

"Streets and parks have immemorially been held in trust for the use of the public, and time out of mind, have been used for purpose of assembly, communicating thoughts between citizens and discussing public questions."[195] In such areas the state may enforce content-neutral time, place, and manner regulations that are "narrowly tailored to serve a significant government interest, and leave open ample alternative channels of communication."[196] Thus, the Supreme Court, assuming for purposes of the case but not deciding that "overnight sleeping in connection with a demonstration is expressive conduct protected to some extent by the First Amendment," upheld a National Park Service regulation that allows persons to hold rallies, even to pitch tents and stay in them, but not to sleep in tents on the Mall in downtown Washington and in Lafayette Park, across the street from the White House.[197] The Court, while not ruling on a law forbidding the display in the Supreme Court building or on its grounds "of any flag, banner, or device designed or adapted to bring into public notice any party, organization, or movement," held the law unconstitutional as applied to side-walks surrounding the Supreme Court building. The solicitor general had argued that since judges, unlike legislators and executives, are supposed to decide cases on the basis only of the record before them, Congress had been justified in outlawing conduct that might create the appearance that judges are subject to outside influences. The Supreme Court refused to buy this contention.[198]

When the state opens up public property beyond streets and parks and designates it a public area, reasonable time, place, and manner regulations are permissible. Judges are not to find that a public forum has been created unless the government in question has clearly designated it as such.

"Public property which is not by tradition or designation a forum for public communication is governed by different standards. . . . In addition to time, place, and manner regulations, the state may reserve the forum for its intended purposes, communicative or otherwise, as long as the regulation on speech is reasonable and not an effort to suppress expression merely because public officials oppose the speaker's view."[199] Moreover, "control over access to a nonpublic forum can be based on subject matter and speaker identity so long as the distinctions drawn are reasonable in the light of the purpose served by the forum and are viewpoint neutral." Thus, as we have noted, a city may ban the posting of handbills on telephone poles and lamp posts. School mail facilities are not a public forum and a school board may keep all unions or associations, other than the one that has won collective bargaining rights, from using the interschool mail system and teacher mailboxes.[200] Military commanders may ban persons from military bases.[201]

A fascinating cluster of issues was raised by a 1980 decision of the California Supreme Court. The United States Supreme Court had previously established that the federal Constitution does not give one a right to go into a privately owned shopping center against the wishes of the owner to distribute handbills or engage in picketing on matters unrelated to the shopping center's own operations.[202] The Supreme Court of California, however, ruled that whatever the United States Constitution provides, the California constitution protects "speech and petitioning, reasonably exercised, even when the centers are privately owned." But what of the rights of the owners of the shopping centers? Can a state compel them to allow their property to be used to express views that they find distasteful? The United States Supreme Court ruled that what California had done in this particular case was all right: it had allowed a group of high school students to set up a card table in the corner of a large shopping center to gather signatures on a petition, even though the owners of the shopping center had ordered them off the property. But the justices carefully limited the holding to the facts of the case before them and emphasized that the decision was not "blanket approval for state efforts to transform privately owned commercial property into public forums."[203]

Does the Constitution require police officers to protect unpopular groups whose public meetings and demonstrations in public forums arouse others to violence? If the answer were no, then the right of unpopular minorities to hold meetings would be seriously curtailed. It is almost always easier for the police to maintain order by curbing the peaceful meetings of the unpopular minority than to restrain those threatening violence. Yet if police were never to have the right to order a group to disperse, public order would be at the mercy of those who might resort to street demonstrations just to create public tensions and provoke street battles.

The Supreme Court has refused to give a categorical answer to the question; the answer depends on the circumstances. In 1951, in *Feiner* v *New York*, the Court upheld the conviction for unlawful assembly of a sidewalk speaker who continued to talk after being ordered to stop by the only two policemen present. There was no evidence that the police interfered because of objection to what was being said. In view, however, of the hostile response of the audience, the police were fearful a riot might ensue that they could not contain or prevent.[204] The *Feiner* case has never been overruled, but since then the Supreme Court has tended to emphasize the need for governments to move under more precisely drawn statutes.

In *Edwards* v *South Carolina*, the Court reversed the conviction of 187 black students for breach of the peace because of their holding a protest meeting in front of the South Carolina State House. The police had been afraid that their gathering would provoke a clash with a crowd of onlookers. After trying to keep the groups apart for forty-five minutes, the police told the students to disperse and when they failed to do so, arrested them. "The Fourteenth Amendment," said the Court, "does not permit a State to make criminal the peaceful expression of unpopular views."[205]

The Supreme Court followed the *Edwards* precedent rather than the *Feiner* when it reversed the conviction under a disorderly conduct statute of Dick Gregory and other demonstrators for failing to obey a police command to stop marching in front of the house of the mayor of Chicago at a time when a large number of onlookers became unruly toward the demonstrators. Although the Supreme Court reversed the decision, the Court made it clear that the situation would have been different if Chicago had acted under ordinances specifically forbidding demonstrations after certain hours in residential areas or making it an offense to disobey a police officer when there is an imminent threat of violence and the police have made all reasonable efforts to protect the demonstrators from hostile bystanders. The Court's objection was to the fact that Gregory and his followers had been convicted of disorderly conduct when there was no evidence they had been acting disorderly.[206]

Again, in *Coates* v *Cincinnati*, the Court held as void for its vagueness and overbreadth an ordinance that forbade three or more persons to assemble on sidewalks and there conduct themselves in a manner annoying to persons passing by. "A city is free to prevent people from blocking sidewalks, committing assaults, obstructing traffic, littering streets, but it must do so by ordinances directed with reasonable specificity toward the conduct to be prohibited. . . . It cannot constitutionally do so through the enactment and enforcement of an ordinance whose violations may entirely depend upon whether or not a policeman is annoyed."[207]

What of public facilities, such as libraries, courthouses, schools, or swimming pools, that are designated to serve purposes other than public assembly? As long as persons use such facilities within the normal bounds of conduct, they may not be constitutionally restrained from doing so. If they attempt, however, by sit-ins or other kinds of demonstrations, to interfere with programs or to appropriate facilities for their own use, a state has constitutional authority to punish, provided it does so under laws that are not applied in a discriminatory fashion and that properly limit the discretion of those enforcing the laws. "The crucial question is whether the manner of expression is basically incompatible with the normal activity of a particular place at a particular time."[208] To illustrate the application of these general rules: A small group of protesters who quietly remained in a library for ten to fifteen minutes to protest racial discrimination, but did not interfere with the operations of the library, could not constitutionally be charged with violating a general breach of the peace ordinance;[209] a group of protesters could be punished for deliberately making a noise that disturbed the peace and good order of a school under an ordinance directly aimed at preventing demonstrations in and around school buildings;[210] because they were thought to be interfering with the operation of the jail, a group of students could be convicted for trespass when, to protest racial segregation and the arrest of a fellow student, they marched into a jailhouse and refused to leave when so ordered by the sheriff.[211]

Right to Associate

"While the freedom of association is not explicitly set out in the Amendment, it has long been held to be implicit in the freedoms of speech, assembly, and petition."[212] (There is another aspect of the freedom of association, a "fundamental element of personal liberty" protected by the due process clause that relates to intimate human relationships such as the family and close friends (see page 247).[213] Thus, although a state college may refuse to grant a student organization the right to use facilities unless it agrees to abide by reasonable campus rules, it may not deny such privileges to an organization because of disapproval of its aims or generalized apprehensions that its activities could lead to disruptions.[214] Before a government may impose a legislative requirement that organizations make public the names of their members, it must demonstrate some compelling and legitimate need to know.[215]

What about the 1974 amendments to the Federal Election Campaign Act of 1971 that compel political parties to maintain records and disclose contributions of more than $10 and disbursements of more than $100? The Supreme Court, conceding that these compelled disclosures could seriously infringe on the rights of association and could have a chilling effect on peoples' exercising the right to associate, somewhat reluctantly upheld these requirements, including their application to minor parties, as necessary and proper ways for the government to enhance voters' knowledge about a candidate's possible allegiances and interests, to deter corruption, and to help enforce contribution limitations.[216] The Court indicated, however, that if a minor party could show that disclosure of its contributors' names might subject such contributors to threats or reprisals or impair the party's ability to receive funds, the disclosure and reporting requirement as applied to that party might well be declared unconstitutional.

True to this promise, in 1982 the Court held that the Ohio campaign law could not be applied to require the Socialist Workers Party to report the names and addresses of campaign contributors, or even the names and addresses of those with whom it did business. "The First Amendment prohibits a state from compelling disclosures by a minor party that will subject those persons identified to the reasonable probability of threats, harassment, or reprisals. Such disclosures would infringe the First Amendment rights of the party and its members and supporters."[217] Democrats and Republicans, however, can still be required to disclose publicly the contributions to their political parties and must hope that the bosses of their contributors are of the same political persuasion.

Recent Supreme Court decisions have applied the right to associate in such a fashion as to strengthen the autonomy of national political parties. National party conventions, rather than the state from which delegates come, have the final say on the seating of delegations and the requirements for participation in the convention.[218] The right of association protected the Connecticut Republican Party when it ignored a Connecticut closed primary law to the extent of opening some of its primaries to independent voters.[219] (The Court made it clear, however, that a political party's right to associate does not necessarily extend, in the face of state law to the contrary, to opening its primaries to members of other parties.) Justice Scalia in dissent contended that if the concept of freedom of association is extended to such casual contacts as that of an independent voting in a party primary, "it ceases to be of any analytic use."

The Supreme Court has rejected the contention of a law partnership that it need not comply with Title VII, which forbids sex discrimination in employment, because of its constitutional right of association.[220] The Court has also sustained the application of state human rights acts to compel the Jaycees and the Rotary Club to admit women. Such acts make it an "unfair discriminatory practice . . . to deny any person the full and equal enjoyment of goods, services, facilities, privileges, advantages . . . of a place of public accommodation because of race, color, creed, religion, disability, national origin, or sex." The Jaycees and Rotarians argued, among other things, that the law interfered with their constitutionally protected right to associate with persons of their own choice for the purpose of expressing their views. Justice Brennan, speaking for the majority in the cases relating to the Jaycees, conceded, "There can be no clearer example of an intrusion into the internal structure or affairs of an association than a regulation that forces the group to accept members it does not desire. Such a regulation may impair the ability of the original members to express only those views that brought them together."[221] However, the Court decided that the Jaycees (and in separate cases the law partnership and the Rotarians) were not purely private organizations and that they had failed to demonstrate that allowing women to become members and to vote would change the content or impact of the organization's speech.

The Court's several opinions have been carefully crafted to try to make clear that the right to associate is constitutionally protected and will take priority over a state public accommodation regulation for many kinds of associations. At one extreme are families and churches; at the other extreme such things as buyer cooperatives or large associations with only nominal membership requirements. The Court indicated that its decision would have been different for associations organized for political, religious, cultural, or social purposes. Factors to be considered in determining whether an organization may constitutionally be covered by antidiscrimination laws are "size, purpose, policies, selectivity, congeniality."[222] Justice O'Connor, in her concurring opinion in the Jaycee case, would have drawn the line between an association that chooses to be expressive, which could not be covered by a public accommodations act and forced to accept memberships, and one that enters the marketplace of commerce in any substantial degree and thus "loses the complete control over its membership that it would otherwise enjoy if it confined its affairs to the marketplace of ideas."

Persons may associate together and engage in boycotts for political purposes. Violence is not entitled to constitutional protection, even if motivated for political purposes, but the mere fact that some violence may flow from a political boycott is not sufficient to permit the imposition of liability on all participants if there is no evidence that they agreed to the use of unlawful means. Thus, the Supreme Court reversed the imposition of damages by Mississippi courts on the NAACP for promoting a boycott of white merchants in Claiborne County as a means of bringing about political, social, and economic change. The First Amendment did not, however, bar recovery of damages from those who engaged in violence or threatened it, for losses directly caused by their unlawful conduct.[223]

The First Amendment offers less protection to secondary political boycotts by trade unions. Secondary boycotts — those against someone other than the workers' own employers — are forbidden by the National Labor Relations Act. After the Soviet Union invaded Afghanistan, the longshoremen's union refused to unload cargoes shipped from the Soviet Union, but the Supreme Court held their refusal to be illegal and unprotected. "We have consistently rejected," wrote Justice Powell for the Court, "the claim that secondary picketing by labor unions in violation of [the National Labor Relations Act] is protected activity under the First Amendment. . . . It would seem even clear[er] that conduct designed not to communicate but to coerce merits still less consideration under the First Amendment."[224]

What of the freedom not to associate? May a state compel lawyers to join bar associations, or may it pass laws allowing employers to make agreements with unions that require workers either to join the union or make payments to it as a condition of employment? To oversimplify a complex problem, laws permitting or compelling such arrangements are constitutional provided individuals are not compelled to make contributions for political or ideological purposes. Compelled contributions may be used to support the professional purposes of a bar association and the collective-bargaining, contract-administration, and grievance-adjustment purposes of a union, including costs of running conventions, costs of social activities related to union programs, and general publication expenses. But nonunion employees have a constitutional right to "prevent the Union's spending a part of their required service fees to contribute to political candidates and to express political views unrelated to its duties as an exclusive bargaining representative."[225] Unions may not take dues from unwilling members or nonmembers in a union or agency shop and then later rebate to them the funds used for political purposes. They must make it possible for such unwilling members to pay the lower amounts initially.[226] Moreover, to pass constitutional muster a union's collection of fees from nonmembers must "include an adequate explanation of the basis for the fee, a reasonably prompt opportunity to challenge the amount of the fee before an impartial decision-maker, and an escrow for the amounts reasonably in dispute while such challenges are pending."[227]

Minnesota raised the troublesome tension between rights to associate and not to do so when it gave unions of state employees, including faculty unions, a special exclusive right (in addition to the regular right to be the collective bargaining agent) "to meet and confer" with administrators and talk with them about matters of common concern beyond issues directly relating to employment. Twenty community college instructors who were not members of the union charged that giving this special privilege to unions deprived faculty members who chose not to join the union of their free speech rights. The Court did not agree: "[The instructors]," wrote Justice O'Connor for the Court, "have no constitutional right to force the government to listen to their views. They have no such right as members of the public, as government employees, or as instructors in an institution of higher education." It is of special interest, at least to faculty members, that Justice O'Connor went out of her way to write, "This Court has never recognized a constitutional right of faculty to participate in policy making in academic institutions. . . . Faculty involvement in academic governance has much to recommend it as a matter of academic policy, but it finds no basis in the Constitution."[228]

Petitioning for Redress of Grievances

Today when we speak of "petitioning the government for the redress of grievances," we call it lobbying. And lobbying is done primarily through associations. Lobbying, like other protected rights, is not immune from regulation. Congress and most states require associations that spend considerable sums of money to influence legislation to register and make public their records. These laws have been upheld, provided *lobbying* is narrowly defined.

Although lobbying is a constitutional right, "Congress is not required to subsidize lobbying." Nonprofit groups may lose their tax-exempt status and contributions to them may no longer be deductible if "a substantial part of the activities" is "carrying on propaganda, otherwise attempting to influence legislation."[229]

Litigation has become an increasingly important means whereby interest groups pursue their public policy objectives. "The right of access to the courts is an aspect of the First Amendment right to petition the Government for redress of grievances," and although governments may regulate to prevent "baseless litigation," they may not halt the prosecution of lawsuits unless these suits lack any reasonable basis in fact or law.[230]

Public Employees and the First Amendment

A troublesome question grows out of the conflict between the constitutional right to engage in political activity, to join political organizations, and to speak freely and the right of the government to regulate the conditions of public employment. Many years ago, public employees had no rights to object to the conditions placed upon the terms of their employment, including those that restricted the exercise of constitutional rights. Justice Holmes, while sitting on the Supreme Judicial Court of Massachusetts, quipped, "A policeman may have a constitutional right to talk politics, but he has no constitutional right to be a policeman."[231] That famous epigram no longer expresses current interpretation of the Constitution. Today "it is clearly established that a State may not discharge an employee on a basis that infringes an employee's constitutionally protected interest in freedom of speech."[232]

Persons may be disqualified, however, from public employment who are actively attempting to overthrow the government by force and who are unwilling to take an oath to support the Constitution. But neither the national government nor the state governments may make it a condition of employment that employees abandon their constitutional rights of freedom of speech or of association. The Court has struck down all except the most narrowly drawn loyalty oath requirements. Among the requirements invalidated are those that bring within their net persons who are members of organizations that may have unlawful purposes but who themselves do not participate in those unlawful activities or share the unlawful purposes.[233]

Although "a public employee does not relinquish First Amendment rights to comment on matters of public interest by virtue of government employment,"[234] when public employees write or speak about matters of only personal interest that relate to their jobs, they may be fired for insubordination or for disrupting their offices. First Amendment protections extend to public employees only for speech on matters of public concern, and then only to employees who serve no confidential, policymaking, or public contact role.[235] Employees who occupy key policy roles may be dismissed for policy differences and for failure, in pursuing their duties, to support the positions of the department. Furthermore, except under the most unusual circumstances, the federal courts will not review the wisdom of a personnel decision by a public agency.

As with all constitutional guidelines, the application of these guidelines to specific cases, is not always easy. The Court ruled that the private communication of a teacher protesting racial discrimination to a school board was constitutionally protected, but circulation of a questionnaire by an assistant district attorney to her fellow staff members right after she had refused to accept a transfer was not.[236] Even more troublesome for the Court was a case that involved the dismissal of a probationary employee from the Harris County, Texas, constable's office. As Justice Powell in concurrence wrote, it was "not easy to understand how this case has assumed constitutional dimensions and reached the Supreme Court of the United States." The employee, reacting to a radio announcement that someone had tried to assassinate the president, had said in a brief conversation with a co-worker, "If they go for him again, I hope they get him." That remark was overheard by another employee, who related it to the constable. He discharged the employee. By five to four, the Supreme Court, making a distinction between a statement that amounts to a threat to kill the president, which is not protected, and a statement such as this one, which could not properly be criminalized at all, concluded that since this employee did not occupy a confidential, policymaking, or public contact role, and since her comment related to matters of public concern, she could not constitutionally be discharged for having made it.[237]

The First Amendment rights of speech and association do not protect government employees from federal and state regulations forbidding civil servants to take "an active part in the political management of political campaigns." The Hatch Act, as the federal law is known, has been twice sustained, despite the contention that it is overbroad, and vague and interferes with the right of association. The Court concluded that it is a reasonable measure to free employees from political pressures and to ensure that they are not coerced into political action in behalf of the party in power.[238] A state may also require certain officeholders to resign if they wish to run for other offices or may make certain officeholders ineligible for certain other posts until after the term for which they were previously elected or appointed has expired.[239]

Among the more amazing decisions of recent years are those in which the Supreme Court has struck down the political patronage system, a system older than the nation. The Court has ruled that those government employees who occupy positions in which party membership is "not relevant" may not be discharged because of their failure to belong to the winning political party. Justice Stevens, providing examples of public employees constitutionally protected from discharge for party reasons, cited a coach of a state university football team. Such a coach, he pointed out, formulates policy, but nonetheless, he argued, "no one could seriously claim that Republicans make better coaches than Democrats, or vice versa." (Justice Stevens apparently does not know very many political partisans.) As examples of officials who could be discharged for political reasons, Justice Stevens mentioned election judges and assistants who help governors write speeches. The immediate cases before the Court involved deputy sheriffs and assistant public defenders.

Although the sheriff and the public defender had been elected in partisan elections, the Court ruled that, once elected, they could not fire their deputy sheriffs and assistant public defenders for belonging to the political party that had lost the election. Justice Powell, in dissent, wondered why the voters, who could also have elected deputy sheriffs and assistant public defenders on party tickets if they had wished, could not delegate to those whom they had elected the authority to hire only those of the winning party faith.[240] So far, no Supreme Court decision has dealt with the power of a president to replace top policy-making officials of the federal executive branch, but the logic of its decisions and the litigious nature of our times suggest that it may not be long before some discharged federal official brings the question to the Court.

AMENDMENT II: MILITIA AND THE RIGHT TO BEAR ARMS

A well regulated Militia, being necessary to the security of a free State,[1] the right of the people to keep and bear Arms, shall not be infringed.

This amendment was designed to prevent Congress from disarming the state militias, not to prevent it from regulating private ownership of firearms. "The Second Amendment guarantees no right to keep and bear a firearm that does not have 'some reasonable relationship to the preservation or efficiency of a well-regulated militia.' "[2] In upholding a federal law making criminal the shipment in interstate commerce of sawed-off shotguns, the Court found no evidence that such weapons had any reasonable relationship "to the preservation or efficiency of a well-regulated militia." The Second Amendment, it held, "must be interpreted and applied" with a view to maintaining a militia. "The Militia which the States were expected to maintain and train is set in contrast with Troops which they were forbidden to keep without the consent of Congress. The sentiment of the time strongly disfavored standing armies; the common view was that adequate defense of country and laws could be secured through the Militia — civilians primarily, soldiers on occasion."[3]

The Second Amendment applies, even to this limited extent, only to the national government. It in no way limits the power of the state and local governments to regulate firearms. As Justice Douglas wrote in an opinion dissenting on another point, "a powerful lobby dins into the ears of our citizenry that gun . . . purchases are constitutional rights protected by the Second Amendment. . . There is under our decisions no reason why stiff state laws governing the purchase and possession of pistols may not be enacted. There is no reason why pistols may not be barred from anyone with a police record. There is no reason why a State may not require a purchaser of a pistol to pass a psychiatric test. There is no reason why all pistols should not be barred to everyone except the police."[4]

AMENDMENT III: QUARTERING OF SOLDIERS

No Soldier shall, in time of peace be quartered in any house, without the consent of the Owner, nor in time of war, but in a manner to be prescribed by law.

Certain remarks of Justice Miller are appropriate here: "This amendment seems to have been thought necessary. It does not appear to have been the subject of judicial exposition; and it is so thoroughly in accord with all our ideas, that further comment is unnecessary."[1]

AMENDMENT IV: SEARCHES AND SEIZURES

The right of the people to be secure in their persons, houses, papers, and effects, against unreasonable searches and seizures, shall not be violated,

Since the Fourth Amendment has been incorporated into the due process clause, the limitation against unreasonable searches and seizures applies to state and local as well as to federal officers. It does not apply to private individuals unless they are operating under instructions from law enforcement officers.

The Constitution does not forbid all searches and seizures but forbids only "unreasonable ones by agents of the government." What distinguishes a reasonable search and seizure from an unreasonable one is "an opaque area of the law."[1] It is also an area in which the justices are divided. The Warren Court took the view that, with few limited exceptions, any search or seizure without a warrant is unreasonable.[2] The Burger Court tended more to the view that "it is not whether it was reasonable to procure a search [or arrest] warrant, but whether the search itself was reasonable."[3] The view of the Rehnquist Court is yet to be established, but the Reagan administration has been especially critical of what it considers shackles on police investigations imposed by judicial interpretations of the Fourth Amendment.

In the application of the Fourth Amendment, each decision often depends on refinements in the facts; the justices are not often of one mind, and the Court has had difficulty in developing generalizable doctrines. We shall try, however, to make some sense of the hundreds of decisions relating to the Fourth Amendment.

In general, and with few exceptions, the distinction between reasonable and unreasonable searches and seizures is that reasonable searches are based on a search warrant or probable cause and unreasonable ones are not. However, there are some searches that are unreasonable, and thus unconstitutional, even if surrounded by the appropriate procedural safeguards. For example, absent a showing of a compelling need, a state could not force a person to undergo surgery to produce a bullet that might be useful evidence to prove his or her guilt, no matter how careful the procedures it used or how many warrants it obtained.[4] For the most part, however, the issues are those of procedure.

Police Detentions and Arrests

The Fourth Amendment protects both people and their property. People have somewhat less protection from searches and seizures than does their property. Although police have no general right to stop people, not all police stops are subject to the Fourth Amendment; in other words, the Fourth Amendment does not require police to have a justification to approach persons just to ask them questions. It is difficult to draw the line between police questioning of someone who consents to respond, which does not raise Fourth Amendment issues, and police constraint, which brings the Fourth Amendment into play. If all that happens is that the police ask questions in a noncoercive atmosphere, there is no detention. But if the person refuses to answer and the police take additional steps to obtain an answer, then the Fourth Amendment applies. (So does the Fifth Amendment's protection against self-incrimination, and so may the Sixth Amendment's right to counsel, see pages 186 — 210). Or if, by means of physical force or a show of authority, police restrain the movement of people, even though there is no arrest, the Fourth Amendment comes into play. (The Supreme Court, in an opinion with Fourth Amendment overtones, declared unconstitutional for vagueness an ordinance giving police authority to ask persons who loiter or wander the streets to give "credible and reliable" identification and to account for their presence.)[5] Here are a few examples of the application of these generalizations: There was no constitutional violation when officers approached a person in an airport and requested identification and the person responded. The situation was not considered a detention. But when the police asked another person if he would consent to a search of his suitcases, and took him to a small room for the search, their actions created an in-custody detention, which requires police to have some objective justification beyond a mere suspicion.[6]

In one of the more controversial decisions of recent terms, the Court in *INS* v *Delgado* gave a green light to the Immigration and Naturalization Service's use of "factory sweeps" to catch illegal aliens. The INS, either with the employer's consent or with a broadly worded search warrant, sends its agents into factories where it thinks illegal aliens may be working and has the agents question all the workers about their citizenship. Having INS agents posted at the exits, said Justice Rehnquist for the majority, did not turn the encounter into a detention. It was merely a classic case of a consensual encounter between individuals and officials.[7] Justice Brennan in his dissent wrote, "It is simply fantastic to conclude that a reasonable person could ignore all that was occurring throughout the factory and have the temerity to believe that he was at liberty to refuse to answer the questions and walk away."[8]

Police may make arrests only when they have "probable cause" (see the second part of this amendment, and the discussion concerning it). Persons found in public places may be detained without probable cause, however, in investigatory stops called Terry stops, after the case for which this exception was first elaborated, *Terry* v *Ohio* (see page 172).[9] Police may make such investigatory stops if they have "some objective manifestation that the person stopped is or is about to be engaged in criminal activity, or that there is reasonable grounds to believe the person is wanted for past criminal conduct."[10] Such investigatory stops cannot continue indefinitely, but the Court has refused to set a time limit. Rather, the test is "whether the police diligently pursued a means of investigation that was likely to confirm or dispel their suspicions quickly." During an investigatory stop, the police may also fingerprint persons "if there is a reasonable suspicion that the suspect has committed a criminal act, if there is a reasonable basis for believing that fingerprinting will establish or eliminate the suspect's connection with the crime, and if the procedure is carried out with dispatch."[11]

The Fourth Amendment clearly covers arrests in which police take people into custody and book them for a crime. For such an arrest, the police must have either an arrest warrant or probable cause to believe that the person has committed a crime. Sometimes the police lack probable cause to make an arrest but have the objective justification to detain a person for questioning and, as a result of the interrogation (but see page 172 for ground rules that apply to such interrogations), get the evidence they need to justify a probable-cause arrest.

Without some exigent circumstance — as when somebody's life is in danger, evidence is about to be destroyed, or the police are in hot pursuit of a person seen committing a *serious* crime — police may arrest without warrant on probable cause only in *public places*, not in a person's home.[12] "Police bear a heavy burden when attempting to demonstrate an urgent need that might justify warrantless searches or arrests in a private home. [Moreover] . . . application of the exigent-circumstances exception in the context of a home entry should rarely be sanctioned when there is probable cause to believe that only a minor offense . . . has been committed."[13]

An arrest may sometimes be justified on the basis of a *search* warrant: a warrant to search for contraband carries with it authority to detain the occupants of the premises while the search is conducted, and if the search uncovers evidence that establishes probable cause to arrest the persons found on the premises, their initial detention does not violate the Fourth Amendment.[14] (A search warrant for particular items in a particular place permits this detention of the persons found there; it does not permit their personal search, except to ensure they do not have dangerous weapons. However, if the search uncovers evidence justifying their arrest on probable cause, then they can be searched to the same extent as if they had been arrested with a warrant.)

The Fourth Amendment not only limits when police may seize people, it also limits *how* they may do so. Under the common law, police could use whatever force was necessary to effect the arrest of a fleeing felon, though not of a misdemeanant. Not so under the Fourth Amendment. A police officer may not seize an unarmed, nondangerous suspect "by shooting him dead," as Justice White rather bluntly put it for the Court.[15] Deadly force may be used only when the officer has probable cause to believe that the suspect poses a threat of serious physical harm, either to the officer or to others. Thus, if a suspect threatens the officer with a weapon or there is probable cause to believe that the suspect has committed a crime involving the infliction or threatened infliction of serious physical harm, and after, where feasible, some warning has been given, then, and only then, the officer may use a weapon that could kill to prevent the escape of the fleeing and dangerous felon.

Police Searches

In contrast to seizures or arrest of persons, what about searches of persons and of their property? "It is a cardinal principle that searches conducted outside the judicial process, without prior approval by a judge or a magistrate, are per se unreasonable under the Fourth Amendment — subject only to a few specifically established and well-delineated exceptions."[16] In fact, however, the number of exceptions keeps growing, and they are not so well delineated.

First, there are a variety of searches by government agents not designed to uncover crimes. Such searches are discussed later. Here we concentrate on exceptions for searches by law enforcement officers. Furthermore, not all inspections are searches. "A truly cursory inspection — one that involves merely looking at what is already exposed to view, without disturbing it — is not a 'search' for Fourth Amendment purposes."[17] Thus, police committed no violation when, without warrant or probable cause, they merely recorded the serial numbers of some stereo equipment. (They did commit a violation, however, when they picked up the equipment, for that action was a search.)[18]

Where the Amendment applies, the exceptions to warrantless searches and seizures by police and customs officials are as follows:

1.   The automobile exception: "The law of search and seizure with respect to automobiles is intolerably confusing. The Court apparently cannot agree even on what it has held previously, let alone on how these cases should be decided."[19] The exception is justified in part because of the mobility of automobiles and in part because persons are not entitled to the same expectations of privacy in their automobiles as in their homes or other places. Police have no general right to stop automobiles or to search the occupants of an automobile. But if officers have probable cause to believe that an automobile is being used to commit a crime, even a traffic offense, or that it contains persons who have committed crimes or that it contains evidence of crimes or contraband, they may stop the automobile, detain the persons found therein, and search them and any containers or packages found inside the car.[20] Officers may conduct a warrantless search of the vehicle even after it has been impounded and is in police custody.[21] The police are not free to roam at will and search things and persons found inside automobiles, but if they have probable cause that would justify the issuing of a warrant, they may engage in such an automobile search without first securing a warrant from a magistrate. For example, if the police have probable cause to think that an automobile contains contraband, they may make a warrantless search of the car and its trunk for that contraband. They may not search the trunk of that car for undocumented aliens. (But if they find undocumented aliens, they may arrest them.) "The scope of a warrantless search of an automobile thus is defined . . . by the object of the search and the places in which there is probable cause to believe that it may be found."[22] The automobile exception applies to fully mobile motor homes in public places,[23] but probably not to trailers on private land.

2.   As noted, officers may make *Terry* stops, brief investigatory stops, which were first justified only when officers had reason to believe they were dealing with armed and dangerous persons but have subsequently been expanded to cover

stops when the police have reason to believe that a person has committed or is about to commit a criminal offense. During such *Terry* stops, police may make *Terry* searches. Such a search must be limited to a quick pat-down to check for weapons that might be used to assault the arresting officer, to check for contraband, to determine identity, or to maintain briefly the status quo while obtaining more information.[24]

3. Officers may make a *Terry* stop and search when they have "reasonable suspicion, grounded in specific and articulable facts, that the person in question was involved in or is wanted in connection with a felony."[25] To illustrate, if the police have a "wanted" flier making it clear that the police department issuing it possessed a reasonable suspicion that the person in question had committed a felony, police may make a *Terry* search even without a warrant or probable cause to arrest.

4. If an officer, under exception 2, stops and frisks a suspect to look for weapons but instead finds criminal evidence that might justify an arrest, then under exception 3 the officer can make a full search. To illustrate: An officer, acting on an informer's tip, approached a man sitting in a car. The officer ordered the suspect to get out of the car, but the suspect merely rolled down the window. The officer saw a bulge on the suspect's waistband. He reached over and into the car and removed a gun from the suspect's waistband. The officer arrested the suspect, although the mere possession of a weapon was not a crime, made a search, and found heroin. Justice Rehnquist, speaking for the Court, said, "The Fourth Amendment does not require a policeman who lacks the precise level of information necessary for probable cause to arrest to simply shrug his shoulders and allow a crime to occur or a criminal to escape." The dissenting justices argued that the majority had ignored the fact that the stop-and-frisk exception to the warrant requirement had been begrudgingly granted only to protect the safety of officers of the law.[26]

5. When making a lawful arrest, either with an arrest warrant or because of probable cause, police may make a warrantless full search of the persons involved, the areas under their immediate control, and all the possessions they take with them to the place of detention.[27]

6. Inventory searches that are part of the routine procedures incident to incarceration of an arrested person are acceptable. These include searches of articles in the possession of the person being arrested, including his or her car and items in the car.[28]

7. When there is probable cause to make an arrest, even if one is not made, limited searches are permitted if necessary to preserve easily-disposed-of evidence, such as scrapings under fingernails.[29]

8. Searches based on voluntary consent are allowed even if the persons who give the consent are not told they have a right to refuse to grant permission.[30]

9. Searches of persons and the goods they bring with them are permissible, under customs and immigration laws, at border crossings.[31] The border search exception also permits officials to open mail entering the country if they have "reasonable cause" to suspect it contains merchandise imported contrary to the law.[32] (The border search exception does not extend to searches by Puerto Rican authorities of persons coming from the continental United States; such persons are not making an international crossing.)[33]

10. The plain-view exception permits officers to search and seize evidence if (1) they are lawfully in a position from which the evidence can be viewed, (2) it is immediately apparent to them that the items they observe are evidence of a crime or are contraband, (3) they discover the evidence "inadvertently" (they may not rely on the plain-view exception as a pretext),[34] and (4) they have probable cause — a reasonable suspicion will not do — that the evidence uncovered is contraband or evidence of a crime.[35]

11. Searches and seizures are permissible under "exigent circumstances," that is, when officers do not have time to secure a warrant before evidence is destroyed or a criminal escapes capture or when there is need "to protect or preserve life or avoid serious injury."[36] Here are some examples of exigent circumstances: Firefighters and police may enter a burning building without a warrant and may remain there for a reasonable time to investigate the cause of the blaze after the fire has been extinguished. However, after the fire has been put out, the emergency is not to be used as an excuse to make an exhaustive, warrantless search for evidence not in plain sight. Police may enter a building in hot pursuit of a fleeing felon or in search of immediate aid needed to save life or to avoid injury and may seize any evidence that is in plain view during the course of their legitimate emergency activities. They may make a prompt warrantless search of an area where, they have reason to believe, a person has been injured or murdered, to see if there are other victims or if a killer is still on the premises.[37] For other than capital crimes, as we have noted, the circumstances justifying a warrantless search of a home must really be urgent and the crime involved must be serious. Films, books and other materials that might be protected by the First Amendment may be seized under the exigent-circumstances exception only if copies of the seized materials are left.

Premises and Persons Protected

The premises and things protected against warrantless police searches include all places where a person has a legitimate expectation of privacy, including hotel rooms, rented homes, apartments of friends, first class mails, offices, desks, and file cabinets at places of work of both private and government employees, and even telephone booths. The Amendment does not, however, cover all places where one has a legitimate right to be; it covers only those where one has legitimate expectations of privacy, "those expectations that society is prepared to recognize as reasonable."[38]

In other words, first, a person has to make clear that he or she has an expectation of privacy, and second, the Supreme Court has to decide that society is willing to recognize that expectation as reasonable.[39] Since no one has a legitimate expectation of privacy in the glove compartment of a car in which one is merely a passenger, or in the numbers one dials into a telephone system, evidence taken from such places can be used even if taken without a warrant.[40] Prisoners have no reasonable expectation of privacy in their cells.[41] Nor may a shopkeeper successfully raise constitutional objections if he offers to sell books and magazines and they are purchased by police officers and used as evidence in a prosecution for the distribution of obscene literature.[42]

In addition, only those whose rights are directly violated have standing to challenge an improper search. One Jack Payner discovered this fact, to his unhappiness. Payner was brought to trial because Internal Revenue Agents had found incriminating evidence against him in his banker's briefcase. The agents had used a female private investigator to lure Payner's banker out to dinner. During the dinner the agents had swiped the briefcase from his apartment, copied documents found in it, and then returned it to the apartment. Federal courts found the agents had knowingly and willfully violated the Fourth Amendment rights of the banker but that Payner had no expectations of privacy in his banker's briefcase. Since Payner's rights had not been violated, evidence taken in the briefcase caper could be used against him.[43]

The Fourth Amendment does not protect open fields. Such fields may be searched by police officers without warrants or probable cause.[44] The amendment does apply, however, to a *curtilage*, the common-law term for the land immediately surrounding and associated with a home. In determining the dividing line between curtilage and open fields, the centrally relevant consideration is "whether the area in question is so intimately tied to the home itself that it should be placed under the home's 'umbrella' of Fourth Amendment protection."[45] This question is to be resolved with reference to four factors: the proximity to the home of the area claimed to be curtilage, inclusion of the area within an enclosure surrounding the home, the nature of the uses to which the area is put, and the steps taken by the resident to protect the area from observation by people passing by. Applying these factors the Court apparently has concluded that most barns on most farms most of the time are not part of the curtilage.[46]

As aerial surveillance and satellite technology become more sophisticated, judges are once again being asked to apply the principles of the Fourth Amendment to the electronic age. The Court ruled that there was no violation of the Amendment when police officers rented an airplane to fly within 1,000 feet above the backyard of a person suspected of growing marijuana. Said the majority, "The Fourth Amendment simply does not require the police traveling in the public airways at this altitude to obtain a warrant in order to observe what is visible to the naked eye."[47] A closely divided Court also held that the Fourth Amendment did not prevent the Environmental Protection Agency from using aerial photography to observe Dow Chemical Company's compliance with the antipollution laws. However, the Court made quite clear that if government agents, going beyond mere eyeballing or the use of conventional cameras commonly used in mapmaking, use "highly sophisticated surveillance equipment not generally available to the public, such as satellite technology," the use of such equipment might well be constitutionally proscribed, absent a warrant.[48] In other words, flying over and taking pictures of people's backyards or of industrial plants presents a different constitutional issue from using aerial observation and modern technology to disclose to the police "those intimate associations, objects or activities otherwise imperceptible to police or fellow citizens."[49]

Searches by Authorities Other than the Police

The Fourth Amendment protects commercial buildings as well as homes, covers civil as well as criminal investigations, and includes searches by government officers other than the police, such as internal revenue agents, probation officers, health inspectors, occupational and safety inspectors, and public school teachers and administrators. But the standards for such administrative searches are much less stringent than those for police searches. When a warrant is constitutionally required for police officers, it may not be issued except as the Constitution stipulates (see page 177). But searches by other officials may take place without warrant or probable cause if they are under "reasonable" regulations.[50]

Take public elementary and secondary school officials. They need not obtain a warrant before searching a student, nor must they have probable cause to believe that the student has violated or is violating a law. Rather, a search by school officials is justified if there are reasonable grounds for suspecting that it will turn up evidence that the student has violated or is violating either the law or a rule of the school and if the search is reasonably related to its objectives and is not excessively intrusive in light of the age and sex of the student and the nature of the infraction.

The Fourth Amendment applies to supervisors of government employees, but a search of offices for noninvestigatory work-related purposes or an investigatory search for evidence of suspected work-related employee misconduct does not require a warrant or probable cause.[51] It is judged merely by the standard of reasonableness. Justice Blackmun, dissenting from this view, was so incensed that he accused the plurality, whose opinion had been penned by Justice O'Connor, of being motivated by a dislike for public employees.[52]

Health, building, and safety inspectors must secure a warrant before they may enter a home or most businesses if the occupants refuse to give them entry.[53] However, in such instances an *administrative search warrant,* rather than a criminal search warrant is all that is required. Inspectors do not have to prove to a magistrate that they have probable cause to believe that violations are taking place; they must prove merely that an inspection is authorized by law, that it is based on a general administrative plan for the enforcement of the law, and that they are acting reasonably to enforce it.

Warrantless searches are permitted for a few kinds of business. First, such searches are permitted for industries "that have such a history of governmental oversight that no reasonable expectation of privacy . . . could exist for a proprietor over the stock of such an enterprise." Liquor and firearms are industries of this type. When entrepreneurs embark on such businesses, they have voluntarily chosen to subject themselves to a full arsenal of governmental regulation.[54] Second, although governments cannot authorize warrantless inspections of all businesses, they may do so for specific businesses when they "reasonably" determine that warrantless searches are necessary to further a regulatory scheme and when the regulatory presence is so comprehensive and so well defined that the owner of the commercial property cannot help being aware that the property will be subject to periodic inspections undertaken for specific purposes. Mines and car junkyards are examples of such pervasively regulated industries. Warrantless inspections, however, even in the context of pervasively regulated businesses, will be deemed to be reasonable only so long as (1) there is a substantial government interest, (2) the warrantless inspections are necessary to further the regulatory scheme, and (3) the regulatory statute performs the functions of a warrant by advising the owner that the search is being made pursuant to the law and by carefully limiting the search in time, place, and scope. Thus, Congress may constitutionally authorize warrantless inspections of the nation's underground and surface mines, and a state may regulate car junkyards even to the extent of allowing police to make warrantless inspections that lead to arrests for criminal violations.[55]

[continued] and no Warrants shall issue, but upon probable cause, supported by Oath or affirmation, and particularly describing the place to be searched, and the persons or things to be seized.

"Our constitutional fathers were not concerned about warrantless searches, but about overreaching warrants. It is perhaps too much to say that they feared the warrant more than the search, but it is plain enough that the warrant was the prime object of their concern."[56] "Since the general warrant, not the warrantless search, was the immediate evil at which the Fourth Amendment was directed, it is not surprising that the Framers placed precise limits on its issuance. The requirement that a warrant only issue on showing of a particular probable cause was the means adopted to circumscribe the warrant power."[57]

When a search warrant is required, a magistrate — a judicial officer — or a clerk of a court who may serve as a neutral judicial officer for such purpose must grant it. Police must appear before such a magistrate and, under oath, indicate they have "probable cause" to believe the search will produce criminal evidence. If it subsequently appears that the police knowingly or recklessly made a false statement to the magistrate, the evidence obtained by the search cannot be used (see the material, later in this section, on the exclusionary rule).[58] The magistrate need not be a legally trained judge, but a prosecutor or a state's attorney will not do, nor will justices of the peace who receive a fee if they issue a warrant but no fee if they refuse to do so.[59]

The magistrate must "perform his 'neutral and detached' function and not serve merely as a rubber stamp for the police."[60] Thus, it was impermissible for a town justice to issue an open-ended search warrant and then go along with the police on a raid of an adult bookstore in which the justice made an on-the-spot decision about which items should be included in the warrant and which excluded. The fact that the judge visited the scene was not the problem: He acted not as a judicial officer, but as an adjunct law enforcement officer. "He did not manifest that neutrality and detachment demanded of a judicial officer."[61]

The "probable cause" that justifies the issuance of a warrant is hard to define; it is a "fluid concept." It requires, however, that a magistrate be able reasonably to conclude, based on the totality of the circumstances, that there is a substantial basis for believing that a search will uncover evidence of wrongdoing.[62] "The task of the issuing magistrate is simply to make a practical, common-sense decision whether, given all the circumstances set forth in the affidavit before him, . . . there is a fair probability that contraband or evidence of a crime will be found in a particular place. And the duty of a reviewing court is simply to ensure that the magistrate had a 'substantial basis for . . . conclud[ing]' that probable cause existed."[63]

The warrant the magistrate issues must specify the places to be searched and the things to be seized. A blanket authorization to search indiscriminately is a *general search warrant* and violates the Constitution. A warrant to search a public place, such a tavern, does not authorize a warrantless search of customers in the place.[64]

A magistrate may issue a warrant to enter any place if the police demonstrate to the magistrate's satisfaction that there is evidence of a crime in that place. That the place is owned by an innocent party or that the person in possession of the things to be searched is not suspected of any law violations makes no constitutional difference.[65] Once a valid search warrant has been obtained, the Fourth Amendment does not prohibit police from using force or stealth to execute the search warrant if that is the only way the a warrant can be effectively executed. When there is a warrant to engage in electronic surveillance, a separate warrant to enter the premises to install the device is not needed and the installation may be done by stealth. In some circumstances, with a warrant, police may break down a door and enter a place.

Suppose the police have probable cause to believe that a person's body contains evidence of a crime. May they make an appropriate intrusion if they have a warrant? May they do so without a warrant? The Amendment protects people "in their persons" as well as in their "houses, papers, and effects." Ultimately, judges must decide if such an intrusion is "reasonable."[66] On one side, the Court has held reasonable the compelled taking of blood from a person who the police have probable cause to believe is guilty of drunken driving. On the other side, as we have noted, to compel a person to submit to surgical removal of a bullet from his or her chest, even with proper warrants and judicial orders, is an unreasonable search.[67]

Electronic Searches

The inventions of science have confronted judges with novel problems in applying the prohibitions against unreasonable searches and seizures. Obviously, the framers of the Fourth Amendment had in mind physical objects such as books, papers, letters, other kinds of written documents, weapons, and other physical evidence. But what of tapping phone wires or using electronic devices to eavesdrop? In *Olmstead* v *United States*, decided in 1928, a bare majority of the Supreme Court held that there was no unconstitutional search unless there was seizure of physical objects or an actual physical entry into a place. Justices Holmes and Brandeis, in dissent, argued that the Constitution should be kept up with the times; the "dirty business" of wiretapping produced the same evil invasions of privacy that the framers had in mind when they wrote the Fourth Amendment.[68]

Forty years later, in *Katz* v *United States*, the Supreme Court adopted the Holmes-Brandeis position: "The Fourth Amendment protects people — and not simply 'areas' — against unreasonable searches and seizures." The use by police officers of electronic devices to overhear a conversation in a public telephone booth is a search and seizure within the meaning of the Constitution. "Wherever a man may be [*since modified to* wherever a person has a legitimate expectation of privacy], he is entitled to know that he will remain free from unreasonable searches and seizures."[69]

After conversations became constitutionally protected, legislatures and judges had to develop rules for the conditions under which conversations would be allowed to be intercepted. The basic federal legislation is contained in the Crime Control and Safe Streets Act of 1968, which makes it a crime for any unauthorized person to tap telephone wires or use or sell electronic bugging devices in interstate commerce. Yet the act authorizes the attorney general to secure permission for federal agents to engage in bugging by applying for a warrant from a federal judge. The attorney general must authorize the wiretapping personally or through an assistant specifically designated for that purpose.[70] At the state level, the act authorizes the principal prosecuting attorney of any state or its political subdivision to apply to a state judge for a warrant approving wiretapping or mechanical devices for felonies.

Judges are to issue warrants only if they decide that probable cause exists that a crime is being, has been, or is about to be committed and that information relating to that crime may be obtained only by the intercept. In addition to intercepts under warrant, the act permits police officers to act without a warrant for forty-eight hours in "an emergency situation relating to conspiratorial activities threatening the national security" or involving organized crime.

The Crime Control Act of 1968 specifically left undisturbed whatever constitutional authority the president might have to authorize, without securing a warrant, bugging and tapping to protect our national security. But the Supreme Court has held that the president's authority to act to protect the nation against foreign attack and violent overthrow does not include the right, without judicial warrant, to authorize electronic surveillance of persons suspected of *domestic* subversion. Justice Powell, speaking for the Court, said, "The danger to political dissent is acute where the government attempts to act under so vague a concept as the power to protect domestic security."[71] The Court pointedly did not rule on the scope of the president's authority to authorize surveillance of foreign agents inside or outside the country.

In 1978, by the Foreign Intelligence Surveillance Act, Congress forbade all officials except those of the National Security Agency — the agency in charge of making and breaking codes — to bug foreign agents, except with a warrant from the United States Foreign Intelligence Surveillance Court. This court, consisting of seven designated federal district judges, grants secret warrants permitting the bugging of foreign agents.

It needs to be noted that as long as the police make no illegal entries and do not violate the laws by using illegal electronic devices, neither the Constitution nor any federal law requires police officers to secure warrants before they resort to undercover tactics, including the use of secret cameras or recording devices on their persons or on undercover agents. Police may use the devices of science to extend the range of their "eavesdropping" by expanding what they can hear, see, film, record, or smell. These "modern devices" include dogs trained to sniff luggage and detect the presence of drugs.[72]

One must choose one's friends with care, for there is no violation of the Constitution if one tells a friend a secret and the friend in turn informs the police. Except inside your own home, and not always even then, if your "friend" is wired for sound so that what you say is transmitted back to police officers, there is no constitutional violation. Similarly, police may listen in on a telephone conversation over an extension phone with the consent of one of the parties to the conversation but without the knowledge of the other.[73]

The Court upheld the warrantless installation of an electronic tracking device, a beeper, inside a container of chemicals being transported in an automobile when it revealed no information that could not have been obtained through visual surveillance.[74] However, the Court is beginning to show some concern about the warrantless use of these electronic devices when they are smuggled inside a person's home, where there is the greatest expectation of privacy.[75]

The Exclusionary Rule

How to enforce the Fourth Amendment? Officers who engage in unreasonable searches and seizures are, under most circumstances, guilty of violating the criminal laws.[76] They can also be sued for civil damages by those whose rights have been violated, and the governments that employ them can also be sued. Victims of unreasonable searches, however, are often poor and lack the knowledge about this right. They are seldom in a position to sue the police. Police and prosecutors are seldom likely to move against fellow officers for engaging in unlawful searches.

To enforce the Fourth Amendment, we rely on the exclusionary rule.[77] (It is also used to enforce the Fifth and Sixth Amendments.) Under this rule, evidence obtained in an improper fashion, that is, in violation of the Constitution or of statute, cannot be introduced against those whose Fourth Amendment rights have been violated. By excluding such evidence, judges hope to deter officers from violating the Fourth (or Fifth or Sixth) Amendment.

There have always been critics of the exclusionary rule. "Why," they quote Justice Cardozo, should the criminal "go free because the constable has blundered?"[78] They argue that the rule is ineffective, that there are more desirable ways to prevent police misconduct, that it keeps relevant and reliable evidence from the trier of the facts, and that it deflects the search for the truth. Defenders of the rule respond that not only does the exclusionary rule have a deterrent effect on police misconduct, but judges, who are also agents of the government, should have no part in violating the Fourth Amendment.[79]

In 1971 the Court began to back away from the full sweep of the exclusionary rule. In *New York* v *Harris* it allowed unconstitutionally obtained evidence to be used to contradict a defendant's testimony and to challenge credibility.[80] As already noted, in *Stone* v *Powell* the Supreme Court told federal district judges that if the constitutionality of the way evidence was secured had been reviewed by state courts, prisoners should not be allowed to use habeas corpus petitions to get another review of these same questions by federal judges.[81]

The major exception to the exclusionary rule is the "objective good faith" one. For years some members of the Court, as well as many outside, have urged the Court to make a good faith exception that would "not require the exclusion of evidence obtained by the police in a reasonable belief that they have obtained it in a constitutional manner."[82] The Court has not gone that far — yet. It has ruled, however, that if a police officer has obtained a search warrant from a magistrate who acted in the proper neutral and detached way, evidence so obtained should not be excluded, even if it subsequently is established that the magistrate lacked probable cause to issue the warrant (*United States* v *Leon*)[83] or if it turns out that the warrant was defective (*Massachusetts* v *Sheppard*).[84] This does not mean that evidence may be used if the police obtained the warrant by knowingly or recklessly submitting false information or if they acted on a warrant that they knew to be improperly issued. The police officers' belief in the validity of the warrant must be "objectively reasonable. An officer's subjective belief, based on ignorance of constitutional requirements, will not protect an invalid warrant." The Court left for another day the question whether the good faith exception would apply to good faith warrantless searches. Cases raising those issues are working their way to the Supreme Court.

Justice Stevens, who, along with Justices Brennan and Marshall, continues to champion the exclusionary rule, vigorously opposed the Court's good faith exception for searches for which police have obtained warrants. He wrote a long and especially bitter dissent, charging that the Court, in effect, had converted the "Bill of Rights into an unenforced honor code that the police may follow in their discretion. The Constitution requires more; it requires a remedy. If the Court's new rule is to be followed, the Bill of Rights should be renamed.[85] He accused his colleagues of having "acquired a voracious appetite for judicial activism in [their] Fourth Amendment jurisprudence, at least when it comes to restricting the constitutional rights of the citizen."[86]

By five to four, the Court has extended the exception to cases in which officers have acted in objectively reasonable reliance on a statute authorizing warrantless administrative searches and the statute is ultimately found to violate the Fourth Amendment. Justice Blackmun for the Court wrote, "A statute cannot support objectively reasonable reliance if, in passing the statute, the legislature wholly abandoned its responsibility to enact constitutional laws. Nor can a law enforcement officer be said to have acted in good-faith reliance upon a statute if its provisions are such that a reasonable officer should have known that the statute was unconstitutional."[87] The exception is not likely to be very significant, since it will apply only to searches occurring before the declaration by a court of the unconstitutionality of such a particular law authorizing administrative searches. It is not likely that there will be many examples of legislative bodies wholly abandoning responsibilities to enact constitutional laws. One also wonders if we really want law enforcement officers to decide for themselves which laws are unconstitutional and thus not to be relied on for the purposes of making administrative searches.

The exclusionary rule does not apply to a grand jury. Such a jury may not instruct its agents to violate the Fourth Amendment and may not issue subpoenas that do, but if illegally procured evidence becomes available to a grand jury, the jury may consider it, even though the evidence may not be used in a subsequent criminal trial.[88] Nor does the exclusionary rule apply to civil proceedings, not even to deportation proceedings to determine eligibility to remain in this country.[89]

AMENDMENT V: GRAND JURIES, DOUBLE JEOPARDY, SELF-INCRIMINATION, DUE PROCESS, AND EMINENT DOMAIN

No person shall be held to answer for a capital, or otherwise infamous crime, unless on a presentment or indictment of a Grand Jury,

---

The Fifth Amendment introduces us to the oldest institution known to the Constitution, the grand jury. It hails from the days of William the Conqueror; the trial, or *petit* (also spelled *petty*) jury, is an offshoot of it (see the Sixth Amendment). Like its English forerunner, the federal grand jury is composed of not more than twenty-three members, of whom any twelve are sufficient to make a *presentment* or return an *indictment* — that is, to accuse some person or persons of an offense against the laws of the United States, on the basis either of evidence gathered by the grand jury itself or of evidence laid before it by a prosecuting officer. Since the "accused" is not being tried, the grand jury's proceedings are secret and one-sided (*ex parte*), only the government being represented. Although persons brought before grand juries have no right to have attorneys with them in the grand jury room, the federal government permits such persons to consult with their lawyers anytime they wish in adjacent quarters.

Grand juries, like all other juries, must be selected without respect to race, sex, or ethnic origin. To discriminate violates the constitutional rights of those who are indicted, as well as the rights of any person who might be denied the opportunity to serve on a grand jury. Systematic discrimination in selection of grand jurors requires reversal of a conviction based on an indictment brought by such a jury. The Supreme Court concluded, however, that reversing the conviction and dismissing the indictment was inappropriate in a case in which the grand jury had been presided over by a foreman alleged to have been selected in a discriminatory fashion. The office of grand jury foreman, unlike the grand jury, is not established by the Constitution and "the ministerial role is not such a vital one that discrimination in the appointment of an individual to that post significantly invades the distinctive interests of the defendant protected by the due process clause."[1]

After an indictment has been returned, it may not be broadened except by the grand jury itself. Any conviction of a defendant for an offense different from those included in the indictment violates the Fifth Amendment. However, "As long as the crime and the elements of the offense that sustain the conviction are fully and clearly set out in the indictment, the right to a grand jury is not normally violated by the fact that the indictment alleges more crimes or other means of committing the same crime."[2]

Indictment by grand jury is the one provision of the Bill of Rights relating to criminal prosecutions that the Supreme Court has not construed to be within the scope of the due process clause of the Fourteenth Amendment. States are, therefore, free to indict by other means, and they have been using the grand jury less and less. At the moment, only twenty-two states require grand jury indictments; three require it only when the crime is punishable by death or life imprisonment. In the others, the prosecuting attorney simply files an *information*, an affidavit that there is evidence available to justify a trial.[3] (To hold a person in custody, however, the prosecutor's information must be followed by a hearing before a magistrate for presentation of evidence showing probable cause.[4])

---

except in cases arising in the land or naval forces, or in the Militia, when in actual service in time of War or public danger;

The significance of this exception goes far beyond merely dispensing with grand jury indictments for persons in the armed forces. This clause, along with Article I, Section 8, giving Congress the power to make "rules for the Government and Regulation of the land and naval Forces;" means that persons subject to trial before military courts are not entitled to the same procedural rights as are civilians.

What persons are subject to trial before military courts? Since 1960 only members of the armed forces have been subject to military trials, and from 1969 to 1987, only for service-connected crimes. In 1987 the Court reversed a 1969 precedent and held that jurisdiction of military tribunals extends to members of the armed services for crimes committed during their military service, whether or not the crimes are service connected.[5] Military jurisdiction does not extend to civilian employees of the armed forces, here or overseas, nor to civilian dependents of military personnel, including those who accompany a member of the armed forces overseas.[6] Nor may persons be tried by the military after they have been discharged, even for crimes committed while they were in the service.[7]

Congress has created a Uniform Code of Military Justice and established a Court of Military Appeals, the so-called GI Supreme Court. That court has extended to armed forces personnel the right to a speedy trial, the right to confront witnesses, the right to protection against unreasonable searches and seizures, the privilege against self-incrimination, the right to public trial, the right to compulsory service of process, and the right to *Miranda*-like warnings (see page 189). Persons within the armed forces ordinarily must exhaust their military appeals from court-martial through the Court of Military Appeals before federal courts will interfere.[8]

---

nor shall any person be subject for the same offense to be twice put in jeopardy of life or limb;

This provision is now extended to the states by means of the Fourteenth Amendment.[9] Although the constitutional language "jeopardy of life or limb" suggests proceedings in which only the most serious penalties can be imposed, "the clause has long been construed to mean something far broader than its literal language."[10] The guarantee consists of three separate constitutional protections. "It protects against a second prosecution for the same offense after acquittal. It protects against a second prosecution for the same offense after conviction. And it protects against multiple punishments for the same offense."[11] The problem with this often-quoted statement, as Justice Rehnquist has pointed out, is that "same offense" is "a phrase deceptively simple in appearance but virtually kaleidoscopic in application."[12]

"Historians have traced the origins of our constitutional guarantee against double jeopardy back to the days of Demosthenes. . . . Despite its roots in antiquity, however, this guarantee seems both one of the least understood and, in recent years, one of the most frequently litigated provisions of the Bill of Rights."[13] Since 1971, when Congress authorized government appeals in all criminal prosecutions except when banned by the double jeopardy clause, the Supreme Court, in a series of confusing decisions, has tried, without much success, to "create order and understanding" about the meaning of double jeopardy. Here is what the Court seems to be saying:

Jeopardy attaches in both national and state jury trials as soon as the jury has been sworn in and, in nonjury trials, as soon as the judge begins to hear the evidence.[14] (In contrast, common law and current English interpretation restrict the limitations against double jeopardy to cases in which there has been a complete trial, ending in acquittal or conviction.)

If a trial ends in acquittal, the double jeopardy clause unequivocably bars reprosecution.[15]

If a trial ends with a guilty verdict, "the general rule is that the Clause does not bar reprosecution of a defendant whose conviction is overturned on appeal," or set aside by the judge.[16] But, if the verdict is set aside because it is based on insufficient evidence, it has the same effect as a judgment of acquittal, "because it means that no rational factfinder could have voted to convict the defendant."[17] However, if the verdict of guilty is set aside because of "the weight of the evidence," the state may reprosecute. Such a reversal does not mean that acquittal was the only proper verdict, but merely that the reviewing court sits as a "thirteenth juror" and disagrees with the jury's resolution of conflicting testimony. "This difference of opinion no more signifies acquittal than does a disagreement among the jurors themselves."[18]

If a trial terminates before a final verdict, the double jeopardy clause may or may not prevent retrial. It prevents retrial if an indictment is dismissed or the case is terminated because the evidence is insufficient to justify conviction. Such action is tantamount to an acquittal.[19] But most midtrial terminations are not likely to prevent reprosecution, despite the Court's generalization that once jeopardy attaches and a trial starts, a defendant is ordinarily entitled to have it run its course and not again to be placed in the agony of having to be retried. For the Court has a counter generalization: "The double jeopardy clause . . . does not offer a guaranty to the defendant that the State will vindicate its societal interest in the enforcement of the criminal laws in one proceeding."[20] Persons may be retried if the jury is unable to agree on a verdict (that is, if there is a *hung jury*); if, at the defendant's request, the judge terminates the proceedings because of the failure of the government to frame the indictment properly; or even if a prosecutor's action causes the judge to declare a mistrial, unless the "prosecutor's actions . . . were done in order to goad the defendant into requesting a mistrial."[21]

The Supreme Court sustained an act of Congress (an act of Congress has never been held to violate the double jeopardy clause) that permits the federal government to ask the court of appeals to review a sentence imposed by a district judge. Under such circumstances, the defendant is not placed in jeopardy again, but merely has to defend against an increase in the severity of the sentence imposed.[22]

A single act may violate several statutory provisions, but the double jeopardy clause prevents prosecution (but not punishment) for a single act separately under several laws or provisions of a law unless "each provision requires proof of a fact that the other does not"; this is the so-called *Blockburger* test.[23] Thus, prosecution for a greater, or more serious, offense may be precluded by prosecution for a "lesser included offense," and vice versa. To illustrate: After Nathaniel Brown's conviction by Ohio for joyriding — taking an automobile without the owner's consent — he could not be tried again for that same act under a different provision against auto theft — joyriding with intent to permanently deprive the owner of possession.[24] Such double jeopardy cases are "fact-bound": trial for a lesser offense does not always preclude trial for a more serious crime. For example, an initial prosecution for assault and battery did not bar a subsequent prosecution for homicide after the victim eventually died from the assault. And the federal government was allowed to prosecute Jonathan Garrett in federal court in Washington in March of 1981 for smuggling from Neah Bay 12,000 pounds of marijuana and, two months later, to prosecute him in federal court in Florida on the charge of engaging in a "continuing criminal enterprise," as a part of which the Neah Bay episode, along with many others, was cited.[25] In each of these cases, a majority of the justices was persuaded that Congress had intended the crimes to be two separate offenses and that the lesser crimes were not "lesser included offenses" in the sense forbidden by the double jeopardy clause.

Although the Court has steadfastly refused to adopt the single-transaction view of double jeopardy — that one robbery or one murder should be treated as one crime regardless of the number of laws broken — nonetheless, it is apparently more likely to bar prosecution for a lesser included offense when there is a single action involved — taking a car, for example — than where there is a continuing series of criminal offenses — being a ringleader in a continuing criminal enterprise.

The double jeopardy clause also prevented the reprosecution of a man named

Ashe after he had been tried and acquitted of participating with others in the armed robbery of one of six men who were playing poker. The acquittal was based chiefly on the matter of identification. Six weeks later Ashe was convicted of robbing another of the poker players. The Supreme Court set his conviction aside because he had already been tried for the offense of being one of the robbers of the poker players. Chief Justice Burger argued in dissent, "What the Court is holding, is, in effect, that the second and third and fourth criminal acts are 'free' unless the accused is tried for the multiple crimes in a single trial."[26]

Although conviction of a lesser offense probably precludes prosecution for the greater offense, the same is not true of a guilty plea to the lesser offense. After Thomas Hill was shot to death in his apartment, Kenneth Johnson was indicted for murder, involuntary manslaughter, aggravated robbery, and grand theft. His guilty pleas to the charges of manslaughter and grand theft were accepted by the court over the state's objection. Johnson then argued that it would be double jeopardy if the state were to prosecute him for murder. The Supreme Court rejected his contention: "The acceptance of a guilty plea to a lesser included offense while charges on the greater offense remain pending . . . has none of the implications of an 'implied acquittal' which results from a verdict convicting a defendant on lesser included offenses rendered by a jury charged to consider both greater and lesser included offenses."[27]

There is no double jeopardy in trying persons both for a substantive offense and for conspiring to commit that same offense.[28] And since "acquittal on criminal charges does not prove that the defendant is innocent; it merely proves the existence of a reasonable doubt as to his guilt," a civil action, which requires less proof, is permissible, provided the purpose of the civil action is remedial and not punitive.[29] Here are two examples: after a person was acquitted of smuggling, the government was allowed to seek forfeiture of the goods alleged to have been illegally brought into the country;[30] and after a person was acquitted of knowingly engaging in selling firearms without a license, the government was allowed to institute civil proceedings to force him to give up the weapons.[31]

The double jeopardy clause does prevent a government from trying delinquents for the same offense in the regular courts after trying them in juvenile courts.[32] (If, after a mere preliminary hearing on whether or not to try a person as a juvenile, a decision were made to transfer the case to adult court, there would not be double jeopardy.)

The double jeopardy clause prevents only trial by the *same government* for the same offense. It does not keep both national and state governments from trying a person for the same act if it violates the law of each government, even if the defendant is acquitted of the charge in the courts of the first government to bring him or her to trial.[33] It should be noted that, although prosecution for the same act by the national and state governments is not forbidden by the Constitution, in most instances federal policy precludes federal prosecution if there has been a previous state prosecution for the same act.[34] (Whenever federal civil rights violations are involved, the Department of Justice is more likely to reverse the presumption against federal prosecution.)

The double jeopardy clause does not bar prosecution of Indians both in tribal courts and in federal courts, since tribal courts, although their jurisdiction is subject to supervision by Congress, receive their jurisdiction from the tribes — independent sovereigns, at least for this purpose — and they are not arms of the federal government.[35] Nor does the clause prevent two or more states from trying a person for the same act.[36] In contrast, trial by both a state and one of its municipalities for the same act is double jeopardy:[37] municipal corporations are creatures of the state, and, constitutionally speaking, a city and its state are the same government. The same is true of the national government and a territorial government, and probably of the national government and the District of Columbia where the U.S. Attorney for the District of Columbia prosecutes both D.C. and federal crimes.

The double jeopardy clause does not apply to sentencing decisions with the same force that it applies to redeterminations of guilt or innocence. On the other hand, due process considerations are often brought to bear. On retrial, if the responsibility for setting a sentence is vested in a jury, a defendant may receive a more severe sentence than was received at the first trial. However, because of the due process clause, if a judge is responsible for the sentence, as is true in most jurisdictions, the judge may not ordinarily impose a harsher punishment than was given in the first trial. If the judge does so, he or she must justify such action in writing, or the reasons for doing so must be otherwise clear.[38] Moreover, a state cannot impose the death penalty on retrial if at the first trial the jury declined to do so, nor may a judge impose the death penalty on a person after the life sentence he or she had initially received has been set aside on appeal.[39]

The double jeopardy clause does not prohibit multiple punishments after a single trial for an act that is contrary to several statutes: "It does no more than prevent the sentencing court from prescribing greater punishment [under each statute] than the legislature intended."[40]

---

nor shall be compelled in any criminal case to be a witness against himself,

---

Originally construed to mean only that persons might not be forced to testify against themselves in criminal prosecutions, this provision has been broadened in a variety of highly significant ways. It is now included within the Fourteenth Amendment as a limitation on the states,[41] thereby permitting a person to claim the right in order to avoid the risk of criminal prosecution by either national or state authorities.[42]

Not only does the Constitution guarantee that people will not have to testify against themselves, but in recent decades it has also been construed to give criminal defendants the right to testify in their own behalf. This right is taken in part from the due process clause, but it also exists as a corollary to the privilege against compelled testimony.[43]

The privilege against self-incrimination is designed, not "to enhance the reliability of the fact-finding determination," but to prevent the use of evidence obtained in a manner "that offends an underlying principle in the enforcement of our criminal law: that ours is an accusatorial and not an inquisitorial system."[44] The individual has no responsibility whatsoever to prove innocence; the government has the full burden to demonstrate guilt. Persons are not entitled to refuse to answer questions merely because the answers might be embarrassing, lead to public ridicule, or incriminate others, but they are entitled to refuse to answer questions that may furnish the police with links to evidence that could result in their being prosecuted, even if the ultimate outcome would be acquittal.

If a government grants immunity from prosecution as broad as the protection provided by the self-incrimination clause, then a witness may be compelled to respond under pain of fine or imprisonment. Often the government would rather have the evidence than prosecute, and for many decades Congress authorized the granting of "transactional immunity," meaning that a person who was denied the right to claim self-incrimination and was compelled to testify could not be prosecuted for any transactions mentioned in the compelled testimony.

In 1970 Congress restricted the immunity. No longer does it grant immunity for any crimes mentioned. The immunity conferred only denies the government the right to use any information derived directly or indirectly from the compelled testimony. The Court has said this "use and derivate use immunity" is coextensive with the Fifth Amendment requirement and that, therefore, persons given "use and derivate use immunity" may not claim the privilege to refuse to answer incriminating questions. However, if they are subsequently prosecuted, the government has to prove that the evidence it proposes to use was derived from legitimate sources wholly independent of the compelled testimony.

Any testimony given under immunity, however, may be used in a prosecution for perjury. It may also be used in most civil suits.[45] Persons previously granted immunity from criminal prosecution may claim the Fifth Amendment right not to respond to incriminating questions in a civil deposition lest that testimony be used against them in a criminal prosecution.[46]

The privilege against self-incrimination protects a person, unless granted immunity, from being compelled to answer incriminating questions put by any government agency, for example, the Federal Trade Commission, if such answers could lead to criminal proceedings against that person. Furthermore, it provides some protection from complying with certain laws — specifically aimed tax laws, for example — when compliance would expose a person to "real and appreciable risk" of self-incrimination by furnishing evidence of illegal activities. For instance, professional gamblers cannot be made to pay a special excise tax on receipts from professional gambling if doing so would provide evidence of their illegal activity.[47] On the other hand, the self-incrimination clause does not prevent a state from requiring drivers involved in accidents to stop and notify the owner or person in charge of the property damaged of their name and address, since such a statute is more general and is not directly aimed at uncovering illegal action.[48]

The clause does not protect against future transgressions of the law; hence, Congress may require persons that sell or give certain kinds of firearms to file with federal authorities the names, addresses, and fingerprints of the transferees. The information provided cannot be used as evidence in a criminal proceeding for a prior or concurrent violation, but failure to file the information may be made a crime, such as the possession of an unregistered weapon.[49]

Nor does this clause, which is limited to criminal prosecutions, preclude Congress from requiring persons in charge of offshore facilities to report any discharge of oil into navigable waters and to pay a penalty for the discharge. Such action may also be a criminal offense, but since the penalty imposed is civil, it does not trigger the protections afforded by the Constitution to a criminal defendant.[50] (The statute provides some limited immunity in that the fact of notification of oil discharge cannot be used against the reporting person as evidence of other crimes.)

The privilege does not prevent the use of admissions made to examining psychiatrists in proceedings designed to determine whether persons are "sexually dangerous" and should be committed to institutions for treatment. This is true even though the commitment proceedings — in this particular instance, in Illinois — are triggered only after the state has brought criminal charges and even though confinement is in a maximum security institution run by the Illinois Department of Corrections. That the purpose is to treat rather than to punish or deter did not persuade a skeptical minority of four justices that this is a civil and not a criminal proceeding.[51]

The self-incrimination clause provides some protection for public employees, who cannot be fired merely for invoking the clause when questioned by their superiors. However, they may be dismissed if they refuse to answer questions directly relating to the performance of their official duties, provided they are not required to relinquish their constitutional immunity nor may such compelled evidence be used against them in subsequent criminal prosecutions. Similarly, unless they are given immunity, contractors may not be denied the right to do future business with a state merely because they have refused to testify before a grand jury about past contracts.[52]

The Supreme Court quickly disposed of the claim that the Solomon Amendment compels persons to testify against themselves. This provision requires men applying for federal student financial assistance to furnish proof that they have registered with the selective service system. It was argued that men who had not registered would be compelled to testify if they applied for such aid. Chief Justice Burger wrote for the Court, "a person who has not registered clearly is under no compulsion to seek financial aid."[53] Justices Marshall and Brennan, who dissented, felt that the problem was not that simple. Wrote Justice Marshall, "If appellees assert their Fifth Amendment privilege by their silence, they are penalized for exercising a constitutional right by the withholding of education aid. If they succumb to the economic coercion either by registering, or by registering but claiming the privilege as to particular disclosures, they have incriminated themselves."[54]

The protection against self-incrimination extends only to testimonial evidence. One cannot claim the right in order to refuse to submit handwriting samples, to give voice samples, to be fingerprinted, to appear in a police lineup, to submit to a breath test, or even to give a blood sample. Moreover, the mere fact that one refused to give fingerprints or submit to a breath test or give blood samples may be used as incriminating evidence in court.[55]

The self-incrimination clause, at least for the moment, also protects against subpoenas for one's *personal* books and papers in one's *own* possession. The important condition is that the material be personal and in one's possession. Tax records in the hands of one's accountant are not protected, for example, nor are books or papers that one might have as a union officer or that belong to a corporation of which one is an officer or that belong to a partnership, nor are the papers of a one-person business firm.[56] However, in the last example the act of producing incriminating documents may be protected, since the mere act of producing them may amount to testifying against oneself. But even this minimal protection for business records should not be read too generously. The Supreme Court, although not there yet, appears to be moving toward Justice O'Connor's position "that the Fifth Amendment provides absolutely no protection for the contents of private papers of any kind."[57]

It is in the area of protection for those accused of a crime that the self-incrimination clause has had its most important and controversial extensions. The clause gives defendants the right to refuse to take the stand at their trials; they may thus refrain from answering any question, incriminating or not. The burden is on the government to prove guilt; the defendant has no responsibility to help. If defendants choose not to take the stand, nothing can prevent jurors from speculating about why they stand mute in the face of a criminal accusation. Yet a prosecutor may not comment about a defendant's refusal to testify.[58] A judge may, and must if requested to do so, use the unique power of the jury instruction to reduce speculation to a minimum by instructing the jurors that a defendant has a constitutional right not to testify and that the defendant's failure to testify should not be used to infer guilt and should not prejudice the jury against the defendant in any way.[59] If defendants do take the stand, the prosecution may cross-examine them on all of their testimony, even including their failure to respond to police accusations and questions before their arrest.

Traditionally, the right to refuse to incriminate oneself applied only at the time of formal trial. But what good was this constitutional protection, or the guarantee of the right to assistance of counsel, or the presumption of innocence, if long before the accused was brought before a judge he or she was detained and, without the help of an attorney, forced to prove innocence to the police? Do not such procedures reduce the courtroom proceedings to a mere formality?

In the 1930s the Supreme Court began to move against such tactics. At first it used the more general due process standards to reverse convictions obtained by using evidence secured by torture, by prolonged psychological coercion, or by involuntary confession. It acted not so much because these practices amount to self-incrimination as because such brutal procedures and the use of coerced confessions, whether true or false, offend constitutional principles.[60] "The use against a defendant of his *involuntary* statement is a denial of due process of law, 'even though there is ample evidence aside from the confession to support the conviction.' "[61]

In 1966, in *Miranda v Arizona*, the Supreme Court abandoned case-by-case determination of where police interrogation had gone too far. It brought the self-incrimination clause into play.[62] The Court announced that henceforth no conviction could stand if evidence introduced at the trial, even though voluntarily given, had been obtained by the police as a result of "custodial interrogation" unless suspects had been (1) notified that they are free to remain silent, (2) warned that what they say may be used against them in court, (3) told they have a right to have their attorneys present during the questioning, (4) informed that if they cannot afford to hire their own lawyers, attorneys will be provided for them, and (5) permitted at any stage of the police interrogation to terminate it. If suspects answer questions in the absence of attorneys, the prosecution must be prepared to demonstrate that the suspects knowingly and intelligently waived their rights to remain silent and to have their own lawyer present. (This burden may have been substantially undermined by *Moran v Burbine*.[63] The Court concluded that there had been no violation of *Miranda* in the use of a confession obtained by police after they failed to inform a suspect that his counsel had tried to communicate with him and had been assured that there would be no further questioning until the next day.) Failure to comply with the *Miranda* requirements will lead to reversal of a conviction, even if other independent evidence would have been sufficient to establish guilt.

Custodial interrogation includes any questioning by police, including Internal Revenue Service agents, when the investigators have fixed on the person questioned for possible criminal prosecution.[64] Custodial interrogations do not depend on whether persons are in custody in a police station or have been placed under formal arrest. They cover all investigations in which persons are deprived of freedom of action "to a degree associated with a formal arrest."[65]

Miranda warnings are not required, however, merely for police to talk with suspects, even in police stations, if suspects have voluntarily gone to the station, are free to go whenever they wish, and are under no legal restraint.[66] Nor are *Miranda* warnings required at routine traffic stops.[67] Nor are such warnings required when a probation officer questions a probationer about an earlier crime or when a person has been called to appear before a grand jury.[68]

The Supreme Court has also created a "public safety" exception to the *Miranda* requirement. In *New York* v *Quarles* the Court was faced with the following facts: On September 11, 1980, officers were patrolling in Queens when a young woman approached the car. She told them that she had just been raped by a man who had then gone into an A & P market and that he was carrying a gun. The officers drove the woman to the store, saw the suspect, frisked him, and discovered he was wearing an empty shoulder holster. After handcuffing him, one officer asked him where the gun was and the suspect said, "The gun is over there," and pointed to some empty cartons. The officer retrieved a loaded .38-caliber revolver, formally placed the defendant under arrest and then read him his *Miranda* rights. The lower courts held that neither the gun nor the defendant's statement "The gun is over there" could be introduced at his trial, since that evidence had been obtained before the *Miranda* warning had been given. The Supreme Court agreed that prior decisions would have required that result but concluded, "There is a 'public safety exception' to the requirement.... We do not believe that the doctrinal underpinnings of *Miranda* require that it be applied in all its rigor to a situation in which police officers ask questions reasonably prompted by a concern for the public safety."[69] The Court, speaking through Justice Rehnquist, acknowledged: "In recognizing a narrow exception to the *Miranda* rule, to some degree we lessen the desirable clarity of that rule."

After a *Miranda* warning has been given and a suspect has requested that an attorney be present, police are in danger of violating the suspect's rights "even if what they say to a suspect is not punctuated by a question mark." In *Edwards* v *Arizona* the Court established a rule that once a suspect asks to have an attorney present, no waiver of that right, however voluntary, can be valid if made in response to further police questioning.[70] "Once a suspect has invoked the right to counsel, any subsequent conversation must be initiated by him."[71] The *Edwards* rule, although dogmatically stated, has not been rigorously applied. Even when a suspect has asked for an attorney, the Court has regularly found conditions that make the *Edwards* rule inapplicable, and the questioning has been allowed. Of course, not all conversation between the police and the accused must cease. Yet, if in such conversations the suspect makes incriminating statements away from counsel, the statements may not be introduced in court against the suspect unless they clearly were not provoked by the police, directly or indirectly.

The *Miranda* doctrine also applies in a modified form to psychiatric examinations initiated by the state. A state may order such examinations to determine whether an accused is mentally competent to stand trial, and the accused is not entitled to have an attorney present during the examination. However, the state may not use any evidence from such an examination to determine guilt or severity of the sentence unless before the examination it gave the suspect a *Miranda* warning and an opportunity to consult with an attorney and made it clear that the suspect did not have to answer incriminating questions.[72]

The *Miranda* prohibitions apply primarily to evidence relating to issues of guilt or innocence. Thus, a prosecutor, to challenge a defendant's credibility, may introduce evidence obtained in violation of the *Miranda* ruling to contradict statements a defendant has volunteered from the witness stand. Otherwise, a defendant might give perjured testimony free from the risk of confrontation with prior inconsistent utterances. However, the exception does put pressure on defendants to refrain from taking the stand in their own defense, since their testimony may open the way for the prosecution to use evidence that could not otherwise be introduced.[73]

Although governments cannot compel persons to incriminate themselves, most cases are disposed of by guilty pleas. Increasingly, such pleas result from bargaining in which prosecutors agree to drop more serious charges in return for defendants' guilty pleas to lesser ones. It was not until 1971 that the Supreme Court, in *Santobello* v *New York*, dispelled any "lingering doubts about the legitimacy of the practice . . . and . . . plea bargaining was no longer shrouded in secrecy and deliberately concealed."[74] A year earlier, in *Brady* v *United States*, the Court had listed the arguments for plea bargaining: "For a defendant who sees slight possibility of acquittal, the advantages of pleading guilty and limiting the probable penalty are obvious. . . . For the State there are also advantages — the more promptly imposed punishment after an admission of guilt may more effectively attain the objectives of punishment; and with the avoidance of trial, scarce judicial and prosecutorial resources are conserved for those cases in which there is a substantial issue of the defendant's guilt or in which there is substantial doubt that the State can sustain its burden of proof. It is this mutuality of advantage that perhaps explains the fact that at present well over three-fourths of the criminal convictions in this country rest on pleas of guilty."[75]

Since *Santobello*, the Court has established ground rules for plea bargaining that ensure that the guilty plea is knowingly made and the prosecutor's promise is upheld. (A prosecutor may withdraw an offer and then the defendant has a right to withdraw a guilty plea.) Counsel must be present during plea negotiations, and a record must be made to show that the plea was knowingly and voluntarily made with a full understanding of its consequences.[76]

---

nor be deprived of life, liberty, or property, without due process of law;

A parallel clause is found in the Fourteenth Amendment as a limitation on the states. The due process clauses of the Fifth and Fourteenth Amendments have resulted in more cases and controversies than any others in the Constitution, although the equal protection clause of the Fourteenth Amendment is quickly catching up. Despite the number of cases, it is impossible to give due process clauses any exact, final, and completely satisfactory explanation. Indeed, the Supreme Court itself has refused to give due process a precise definition, stating that it prefers to rely on "the gradual process of judicial inclusion and exclusion."[77]

The due process clause restricts the actions of governments, not of private individuals. A question that for decades was significant only for the application of the equal protection clause (see page 247) has now become an issue in the application of the due process clauses; namely, when is an action an action of the state or an action taken under color of law, and when is it merely private action? In part, the question has become more important because of the Supreme Court's more liberal construction of 42 U.S.C. 1983 permitting persons to bring suits against those who act under color of law "to deprive them of any right secured by law or the Constitution." In part, the issue of what is and what is not state action comes about because of the more expansive application of the protections of the due process clauses to more and more arenas.

When we get to the equal protection clause we will discuss at greater length the factors that cause the Court to decide that state action is involved. (The Fifth Amendment contains no equal protection clause, but the Supreme Court has interpreted the due process clause of the Fifth Amendment [*Bolling* v *Sharpe*] to limit the national government in precisely the same way that the equal protection clause of the Fourteenth Amendment limits states.[78]) Here are a couple of examples: A private nursing home transferred Medicaid patients, whose expenses were paid by federal and state funds, to a facility that provided lower levels of care, after a utilization review committee, required by federal regulations, concluded that the lower level was appropriate for the patients. The patients argued they had been denied due process because they had not been given a proper hearing. The Supreme Court said that the due process clause did not apply. True, the nursing home was extensively regulated by the state — the state paid the expenses — but the decision about the appropriate level of care turned on medical judgments made by private parties, and the nursing home was not performing a function that has traditionally been the exclusive prerogative of the state.[79] On the other hand, when a creditor using procedures established by Virginia law went into a Virginia court to attach property of one of his debtors, the debtor was allowed to sue the creditor under Section 1983 on the grounds that the creditor, acting under color of state law, had violated the debtor's due process rights.[80]

The Court has expanded the meanings of *property* and, especially, *liberty* within the due process clause. Originally, *liberty* meant freedom from physical restraint; it has been expanded to denote "not merely freedom from bodily restraint but also right of the individual to contract, to engage in any of the common occupations of life, to acquire useful knowledge, to marry, to establish a home and to bring up children, to worship God according to the dictates of his own conscience, and generally to enjoy those common law privileges long recognized as essential to the orderly pursuit of happiness by free men."[81] Also now included in the liberty protected by due process is the right of privacy, a largely undefined right, within which "marital privacy" has received the most protection.

The Court has so expanded the term *liberty* as to blur the distinction between a privilege — something given by the government as a matter of grace — and a right — something to which one is entitled. Until 1937 the most important part of this "new liberty" protected by the Supreme Court was "liberty of contract,"[82] that is, business liberty. Since 1937 the Supreme Court has abandoned the doctrine of "liberty" of contract, but its action did not foreshadow a return to the old narrow conception of liberty. On the contrary, the liberty of the Fifth and Fourteenth Amendments has been expanded to include the basic civil liberties.

Property, too, has been expanded. At one time thought to be primarily physical things, property now includes a whole bundle of rights. Welfare, housing, education, employment, professional licenses, and so on are now more and more matters of entitlement, and to deprive someone of them calls into play some form of due process protection.[83] Unlike the liberty protected by the due process clause, which liberty comes from the Constitution itself, property interests are not created by the due process clause itself. Rather, the clause extends various *procedural* safeguards to property interests created by other parts of the Constitution or, more commonly, by state law.[84]

Despite the expansive interpretations of liberty and property, "not every grievous . . . loss invokes procedural protections of the Due Process Clause."[85] For example, nontenured faculty members at state colleges or universities have no property or liberty right in their jobs that flows from the Constitution. (The state, by its own laws and procedures, can confer property rights in teaching jobs, and if it does so, then it cannot take such rights away without due process.) True, teachers are entitled to freedom of speech, along with everybody else, and they cannot be denied that freedom without due process, but "the interest in holding a job at a state university, simpliciter, is not itself a free speech interest . . . nor one that cannot be denied without procedural due process."[86]

One has no liberty right to a government job, but one may have a property right conferred by law. If a law confers some kind of security of employment, employees may not be dismissed without appropriate due process.[87] Even if there are no property rights in a job, if government employees, at least most of them, are dismissed because they belong to a different party from the one that won the last election or merely because they have exercised First Amendment rights of speech or association, such action might be a denial of First Amendment rights and thus unconstitutional.[88] If the reasons for a dismissal are publicized, the publicity might amount to governmental imposition of a stigma on a person, which would infringe on that person's liberty and thus require some kind of due process.[89]

Prisoners do not have any rights to due process before being denied a parole or a reduction in the length of their sentences.[90] (A prisoner does have a right to due process before having a parole, once granted, taken away. "There is a difference between losing what one has and not getting what one wants.") Prisoners must be provided reasonable opportunities to exercise their religious freedoms, and to petition the government and must not be subject to cruel and unusual punishments. A prisoner, however, has no liberty right to be transferred from one prison to another, whether in the same state or in another state (but see page 197).[91] Nor do prisoners, even those being held in pretrial detention, have a liberty right to have contact with members of their families or friends who come to visit them.[92]

"Once it is determined that due process applies, the question remains what process is due."[93] There are two kinds of due process: *procedural* and *substantive*. Procedural due process applies to the methods by which the law is enforced. It requires, to paraphrase Daniel Webster's famous definition, a procedure that hears before it condemns, proceeds upon inquiry, and renders judgment only after [a] trial or hearing of some sort in which the essentials of justice have been preserved. Or as the Court has said more recently, "the fundamental requirement of due process is the opportunity to be heard at a meaningful time and in a meaningful manner."[94]

There are several ways in which a law itself may violate procedural due process. First, "a statute which either forbids or requires the doing of an act in terms so vague that men of common intelligence must necessarily guess at its meaning and differ as to its application violates the first essential of due process of law."[95] Not only does a vague statute run the risk of entrapping the innocent, but it also "impermissibly delegates basic policy matters to policemen, judges, and juries . . . on an *ad hoc* and subjective basis, with the attendant dangers of arbitrary and discriminatory application."[96] A vague statute "furnishes a convenient tool for 'harsh and discriminatory enforcement by local prosecuting officials,' "[97] . . . "confers on police a virtually unrestrained power to arrest and charge persons with a violation,"[98] and "entrust[s] lawmaking to the moment-to-moment judgment of the policeman on the beat."[99]

Examples of statutes that have been struck down for vagueness are "a suspicious person ordinance," providing that any persons found on a street at late or unusual hours of the night without any visible or lawful business and who did not give satisfactory accounts of themselves, might be fined or imprisoned,[100] and a statute requiring persons who loitered or wandered on the streets, under circumstances that made police suspicious, to provide "credible and reliable" identification to account for their presence when asked by a police officer to do so.[101] A similar fate befell a vagrancy ordinance declaring to be vagrants a wide variety of ill-defined classes such as "rogues and vagabonds," "dissolute persons who go about begging," "common night walkers," and so on.[102] Yet another example: A Pennsylvania statute that was held void for vagueness made doctors criminally liable who, after determining that a fetus "is viable or . . . may be viable," failed to exercise "that degree of professional skill, care, and diligence necessary to preserve the life and health of the fetus" and to adopt the particular abortion technique "which would provide the best opportunity for the fetus to be aborted alive so long as a different technique would not be necessary in order to preserve the life or health of the mother."[103]

On the other side, the Court ruled that an ordinance requiring a business to obtain a license if it sells any items "designed or marketed for use with illegal cannabis or drugs," that is, if it is a "head   shop," was not unconstitutionally vague on its face.[104] The Court also upheld an ordinance directing the chief of police, prior to making a recommendation, to consider whether an applicant for a license to run a coin-operated amusement center has any "connection with criminal elements." The Court pointed out that, although the ordinance would be too vague to convict a person of the offense of having such a connection, and might even be too vague to support the denial of a license, the Constitution does not preclude a city from giving vague directions to officials who are authorized to make investigations and recommendations to the city council.[105]

A second way in which a law itself may violate procedural due process is by creating an improper burden of proof. For most civil proceedings, the preponderance-of-evidence standard — the side with the most evidence wins — meets due process requirements, but in some proceedings due process may impose a "clear and convincing" evidence standard.[106] For criminal trials there must be a presumption of innocence. Due process places the burden on the government in criminal prosecutions to prove guilt beyond a reasonable doubt. The state must present proof of every fact necessary to constitute the crime with which a defendant is charged.[107] This burden cannot be shifted by a law that creates a presumption of criminal guilt, unless the fact the law infers "is more likely than not . . . to flow from the fact proved."[108] For example, the Court has declared unconstitutional laws creating the presumption that possessors of marijuana or cocaine obtained the drugs through illegal importation.[109] The constitutionality of such a presumption in the case of heroin has been sustained, since little, if any, heroin is made in this country, virtually all heroin is illegally imported, and anyone convicted of its possession has more likely than not obtained it illegally.[110]

A third way a law can violate procedural due process is to take away a liberty or property interest without a hearing. Here are just a few examples of laws declared unconstitutional on such grounds: a law providing for automatic revocation of a driver's license after an accident,[111] a law permitting the listing in liquor stores of the names of persons who have engaged in "excessive drinking" and forbidding sales of liquor to such persons, with no provisions for those whose names were listed to be first notified and given a hearing,[112] and a law disqualifying unwed fathers as fit parents without giving such fathers a hearing to determine their fitness.[113]

When a hearing is required, it must be a proper one. What is a proper hearing depends on the interests involved. In a courtroom, due process requires the full panoply of rights outlined in the Constitution. Yet courtroom due process goes beyond the specific provisions of the Bill of Rights. A court could follow each particular provision of the Bill of Rights and still deny due process if, for example, the judge, in manner or mood, showed bias toward the defendant or if the judge had a financial interest in the outcome of the trial. In other words, due process requires fundamental fairness, a fair and impartial trial.[114] Thus, it is impossible to provide a fair trial for a person not mentally competent to understand the nature of the proceedings, or not able to consult with counsel or to assist in the preparation of a defense.[115]

To give examples of the kind of process that is due in the criminal law context: A juvenile cannot be declared delinquent without a hearing in which the juvenile is given the right to confront hostile witnesses and to cross-examine them, to present oral evidence, and to be represented by counsel. The level of proof to demonstrate delinquency must be the same as that required in a criminal trial, namely, proof beyond any reasonable doubt, but the juvenile is not entitled to have the decision made by a jury. Furthermore, after a hearing and a finding of a "serious risk" that a juvenile "may before the return date commit an act which if committed by an adult would constitute a crime," a juvenile may be kept in preventive detention for a limited time.[116] (For preventive detention for adults, see page 213)

Due process does not necessarily require that criminal procedures be used in noncriminal proceedings. The question in each instance is what must be done to ensure fundamental fairness. It is hard to generalize because of the wide variety of governmental proceedings involved. Among the many forums in which procedural due process is required are disbarment proceedings, determinations of eligibility for welfare payments, parole and probation revocations, legislative contempt proceedings, congressional committees and administrative tribunals, disciplinary proceedings in state universities, colleges, and public schools, and proceedings for confinement in mental institutions.[117]

In debating the requirements of due process in noncourtroom proceedings, the Court asks three questions, outlined in its decision in *Mathews* v *Eldridge*: (1) What are the private interests at stake? (2) What is the government's interest? (3) What are the risks the procedures used will lead to an erroneous decision?[118]

In emergency situations, when protection of public health and safety is paramount, summary administrative actions may be taken. For example, an unsafe mine may be closed or a passport revoked merely with a statement of reasons and an opportunity for a prompt postrevocation hearing.[119] The national government may seize property being brought illegally into the country and follow with a hearing later, but it cannot keep noncontraband property without holding a hearing within a reasonable time. The Court recently held that an eighteen-month delay in filing civil proceedings for forfeiture of currency, which had been seized by customs officials because it had not been properly listed on a form, was not a denial of due process.[120] However, these are unusual situations. In all but these few emergency situations, due process requires, at a minimum, adequate notice and an opportunity to be heard before the deprivation of the protected liberty or property interest.

Hearings do not have to be formal or adversary in nature. To illustrate: A student is entitled to notice and to an informal hearing (unless the student's presence poses a continuing danger to persons or property) before being suspended from a public school for disciplinary reasons, but the hearing may be informal, perhaps only a brief talk with the principal.[121] For long-term expulsion the procedures must be a little more formal, but dismissal from a state college or university for academic reasons calls for even less rigorous procedures, no hearing whatsoever being required.[122] A municipally owned utility, before terminating service for failure to pay bills, must notify customers of procedures that permit them to protest the proposed termination.[123] Apparently the federal government must provide some kind of hearing procedure for persons whose claims under the Medicare program have been turned down, but a review by a hearing officer, who does not have to be a lawyer, appointed by insurance carriers under contract from the government, without further judicial review, is sufficient.[124]

To give more examples of the kind of process due: Before children may be taken by the government from the custody of natural parents, those parents must be given an opportunity to be heard in a rather formal proceeding, and the state is required to support by "clear and convincing proof " its allegations that the children's welfare requires such an action.[125] Parents do not, however, have an automatic right to court-appointed counsel in such a proceeding: the trial judge must make a decision in each instance whether or not due process requires the assistance of counsel. In fact, the Court has suggested that due process probably requires the automatic appointment of counsel for indigents in noncriminal proceedings only in situations in which they "may be deprived of physical liberty."[126]

Admissions to mental institutions have caused considerable litigation. Children are entitled to due process before they can be placed by their parents in mental institutions, but due process does not require a formal adversarial hearing, merely a neutral medical determination by a doctor or other professional.[127] Prisoners, however, even though not entitled to due process before being transferred from one prison to another, are entitled to such protection before being taken from prison and placed in a mental hospital, even if the placement is for a period within the period of their sentence. Moreover, before being transferred to a mental hospital, a prisoner must be given written notice, a hearing before an independent decision maker, an opportunity to present evidence and cross-examine witnesses, and a written statement of the decision.[128]

An issue that has caused considerable division within the Court, and some heat, is the due process requirements for state proceedings that afford relief for creditors against delinquent debtors. Before the garnishment of wages there must be a hearing.[129] (Garnishment is a process by which an employer is ordered by a court to pay directly to an employee's creditors amounts deducted from the wages due the employee.) A hearing is necessary before goods sold on the installment plan can be repossessed.[130] A prerepossession hearing is not necessary if a judge orders a sheriff to take possession of property in which title is still vested in the seller.[131] A hearing is necessary before a creditor can place a hold on and garnish a bank account.[132]

The special preserve and the most deferred-to competence of judges is to determine the requirements of procedural due process. But even about such issues judges are not of one mind. For example, when Congress authorized the secretary of labor to order the immediate reinstatement of employees who claimed they had been discharged for refusing to operate trucks that were not in compliance with applicable safety standards, with a hearing for their employers to follow later, the justices reached a variety of conclusions about whether such procedures complied with due process. Justices Marshall, Blackmun, Powell, and O'Connor said no and that due process requires the secretary of labor, before ordering an employer to reinstate an employee, to give the employer notice of the employee's allegations, notice of the substance of the relevant supporting evidence, an opportunity to submit a written response, a chance to meet with the investigating official, and an opportunity to present statements from rebuttal witnesses. But to these justices, due process does not require that the employer be allowed to confront and cross-examine witnesses before the employee is reinstated, provided a prompt postreinstatement hearing is made available. Justices Brennan and Stevens, although agreeing that Congress had not provided due process for employers, contended that due process also requires that the employer be given a chance before reinstatement to cross-examine witnesses and test the evidence in an adversary proceeding. On the other side, Chief Justice Rehnquist and Justices White and Scalia thought that this situation had provided due process.[133]

Whereas procedural due process places limits on the manner in which governmental power may be exercised, *substantive due process* withdraws certain subjects from the full reach of governmental power regardless of the procedures used. Substantive due process requires that the Court be convinced that a law — not merely the procedures by which the law would be enforced, but its very purpose — is fair, reasonable, and just.

Before 1937 the Supreme Court used substantive due process and the expanded definition of liberty to strike down many laws that the justices thought unreasonable regulations of business liberty. Indeed, the Supreme Court for a time became the final arbiter of our economic and industrial life. During that period the Court struck down laws regulating hours of labor, establishing minimum wages, regulating prices, forbidding employers to discharge workers for union membership, and so on, on the grounds that they were unreasonable interferences with the liberty of employers and employees to contract with one another.[134] Since 1937 the Supreme Court has refused to apply substantive due process to laws regulating the economy.[135] This rejection does not mean that the Court has abandoned the doctrine of substantive due process. Quite the contrary, the doctrine has been given new life as a judicially imposed limitation on both state and federal governments' power to regulate civil liberties and civil rights.

Closely related to the revival of the doctrine of substantive due process, and often merging with it, has been the Supreme Court's development of new tests to determine whether or not a state or federal law deprives a person of the equal protection of the law. A specific clause in the Fourteenth Amendment forbids such deprivation by the states. No such clause applies to the national government, but the Supreme Court has construed the due process clause of the Fifth Amendment to incorporate an equal protection requirement. The equal protection clause, as presently interpreted, has many similarities to substantive due process. Indeed, it is sometimes difficult to determine whether the Supreme Court is striking down a law because it violates the due process clause or because it is a denial of equal protection. This merging of the two provisions is especially pronounced when the Court invokes its relatively new doctrine against "irrebuttable presumptions."

Take several examples: The Supreme Court declared unconstitutional a federal law aimed at preventing middle-class college students from getting food stamps. The law made ineligible for food stamps any household that contained any person over the age of eighteen who had been claimed as a tax dependent the prior year by somebody not living in that house. The Supreme Court ruled that the law created an unreasonable irrebuttable presumption because there is often no relation between the need of a household and the fact that it contains a person claimed the year before as a tax dependent by someone not living in the house.[136] Along the same lines, when Congress, to deny food stamps to "hippie communes," declared ineligible for such stamps any household containing an individual not related to any other member of the household, the Supreme Court declared the "classification to be wholly without any rational basis."[137] And then there was the regulation of the Cleveland Board of Education that no pregnant teacher should be allowed to teach beyond the fifth month of her pregnancy or to return to work until her child was three months old. Justice Stewart announced in *Cleveland Board of Education* v *LaFleur* that the "maternity leave rules directly affect 'one of the basic civil rights of man [sic],' " that they were "wholly arbitrary and irrational," and that they hence violated the due process clause of the Fourteenth Amendment.[138]

In a case of some interest to students, teachers, and university administrators, the Supreme Court, assuming that federal judges may review academic decisions of public universities and colleges under substantive due process standards, has concluded, "When judges are asked to review the substance of a genuinely academic decision, such as the dismissal of a student, they should show great respect for the faculty's professional judgment. Plainly, they may not override it unless it is such a substantial departure from accepted academic norms as to demonstrate that the person or committee responsible did not actually exercise professional judgment."[139]

For a while, the Court applied substantive due process but was reluctant to admit that it was doing so. However, in recent years, it has openly begun to inspect laws for "reasonableness." For example, the Court declared unconstitutional an ordinance limiting occupancy in homes to single families and defining single families in a way that excluded a grandmother living with two grandchildren who were cousins rather than brothers. Justice Powell, speaking for a plurality of four, conceded that "substantive due process has at times been a treacherous field for this Court. There *are* risks when the judicial branch gives enhanced protection to certain substantive liberties without the guidance of the more specific provisions of the Bill of Rights. As the history [of the earlier use of due process to strike down many welfare laws] demonstrates there is reason for concern lest the only limits to such judicial intervention become the predilections of those who happen at the time to be members of this Court. That history counsels caution and restraint. But it does not counsel abandonment." Justice White, in dissent, reminded his colleagues "that the Court has no license to invalidate legislation which it thinks merely arbitrary or unreasonable. . . . The Court should be extremely reluctant to breathe still further substantive content into the Due Process Clause so as to strike down legislation adopted by a state or a city to promote its welfare. Whenever the Judiciary does so, it unavoidably preempts for itself another part of the governance of the country without express constitutional authority."[140]

Perhaps the most celebrated, certainly the most controversial, illustration of the modern Supreme Court's use of substantive due process is its ruling, in *Roe* v *Wade* that the constitutionality of a state's regulation of abortions varies with the trimester of a woman's pregnancy.[141] During the first trimester (about the first three months), it is unreasonable and unconstitutional for a state to interfere with a woman's right to choose an abortion or to interfere with her doctor's medical judgments about how to carry it out. During the second trimester, the state's interest in protecting the health of women who undergo abortions becomes compelling, and a state may make reasonable regulations about how, where, and when abortions may be performed. During the third trimester, the state's interest in protecting the unborn child is so important that the state can proscribe abortions altogether, except when necessary to preserve the life or health of the mother.

Four years later, in *Maher* v *Roe*, the Court concluded that although a woman has the constitutional right to an abortion during the early months of pregnancy, she has no right to have the state pay for it. A state may refuse to pay the medical expenses for poor women for nontherapeutic abortions, even if the state covers medical expenses related to childbirth.[142] Several years later, in *Akron* v *Akron Center for Reproductive Health*, the Court held that the state of medical science had so progressed that most abortions during the early part of the second trimester could be performed safely in a doctor's office. Thus, a state regulation requiring all such abortions to be performed in a hospital, along with some other state regulations, unduly burdened a woman's constitutional right to an abortion.[143]

The abortion decisions continue to divide the nation. What divides the nation for an extended period of time almost always divides the Court. In the most recent decision, *Thornburgh* v *American Coll. of Obst. & Gyn.*, which is clearly not the last word on this subject, five justices joined in striking down a Pennsylvania law requiring that a patient seeking an abortion be given certain information, that the action be reported to public authorities, that a second physician be present during the abortion except in emergencies, and that a doctor use a particular standard of care when aborting a viable fetus. The dissent of Justice White, joined by Justice Rehnquist, Justice O'Connor, and Chief Justice Burger, is notable for its strong language, reflecting strong feelings. Justice White accused the majority of having a "warped point of view" and following a "tortuous path." Justice O'Connor stated, "Today's decision . . . makes it painfully clear that no legal rule or doctrine is safe from ad hoc nullification by this Court when an occasion for its application arises in a case involving state regulation of abortion."[144] Whatever one thinks about the issue, surely Justice O'Connor is right that the differences among the justices are generating as much heat as light. Nonetheless, the opinions in *Thornburgh* v *American Coll. of Obst. & Gyn.* are worthy of close attention in one more round of the never-ending debate about the proper role of the courts in a democracy and about the use and alleged abuse of the doctrine of substantive due process.

The Court, by five to four, refused to extend to homosexual activity what it described as this "fundamental individual right to decide whether or not to beget or bear a child," which comes from the abortion line of cases and from cases declaring unconstitutional state laws restricting or forbidding the sale of contraceptives. The dissenters angrily responded that the Court's unwillingness to strike down the Georgia antisodomy law was a betrayal of a value deeply rooted in our nation's history, namely, that governments have no right to deprive individuals of the choice of how to conduct their most intimate relationships. Sex practices in private bedrooms between consenting adults, said the dissenters, are protected by the Constitution against governmental regulation.[145]

All these conclusions about what is and what is not a reasonable state regulation stem from the words "nor shall any State deprive any person of life, liberty, or property, without due process of law," in the Fourteenth Amendment. In fact, as the Court has written somewhat apologetically, "while our decisions . . . do not form checkerboard bright lines between black squares and red squares," today substantive due process is likely to be bound by "the individual's freedom of choice with respect to certain basic matters of procreation, marriage, and family life."[146]

---

nor shall private property be taken for public use, [without just compensation, *discussed later*]

This clause was the first provision of the Bill of Rights to be incorporated in the Fourteenth Amendment and thus to be made applicable to the states.[147] (A regulation that "goes too far" may also violate the due process clause.[148]) This clause places a restriction on the government's power of *eminent domain* — that is, the power to take property for public use.

Although the clause refers to private property, the national government may take property belonging to a local government, as may a state, but an interesting question not definitively decided is whether the national government may take property owned and used by a state for a direct governmental purpose.

Property may be taken under eminent domain, even if the owner is fairly compensated, only for public use. In *Hawaii Housing Authority* v *Midkiff*, the Supreme Court put to rest the notion that the words "public use" should be read literally to mean that the taken property must be owned and operated by a government and open to use by the public. The Hawaii legislature in 1967 had adopted a land reform act empowering authorities to condemn the land of large landowners, transfer ownership of the condemned land to tenants, and lend funds or arrange for the financing of the land so purchased. The landowners who lost their property argued that the act violated the Constitution in that it took property from one person and made it available to others for their own private use. The Court of Appeals for the Ninth Circuit agreed. In its judgment, the act was simply "a naked attempt on the part of the state of Hawaii to take the private property of A and transfer it to B solely for B's private use and benefit." But the Supreme Court said that although "one person's property may not be taken for the benefit of another private person without a justifying public purpose, even though compensation be paid,"[149] it can be taken if it serves a public purpose. It is the legislature which determines what constitutes a public use. "The Court . . . will not substitute its judgment for a legislature's judgment as to what constitutes a public use unless the use be palpably without reasonable foundation.... The Hawaii Legislature's judgment to break up land oligopolies and correct the evils associated with such concentrated landownership was a classic exercise of a State's police powers and clearly serves a public use."[150]

The question of what constitutes a *taking* for purposes of the Fifth Amendment has occupied a considerable portion of the Court's time, most especially in recent years. In fact, the taking jurisdiction of the modern-day Supreme Court has become a new battleground, replacing pre-1937 substantive due process, in the war between those who favor governmental regulation, especially of land development, and those who are suspicious of such government actions.

Ordinarily, but not always, a taking must be direct, some kind of permanent physical occupation authorized by the government. Taxes are not takings, even if a tax is so stiff as to drive a person out of business.[151] Government regulations are not ordinarily considered takings and do not ordinarily require compensation (but see page 203), even if the government action results in a property loss. There is not a taking if a land use regulation "substantially advances legitimate state interests" and does not deny an owner "economically viable use of his land."[152] But a regulation that goes "too far" may be considered a taking.

Price control regulations are not takings unless the rates set are considered by the courts to be confiscatory.[153] Nor does the government have to pay damages when it temporarily occupies a building in the course of restoring order in a riot situation.[154] Land use regulations are ordinarily not takings; for example, a government may designate a building a "historic landmark" and may impose on the owner of such a building requirements for its maintenance and restrictions on its development without having to pay "just compensation," as the owners of Grand Central Terminal in New York discovered. They were denied the right to make changes in the structure, changes that would have increased their rental returns.[155]

On the other side, even when title is left in the hands of the owners, sometimes the courts will find that the government has "taken" property and owes compensation to its owners. To illustrate: If airplanes take off and land over property adjacent to airports at such levels that the land is no longer suitable for its prior use, say, raising chickens, this is a compensable taking.[156] Similarly, the Supreme Court indicated that if in fact a congressional scheme to keep the bankrupt northeastern railroads operating resulted in such significant losses to them that it amounted to an "erosion taking," the government would be liable for just compensation for having taken railroad property by forcing them to continue to operate at huge losses.[157] Along these same lines, the government must provide compensation if it wants to provide public access to a private lagoon that the owners have dredged out at their own expense to make it accessible to the ocean.[158]

Recent taking cases illustrate how difficult the drawing of constitutional lines is and how often where they are drawn rests ultimately on ideas of fairness and justice rather than precise constitutional language. In 1922 Justice Holmes, the leading light of judicial deference, speaking for the Court in *Pennsylvania Coal Co.* v *Mahon*, held that Pennsylvania had gone too far when it restricted the mining of coal on land owned by mining companies if it might cause damage to buildings on adjacent land.[159] This restriction, said Justice Holmes, took the mine owners' property from them for the benefit of the few people whose buildings might be damaged. For sixty-five years the case was cited as an example of regulation that went too far. Then in 1987, by a five-to-four vote, the Supreme Court, distinguishing but not overruling *Mahon*, upheld another Pennsylvania law requiring miners to leave a certain amount of coal — 27 million tons — in the ground for support of buildings and to pay for damage to structures, even if the surface owners had waived any claim to such damages when they sold the rights to mine under their land. The coal that had to be left underground, a limitation on the miners' purchased interest in mining the coal, was not a taking, said the majority, but a regulation in the public interest.[160]

In the same term, following this less rigorous application of the taking clause, the Court signaled, in a pair of cases, a more restrictive application of the clause to governmental land regulations. The first, *First English Evangelical Lutheran Church v Los Angeles County*, warned governments that they may have to pay compensation for regulations that are subsequently judged to be takings. The second, *Nollan v California Coastal Commission*, established that governments may not impose mitigating conditions on land use without paying just compensation, unless there is a substantial relation between the governmental purpose and the condition imposed. The particular case before it was an attempt by the California Coastal Commission to deny a permit to remodel a beach home unless the owners agreed to extend public access to the beach. The Court held there was no relation between the remodeling and public access and that this was a taking entitled to just compensation.[161] Justice Scalia, for the Court, stated that the commission's action is the "same as if California law forbade shouting fire in a crowded theater, but granted dispensations to those willing to contribute $100 to the state treasury. . . . In short, unless the permit condition serves the same governmental purpose as the development ban, the building restriction is not a valid regulation of land use but an 'out-and-out plan of extortion.' "

---

without just compensation.

In cases of disagreement between the government and the individual about what price is just, decision is referred to a disinterested body; ultimately, a court of law makes the final decision. What is just compensation is not always an easy question to answer. By and large, "the owner is entitled to receive what a willing buyer would pay in cash to a willing seller at the time of the taking."[162] An owner is not entitled to compensation for the special value of the property to the owner: an old, broken-down house that is loved dearly will still bring only compensation for an old, broken-down house. When the property is owned by a public entity, that entity is entitled to no more than the fair market value of the condemned property even if it will cost more to acquire a substitute facility that the entity has a duty to acquire.[163]

What happens if, after a long-drawn-out legal battle, there is a final judicial determination that a regulation was in fact a taking? The government involved may amend the invalid regulation, withdraw it, or exercise eminent domain and pay compensation. But what about the losses while the proceedings are taking place? Does the Constitution confer a right to compensation for these "temporary takings"? In an important *inverse condemnation* — the right to sue for compensation — decision (*First English Evangelical Lutheran Church v Los Angeles County*) that will spawn considerable additional litigation and may, as the Court conceded, significantly slow down land use regulations, the Court, considering an ordinance that denied a church all use of its property for a considerable period of time, decided that the church was entitled to just compensation for that temporary taking. The Court limited its holding to the facts of the case and did not "deal with the quite different questions that would arise in the case of normal delays in obtaining building permits, changes in zoning ordinances, variances, and the like which are not before us."[164]

Another interesting taking and compensation case involved Indian lands. In 1980 the Supreme Court ruled that the national government had exceeded its powers to abrogate Indian treaties and to manage tribal lands and, in 1877 had acted in bad faith by taking the Black Hills from the Sioux Indians. The Indians, ruled the Court, were entitled to the $17 million that the Black Hills had been worth in 1877, plus 5 percent annual interest compounded since then, for a total of almost $100 million.[165]

AMENDMENT VI: CRIMINAL COURT PROCEDURES

In all criminal prosecutions, the accused shall enjoy the right to a speedy [trial]

"This guarantee is an important safeguard to prevent undue and oppressive incarceration prior to trial, to minimize anxiety and concern accompanying public accusation, and to limit the possibilities that long delay will impair the ability of an accused to defend himself."[1] This right differs from other constitutional rights in that "there is a societal interest in providing a speedy trial which exists separate from, and at times in opposition to, the interests of the accused," who often finds delay to his or her advantage. It also differs in that if it is determined that a defendant has been denied a speedy trial, the only remedy is the drastic one of dismissal of the charges without the possibility of their reinstatement, for the fault is not correctable, as are other violations of the Sixth Amendment, by a retrial.[2]

A trial clearly may be "speedy" in a legal sense even though it admits of considerable delay, especially delays caused by the counsel for the accused. "The many procedural safeguards provided an accused mean that the ordinary procedures for criminal prosecution are designed to move at a deliberate pace."[3] But when Texas failed for six years to try a prisoner in a federal penitentiary who had requested that the state proceed with its charges against him, Texas failed to meet the constitutional requirement, and the state had to dismiss its charges against him.[4]

The speedy trial requirement applies to states through the Fourteenth Amendment. The constitutional right to a speedy trial starts from the time a person has been formally charged, not from the time of arrest. There is no right to "speedy arrest." (Federal law, however, now starts the clock from time of arrest for federal crimes or from the time the police discover evidence of a crime.) Nor does the speedy trial guarantee apply when the government, acting in good faith, has formally dropped charges and then later reinstates them. However, undue and prejudicial delay by the prosecution before arrest or indictment, or between dropping charges and reinstating them, could create a due process claim.[5] The Supreme Court has refused to give the words "speedy trial" any precise time limit.[6] Rather, the Court has listed four factors that must be taken into account in determining whether the right to a speedy trial has been violated: the length of the delay, the reasons for the delay, a defendant's demand for waiver of the right to an immediate trial, and any disadvantage to a defendant because of the delay.[7]

Congress had adopted a law designed to expedite criminal trials in federal courts. The 1974 Speedy Trial Act, openly opposed by many federal judges as an ineffective congressional interference in court business, provides time limits for various stages of a case, from arrest through indictment to trial, with some exclusions of time for various purposes. If any of the specified deadlines is not met, the judge is to decide whether to dismiss the charges with prejudice, which will bar reprosecution, or to dismiss them without prejudice, which will allow for reprosecution. Although it is not clear that defendants' causes are advanced when charges against them are dropped without prejudice, such action expresses a congressionally defined goal that justice should move more swiftly in the future than it has in the past.

---

and public trial,

A public trial is essential for due process and therefore is a right secured to defendants in state as well as federal courts.[8] The right to a public trial belongs to defendants and not to television camera operators, photographers, or newspaper reporters. The requirement of a public trial is satisfied if the members of the public and press have an opportunity to attend the trial and to report what they observe. The press does not have a right to be allowed to broadcast or tape the trial. Nor does the First Amendment grant the press any right to information about the trial superior to that of the general public.[9]

In 1979, in *Gannett Co.* v *DePasquale*, the Supreme Court went so far as to declare that because the Sixth Amendment confers rights on defendants — not the press or the public — a judge could, with the consent of the defendant, close a judicial hearing to the public. The case involved a pretrial hearing, but Justice Stewart, writing for the Court, used the word *trial*. The decision created such adverse criticism, however, especially from the press, that three justices felt compelled to find an occasion to emphasize that the *Gannett* decision applied only to preliminary hearings.[10] A year later, in *Richmond Newspapers, Inc.* v *Virginia* (as noted on page 155), the Court interpreted the First Amendment to limit severely the scope of the *Gannett* decision. Since then *Gannett* has been even further restricted. An accused has a Sixth Amendment right to insist on a public trial, including a pretrial suppression hearing, and judges' authority to close trials or preliminary hearings is limited to those few instances when they can show an overriding need to do so.[11]

There is no constitutional right to a private trial. A state may permit the televising of trials notwithstanding the objections of the defendants.[12] However, the televising of a trial might create such distractions that it denies the defendant due process. And if a judge allows news people to hound witnesses or permits the prosecutor to make damaging statements to the press that deprive the defendant of a right to trial by an impartial jury free from outside influences, such actions create due process problems. As the Supreme Court said, "Trial courts must take strong measures to ensure that the balance is never weighted against the accused."[13]

by an impartial jury

Despite the fact that Article III requires for all federal crimes a trial by jury in the state in which a crime was committed, the right was considered so important that it was further guaranteed by the Sixth Amendment. The Fourteenth Amendment "guarantees a right of jury trial in all [state] criminal cases which, were they tried in a federal court, would come within the Sixth Amendment's guarantee of trial by jury."[14]

Trial by jury is a constitutional requirement for serious but not petty crimes. Petty offenses are those punishable by no more than six months in prison and a $500 fine.[15] The jury trial requirement applies to convictions for criminal contempt if the penalty imposed exceeds imprisonment for six months.[16] It does not apply to civil contempt or to other noncriminal proceedings, such as deportation or loyalty and security hearings.

Trial by jury was once thought to include all the elements recognized by common law at the time the Constitution was adopted, the most important being a jury of exactly twelve members and the requirement of a unanimous verdict for conviction. In 1970, however, the Supreme Court decided that a twelve-person jury is not an "indispensable component of the Sixth Amendment."[17] A jury composed of at least six people will do. Fewer than six, the Court has decided, promotes inaccurate and biased verdicts, causes lack of consistency in verdicts, and prevents juries from adequately representing a cross-section of the community. Moreover, reduction below six provides no particular saving in court time or costs.[18] (Although the Sixth Amendment no longer requires a twelve-member criminal jury, most states and the federal government continue to use such juries.)

Unanimity is constitutionally required for conviction in federal courts, but not in state courts. This result came about because Justice Powell, who had the swing vote on the issue, took the view that the Sixth Amendment, which applies to the federal government, calls for unanimous verdicts but that the Fourteenth Amendment, which applies to the states, while requiring states to use juries for serious crimes, does not require that state juries be unanimous for conviction. How much less than unanimous is not clear. The Court has approved convictions by the votes of nine jurors out of twelve.[19] The Court has said, however, that if a state uses the minimum number of jurors permitted under the Constitution — that is, six — the decisions must be unanimous.[20]

Defendants may waive the right to a jury trial, but a judge may insist on a jury trial even against the wishes of the defendant, for there is no constitutional right *not* to be tried by a jury.[21] However, defendants can, by a plea of guilty, waive the right to any kind of trial.

A person is entitled to trial by an impartial jury, which means a jury drawn from a panel that represents a "fair cross section" of the community and that has had no person excluded because of race, sex, national origin, or religion. The fair-cross-section requirement applies to the panels — venires, they are called — from which juries are drawn, not to the actual composition of the jury itself.[22] A defendant does not have to be a member of an excluded class to object to a trial by a jury from which persons have been excluded because of race, sex, national origin, or religion; that is, a white person may object to the absence of black people, and a man to the absence of women.[23]

Practices or statutes that bias the selection of particular categories of persons may run afoul of this fair-cross-section requirement. Thus, a Missouri statute was declared unconstitutional that allowed women, but not men, to be excused from jury duty merely by so requesting.[24] There is no violation of the Constitution, however, if a judge exempts women from service who request it because of the need to stay home with small children, even if the granting of such requests results in an all-male jury.

To ensure that the jury is impartial, both the prosecution and the defense have a right to question prospective jurors about their possible biases. A capital defendant accused of an interracial crime is entitled, on request, to have prospective jurors informed of the race of the victim and questioned on the issue of racial bias.[25] Except for such cases, there is no automatic constitutional rule that permits a defendant to question jurors about racial prejudice. If the trial court determines, however, that "there are substantial indications of the likelihood of racial or ethnic prejudice affecting the jurors in a particular case," it may permit such questions. The Supreme Court has also left to the discretion of the trial judge whether defendants with beards may interrogate potential jurors about their possible prejudice against bearded persons.[26] Of a more serious nature, at least to persons without beards, the Court has ruled that a jury from which persons have been excluded because of their general objections to the death penalty cannot be impartial in choosing between a sentence of life and a sentence of death and that such a jury does not represent a fair cross-section of the community.[27] Jurors may be excluded, however, if they make it "'unmistakably clear' that they would 'automatically' vote against capital punishment without regard to the evidence or that their attitude toward penalty would prevent them from making an impartial decision as to the defendant's 'guilt.' "[28] Or, as the Court more recently explained about the constitutionality of "death-qualified" juries, a juror may be excluded when his (or her) views would "prevent or substantially impair the performance of his duties as a juror in accordance with his instructions and his oath."[29]

Interesting equal protection clause questions related to the impartial jury requirement are raised by the long-established practice of giving both prosecution and defense the right to challenge peremptorily and exclude from the jury a certain number of people. Potential jurors removed by peremptory challenges are in addition to the unlimited number that the judge may remove for cause on the recommendation of the prosecutor or the defense attorney. No reason has to be given for a peremptory challenge: one can excuse fat people or tall people or people with college degrees or people without them or rich people or poor people — any person or group of persons one wishes.

Until recently a state prosecutor could, through peremptory challenges, exclude all white people or all black people from a jury. However, in Batson v Kentucky the Supreme Court held, not for Sixth Amendment reasons of ensuring an impartial jury, but for equal protection reasons, that a prosecutor's use of peremptory challenges to exclude all blacks from a jury trying black defendants establishes a prima facie case of purposeful racial discrimination.[30] The burden then shifts to the prosecution to provide a neutral explanation that relates to the particular case. It will not do merely to assert that black jurors as a group will be unable to consider impartially the case against a black defendant.[31]

of the State and district wherein the crime shall have been committed, which district shall have been previously ascertained by law,

Early English juries were always from the neighborhood of the accused, which was sometimes an advantage for the accused, sometimes not. One of the grievances against George III was that his government had forced American colonists to stand trial in England for offenses alleged to have been committed in America. To prevent the national government from using such procedures, both Article III and the Sixth Amendment require trials to be held in the state in which the crime was committed (the Sixth Amendment adds district). Defendants may, however, petition for removal of the trial from the district on the grounds that the community has been so inflamed and prejudiced against them that it would be impossible to select a fair and impartial jury in the district in which the crime was committed.

---

and to be informed of the nature and cause of the accusation;

A statute must state precisely the acts that are forbidden and must include all the ingredients essential to a proper judgment of guilt of the crime. A law violates this requirement if it is so vague as to provide no clear notice that an action has been made criminal and no clear standard to guide judge and jury in determining guilt.

---

to be confronted with the witnesses against him;

This clause provides two types of protection for criminal defendants: the right physically to face those who testify against them and the right to conduct cross-examination. The cases involving the clause fall into two general categories: (1) cases that relate to the admission of testimony by a person not available for cross-examination and (2) cases in which the opportunity to cross-examine has been restricted by law or by a court ruling.[32]

Under most circumstances a witness's evidence cannot be introduced at a trial unless the witness is available for cross-examination.[33] The prosecution must either produce the accusatory witnesses or demonstrate their unavailability. If witnesses are shown to be unavailable, their written statements can be used only when there are ample "indicia of reliability."[34] Other exceptions to face-to-face accusation are certain deathbed statements, evidence given at a prior trial by a witness who has since moved to a foreign country, and evidence given at a preliminary hearing by a witness no longer available to testify.[35]

The Court recently sustained the exclusion of a defendant from a hearing held to determine the competency of two child witnesses to testify against him at a subsequent trial for child sexual molestation. The Court did so because the purpose of the hearing was to establish whether the children were able to remember basic facts and to distinguish between telling the truth and telling a lie, because the defendant's attorney was allowed to remain to cross-examine, and because the defendant would have an opportunity for full and effective cross-examination of the two witnesses during the trial. The dissenters argued that the clause plainly envisions that witnesses against the accused shall testify in the defendant's physical presence; its purpose is not merely to secure the right of cross-examination. "Not until today," wrote Justice Marshall for the three dissenters, "has this Court gone so far as to substitute a defendant's subsequent opportunity for cross-examination for his right to confront adverse witnesses in a prior testimonial proceeding."[36]

Defendants may lose their right to confront adverse witnesses if they engage in such disruptive behavior that their trials cannot proceed as long as they remain in the courtroom, or if they voluntarily absent themselves from the proceedings.[37] On the other side of the ledger, a state may not introduce at a trial the accusatory statements of juveniles whose anonymity it wishes to preserve.[38]

A difficult problem is how to handle the confessions of nontestifying codefendants. Although it is ordinarily assumed that juries will follow instructions, defendants are deprived of their rights under the confrontation clause when the confessions of nontestifying codefendants naming them as participants in a crime are introduced at a joint trial, even if the jury is instructed to consider a confession only against the defendant who made it.[39] The codefendant's confession is admissible, however, if it is edited to omit any reference to other defendants.[40]

The right to confront witnesses does not require the government to make pretrial disclosure of any and all information that might be useful to defendants. However, the failure of the state to produce material evidence in its possession could raise serious due process considerations.

---

to have compulsory process for obtaining witnesses in his favor,

---

Under eighteenth-century English common law, persons accused of felonies or treason were not allowed to introduce any witnesses in their own defense. England abolished this general disqualification in 1787 but retained a number of restrictions on the kind of witnesses who could be called. For a while we followed English practices, but in 1918 the Supreme Court declared that all persons of competence who may have knowledge of the facts involved in a case should be allowed to be called, with a few exceptions. Among these exceptions is the husband-wife privilege, but it has been limited. A husband may no longer deny his wife, and vice versa, the right to testify if she (or he) wishes to do so.[41] However, the common-law testimonial privileges protecting communications between lawyer and client, priest and penitent, and doctor and patient still give to those involved in such communications the privilege of refusing to testify if they wish to claim it. The disqualification of witnesses because of mental infirmity or infancy remains undisturbed.

The Supreme Court "has had little occasion to discuss the contours of the Compulsory Process Clause.... At a minimum ... criminal defendants have the right to the Government's assistance in compelling the attendance of favorable witnesses at a trial and the right to put before a jury evidence that might influence the determination of guilt."[42] A state has no authority to compel the attendance in its court proceedings of witnesses outside its jurisdiction. Nonetheless, it must make a good faith effort to secure witnesses for the defense wherever they are.[43]

The clause, which has been incorporated into the due process requirement of the Fourteenth Amendment,[44] does not by its terms grant criminal defendants the right to secure the attendance and testimony of any and all witnesses; it guarantees them only "compulsory process for obtaining *witnesses in their favor*." Thus, defendants cannot establish a violation of their constitutional right to compulsory process merely by showing that the government has not helped to produce a witness; they must make some "plausible showing of how" the witness's testimony would have been both material and favorable to their defense.[45]

---

and to have the Assistance of Counsel for his defence.

What was once a right of defendants to be represented by an attorney during trial, provided they could afford to obtain such assistance, has now become a positive obligation — for federal authorities since *Johnson* v *Zerbst* (1938) and for state authorities since *Gideon* v *Wainwright* (1963) — to secure lawyers for those who are unable to pay for their own.

"Where assistance of counsel is a constitutional requirement, the right to be furnished counsel does not depend on request."[46] Unless the record clearly shows that defendants, with full awareness of what they were doing, waived their right to counsel, the absence of such counsel will render criminal proceedings unconstitutional. To complicate the issue, the right to assistance of counsel includes the right *not* to be assisted by counsel, provided the record clearly shows that defendants — again with full awareness of what they were doing — asked the judge for the right to defend themselves.[47] Although a judge must grant such a request, the appointment of standby counsel by the judge does not violate defendants' rights to conduct their own defense, provided the standby counsel's participation does not interfere with the defendants' actual control over the presentation of their defense and cannot reasonably be thought to have undermined the defendants' appearance before the jury in the status of representing themselves.[48]

"The Sixth Amendment right to counsel does not attach until after the initiation of formal charges."[49] (Under the Fifth Amendment, however, persons not formally accused of a crime but subject to custodial interrogation have the right to refuse to answer questions until furnished with an attorney.) After criminal charges have been initiated, whether by formal charge, preliminary hearing, indictment, information, or arraignment, defendants are entitled to have a lawyer at their side whenever and wherever they appear and substantial rights may be affected. Included are occasions when defendants are subject to identification by victims, as in lineups (but not when arrays of photographs are used); preliminary hearings; the trial itself, of course; the time when the judge instructs the jury; and the sentencing.[50]

Confessions and other evidence secured in violation of the right to the assistance of counsel are subject to essentially the same exclusionary rules as are applied to enforce the Fourth Amendment. And what police and prosecutors may not do directly — namely, cross-examine defendants without counsel when counsel has been requested — they may not do indirectly. For example, although there is no constitutional prohibition against the use of undercover agents, prosecutors violated the Sixth Amendment when they instructed a paid informer in the same jail with the accused to listen for and report any damaging statements made by the accused. The government had intentionally created a situation likely to induce the accused to make incriminating statements without the assistance of counsel.[51] In short, after being formally charged with a crime, the accused has a right to communicate with the state only through his or her lawyer.

Perhaps the decision that went to the limit of the application of this principle was the five-to-four holding in *Brewer* v *Williams* (1977). That decision reversed a conviction for murdering a child because it was based on a confession made to the police while they were transporting the accused to jail after his attorney had requested that he not be questioned that evening. The police had induced the confession by telling Williams that because it was snowing so hard, the child might not be able to have "a Christian burial" unless he told them where the body could be found.[52] (On retrial, Williams was convicted again. This time his conviction was sustained.[53])

When a right of appeal has been established by statute (all jurisdictions now provide at least one appeal for all criminal convictions), a defendant is constitutionally entitled to the help of an attorney in making the first appeal.[54] (This right to an effective attorney for an appeal was held to be guaranteed by due process rather than Sixth Amendment considerations, but it seems that the Court, although saying "due process," was thinking Sixth Amendment.) For other appeals, a state need not furnish attorneys at public expense.[55] If placed on probation, a person is entitled to legal help whenever there is a hearing to revoke probation.

In some jurisdictions, when persons are unable to afford their own counsel, judges assign them lawyers from the community. However, the growing practice in the larger states and cities is to create and support from tax funds an office of public defender. Congress now requires each federal district court to have an organized plan to ensure that indigents are adequately represented.

A defendant unable to afford counsel is not entitled to the attorney of his or her choice and is not guaranteed a "meaningful attorney-client relationship," only that counsel will be competent.[56] How competent? The Sixth Amendment right to counsel is the right to the *effective* assistance of counsel. However, the burden is on the defendant to prove that counsel provided was not effective, and the defendant must show, first, that counsel's performance was deficient because of serious errors and, second, that this deficient performance did in fact prejudice the defense to such an extent that the defendant was deprived of a fair trial.[57]

Does the right to the assistance of counsel — or its more significant corollary, the right to have the government furnish and pay for counsel if one cannot afford it — extend only to trials for serious offenses or to all trials? "No accused may be deprived of his liberty as the result of any criminal prosecution, . . . whether or not a jury trial is required . . . in which he was denied the assistance of counsel."[58] The only trials exempt from the assistance-of-counsel requirement are those in which fines are the sole penalty actually imposed.[59] This requirement differs from that for jury trials. A jury trial must be offered for any crime for which imprisonment for more than six months may be imposed, even if in fact only a fine is levied.

The Sixth Amendment protects the right to the help of a trained lawyer, but the Supreme Court, proceeding more from due process than Sixth Amendment considerations, has established a variety of conditions under which psychiatric or clinical psychological help is constitutionally necessary. For example, when defendants in a criminal prosecution make a preliminary showing that their sanity at the time of the offense is likely to be a significant factor at their trial, they are entitled access to a psychiatrist even if they cannot otherwise afford such professional help. They are also entitled to such help at the time of sentencing if a question of their future dangerousness is involved.[60]

AMENDMENT VII: TRIAL BY JURY IN COMMON-LAW CASES

In Suits at common law, where the value in controversy shall exceed twenty dollars, the right of trial by jury shall be preserved, and no fact tried by a jury, shall be otherwise re-examined in any Court of the United States, than according to the rules of the common law.

This provision refers to litigation in federal courts and has *not* been incorporated into the due process requirement of the Fourteenth Amendment. It concerns suits at common law and it does not prevent the two parties from dispensing with a jury with the consent of the court. It does not apply to equity proceedings, which are seldom before a jury.

For many years it was generally thought that the constitutional right to jury trial extended only to actions arising under the common law, not to those arising out of statutes enacted by Congress. In 1974 the Supreme Court declared the contrary: "The Seventh Amendment does apply to actions enforcing statutory rights, and requires a jury trial upon demand, if the statutes create legal rights and remedies, enforceable in an action for damages in the ordinary courts of law."[1]

The amendment guarantees a jury trial to determine liability in actions by the government seeking civil penalties. It does not, however, guarantee that a jury will establish the amount of the penalty. Congress, if it wishes, can give to a judge the responsibility for assessing the penalty.[2]

The Seventh Amendment does not require that the jury be of the size and character known in common law. A jury of six members is satisfactory.[3] Most federal district courts are presently employing for civil cases some form of jury with fewer than twelve members. There is no holding whether less than unanimity would be permissible.

AMENDMENT VIII: BAIL AND CRUEL AND UNUSUAL PUNISHMENTS

Excessive bail shall not be required,

Until the Court's decision in *United States* v *Salerno* (1987), bail higher than might reasonably be calculated to ensure the presence of a defendant at trial was thought "excessive."[1] Since persons are to be considered innocent until their guilt has been determined by trial, the sole constitutional justification for bail was to prevent flight. Except for persons accused of capital crimes — because under some circumstances no amount of bail might be sufficient to ensure their presence at trial — this phrase was thought to guarantee that no person could be detained without bail until after conviction.

In *United States* v *Salerno* the Court upheld the preventive detention provisions of the Bail Reform Act of 1984 against the charge that they violated both the due process clause and the Eighth Amendment. That act, similar to laws in thirty or so states, authorizes federal judges to deny bail to "dangerous persons" charged with certain felonies, including serious drug offenses, crimes of violence, and crimes in which firearms were used or possessed. Suspects are entitled to a hearing on the matter within five days. Judges (in fact most hearings are before magistrates) must explain in writing why they believe there is clear and convincing evidence that no conditions of pretrial release can reasonably ensure the safety of other persons and of the community. Detention orders may be appealed.

In sustaining the law, Chief Justice Rehnquist stated for the Court, "This Clause . . . says nothing about whether bail shall be available at all. . . . We believe that when Congress has mandated detention on the basis of a compelling interest other than prevention of flight, as it has here, the Eighth Amendment does not require release on bail."[2]

---

nor cruel and unusual punishments inflicted

This ban limits government in three ways. First, it limits barbaric punishments, such as burning at the stake, crucifixion, breaking on the wheel, use of the rack and the thumbscrew, and service in chains at hard labor. "Moreover, the Eighth Amendment's proscriptions are not limited to those practices condemned by the common law in 1789 . . . [T]he Amendment also recognizes the evolving standards of decency that mark the progress of a maturing society."[3] The Eighth Amendment limits the conditions in which a state may operate its prisons and treat those convicted of crimes. Federal judges have declared unconstitutional the manner in which at least twenty-four states operated their prisons, in some cases their entire prison systems.

"The Constitution does not mandate comfortable prisons," and to the mere extent that conditions "are restrictive and even harsh they are part of the penalty that criminals pay for their offenses."[4] To prove cruel and unusual punishments in the operation of prisons, the standard ordinarily applied is "unnecessary and wanton" infliction of pain, but in the case of a riot, there must also be evidence that the force used to restore order was so wanton and unjustified that it was "tantamount to a knowing willingness that it occur."[5] "Double-celling" is not a violation. But when governments confine persons without proper diet in excessively crowded and unsanitary conditions and knowingly deny prisoners needed medical care, they violate the Constitution.[6]

Second, the clause prohibits punishments that are "grossly out of proportion to the severity of the crime or that make no measurable contribution to acceptable goals of punishment and hence are nothing more than the purposeless and needless imposition of pain and suffering." For example, the Court set aside the sentence of death for the crime of rape of an adult woman in the absence of additional physical attack or abuse.[7]

Outside the context of capital punishment, successful challenges to the proportionality of particular sentences have been exceedingly rare but not unknown. Although the Supreme Court said the proportionality principle would come into play if, say, a legislature made overtime parking a felony punishable by life imprisonment, it held that the Eighth Amendment did not prevent Texas from applying its recidivist statute to William James Rummel. The Texas statute calls for the mandatory life imprisonment of any person convicted for a third time of a felony. Rummel's convictions were for relatively minor offenses: fraudulent use of a credit card to obtain $80 worth of merchandise, passing a forged check in the amount of $28.36, and accepting $120.75 to repair an air conditioner that he never intended to repair.[8] Two years later the Court reaffirmed its unwillingness to get involved in the review of the proportionality of sentences and refused to set aside a forty-year sentence and a $20,000 fine for the crime of intending to distribute nine ounces of marijuana. The Court reaffirmed that for crimes classifiable as felonies, the length of the sentence imposed is purely a matter of legislative prerogative.[9]

Then just a year later, Justice Powell and the other dissenting justices in the *Rummel* case, along with Justice Blackmun from the *Rummel* majority, while insisting that their decision "is entirely consistent with" the *Rummel* ruling, rejected the view that the prohibition against disproportionate sentences applies only to cases involving capital punishment. They set aside South Dakota's sentencing of Jerry Helm to life in prison without possibility of parole after his conviction for his seventh nonviolent felony. For determining whether punishments are disproportionate, the Court majority set forth three guidelines: (1) the gravity of the offense and the harshness of the penalty, (2) the sentences imposed on other criminals in the same jurisdiction, and (3) the sentences imposed for the commission of the same crime in other jurisdictions.[10] Chief Justice Burger, with whom Justices White, Rehnquist, and O'Connor joined in dissent, accused the majority of ignoring the *Rummel* decision and of adopting a view that amounts to nothing more than a determination "that a sentence is unconstitutional if it is more severe than five justices think appropriate."

Third, the clause limits what can be considered a criminal offense. For example, merely being addicted to drugs or being a chronic alcoholic cannot be made a crime, for making it a crime would inflict punishment simply for being ill.[11] However, being drunk in public or buying drugs or possessing them can be made criminal, for such statutes punish persons, not for being ill, but for their behavior.[12]

The Eighth Amendment prohibition against cruel and unusual punishments applies only to criminal sanctions; it does not protect public school children from corporal punishment by their teachers. As far as protecting the students' due process, the Supreme Court in essence sent complaints about corporal punishment to the state courts.[13]

What of capital punishment? After much soul-searching and many decisions, the Supreme Court ruled that the death penalty is not per se cruel and unusual punishment for the crime of murder. But it must be properly imposed. Death is different from any other punishment, both in severity and finality. The sentencing process as well as the trial itself must satisfy both due process and Eighth Amendment requirements.[14]

The Court, although four justices do not agree, has made it clear that "the death penalty may be properly imposed only as to crimes resulting in the death of the victim."[15] For a while the Court's standard was that no one could be given the death penalty who was not actually the "triggerman" convicted of having killed, attempted to kill, or intended to kill someone. Merely having participated in a felony in which persons were killed by others would not do. In fact, there was some language that seemed to suggest that the death penalty could properly be imposed only on those who had committed an "outrageously wanton and vile murder."[16] However, the Rehnquist Court, reflecting new conservatism, has modified that standard and announced that persons participating in felonies may be given the death penalty even if they did not kill or intend to kill anybody, provided their participation in the felony was "major" and showed a reckless indifference to human life.[17]

A state may not leave the decision whether to impose capital punishment on a particular defendant solely to "the untrammeled discretion of a jury."[18] Nor may a state adopt a vague standard to guide judges and juries in distinguishing between those persons convicted of murder who will be subject to the death penalty and those who will not.[19] The state must ensure that whoever imposes the penalty—judge or jury—does so only after careful consideration of the character and record of the person convicted and the circumstances of a particular crime. The automatic use of the death sentence for every person convicted of a specified capital offense—for example, murder of a police officer or murder while serving a life sentence—will not do.[20] It is essential that the capital sentencing decision allow for any mitigating circumstances that may be relevant to either the particular offender or the particular offense. "The sentencer may not refuse to consider or be precluded from considering any relevant mitigating evidence" which the defendant wishes to present.[21] On the other hand, a state may not present to a jury during the sentencing phase of a capital murder trial a victim's statement describing the effect of the crime on the victims and their families or set forth the opinions of family members. Such evidence, said the Court, "creates a constitutionally unacceptable risk that the jury may impose the death penalty in an arbitrary and capricious manner."[22]

Most states leave to the jury the responsibility, after guilt has been established, of deciding whether the sentence should be life or death. Three states—Florida, Alabama, and Indiana—allow a judge to override a jury's recommendation of life imprisonment, and the Court has concluded that "placing the responsibility on a trial judge to impose the sentence in a capital case is [not] so fundamentally at odds with contemporary standards of fairness and decency" that the practice violates either the Eighth Amendment or the due process clause of the Fourteenth.[23]

In 1987 a substantial attack was made on the death penalty, based on persuasive statistical evidence that in Georgia those convicted of murdering a white person were much more likely than those convicted of murdering a black person to be given a death sentence. The evidence, it was argued, showed that the death penalty in Georgia was being imposed under a sentencing procedure that created a substantial risk that punishment would be inflicted in an arbitrary and capricious manner. A majority of the Court rejected this argument on the grounds that the sentence of death for the crime charged was not disproportionate merely because other defendants did not receive the death penalty. The dissenters responded that the evidence conclusively proved that in Georgia a jury would more likely than not have spared the defendant's life if his victim had been black, and they said that this fact alone demonstrated that the sentencing procedures of Georgia, in addition to violating the equal protection clause, by their arbitrariness amounted to cruel and unusual punishment.[24]

The Eighth Amendment forbids the execution of any person who is insane at the time of the execution and requires that a state provide an opportunity for some kind of hearing on this issue to dispose of claims of insanity.[25]

AMENDMENT IX: RIGHTS RETAINED BY THE PEOPLE

The enumeration in the Constitution, of certain rights, shall not be construed to deny or disparage others retained by the people.

This amendment embodies the dominant political thought of eighteenth-century America, which taught that before the establishment of government, people existed in a state of nature and lived under the natural law, which endowed them with certain natural rights. When, by mutual consent, people created government, they granted to it their natural right of judging and executing the natural law but retained the rest of their natural rights. In accordance with this theory, the Bill of Rights did not *confer* rights but merely *protected* those already granted by the natural law. The Ninth Amendment made it clear that the enumeration of rights to be protected did not imply that the other natural rights not mentioned were abandoned.

Although mentioned in passing,[1] until 1965 no law had been declared unconstitutional because of disparagement of any of these unenumerated rights, nor had there been any suggestion that this amendment limited the powers of the states. Then the Court ruled that a Connecticut law forbidding the use of contraceptives violated the right of marital privacy and stated that this right is "within the penumbra of specific guarantees of the Bill of Rights" and is one of the fundamental rights reserved by the Ninth Amendment to the people against disparagement by a state or the national government.[2] More recent decisions tend to peg the right of privacy on the protections of the due process clauses of the Fifth and Fourteenth Amendments.

Among the other rights found in the Ninth Amendment, but always in connection with other constitutional provisions, arc the right to be presumed innocent, the right to be judged by a standard of proof beyond a reasonable doubt of guilt in a criminal trial, the right to travel among states, and the right to attend a criminal trial.

After the incorporation of most of the specific provisions of the Bill of Rights into the Fourteenth Amendment, some anticipated that the "glittering generalities" of the Ninth Amendment would become a new constitutional battleground. But the justices who want to protect from governmental intrusion what they consider basic rights not otherwise specifically secured in the Constitution have found the language of the due process and equal protection clauses sufficiently commodious to suit their needs.

AMENDMENT X: RESERVED POWERS OF THE STATES

The powers not delegated to the United States by the Constitution, nor prohibited by it to the States, are reserved to the States respectively, or to the people.

This amendment was adopted to assuage fears. It does not alter the distribution of powers between the national and state governments. It adds nothing to the Constitution; in the words of Justice Stone, "It is merely a truism."[1] Nonetheless, for a hundred years after John Marshall's death, the Supreme Court from time to time held that some of the reserved powers of the states were sovereign powers and hence set a limit to the delegated powers of the national government. When the national government used its specifically granted taxing and spending powers in such a way that agricultural production was regulated, its action was held by the Supreme Court, in *United States* v *Butler* (1937), to be repugnant to this amendment, since the regulation of agriculture is a power reserved to the states.[2] Earlier the Supreme Court had ruled that since the power to regulate conditions of employment is reserved to the states, Congress could not use its powers to regulate interstate commerce (*Hammer* v *Dagenhart*) or to tax

(*Child Labor Tax Cases*) for the purpose of driving employers of children out of the interstate market.[3] In short, under the doctrine of dual federalism, the Supreme Court used the Tenth Amendment to limit some of the enumerated powers of the national government.

Subsequently, however, the Court reversed *Butler, Dagenhart,* and the *Child Labor Tax Cases* and returned to Marshall's view that the Tenth Amendment and the reserved powers of the states do not limit the national government in exercising the powers given it by the Constitution.[4] Today it makes no constitutional difference whether or not an act of Congress touches or governs matters otherwise subject to state regulation. Congressional regulation supersedes any conflicting state regulation.

When it comes to the application of national laws directly to the states, that is, to the way that states and local governments exercise their powers, "the Tenth Amendment . . . is not without significance." It declares "the constitutional policy that Congress may not exercise power in a fashion that impairs the States' integrity or their ability to function effectively in a federal system."[5] Yet, as already noted, after a temporary flirtation with the doctrine of dual federalism in *National League of Cities,* the Court by a five-to-four vote in *Garcia* v *San Antonio Metropolitan Transit Authority* returned to the more traditional view that the Tenth Amendment is not to be construed as setting any substantial judicially enforceable limits on the national government's full exercise of the powers granted to it. In essence the Court told the states to look to the structure of federalism — that states are represented in the Senate, that members of the House of Representatives champion their districts, that electoral votes for President are cast by states — and not to the federal courts to protect them from overreaching federal power. Justice Powell, writing for the dissenters, accused the majority of failing "to recognize the broad, yet specific areas of sovereignty that the Framers intended the States to retain. Indeed," he continued, "the Court barely acknowledges that the Tenth Amendment exists. . . . The Court recasts the language [of the Tenth Amendment] to say that the States retain their sovereign powers 'only to the extent that the Constitution has not divested them of their original powers and transferred those powers to the Federal Government.' "[6]

The relationships between the national government and the state governments are not symmetrical. The national government represents all the people, each state only some of them. Although national regulations may be applied to the states, no state may tax or otherwise regulate a federal agency, except with the consent of Congress. To give one of many examples: No state may levy any tax on liquor sold for use in military installations.[7] But Congress can collect from the states aircraft registration fees for helicopters, including state-owned helicopters used for police work.[8]

Note that the Tenth Amendment does not say that powers not *expressly* delegated to the United States are reserved to the states. The framers of the Tenth Amendment specifically rejected such a statement, for its adoption would have seriously curtailed the scope of natural powers. Moreover, it should be emphasized that the states must exercise their reserved powers subject to the national government's supremacy and to national constitutional limitations. For example, states have the reserved power to establish public schools, but they may not exercise this power contrary to the Fourteenth Amendment or to any other constitutional limit. Nor may they exercise it in such a way as to conflict with national regulations — for example, by compelling an eighteen-year-old drafted to serve in the United States armed forces to attend school.

The national power to raise and support armies and navies takes precedence over a state's power to educate.

PRE-CIVIL WAR AMENDMENTS

AMENDMENT XI: SUITS AGAINST STATES

The Judicial power of the United States shall not be construed to extend to any suit in law or equity, commenced or prosecuted against one of the United States by Citizens of another State, or by Citizens or Subjects of any Foreign State.

This amendment was proposed March 4, 1794 and proclaimed January 8, 1798.

Article III, Section 2, paragraph 1, among other things, extends the judicial power of the United States to "cases and controversies between a state and citizens of another state." During the struggle over ratification of the Constitution, many persons objected to this clause on the ground it would permit a private individual to hail a state before a federal court; they were assured by Hamilton and others that because of the doctrine of "sovereign immunity," no state could ever be sued without its own consent. In 1792, however, the Supreme Court applied the literal terms of the Constitution and upheld the right of the federal courts to take jurisdiction in a case commenced by a citizen of South Carolina against Georgia.[1] Since many states were in default on their debts, there was a great alarm lest a series of similar suits result. Immediately after the Supreme Court's decision, the Eleventh Amendment was proposed, and its ratification in effect "recalled" the decision.

The amendment in its literal terms only immunizes a nonconsenting state against federal court suits in law and equity brought by citizens of another state or by citizens of a foreign state. It has always been construed, however, to incorporate the doctrine of sovereign immunity and thus to extend to states immunity from suits of all kinds, including those in admiralty brought by foreign nations and, more importantly, those by a state's own citizens,[2] although some justices continue to argue that the amendment "bars federal court suits against States only by citizens of other States," not by its own citizens.[3]

The amendment immunizes states against suits brought against them in federal courts. It does not immunize counties, cities, school boards, or regional authorities created by interstate compact.[4] It does not protect a state against suit in the courts of another state.[5] The immunity does not depend on the state's being named as a party; it includes suits in which private individuals seek to impose a liability that must be paid from public funds. Thus, the amendment barred a federal district court from ordering Illinois officials to award retroactive welfare benefits they had wrongfully withheld.[6]

If a state commences a prosecution in a state court, the Eleventh Amendment does not prevent the person prosecuted from appealing the decision of a state court to the Supreme Court. The taking of the case from state courts to the Supreme Court is not considered the initiation of a new case by the individual against the state; it is merely the continuation of the one originally commenced or prosecuted by the state.

The Eleventh Amendment must be read in connection with other constitutional provisions, most especially the Fourteenth Amendment, which to some extent has modified the Eleventh. When Congress exercises authority granted to it by Section 5 of the Fourteenth Amendment, it can open federal courts to suits against state officials "which are constitutionally impermissible in other contexts."[7] The Court has also assumed "without deciding or intimating a view of the question, that the authority of Congress to subject unconsenting states to suit in federal court is not confined" to the Fourteenth Amendment. However, if Congress intends to override Eleventh Amendment immunity, its intent "must be expressed in unmistakably clear language." Moreover, Congress may make a state's participation in a federal program conditional on the state's willingness to waive its immunity, but the state must waive its immunity in express language or by such "overwhelming implications from the text as [will] leave no room for any other reasonable construction." (The Court in 1987 overruled a holding that permitted tacit state consent.[8])

In the landmark case *Ex parte Young*, the Supreme Court declared that the Eleventh Amendment does not prevent federal courts, on the application of private individuals, from restraining state officers who are acting unconstitutionally.[9] By the principle of the *rule of law*, a state officer who acts beyond the law ceases to be an officer and thus ceases to be a representative of the state. However, when state officers act beyond the law, their action is nevertheless state action for the purposes of the Fourteenth Amendment. This result is inconsistent but fortunate for the protection of constitutional rights.

Debates over the meaning of the Eleventh Amendment continue to stir deep passions and illustrate that what appear to be relatively technical and non-substantive issues can generate considerable heat and have major policy consequences. Justice Brennan leads a minority of four justices who would narrowly construe the Eleventh Amendment to preserve maximal freedom for those who believe that their constitutional rights have been violated to seek vindication in federal courts. The differences between the two sides is seen over the question how to apply *Ex parte Young*. That decision clearly opens federal courts to private individuals to protect them from alleged violations by state officials of *federal* laws and the *federal* Constitution. Should the federal courts provide similar protection against allegations of violations by state authorities of their own state constitutions and state laws? Justice Powell, speaking for the Court majority, refused in *Pennhurst II*, as the case came to be called, to extend the *Young* doctrine to such suits. As he said in a reaffirmed decision, such action "would emasculate the Eleventh Amendment."[10]

Although the Eleventh Amendment does not bar injunctive relief to prevent state officials from acting or continuing to act in an unconstitutional fashion, it does prevent suits for money damages to recover from *state* funds (in contrast to personal funds of the state officials) for past misconduct by state or local officials. The distinction is between actions that are designed to bring an end to ongoing and present violation of federal law and suits designed to compensate for past violations of federal law.[11]

Congress has authorized civil suits against officials who have willfully deprived persons of their constitutional rights, even if they acted under color of law, that is, on behalf of the government. (Any action in an official role is under color of law, whether or not the specific action is authorized.) To collect damages from officials, one must prove they acted knowingly or with malicious intent to deprive persons of their constitutional rights.[12] Damages may be collected only from the state officials, not from the state.[13] Municipalities, in contrast to states, may be required to pay compensatory damages for wrongs by their officials, even if done in good faith, if they were done according to policy or custom.[14]

Unlike other officials, judges have absolute immunity and cannot be sued for their judicial acts, even when such actions are in excess of their jurisdiction and are malicious or corrupt.[15] Nonetheless, judges may be liable for the payment of attorneys' fees for injunctive actions, actions designed not to collect damages but to prevent them from interfering with rights in the future.[16] Prosecutors, who have almost as much immunity from federal suits in the performance of their responsibilities as do judges,[17] are also subject to liability for payment of attorneys' fees for actions to enjoin them from acting improperly in the future.

AMENDMENT XII: ELECTION OF THE PRESIDENT

The Electors shall meet in their respective states and vote by ballot for President and Vice-President, one of whom, at least, shall not be an inhabitant of the same state with themselves; they shall name in their ballots the person voted for as President, and in distinct ballots the person voted for as Vice-President, and they shall make distinct lists of all persons voted for as President, and of all persons voted for as Vice-President, and of the number of votes for each, which lists they shall sign and certify, and transmit sealed to the seat of the government of the United States, directed to the President of the Senate; — The President of the Senate shall, in the presence of the Senate and House of Representatives, open all the certificates and the votes shall then be counted; — The person having the greatest number of votes for President, shall be the President, if such number be a majority of the whole number of Electors appointed; and if no person have such majority, then from the persons having the highest numbers not exceeding three on the list of those voted for as President, the House of Representatives shall choose immediately, by ballot, the President. But in choosing the President, the votes shall be taken by states, the representation from each state having one vote; a quorum for this purpose shall consist of a member or members from two-thirds of the states, and a majority of all the states shall be necessary to a choice. *And if the House of Representatives shall not choose a President whenever the right of choice shall devolve upon them, before the fourth day of March next following, then the Vice-President shall act as President, as in the case of the death or other constitutional disability of the President. [emphasis added].* — The person having the greatest number of votes as Vice-President, shall be the Vice-President, if such number be a majority of the whole number of Electors appointed, and if no person have a majority, then from the two highest numbers on the list, the Senate shall choose the Vice-President; a quorum for the purpose shall consist of two-thirds of the whole number of Senators, and a majority of the whole number shall be necessary to a choice. But no person constitutionally ineligible to the office of President shall be eligible to that of Vice-President of the United States.

This amendment was proposed December 8, 1803, and declared in force by the secretary of state September 25, 1804.

The emphasized portion of this amendment has been superseded by the Twentieth Amendment and modified by the Twenty-fifth.

The presidential electoral system is the classic example of how custom and usage have amended and democratized the Constitution. As previously mentioned, the authors of the Constitution expected electors to be distinguished citizens who would in fact, as well as in form, choose the president and the vice president. Their expectations were not fulfilled because of the rise of national political parties. By the election of 1800, electors had come to be party puppets, pledged in advance to vote for the candidates nominated by their respective parties. In that election the Republican-Democratic electors were in a majority. Since under the original provisions for selecting the president and the vice president each elector voted for two individuals without indicating which was his choice for president and which for vice president, Aaron Burr, the Republican-Democratic candidate for vice president, received the same number of electoral votes as Thomas Jefferson, the Republican-Democratic candidate for president. This circumstance transferred the election to the House of Representatives, where the Federalists were in control. Although many Federalists favored Burr as the lesser of two evils, Alexander Hamilton threw his great influence on the side of Jefferson, who was finally elected on the thirty-sixth ballot. The Twelfth Amendment was designed to prevent such a situation from occurring again.

The two major differences between the Twelfth Amendment and the original provisions of the Constitution, which were repealed by it, are as follows: First, today electors are required to cast separate votes clearly designating their choice for president and their choice for vice president. Second, in the event no person receives a majority of the electoral votes for president, the House of Representatives chooses from the three persons with the most electoral votes (rather than five, as in the original provision). Each state has one vote in the House. If no person receives a majority of the electoral votes for vice president, the Senate chooses between the two persons with the most electoral votes, each senator having one vote.

Today presidential and vice-presidential candidates are chosen by political parties in national nominating conventions. On the first Tuesday after the first Monday in November, the voters select the electors, who are morally pledged to cast their electoral votes for the candidates chosen by their particular national convention. In most states the electors' names do not even appear on the ballot; only the names of the candidates to whom they are pledged appear. Thus the electors have been reduced to automatons and the electoral college, as the electors are known collectively, to an automatic registering device.

The development of the two-party system had another consequence for the electoral college that the framers did not anticipate. It greatly lessened the probability that the House of Representatives would be called on to make the final selection. Only once since 1801 has the House exercised this duty. In the election of 1824, before the full development of our party system, Andrew Jackson, John Quincy Adams, and William Crawford received the most electoral votes, but not one of them had a majority. The House, voting by states, chose John Quincy Adams. The only time the Senate has been called upon to make the final selection for the vice presidency was in 1837, when it favored Richard M. Johnson over Francis Granger. With only two major political parties there is no dispersion of the vote, and one party is assured of a majority of the electoral votes. Whenever a strong third party develops, such as George Wallace's American Independent Party in the 1968 election (and John Anderson's independent candidacy in 1980), the probability of final selection by the House and Senate is greatly increased.

All the states except Maine now provide for the selection of electors on a general statewide, straight-ticket basis. Each voter casts one vote for all the electors of one party or independent candidate. This statewide, straight-ticket voting means that the party that receives the most popular votes in a state receives all that state's electoral votes. For example, in 1984 Reagan (that is, the Republican electors) received 59 percent of the popular vote in New York; Mondale received 41 percent. Ronald Reagan, nevertheless, received all thirty-six of New York's electoral votes.

It is even possible for a person to obtain a majority of the total popular vote without receiving a majority of the electoral votes. Let us take a hypothetical case involving two states to illustrate this point:

State X (15 electoral votes):   255,000 Republican popular votes
    250,000 Democratic popular votes
State Y (5 electoral votes):   20,000 Republican popular votes
    50,000 Democratic popular votes

Results:
Republican popular votes: 275,000   Republican electoral votes: 15
Democratic popular votes: 300,000   Democratic electoral votes: 5

Such a thing happened in 1876, when Tilden received more popular votes but lost the electoral vote to Hayes, and again in 1888, when Cleveland, despite his larger popular vote, was defeated by Harrison.

Despite the widely supported view that the electoral college needs to be reformed, it has been difficult to secure agreement about what reforms should be made. The 1980 elections temporarily revived and intensified the concerns about the risks inherent in our present arrangements: if John Anderson had secured enough electoral votes to keep either major party candidate from obtaining a majority, electors might have been tempted to exercise some discretion, or, more probably, the election would have been thrown into the House of Representatives, where the Anderson supporters might have had the balance of power votes necessary to determine the presidential choice between the two major-party candidates. The chaos that could result from the installation of a president selected through such procedures is hard to exaggerate.

For many years amendments have been introduced in Congress to change the procedures for electing the president and the vice president. Representatives of the less populous states have opposed proposals to provide for direct popular election. Since states have as many electoral votes as they have senators and representatives, the smaller states carry greater weight in the electoral college than they would in a nationwide direct election. Some people have proposed that we do away with the individual electors but retain the system of electoral votes and distribute a state's electoral vote in the same ratio as its popular vote. Such a change would eliminate any danger of an elector's disregarding the wishes of the voters (as happened in 1956, 1960, 1968, and 1972), lessen the influence of strategically located minorities, weaken the one-party system where it now exists, and ensure the election of the candidate with the largest popular vote. This change has been opposed by those who fear it would weaken the influence of people living in large cities, who often have the balance of power in presidential elections. These same objections hold even more strongly against proposals to have electors chosen by congressional districts rather than on statewide tickets.

CIVIL WAR AMENDMENTS

The Thirteenth, Fourteenth, and Fifteenth Amendments were adopted after and as a result of the Civil War. They were, so to speak, the terms of surrender dictated by the North to the South. Congress, for example, insisted that the southern states ratify the Fourteenth Amendment before federal troops were withdrawn and the states restored to full participation in Congress.

The purpose of these three amendments was to free the black slaves, grant them citizenship, and protect their rights, especially the right to vote, against infringement by the states. As Justice Miller wrote, "No one can fail to be impressed with the one pervading purpose of them all, . . . the freedom of the slave race, the security and firm establishment of that freedom, and the protection of the newly-made free man and citizen from the oppressions of those who formerly exercised unlimited dominion over him."[1] Clearly the purpose of these amendments was to deprive the states of the "right" to impose disabilities on blacks because of their race, color, or previous condition of servitude. It was to take almost three-quarters of a century, however, before the Civil War amendments were to be used for this purpose.

AMENDMENT XIII: SLAVERY

Section 1

Neither slavery nor involuntary servitude, except as a punishment for crime whereof the party shall have been duly convicted, shall exist within the United States, or any place subject to their jurisdiction.

This amendment was proposed on January 31, 1865, and declared in force by the secretary of state on December 18, 1865.

Before the adoption of this amendment, each state could determine for itself whether or not slavery should be permitted within its borders. The Thirteenth Amendment deprived both the states and the national government of that power. The amendment was aimed at black slavery. Without violating the amendment, a government may still compel persons to help build public roads (under the common law, men could be drafted for a certain number of days every year for this purpose, although in some cases, payment of taxes exempted them from such duties), to pay alimony, or to serve on a jury, in the militia, or in the armed forces.

Several state laws that made failure to work after receiving money *prima facie* evidence of intent to defraud have been held contrary to the Thirteenth Amendment. In effect, such laws made it a crime punishable by imprisonment to fail to work after securing money on the promise to do so.[2] They established a condition of *peonage*, involuntary servitude forced on a person to work off a debt.

Section 1 of the Thirteenth Amendment is one of the two provisions of the Constitution that an individual can violate directly and that is self-executing (the other is the Twenty-first Amendment). By its "own unaided force and effect" the Thirteenth Amendment abolished slavery and established universal freedom.

After all these years, the Supreme Court has not decided "whether the Thirteenth Amendment itself reaches practices with a disproportionate effect as well as those motivated by discriminatory purpose, or indeed whether it accomplished anything more than the abolition of slavery."[3]

Section 2

Congress shall have power to enforce this article by appropriate legislation.

"Whether or not Section 1 by its own force did anything more than abolish slavery is still an open question. But it is no longer open that under Section 2 Congress has the power to determine what are the badges and incidents of slavery, and the authority to translate that determination into effective legislation."[4] This more expansive interpretation of congressional power is of recent origin. Before 1968 the prevailing view was that all Section 2 did was to give Congress power to prevent the imposition of slavery and peonage, narrowly defined. Hence, it was ruled that Congress had no power under Section 2 to legislate against racial discrimination.[5]

Then, in *Jones* v *Mayer*, the Supreme Court construed Section 2 in a significantly new way, or some would say the Court finally got around to interpreting the section as its framers intended. The case grew out of a suit filed by Mr. and Mrs. Joseph Lee Joncs against a developer in St. Louis County, Missouri, who refused to sell them a home because Mr. Jones was black. The Joneses cited an almost unused section of the Civil Rights Act of 1866, enacted pursuant to the Thirteenth Amendment, that reads, "All citizens of the United States shall have the same right, in every State and Territory, as is enjoyed by white citizens thereof to inherit, purchase, lease, sell, hold, and convey real and personal property." Few thought that the Joneses had a good case; almost 90 years earlier, the Court had ruled that Congress lacked power under the Fourteenth Amendment (see page 250) to legislate against discrimination unless it was imposed or supported by governmental action. The Thirteenth Amendment was thought to cover only slavery; the Civil Rights Act of 1866 had always been construed to cover only state-imposed discrimination. Besides, in 1968 Congress had just passed a civil rights act covering discrimination in housing, which many thought superseded any impact the 1866 law might have had.

As anticipated, the district court dismissed the complaint and the court of appeals affirmed the decision, both courts concluding that the Civil Rights Act of 1866 applied only to state action and did not reach private refusals to sell. But the Supreme Court reversed the decision. Significant beyond the immediate facts of this case was the Supreme Court's interpretation of Section 2 of the Thirteenth Amendment. Justice Stewart, speaking for the Court, proclaimed,

> The Thirteenth Amendment authorized Congress to do more than merely dissolve the legal bond by which the Negro slave was held to his master; it gave Congress the power rationally to determine what are the badges and the incidents of slavery and the authority to translate that determination into effective legislation. . . .
>
> When racial discrimination herds men into ghettos and makes their ability to buy property turn on the color of their skin, then it too is a relic of slavery. . . .
>
> At the very least, the freedom that Congress is empowered to secure under the Thirteenth Amendment includes the freedom to buy whatever a white man can buy, the right to live wherever a white man can live. If Congress cannot say that being a free man means at least this much, then the Thirteenth Amendment made a promise the Nation cannot keep.[6]

Since the Jones decision the Supreme Court has several times reaffirmed its validity.[7] Furthermore, it has ruled that Congress intended the civil rights act passed during Reconstruction to protect not merely blacks but "identifiable classes of persons who are subject to intentional discrimination solely because of their ancestry or ethnic characteristics, such as Jews and Arabs."[8]

In short, Section 2, as now construed, gives Congress the authority to enact whatever legislation is necessary and proper to overcome all incidents and badges of slavery, no matter their source.

AMENDMENT XIV: CITIZENSHIP, PRIVILEGES AND IMMUNITIES OF UNITED STATES CITIZENSHIP, DUE PROCESS, AND EQUAL PROTECTION OF THE LAWS

Section 1

All persons born or naturalized in the United States, and subject to the jurisdiction thereof, are citizens of the United States and of the State wherein they reside.

This amendment was proposed June 13, 1866, and declared in force by the secretary of state July 28, 1868.

In the *Dred Scott* case (1857), Chief Justice Taney had declared that the framers did not include blacks as part of the sovereign "people of the United States"; he had written: "[Negroes] were not intended to be included, under the word 'citizen' in the Constitution, and can therefore claim none of the rights and privileges which that instrument provides for and secures to citizens of the United States. On the contrary, they were at that time considered as a subordinate and inferior class of beings, who had been subjugated by the dominant race, and, whether *emancipated or not* [italics added], yet remained subject to their authority, and had no rights or privileges but such as those who held the power and the government might choose to grant them."[1] The opening sentence of the Fourteenth Amendment reversed this decision.

Persons born in the United States but not subject to the jurisdiction thereof are children of foreign diplomats and children born of alien enemies in the event of a hostile occupation of the United States. Although the Native American tribes are subject to the jurisdiction of the United States, they have been considered a special category, and the Fourteenth Amendment did not directly confer citizenship on them. However, all Native Americans are now citizens of the United States by act of Congress. All other children born in the United States become citizens even if their parents are aliens.

The clause confers citizenship by the principle of *jus soli* — that is, by reason of place of birth; it does not prevent Congress from conferring citizenship by *jus sanguinis* — by reason of blood. Citizenship may also be acquired by naturalization.

The Constitution confers citizenship on all persons born or naturalized in the United States. Although naturalization secured by fraud may be canceled through proper judicial action and persons may under certain conditions voluntarily renounce their citizenship, what the Constitution confers, Congress cannot constitutionally take away. At various times Congress has tried. It has declared that persons who did certain things — for example, voting in elections in other nations, joining the military forces of another nation, and leaving the United States during time of war to avoid the draft — would be construed as having expatriated themselves and would be subject to having their citizenship taken from them by judicial action. The Supreme Court, however, has held those provisions unconstitutional. "In the last analysis expatriation depends on the will of the citizen rather than on the will of Congress and its assessment of his conduct."[2]

Congress has the power, nonetheless, to declare that persons who perform certain acts, for example, swearing allegiance to another country, create a presumption that they intend to relinquish citizenship. In such an instance a court may take citizenship away if the government proves by a preponderance of the evidence that the person both voluntarily performed the expatriating act and did so with the "intent to abandon citizenship."[3]

The Fourteenth Amendment confers citizenship only on persons born or naturalized in the United States. Congress can confer citizenship on others. It has done so for children born to American citizens outside the United States. Since it is Congress (not the Constitution) that confers this citizenship, Congress may set reasonable condition on the obtaining and retaining of such citizenship. Thus, the Court sustained a provision expatriating persons born outside the United States to a citizen parent and an alien if such persons do not return to the United States and live here for five continuous years between the ages of fourteen and twenty-eight (since changed to two years).[4]

Section 1

[continued] No State shall make or enforce any law which shall abridge the privileges or immunities of citizens of the United States;

After the adoption of the Thirteenth Amendment, several Southern states that had been restored by President Johnson promptly adopted legislation that, in the words of Justice Miller, "imposed upon the colored race onerous disabilities and burdens, and curtailed their rights in the pursuit of life, liberty, and property to such an extent that their freedom was of little value." Those laws convinced Congress, again to quote Miller, "that something more was necessary in the way of constitutional protection to the unfortunate race who had suffered so much."[5] Accordingly, Congress insisted on the ratification of the Fourteenth Amendment as a condition of its agreeing to restoring Southern state governments to full participation in the government of the Union. Despite the obvious purpose of the Fourteenth Amendment, to protect blacks from the "oppressions of those who had formerly exercised unlimited dominion" over them, it was not until the 1940s that the amendment was used primarily for this purpose. And it has not been the privileges and immunities clause that has been used, but rather the due process and equal protection clauses.

The Supreme Court, in the *Slaughter House Cases*, so narrowly construed the privileges and immunities clause in the very first case in which the Fourteenth Amendment came before it that it has never had much significance. The Court held that there are two distinct citizenships, state and federal, and that the "fundamental" civil and political rights that we enjoy are privileges or immunities stemming from *state*, not *United States*, citizenship. In other words, this clause conferred no new rights on United States citizens but merely made explicit a federal guarantee against abridgment of already established rights.

The privileges and immunities of United States citizens (which this clause forbids states to abridge) are those that owe their existence to the Constitution and the laws and treaties of the United States, such as the right to travel in the United States, the right to engage in interstate and foreign commerce, the right to the protection of the national government on the high seas and in foreign countries, and the right to vote in primaries and general elections in which members of Congress and presidential electors are chosen and to have that vote properly counted. And although the Supreme Court in past decisions has held that some important rights are not privileges or immunities of United States citizens — such as the right to be secure in one's home, the right to refuse to give self-incriminatory evidence in state courts, the right to engage in a legal occupation, the right to attend public schools, the right to vote in state elections[6] — the significance of those decisions has been undermined by more recent rulings. Those rights may not be privileges of United States citizens, but today they are protected by the due process and equal protection clauses of the Fourteenth Amendment. Furthermore, with the expansion of federal civil rights laws, there are a large number of such rights that owe their existence to federal laws and are thus protected from state (or private, for that matter) abridgment.

Section 1

[continued] nor shall any State deprive any person of life, liberty, or property, without due process of law;

It should be emphasized that this clause, as well as the privileges and immunities clause and the equal protection clause, is directed to the states, their officials, and local governments. Private wrongs — wrongful acts of private individuals — if not sanctioned in some way by a state, do not violate the Fourteenth Amendment.

As has been noted, after the Supreme Court's interpretation of the privileges and immunities clause rendered it ineffective as a protector of "fundamental rights," an attempt was made to make the due process clause serve this purpose, an attempt that was not completely successful until the 1960s. The Supreme Court still has not gone so far as to make the due process clause of the Fourteenth Amendment a mirror image of the Bill of Rights, although as noted, most provisions of the Bill of Rights have been incorporated into the due process clause.

Section 1

[continued] nor deny to any person within its jurisdiction the equal protection of the laws.

The equal protection clause, often merging into substantive due process, is the Court's major instrument for scrutinizing state regulations. There is no equal protection clause limiting the national government; however, just as the due process clause of the Fourteenth Amendment has been used to apply provisions of the Bill of Rights to the states, so has the due process clause of the Fifth Amendment been used to prevent national discriminatory legislation.[7]

When a state law is challenged as a violation of the equal protection clause, the Court chooses among three different *tiers* or tests. The lowest, or least stringent, is the traditional rational basis test. Under this test, "it's enough that the State's action be rationally based and free from invidious discrimination."[8] "It does not offend the Constitution merely because the classification is not made with mathematical nicety or because in practice it results in some inequality."[9] When using this test, the justices emphasize that the Constitution does not forbid governments from making distinctions among people, for it could not legislate without doing so. What it forbids is unreasonable classification when there is no relation between the classes the law creates and permissible governmental goals. When the act relates to social and economic legislation and does not employ suspect classifications (see page 230) or impinge on fundamental rights (see page 229), it must be upheld against equal protection attack if the legislative means are rationally related to a legitimate governmental purpose. Moreover, such legislation carries with it a presumption of rationality that can only be overcome by a clear showing of arbitrariness and irrationality.[10]

The rational basis test has been applied primarily to legislation impinging on business activities or the distribution of public benefits under general legislation such as social security. It essentially means that any law is constitutional so long as it serves some legitimate governmental purpose, even if not the purpose stated by the legislature.[11]

Various justices — Powell, Brennan, Marshall, and Stevens — have at times argued that the rational basis test should be firmed up slightly. They claim that when the legislature has made clear the purpose it intends a statute to serve, thus assuring the courts that the legislature has made a conscious policy choice, such action should receive "the most respectful deference." But when no clear legislative purpose appears from a reading of the statute and the only purpose before the Court is one stated by a government lawyer litigating the constitutionality of the statute, then the Court should require that the classification bear a "fair and substantial relation" to the asserted purpose. "While the absence of a clear statement of purposes need not doom a statute under rationality review, our task must always be to determine whether a particular rational purpose *actually* motivated the Legislature."[12] "This marginally more demanding scrutiny indirectly would test the plausibility of the tendered purpose."[13] However, a majority of the Court has rejected this construction of the rational basis test, and it is probably accurate to say, as Justice Stevens has charged, that once the Court decides that the rational basis test should be applied, "any 'conceivable basis' for a discriminatory classification will repel a constitutional attack . . . [and] judicial review . . . constitute[s] a mere tautological recognition of the fact that Congress [or a state legislature] did what it intended to do."[14] However, there have been rare occasions on which the Court has used the equal protection clause to hold a state purpose improper. For example, by five to four the Court declared that Alabama's goal of encouraging the formation of new Alabama insurance companies by imposing a higher tax on premiums paid for insurance from out-of-state companies was not a legitimate state purpose.[15]

The top tier, or most stringent scrutiny, under the equal protection clause reverses the normal presumption of constitutionality: a state must demonstrate that its actions serve a "compelling governmental interest" and that it has "adopted those means to accomplish the intended ends that put the least possible restraint on the fundamental right in question."[16]

There is also a middle tier. This test is not as rigid as the compelling-state-interest test or as relaxed as the rational basis test. This intermediate tier, often called *heightened scrutiny* to contrast with the *stringent scrutiny* requirement of the top tier, requires that the law be more than a rational means to a legitimate governmental end but not that it be the least restrictive means to accomplish a compelling government interest. Rather the law must serve "important governmental objectives and must be substantially related to the achievement of these objectives."[17] This intermediate tier applies when the law affects neither a suspect class nor a fundamental right but involves an almost suspect, or a "disfavored," classification.

Obviously it makes a substantial difference which kind of equal protection test is applied. If the Court uses the lower tier test, it seldom declares a law unconstitutional. If it decides that the upper tier analysis should be used, it almost never declares the law constitutional. If it decides that the middle tier test applies, the outcome is more difficult to predict. What, then, determines which test is to be applied? Although various critics, including some of the justices, contend that judges make up their minds about the results and then choose the level of scrutiny to fit, the established doctrine is that the upper tier test applies only if the law impinges on fundamental rights or deals with suspect classifications.

Which rights are fundamental and which are not? The justices have not been very clear on this point. Beyond those rights "readily identifiable in the Constitution's text," the Court, "[s]triving to assure itself and the public" that much more is involved than "the imposition of the Justices' own choice of values," has given various formulations over the years. One is that fundamental liberties are those " 'implicit in the concept of ordered liberty,' such that 'neither liberty nor justice would exist if [they] were sacrificed.' " Another formulation characterizes these rights as "those liberties that are 'deeply rooted in this Nation's history and tradition.' "[18]

Clearly, it is not a right's importance that makes it fundamental in a constitutional sense. For example, the rights to food, shelter, and education are basic, but they are not in a constitutional sense fundamental rights. They are not rights the Constitution "explicitly or implicitly" guarantees. The following rights, among others, have been declared fundamental in a constitutional sense: free speech, freedom of religion, freedom to associate, personal privacy, freedom to travel in the United States (but not abroad) if one is under no legal restraint and is not fleeing from officials, access to the courts, the right to marry, freedom from government interference with marital privacy, and the right to obtain an abortion during the early stages of pregnancy (a right deriving from the right to privacy — the right of women to make "intimate decisions" affecting their bodies).[19]

The Court, although refusing to extend the protection of fundamental rights to education, has reserved the question "whether a minimally adequate education is a fundamental right and whether a statute alleged to discriminatorily infringe that right should be accorded heightened equal protection review."[20] Thus, although there is no fundamental right to an adequate or good education, there may be one to at least enough education to be able to read and write.

The Supreme Court has refused to extend the fundamental right of marital privacy to the right of homosexuals to engage in consensual sodomy, because that right of privacy does not relate to procreation, marriage, or the right to decide whether or not to beget or bear a child.[21]

The suspect classification criterion grew out of what may be the most famous Supreme Court footnote of all time, footnote 4 in Justice Stone's opinion in *United States* v *Carolene Products Co.* In that footnote Justice Stone indicated that judges should subject certain kinds of legislation to greater constitutional scrutiny, including statutes directed at discrete and insular religious, national, or racial minorities.[22] Taking off from this language Justice Powell explained that the traditional criteria for determining which groups fall into a suspect, and therefore especially protected, class are "an immutable characteristic determined solely by the accident of birth, or a class saddled with such disabilities, or subjected to such a history of purposeful inequal treatment, or regulated to such a political powerlessness as to command extraordinary protection from the majoritarian political process."[23] Classifications based on race or national origin (or, as it is now called, ethnicity) are clearly suspect. And as far as states are concerned, so is alienage (the condition of being alien), although because of Congress's power to regulate immigration, national legislation affecting aliens is not subject to the same rigid scrutiny as are state laws.[24] Religion is probably a suspect classification, although there is no specific Supreme Court decision to this effect other than those stemming from the First Amendment.

The intermediate tier test applies to laws that deal with disfavored classifications, which at the moment include illegitimacy and sex. "Illegitimacy is analogous in many respects to the personal characteristics that have been held to be suspect," wrote Justice Powell for the Court. "We nevertheless conclude that the analogy is not sufficient to require our most exacting scrutiny."[25] Yet, in reviewing laws imposing disabilities on illegitimate children, the Court has made it clear that the intermediate test to scrutinize such laws is "not a toothless one."[26]

As to gender-based classifications, the Supreme Court has waffled. At one time it came close to declaring sex classifications suspect. More recently it has treated such classifications as merely disfavored.

Judicial constructions of the equal protection clause are instructive in showing how judges move from the simple to the complex. As they are presented with new applications of old rules, they proceed to make distinctions that are more and more refined until the picture becomes so confused and complicated that the judges try to rationalize past decisions and again provide more similar guidelines. We started with an interpretation of the equal protection clause that used one test — the rational basis test. Then the judges added a more stringent requirement — an overriding public purpose. Then they came up with a test to be applied in some instances that is less rigid than the overriding-public-purpose test, but more demanding than the rational basis test; that test is whether a law is "substantially related to important governmental objectives." And now there is a tendency to break the rational basis test into two tests — one when the legislature has clearly stated the purposes it wants to achieve, and another when it has not. Perhaps the next step will be a completely new restructuring and new guidelines.

To summarize, the Supreme Court has been using the equal protection clause and a multi-tiered analysis to differentiate among various kinds of state laws and to subject these laws to varying degrees of scrutiny. Critics of the newer, more rigid equal protection tests contend that the judges are substituting their own policy judgments for those of the legislatures. Justice Rehnquist, for example, has written in dissent, "this Court seems to regard the Equal Protection Clause as a cat-o'-nine-tails to be kept in the judicial closet as a threat to legislatures which may, in view of the judiciary, get out of hand and pass 'arbitrary,' 'illogical,' or 'unreasonable' laws. In enforcing the generalities of the Equal Protection Clause, judges are in the position of Adam in the Garden of Eden and the Court's decisions can fairly be described as an endless tinkering with legislative judgments, a series of conclusions unsupported by any central guiding principle."[27] From the opposite side of the Court, Justice Marshall is also no fan of the "intellectually disingenuous 'two-tier' equal protection analysis."[28] He believes it does not describe the more subtle analysis that the Court should undertake. And from what might be called the middle of the Court, Justice Blackmun has expressed his "unrelieved discomfort with what seems to be a continuing tendency in this Court to use as tests such easy phrases as 'compelling state interest' and 'least drastic means.' . . . I have never been able fully to appreciate just what a compelling state interest is. If it means 'convincingly controlling,' or 'incapable of being overcome upon any balancing process,' then of course, the test merely announces an inevitable result, and the test is no test at all. And, for me, 'least drastic means' is a slippery slope and also the signal of the result the Court has chosen to reach. A judge would be unimaginative indeed if he could not come up with something a little less 'drastic' or less 'restrictive' in almost any situation, and thereby enable himself to vote to strike legislation down."

Let us see how the tests have been applied. The rational basis test was applied to sustain an Illinois law that exempted individuals from personal property taxes but imposed such taxes on corporations. "Where taxation is concerned and no specific federal right, apart from equal protection, is imperiled, the States have large leeway in making classifications and drawing lines which in their judgment produce reasonable systems of taxation."[29] There was no constitutional violation in the Texas practice of providing educational revenues for local schools largely from local property taxes, even though the practice produced fewer dollars to educate children in poor districts than to educate children in districts where more valuable property was located.[30] The village of Belle Terre, New York, had authority to adopt zoning regulations that effectively excluded anyone except single families and groups of no more than two individuals from occupying houses in the village. Six students at the State University of New York at Stony Brook challenged the ordinance as violating their rights, but the Court said, "The police power is not confined to elimination of filth, stench, and unhealthy places. It is ample to lay out zones where family values, youth values, and the blessings of quiet seclusion and clean air make the area a sanctuary for people."[31]

Still more examples of the application of the rational basis test: A state may deny unemployment benefits to those who attend day schools while making them available to those who attend night school, it being reasonable to assume that those who go to school during the day are less likely to be available for employment than are those who go to school after the workday.[32] New York could subject harness-racing trainers to more drastic restrictions than Thoroughbred-racing trainers because of a legislative determination that the former kind of activity justifies more stringent regulation.[33] Minnesota could ban the sale of milk in plastic nonreturnable bottles while allowing its sale in paperboard nonreturnable cartons.[34] Congress could alter the benefits of those eligible for both railroad retirement and social security payments.[35]

Congress could provide death benefits to widows, widowers, and divorced spouses responsible for the care of minor children but deny such aid to unwed mothers.[36]

Congress could authorize survivor's benefits to widows who remarried after age 60 and not to surviving divorced and remarried spouses. "Governmental decisions to spend money . . . in one way and not another are 'not confined to the courts. The discretion belongs to Congress, unless the choice is clearly wrong, a display of arbitrary power, not an exercise of judgment.' "[37] Congress could permit veterans' organizations, but no others, to engage in lobbying activities without jeopardizing their tax-exempt status. "Our country has a long-standing policy of compensating veterans for their past contributions by providing them with numerous advantages."[38]

Until recently, in almost every instance, when the Court concluded that the rational basis test applied, it was in effect concluding that the law was constitutional. After all, if a majority of a state legislature has voted for a particular law, it is rather presumptuous for judges to declare that the legislators have acted without any rational basis. Moreover, until recently the rational basis test was used almost exclusively to judge legislation regulating businesses and was applied to reflect the perspective of some justices that judges should let legislatures regulate business and adopt tax policies almost as they wished. Recently, however, the Supreme Court ruled that Alaska had failed to pass even the minimal test when it proposed to distribute income derived from its oil revenues to its citizens in varying amounts based on the length of each citizen's residency in Alaska. In language reminiscent of Justice Holmes, who at the beginning of the century often reminded the then conservative majority that it had no mandate to impose its views on states, Justice Rehnquist, the Court's most conservative member wrote, "In striking down the Alaskan scheme, the Court seems momentarily to have forgotten 'the principle that the Fourteenth Amendment gives the federal courts no power to impose upon the States their view of what constitutes wise economic or social policy.' "[39] The Court has continued to second-guess the rationality of legislators. The Court told Vermont that it was "wholly arbitrary" for it to charge new Vermont residents a use tax to register cars purchased out of state while exempting old Vermont residents from the same tax for cars they purchased out of state.[40] After specifically refusing to hold that the mentally retarded are a quasi-suspect classification calling for a more exacting standard of judicial review than is normally accorded economic and social legislation, the Court held that a city had violated the rational basis test by requiring a special zoning use permit for homes for a group of mentally retarded persons when it did not require such permits for other multiple-dwelling units. The requirement, said the majority, appeared to have been based on an irrational prejudice, not a rational basis.[41]

A couple of months after the equal protection clause was used to tell Alabama it could not favor Alabama-chartered insurance companies (see page 229),[42] the Court held that the clause does permit states to favor in-state and regional banks. The difference appears to be that the Court interprets the equal protection requirement to permit laws motivated by legislative desires to protect consumers, but not those designed merely to favor local businesses.[43]

The Court has also, in the words of the dissenting justices, patched "together bits and pieces of what might be termed quasi-suspect-class and quasi-fundamental-rights analysis"[44] to declare unconstitutional a Texas statute denying illegal alien children the right to a free public education. Although illegal aliens are not a suspect class and the right to an education is not a fundamental right, the Court nonetheless held that Texas had to "offer something more than a rational basis for its classification."[45]

Texas failed to prove to the justices' satisfaction that its action was justified by a substantial state interest in saving money or discouraging illegal aliens from moving to Texas.

One of the most judicially favored fundamental rights is the constitutional right to travel. This right, having various constitutional sources, ensures new residents who move into a state the same rights to vital governmental benefits and privileges in the state to which they migrate as are enjoyed by long-term residents. As already noted (page 115), Article IV, Section 2, protects citizens who move from one state to another, and those protections often merge with equal protection considerations (the latter also extending to aliens as well as to citizens). Durational residency requirements for eligibility for certain benefits are suspect because of their impact on the right to travel (see page 116). However, the right to travel does not include the right to take with one benefits of the place from which one came; therefore, Congress may limit social security benefits to the residents of the states and the District of Columbia and may exclude persons who move to Puerto Rico.[46] Nor does it impermissibly infringe on the right to travel for a state to set a harsher criminal penalty for parents who abandon their children and leave the state than for parents who abandon their children but remain in the state.[47]

Here are more examples of state actions that impinged on fundamental rights and therefore were subject to rigorous judicial scrutiny resulting in their being declared unconstitutional: laws making property ownership a requirement for serving on a school board;[48] requirements that allowed only persons who had paid some kind of property tax to vote in city bond elections;[49] requirements that permitted only parents or taxpayers to vote in school board elections;[50] laws making it a crime for a doctor to prescribe a contraceptive device to an unmarried person, but not to a married one;[51] laws denying unwed fathers, but not unwed mothers, an opportunity to take custody of children on the death of the other parent;[52] the provision of religious services for Christians and Jews in prisons, but not for Buddhists;[53] and laws imposing such high fees on candidates in primaries that it is difficult for those without funds or without backers to run.[54]

The most suspect of suspect classifications is race. The Fourteenth Amendment, and most especially its equal protection clause, was adopted precisely for the purpose of protecting blacks against discrimination by state and local governments, so we have had more constitutional experience with classifications based on race than we have had with other suspect classifications. In 1984 the Court reminded us that "a core purpose of the Fourteenth Amendment was to do away with all governmentally imposed discrimination based on race. Classifying persons according to their race is more likely to reflect racial prejudice than legitimate public concerns; the race, not the person, dictates the category. Such classifications are subject to the most exacting scrutiny; to pass constitutional muster, they must be justified by a compelling governmental interest and must be 'necessary . . . to the accomplishment' of its legitimate purpose."[55] Earlier the Court had spoken against racial classifications in more emphatic terms, calling them "odious to our system" and "in most instances irrelevant."[56]

Although the Fourteenth Amendment was adopted for the protection of the recently freed slaves, at first it was not applied in that regard. In fact, in *Plessy* v *Ferguson* (1896) the Supreme Court held that a state could compel racial segregation in the use of public facilities, provided equal facilities were available for all races. Only Justice

Harlan dissented, saying, "In view of the Constitution, in the eye of the law, there is in this country no superior, dominant ruling class of citizens. There is no caste here. Our Constitution is color-blind, and neither knows nor tolerates classes among citizens. In respect of civil rights, all citizens are equal before the law."[57]

Under the guise of the "separate but equal" formula, Jim Crow laws, as segregation laws came to be known, were passed in southern states to cover all phases of life from birth to death, from hospitals to burial grounds. For decades, the facilities provided for blacks were separate but not equal. In the 1940s the Supreme Court began to insist that states must either stop requiring segregation in the use of public facilities or start providing blacks with exactly equal facilities.

Finally, in the spring of 1954, in *Brown* v *Board of Education*, the Supreme Court reversed its 1896 holding as applied to public schools and ruled that "separate but equal" is a contradiction in terms and that segregation is itself discrimination.[58] In the years that immediately followed, all forms of segregation in public facilities were declared unconstitutional. Furthermore, the Constitution requires authorities not merely to *cease* discriminating, but also to take action to remedy the consequences of their past segregative conduct. However, the amount of action required to overcome past discrimination varies with the area: the most is required in the case of public schools, the least in the case of such things as 4-H clubs, which southern states used to operate on a segregated basis. In the case of schools, states must take positive steps to overcome the effects of prior segregative practices. In the case of the 4-H clubs, all the Constitution requires is the disestablishment of segregated clubs and nondiscrimination against any person who seeks to join them.[59]

A year after its decision in *Brown* v *Board of Education*, the Court, in the second *Brown* decision, ordered school boards to proceed with all deliberate speed to desegregate public schools at the earliest practicable date.[60] In 1969, fifteen years after its first ruling that school segregation was unconstitutional, and in the face of massive resistance to compliance in many parts of the South, the Supreme Court withdrew its earlier grant of time to school authorities to work out the problems in bringing about desegregation. The Court stated: "The time for mere 'deliberate speed' has run out.... Delays in desegregating school systems are no longer tolerable.... The burden of a school board today is to come forward with a plan that promises realistically to work and promises realistically to work now."[61] In 1964 Congress had authorized the Department of Justice to enter the fray by filing school desegregation suits. It also stipulated in Title VI of the Civil Rights Act that "No person ... shall on the ground of race, color, or national origin, be excluded from participating in, be denied the benefits of, or be subjected to discrimination under any program or activity receiving federal financial assistance," which meant that federal funds could be cut off from any district that refused to desegregate. By the time schools opened in the fall of 1970, de jure segregated school systems had been abolished. No longer was any school legally defined to be for blacks or for whites.

If schools were previously legally segregated, authorities have a duty to take positive action to overcome the past segregation. School authorities and judges formulating desegregation decrees, may require, as a means of dismantling a previously legally segregated school system, the assignment of pupils and teachers to schools on a racial basis. "Just as the race of students must be considered in determining whether a constitutional violation has occurred so must race be considered in formulating a remedy. To forbid, at this stage, all assignments made on the basis of race, would deprive school authorities of the one tool absolutely essential to the fulfillment of their constitutional obligation to eliminate existing dual schools systems."[62]

For schools in which segregation is not the result of prior intentional governmental action, there is no constitutional requirement that authorities act to integrate the schools. In determining appropriate remedies, the Court has continued to maintain a distinction between school districts where racial imbalance is the continuing consequence of a prior segregated school system or the result of purposeful intent to segregate and districts where racial imbalance is not the result of governmental segregative purposes.[63] In school districts that were previously intentionally segregated, judges may impose systemwide remedies and force authorities to take a positive action to disestablish any vestiges of a dual school system. Where racial imbalance is not the result of purposeful governmental action, judges lack any such authority. Therefore, a crucial finding is whether or not any racial imbalance that exists is a consequence of prior violations of the equal protection clause.

When it is found that racial imbalance is the result of prior segregative governmental action, judges formulating desegregation decrees may require remedial programs[64] and, if necessary, the busing of pupils from one school within the district to another. Busing has been a highly controversial constitutional and political issue. Of course, many children have long been bused to schools, but as a means to overcome previously required segregation, many feel that busing is evil.

In a unanimous but cautiously worded decision, the Supreme Court held in Swann v Charlotte Mecklenburg Board of Education (1971) that a federal judge has authority to order, among other things, that students be bused a reasonable distance beyond their own neighborhoods as a means of eliminating all vestiges of state-imposed segregation. No students should be bused so far that the time or distance of travel presents risk to their health or impinges on the educational process. The Court rejected the notion that the constitutional command to desegregate means that every school in every community must always reflect the racial composition of the school system as a whole. Exact racial balance is not required. And "all things being equal with no history of discrimination, it might well be desirable to assign pupils to schools nearest their homes." But in districts that previously operated segregated systems, "desegregation plans cannot be limited to walk-in schools."[65]

What about interdistrict busing? In many cities blacks are crowded into the central city and there has been "white flight" to the suburbs. In such situations it is difficult to achieve integration if the central-city and suburban schools are considered separately. But unless it is demonstrated that school district lines have been drawn for the purpose of maintaining segregation and that the suburban districts are being operated in a racially discriminatory fashion, a judge may not require cross-district busing.[66]

Although the Constitution does not require states to take corrective action to overcome de facto segregation, states may act to create racial balance in their public schools if they wish. In March of 1978 the Seattle School Board decided that mandatory reassignment of students was necessary to eliminate the racial isolation in its schools, caused by segregated housing patterns. This action generated so much opposition that a statewide initiative measure forbidding any board to order mandatory reassignment of students for the purpose of achieving racial balance was overwhelmingly approved. The Supreme Court, however, struck down this action, not because the state of Washington had an obligation to provide such busing, but because the initiative petition had a racially discriminatory purpose and Washington had unconstitutionally distorted its political process to place special burdens on the ability of blacks to achieve legislation they felt would benefit them.[67]

On the very same day, however, the Supreme Court refused to overturn a California action, also adopted as the result of an initiative, that stripped California courts of the power to order mandatory busing unless it was necessary to remedy a violation of the United States Constitution. The consequence of the action was to set aside a busing plan that the California courts had imposed on Los Angeles on the grounds that the California Constitution required school boards to overcome racial segregation regardless of whether it was de facto or de jure. The United States Supreme Court held that the mere repeal of legislation not required by the federal Constitution in the first place is not unconstitutional. California, having by the action of its courts gone beyond the requirements of the federal Constitution, was free to return by the action of its voters to "the standard prevailing throughout the United States." Those who had initiated the action were not motivated, said the Supreme Court, by discriminatory purposes. Moreover, even though California courts could no longer order school boards to adopt busing to overcome de facto segregation, the boards themselves, unlike those in Washington, retained the power to adopt such busing.[68] In short, it is unconstitutional for a state to take from a school board the power to order mandatory busing to overcome racial imbalance not caused by the state, but it is all right for the state to take from its courts the power to order such busing without a finding of a violation of the United States Constitution. Thus do our justices weave distinctions that others sometimes have difficulty in understanding.

Brown v *Board of Education* applied only to public schools. Since that decision, the Supreme Court has declared unconstitutional laws requiring segregation in any public facility or place. Any use of governmental power to keep people of different races apart is clearly unconstitutional.[69] Today any law or government practice that invidiously discriminates against any person because of race is unconstitutional. Nowadays governmentally sanctioned discriminatory action is not likely to be overt, although there are still examples. Two decades ago the Court had to set aside state laws making marriage between persons of different races illegal.[70] And as late as 1984, the Court had to reverse a state court's decision to take from a mother custody of her child because of her remarriage to a person of a different race.[71] The Court did so unanimously and in one of its briefest opinions in recent years. Much more common are more subtle kinds of discrimination.

How is discrimination to be proved? If a law should classify persons based on a suspect classification, such as race, or a semi-suspect classification such as sex, the mere fact that the law has a discriminatory effect raises serious equal protection claims. However, for laws or practices that are not based "on an overtly discriminatory classification,"[72] the mere fact that a law or governmental practice has a differential impact on persons of different races (or sexes) does not by itself establish the law as unconstitutional. "The invidious quality of a law claimed to be racially discriminatory must ultimately be traced to a racially discriminatory purpose. Disproportionate impact is not irrelevant, but it is not the sole touchstone of an invidious racial discrimination forbidden by the Constitution. Standing alone, it does not trigger the rule that racial classifications are to be subjected to the strictest scrutiny and are justified only by the weightiest of considerations."[73]

"Once racial discrimination is shown to have been a 'substantial' . . . factor behind enactment of the law, the burden shifts to the law's defenders to demonstrate that the law would have been enacted without this factor."[74] Examples of discriminatory intent being shown are rather rare these days since legislators who intend to discriminate are not likely to admit it. Such was not the case with respect to a provision of the Alabama Constitution adopted in 1901, which added misdemeanors to the crimes covered by provisions disenfranchising persons convicted of crimes involving moral turpitude. The whole purpose of the provision, said those who worked for its adoption, was to disenfranchise blacks. Although the state argued that regardless of the original purpose, events occurring since then had made the provision legitimate, the Supreme Court, "without deciding whether [that provision] would be valid if enacted today without any impermissible motivation," concluded that it had been adopted with the desire to discriminate, continued to have that effect, and was thus unconstitutional.[75]

The fact of disproportionate effect, although by itself not proof of discrimination, is not unimportant. For if a government practice or law adversely affects members of one race, the burden of proof often shifts to the government to demonstrate that it has not engaged in discriminatory conduct.[76] For example, if a test has a racially discriminatory impact, or if in some districts none or only a few members of a race or ethnic group are called for jury service, the burden shifts to the government to show that the results are not the consequence of an intent to discriminate.

Discriminatory impact, however, does not always shift the burden. A defendant in a Georgia murder case presented powerful statistical evidence that in that state there was a great disparity in the imposition of the death sentence based on the race of the murder victim and to a lesser extent the race of the defendant. According to an analysis of 2,000 Georgia murder cases tried during the 1970s, taking into account 230 variables that could have explained the disparity on nonracial grounds, defendants charged with killing a white person were 4.3 times as likely to receive a death sentence as defendants charged with killing a black person. Black defendants who killed white victims had the greatest likelihood of receiving the death penalty. The majority, speaking through Justice Powell, rejected this analysis as evidence of discriminatory intent and distinguished this rejection from the Court's willingness to accept statistics as proof of intent to discriminate with respect to employment and in the selection of juries in particular districts. In jury sentencing, the statistics relate to many juries, with many other variables to be explained, and the various juries have no opportunity to explain the statistical disparity. Moreover, discretion is essential to the criminal justice process and is the very essence of judicial verdicts and sentencing. Nor could the evidence be considered persuasive in proving that the state of Georgia as a whole had violated the equal protection clause by adopting its capital punishment statute and allowing it to remain in force despite its alleged discriminatory application. For such an argument to prevail, argued Justice Powell, it would have to be established "that the Georgia legislature enacted or maintained the death penalty statute *because of* an anticipated racially discriminatory effect."[77] Justice Blackmun, speaking for himself and Justices Marshall, Brennan, and Stevens, argued that the defendant had established a prima facie case of discriminatory intent and that the burden had then shifted to Georgia to demonstrate that the challenged effect was due to permissible racially neutral selection criteria, which it had failed to do. Although there was no evidence of racial discrimination in the case before them, the dissenters would have reversed, and some would have narrowed the class of defendants eligible for the death penalty to those that had committed such heinous murders under such bizarre circumstances that, according to the study, prosecutors would consistently seek and juries would consistently impose the death penalty, without regard to the race of the victim or the race of the offender. (Justices Marshall and Brennan are against the death penalty for any person.)

In a series of cases that overlap Fifteenth Amendment considerations, the Court has moved back and forth over the question of the evidence necessary to prove discrimination in at large election systems — those in which city council members or county representatives are elected citywide or countywide rather than by election districts. The effect of such systems in most cities, even if there is a substantial black minority population, is to keep the city council all white. The constitutional standard under the Fourteenth Amendment is the same as under the Fifteenth: there must be evidence of an *intent* to discriminate.[78] But even if no or few blacks get elected, it is hard to prove that it was the intent of those who established the system, and it is even harder to prove that it is the intent of those who maintain it.

What is not unconstitutional, however, may be illegal. Most recent civil rights statutes (not the older civil rights statutes) have been interpreted or legislatively modified to forbid actions that have a discriminatory effect even if there is no intent to discriminate. Congress, in amending the Voting Rights Act of 1965 in 1982, under the authority of Section 5 of the Fourteenth Amendment and Section 2 of the Fifteenth, stated that although blacks have no legal right to have members elected in numbers equal to their proportion in the population, where blacks make up a substantial proportion of the population, the fact that few or none of them get elected because of some practice or procedure, such as at-large elections, is part of the "totality of circumstances" judges may take into account to determine if there has been a violation of the act.

Congress, in Title VI of the Civil Rights Act of 1964, has also stipulated that most federal grants are not to be used in any way to discriminate against blacks, women, the aged, or the disabled. For most programs, Congress has made it illegal to use federal funds for practices that have a discriminatory effect even if those practices fall short of being unconstitutional because there is no proof of discriminatory purpose. For example, Title VII of the Civil Rights Act of 1964 provides that even though a job standard or a test to determine eligibility for employment may be neutral on its face, if it has a differential impact on persons by race or sex, even if there is no intent to discriminate, the burden shifts to the employer to demonstrate that the requirement has a manifest relationship to the employment in question.[79] On the other hand, the Civil Rights Act of 1866 (now 42 U.S.C. 1981), although covering private as well as governmental discrimination, reaches only purposeful discrimination.[80] It provides that "all persons within the jurisdiction of the United States shall have the same right in every State and Territory to make and enforce contracts, to sue, be parties, give evidence, and to enjoy the full and equal benefit of all laws and proceedings for the security of persons and property as is enjoyed by white citizens." To win a suit under Section 1981, plaintiffs must prove purposeful discrimination.

Affirmative Action

What if governments adopt programs to remedy disadvantages that minorities suffer because of the lingering effects of past discrimination against them? What if governments adopt programs, or require private employers to adopt race-conscious remedies, popularly known as *affirmative action* by those who support them and as *reverse discrimination* by those who oppose, that provide special protections for minorities? Do such programs create suspect classifications? Are they unconstitutional? There has been no more hotly debated constitutional issue in our time than this one.

Where do we stand with respect to affirmative action programs? In recent years the Supreme Court has dealt with the issue of affirmative action almost a dozen times. The justices, like the rest of the nation, are not of one mind on these issues and have never been able to muster clear majorities behind a definitive set of doctrines. Yet the following seem established:

1. Congress, in implementing the Fourteenth Amendment, has great latitude in deciding what actions might be needed to overcome past discrimination against blacks, other minorities, and women, including requiring minority set-asides in public construction projects.[81]

2. Most provisions of most congressional civil rights acts, however, set limits on private employers and trade unions similar to constitutional constraints. For example, Title VII of the Civil Rights Act of 1964, which outlaws discrimination in interstate employment because of race or sex, also specifically states that it should not be used "to require . . . any employer to grant preferential treatment" to any person or group because of imbalance in the employer's work force. Affirmative actions forbidden by the Constitution are likely to be forbidden by current civil rights acts, and those forbidden by statute are likely to be forbidden by the Constitution.

3. State officials, such as regents of a public university or public employers, are subject to the equal protection clause and may not take race or sex into account, even in a positive manner, merely to overcome past social injustices or to provide role models.[82] But as long as they do not completely disqualify members of one sex or race from participation in programs or employment they may take race and sex into account as plus factors to achieve an appropriately balanced student body or employment force.[83]

4. Nonetheless, in a remedial context there is no requirement that governments "act in a wholly color-blind fashion."[84]

5. Although the goal of achieving a racially balanced work force will not by itself justify an affirmative action program, public and private employers may adopt affirmative action programs to overcome "manifest imbalances" that reflect underrepresentation of women in traditionally segregated job categories.[85] Similarly, an employer may adopt training and other programs that give a temporary preference in hiring and promotion to minorities in order to overcome manifest racial imbalances.[86] Note that such preferences are not justified with respect to layoffs (see item 12).

6. An individual finding by a court that a particular entity seeking to institute an affirmative action program has committed discriminatory acts in the past is not necessary.

7. Persons who benefit from particular affirmative action programs need not be the specific individuals who have suffered the discrimination in the past. The purpose of affirmative action is not to make identified victims whole, but rather to dismantle prior patterns of employment discrimination and to prevent discrimination in the future.[87]

8. "As part of this Nation's dedication to eradicating racial discrimination, innocent persons may be called upon to bear some of the burdens of the remedy."[88]

9. Goals that measure achievement and set forth objectives for hiring or promoting particular numbers of minorities are permissible.

10. Quotas that require an employer to hire or promote a particular number of minority employees, or else automatically suffer penalties, are not generally favored but may be adopted for limited periods of time to overcome specific findings of past egregious discrimination.[89]

11. After court findings of past discrimination, quota promotions or openings may be mandated as remedies, but only for as long as necessary to overcome the past discrimination.

12. The means of overcoming past discrimination may not impose disproportionate harm on the interests of innocent individuals adversely affected by a plan's racial preference. Thus, the Court does not favor affirmative action programs in layoffs, without a specific judicial finding, but accepts them in hiring and promotion. Temporary hiring goals for minorities may be permissible, whereas layoffs of nonminorities would not be. "Denial of a future employment opportunity is not as intrusive as loss of an existing job. . . . While hiring goals impose a diffuse burden, often foreclosing only one of several opportunities, layoffs impose the entire burden of achieving racial equality on particular individuals. The burden is too intrusive."[90]

As a result of these decisions, we can conclude, at least tentatively, that the Constitution does not forbid all affirmative action programs or exclude all governmentally sanctioned racial classifications. However, such classifications are to be approached with considerable caution.

Where does all this Supreme Court decision making leave us with respect to race? The Court still firmly adheres "to the traditional view that racial classifications that stigmatize — because they are drawn on the presumption that one race is inferior to another or because they put the weight of government behind racial hatred and separatism — are not only suspect, but outlawed."[91] A majority still adhere to the view that all practices and all programs that classify people by race or ethnic origin are suspect and should be subject to strict judicial scrutiny. However, if a race-conscious remedy has been carefully created to help minorities overcome present effects of past discrimination, it may be constitutionally permissible, especially if the remedy has been adopted by Congress.

Classifications Other Than Race

The decisions regarding state laws relating to aliens "have not formed an unswerving line."[92] So far as the states are concerned, "restrictions on lawfully resident aliens primarily affecting economic interests are subject to heightened judicial scrutiny," but such "strict scrutiny is out of place when the restriction primarily serves a political function. . . . Some state functions are so bound up with the operation of the State as a governmental entity as to permit the exclusion from those functions of all persons who have not become part of the process of self-government."[93] In other words, some state laws regulating aliens are subject to strict scrutiny, some are not.

The Court has declared unconstitutional laws imposing a blanket prohibition against all public employment of aliens, forbidding them to practice law or civil engineering, denying them financial assistance for higher education, and depriving them of the right to serve as notaries public.[94] Yet, although the Court has recently said that the political exception is to be narrowly construed, that exception has been used to uphold state regulations that exclude aliens from serving as state police officers, probation officers, and public school teachers and that keep aliens from voting, serving on juries, and fulfilling "important nonelective executive, legislative, and judicial positions."[95]

In 1982 Justice Brennan, speaking for the Court, ignored the whole question whether lawfully admitted aliens should be treated as a suspect classification and, resorting to federal supremacy principles, set aside a practice of the University of Maryland of charging nonimmigrant aliens (children of diplomats and persons who work for international associations) out-of-state tuition. Said the Court, "State regulation not congressionally sanctioned that discriminates against aliens lawfully admitted to the country is impermissible if it imposes additional burdens not contemplated by Congress."[96] In his dissenting opinion, in which Chief Justice Burger joined, Justice Rehnquist argued that there is reason to doubt whether political powerlessness is any longer a legitimate reason for treating aliens as a "suspect classification" deserving of "heightened judicial solicitude."[97]

Then, in 1984, after appearing to have been wavering on the issue, the Court, in an opinion in which every justice except Rehnquist joined, reaffirmed in rather strong language that so far as state regulation is concerned, aliens are to remain a suspect classification other than for the political exception, and that exception is to be narrowly construed; "otherwise the exception will swallow the rule and depreciate the significance that should attach to the designation of a group as a 'discrete and insular' minority for whom heightened judicial solicitude is appropriate."[98]

Classifications based on illegitimacy are no longer considered suspect and thus subject to the Court's most exacting scrutiny. However, "in view of the history of treating illegitimate children less favorably than legitimate ones," the Court has "subjected statutory classifications based on illegitimacy to its heightened intermediate test." The scrutiny applied to them is not a "toothless one." A classification based on illegitimacy is unconstitutional unless it "bears an evident and substantial relation to the particular . . . interests [the] statute is designed to serve."[99]

Poverty is not ordinarily a suspect classification. A state has no constitutional duty to see to it that school districts where most people are poor have the same funds for their schools as do districts where many of the people are well-to-do.[100] Poverty, however, is not always without significance in equal protection analysis. Laws that prevent the absolutely destitute, rather than those who are merely poor, from being able to enjoy some legal benefits because of their poverty have received close judicial scrutiny and have been declared unconstitutional.[101] And although the right to run for office is not a fundamental right, the Court has been especially suspicious of filing-fee provisions that may make it difficult for those without funds to run for office, since "economic status is not a measure of a prospective candidate's qualifications to hold elective office, and a filing fee alone is an inadequate test of whether a candidacy is serious or spurious."[102]

The equal protection clause, often combined with due process considerations, also provides some protection for the poor in courtroom situations. In addition to forbidding discrimination in the administration of justice, the clause imposes on states a limited positive obligation to see to it that the poor have treatment equal to that of persons who can afford proper legal counsel, investigators, appeals, and so on. If a state makes a transcript a requirement for an appeal, it must furnish transcripts to those unable to afford them.[103] As mentioned earlier, for the one appeal each state provides as a matter of right, it must provide indigents with attorneys to help them carry their appeals to the next higher court; the state does not, however, have to provide an attorney at public expense for discretionary appeals, including those to the United States Supreme Court.[104]

Although defendants' poverty in no way immunizes them from punishment, "a state cannot force into jail those who cannot pay fines or it cannot revoke probation because of failure to pay a fine or restitution upon which probation had been conditioned." A state may imprison someone for willfully refusing to pay court costs or a fine or for failing to make a genuine effort to get a job or borrow the money to pay the fine; it cannot imprison a person solely because he or she lacks the resources to pay.[105]

In contrast to criminal prosecutions, where the state "hails a defendant into court," states have less of an equal protection and due process obligation to provide the poor with equal access to the civil courts. Yet even here there are some constitutional requirements. A state may not, for example, deny access to its courts to those unable to pay filing fees for a divorce. The right to marry and to get a divorce are basic rights, and the state has a monopoly in regulating the marital relationship: to deny the poor access to the courts is, in effect, to deny them a divorce.[106] In contrast, the United States may deny access to its courts to persons unable to pay a small fee for filing a bankruptcy petition. There is no constitutional right to be absolved of one's debts, and there are ways of handling debts other than by becoming legally bankrupt. As Justice Stewart said in dissent, "Some of the poor are too poor even to go bankrupt."[107] A state may also collect a general filing fee from those wishing to appeal decisions of welfare agencies.[108] And although the precise grounds were denial of due process, the equal protection aspect was prominent when the Supreme Court ruled that a state must pay for the blood-typing of a person involved in a paternity suit who lacks the funds to pay for the test.[109]

The equal protection clause also prohibits states from imposing poll taxes as a condition of eligibility to vote; this prohibition is apart from that contained in the Twenty-fourth Amendment. Even if there is no evidence that a poll tax might discriminate against blacks or the poor, it establishes an unreasonable classification based on wealth. "Wealth, like race, creed, or color, is not germane to one's ability to participate intelligently in the electoral process."[110]

Congress has made some age classifications illegal, but age is not a suspect classification. The Court has never struck down a law because of an unconstitutional age classification. On the contrary, it has sustained a law of Massachusetts disqualifying persons from being state police officers after age fifty, and an act of Congress making retirement from the foreign service compulsory at age sixty.[111]

Mentally ill persons, according to some of the lower federal courts, should be considered a suspect classification. The mentally ill, they argue, "historically have been subjected to purposeful and unequal treatment; they have been relegated to a position of political powerlessness; and prejudice against them curtails their participation in the pluralist system and strips them of political protection against discriminatory legislation."[112] But so far the Supreme Court has sidestepped the issue.

What of classifications based on sex? It was 1971 before any classification based on sex was declared to violate the equal protection clause. Before that, state laws excluding or restricting women's participation on juries had been sustained, as well as many laws purporting to provide special protection for women, such as one in Ohio forbidding any woman other than a wife or daughter of a tavern owner to serve as a barmaid.[113] (The Civil Rights Act of 1964 made illegal rules or regulations of companies affecting interstate commerce that discriminate against persons because of sex, for example, a company regulation denying employment to women with preschool-age children but not to men with such children.[114])

In the fall of 1971, a unanimous Court stated in *Reed* v *Reed* that the arbitrary preference Idaho gave fathers over mothers in the administration of their children's estates "cannot stand in the face of the Fourteenth Amendment's command."[115] Soon after, in *Frontiero* v *Richardson*, the Court invalidated a federal law that permitted a serviceman to claim his wife as his dependent but allowed a servicewoman to claim her husband as a dependent only if he was in fact dependent on her for more than half of his support. Justice Brennan wrote for a plurality that "there can be no doubt that our Nation has had a long and unfortunate history of sex discrimination. Traditionally, such discrimination was rationalized by an attitude of 'romantic paternalism' which, in practical effect, put women not on a pedestal, but in a cage."[116]

Among the sex-based distinctions declared unconstitutional since then are the following: a law specifying that males are entitled to child support from their fathers until they are twenty-one but females only until they are eighteen;[117] a state law prohibiting the sale of beer to males under twenty-one but to females under eighteen;[118] laws making women but not men eligible for alimony;[119] laws giving unwed mothers, but not unwed fathers, the right to consent to the adoption of their children;[120] social security provisions providing aid to children with unemployed fathers but not to those with unemployed mothers;[121] and the policy of the Mississippi University for Women of limiting enrollment to women in its school of nursing (as well as all its other schools).[122] Nor may governments — and because of the equal protection interpretation of the due process clause of the Fifth Amendment (see page 191), members of Congress are included — discriminate because of sex in the selection of public employees.[123] (Note that a good many of the laws were struck down because they discriminated against men.)

On the other side, the Court has sustained some sex-based distinctions, and it is likely to continue to do so, especially since the failure to ratify the Equal Rights Amendment. Upholding a Florida law granting a $500 exemption from the state property tax to widows but not to widowers, the majority said, "There can be no dispute that the financial difficulties confronting the lone woman in Florida or in any other State exceed those facing the man." The dissenters pointed out that there are such things as rich widows and poor widowers and argued that the need for the exemption would not appear to be related to one's sex.[124] A regulation was upheld that permitted male naval officers only nine years in which to be either promoted or discharged, while providing thirteen years for women, because women have less opportunity within the naval service for promotion.[125] A social security regulation was sustained giving women but not men the right to eliminate some low-earning years from the calculation of their retirement benefits in order to compensate them for past economic discrimination.[126] Congress may give preference in admission to the country to alien mothers of illegitimate children over alien fathers of such children.[127] A state may treat fathers of illegitimate children differently from mothers of such children — for example, by requiring that mothers must always be notified prior to the adoption proceedings of their children but that only those fathers who have shouldered some responsibility or acknowledged their responsibility for their children must be notified.[128]

A narrowly divided Court sustained the conviction by California of a seventeen-year-old male for the statutory rape of a sixteen-year-old female under a law that makes it a crime for a male to have intercourse with a female under eighteen, but not for a female to have intercourse with an under-age male. The Court majority argued that such a law was based, not on archaic assumptions about the proper role of the sexes, but on a legitimate state interest in avoiding teenage pregnancies, and that since only women can become pregnant, men and women are not similarly situated with respect to the risks associated with pregnancy. The minority argued that the law discriminated against men and the state could have accomplished its objectives just as well with a gender-neutral law making it a crime for both teenage men and women to engage in sex.[129]

Veterans' preference laws have also been sustained, even though such laws adversely affect women. The Supreme Court upheld a Massachusetts law giving veterans a lifetime preference in public employment, because the law reflects no purpose to discriminate against women, but is designed to favor those who have served in the armed forces, male and female.[130] And as already noted, the Court upheld the power of Congress to order the registration of males and not of females for potential military conscription, largely on the grounds that only men could be assigned to combat duty. "This is not a case," wrote Justice Rehnquist for the majority, "of Congress arbitrarily choosing to burden one of two similarly situated groups, such as would be the case with an all-black or all-white, or an all-Catholic or all-Lutheran, or an all-Republican or all-Democratic registration. Men and women, because of the combat restrictions on women, are simply not similarly situated for purposes of a draft or registration for a draft." The dissenters did not challenge the exclusion of women from combat posts, but charged the Court with placing its "imprimatur on one of the most potent remaining public expressions of 'ancient canards about the proper role of women' by categorically excluding women from a fundamental civic obligation." The armed forces, they argued, need many people beyond those given combat assignments. Women are presently serving with great glory and honor in the armed forces and should not be excluded from the obligation to register, which can be divorced from conscription, since the purpose of the registration requirement is "to provide an inventory of what the available strength is within the military qualified pool in this country."[131]

To summarize, classifications based on sex are not subject to scrutiny as severe as are those based on race, but to sustain a classification based on sex the burden is on the government to show that it serves "important governmental objectives" and is substantially related to the achievement of these objectives. Treatment of women differently from men is forbidden when supported by no more substantial justification than "archaic and overboard generalizations," "old notions," and "the role-typing society has long imposed upon women."[132]

What is allowed by the Constitution, however, may still be illegal. Congress has used its powers to make sex-based distinctions illegal in many areas of employment and education. For example, a state may not under the terms of the Civil Rights Act of 1964, Title VII, require that prison guards be over 5 feet 2 inches tall and weigh more than 120 pounds, because the impact of such a law discriminates against women. (On the other hand, the practice of denying women the right to be prison guards in all-male, maximum security institutions is not illegal.[133]) Similarly, the Civil Rights Act of 1964 made illegal the practice of the Los Angeles Department of Water and Power of charging women more than men for pension benefits.[134] Although women live longer than men, the statute makes it unlawful to discriminate against any individual because of such individual's race, color, religion, sex, or national origin and precludes treatment of an individual woman differently from a man, even though, "unless women as a class are assessed an extra charge, they will be subsidized, to some extent, by the class of male employees."[135]

In his opinion in *Regents of the University of California* v *Bakke*, Justice Powell suggested that preferential programs designed to assist women offer fewer constitutional obstacles than those "premised on racial or ethnic criteria." With respect to gender he wrote, "there are only two possible classifications. The incidence of the burdens imposed by preferential classification is clear. There are no rival groups who can claim that they, too, are entitled to preferential treatment. Classwide questions as to the group suffering previous injury and groups which fairly can be burdened are relatively manageable for reviewing courts."[136] On the other side, the Fourteenth Amendment was intended to protect blacks, not women, and its extension to sex discrimination is of recent origin. Of almost a dozen cases relating to affirmative action, only one has related directly to sex discrimination, but in that one the Court held that neither the Constitution nor the Civil Rights Act, Title VII, forbids public employers from giving preference to women in promotions "to positions within a traditionally segregated job classification in which women have been significantly underrepresented."[137]

Voting

The equal protection clause also protects access to the ballot and voting power. Except where the Constitution provides otherwise, as with respect to apportionment of presidential electors and senators among the states, the equal protection clause prohibits most electoral schemes that give one person's vote more weight than another. Thus, Georgia's county unit system for counting votes for governor had to go because it gave rural voters a much greater voice in the selection of statewide executive officers than voters living in cities.[138] An Illinois law suffered the same fate because it gave more weight to rural than to urban signatories on petitions to secure a place on statewide ballots, by requiring that of the 25,000 signatures needed, at least 200 must come from each of 50 of the state's 102 counties.[139] But certain special purpose units of government, such as water control or irrigation districts, that perform limited functions affecting definable groups have been permitted to distribute votes according to the value of the land owned,[140] and the one-person — one-vote principle does not apply to the selection of judges.[141]

As previously noted, the Supreme Court has applied equal protection considerations to insist that state legislatures be apportioned on the basis of population.[142] In the forty-nine two-chambered state legislatures (Nebraska has only one chamber), the membership of both chambers must be based on population.[143] The requirement of equal population districts also covers all local government units that exercise legislative functions, such as county commissions[144] and junior college districts.[145] Local units do not, however, have to meet such precisely mathematically equal standards as those required for congressional districts, nor do state legislatures have to meet the same rigid standards for their own districts as they are required to meet when laying out congressional districts.[146] (If a legislature fails to reapportion when required to do so, the task may fall to a federal judge. The Supreme Court has instructed the judges to avoid multimember districts and has told them that they are obliged to achieve more population equality among districts than might be required if the legislature had proposed the reapportionment plan.[147])

The latest group to secure judicial protection against discrimination in the drawing of electoral district lines are the major political parties. In the past they had to depend on their own political strengths. Gerrymandering, which is about as old as the Republic, is the practice of the party controlling a legislative body to try to draw the legislative district lines in such a fashion as to make any given number of votes for their party produce the largest number of winning legislators. It can be done by a variety of techniques, one of which is to draw the lines in such a fashion that all the opposition voters are concentrated in as few districts as possible, known as "stacking," or by splitting the opposition voters into as many districts as possible so that they will never carry an election, known as "cracking."[148] With the use of computers it is now possible to draw election district lines so that there are equal numbers of people in each district depending on how the lines are drawn, insuring that one party gets more seats than if the lines were drawn another way.

The Supreme Court has held that political gerrymandering is justiciable but has been unable to come up with a standard to guide federal judges in deciding which gerrymandering is unconstitutional and which is not. A plurality has announced a complicated test that requires proof not only that there has been an intent to discriminate — which gerrymandering is by definition — but also that the effect has been to "consistently degrade a voter's or a group of voters' influence on the political process as a whole." The plurality emphasized that a single election cannot be relied on to prove unconstitutional partisan discrimination; there must be proof that a party has been consigned to minority status for a decade, with no hope of doing any better after the next reapportionment. Clearly this is not the last word on the subject.[149]

State Action

All of the preceding discussion has related to discrimination imposed by government action. Discrimination by private individuals may violate a law, but such action does not violate the equal protection clause or, as we have seen, the due process clause unless it is aid-supported or positively encouraged by the state. Thus, one of the more important issues growing out of the equal protection and due process clauses is what is and what is not state action.

The Supreme Court inspects closely whenever there is a suspicion of state involvement in discriminatory conduct. To certain traditional sovereign functions exclusively reserved to governments, the Fourteenth Amendment applies regardless of who actually does the discriminating. Thus, if a state delegates responsibility for running elections, including primaries, to private associations such as political parties, the action of party officers is state action subject to constitutional restraint.[150] Similarly, if a state allows a private corporation to perform the municipal functions of running a company town, the action of company officials is state action.[151]

On the other side, the management of a private shopping center is not state action, nor is the action of a private warehouse operator, or a private utility, even though its franchise is given to it by a state.[152] Although Congress has by law subjected private schools to some equal-protection-like restraints and conditioned nonprofit status for educational institutions on their not discriminating because of race, private schools are ordinarily not subject to constitutional limitations. Providing an education, unlike holding elections, is not a function that has traditionally been "the exclusive prerogative of the State."[153]

Covenants placed in deeds to restrict the use of property to persons of particular races or religions are not by themselves state action (although they may violate federal and state laws), but no court or public official may help to enforce such covenants.[154] A liquor license granted by the state does not make the discriminatory action of a private club state action,[155] yet when a state leased space to a restaurant in a building designed to provide public parking, the action of the restaurant was no longer considered "purely private" and became subject to equal protection limitations.[156]

Sometimes when a state does nothing, or tries to do nothing, it may still be supporting, encouraging, or abetting discriminatory conduct. The mere repeal of race-related legislation or policies not required in the first place by the Constitution is not necessarily unconstitutional, but it may be. Take, for example, California's action when it adopted a constitutional amendment that repealed previously existing legislation forbidding racial discrimination in the private sale of houses and, in addition, explicitly made nondiscriminatory housing legislation unenforceable. It was argued that no state action was involved when individuals refused to sell property to black people. But the Court concluded that when California amended its Constitution, it was not being neutral. Rather it was encouraging discrimination by making it more difficult for black people than for white people to buy homes. This was state action forbidden by the Constitution.[157] On the other hand, as we have also noted, California's action was ruled constitutionally neutral when it repealed legislation encouraging judges to order busing and forbade them to so unless required to by the U.S. Constitution (see page 236).[158]

In summary, "while the principle that private action is immune from the restrictions of the Fourteenth Amendment is well established and easily stated, the question whether particular conduct is 'private,' on the one hand, or 'state action' on the other, frequently admits of no easy answer."[159]

The conflict over whether a particular act is strictly that of a private individual or is that of the state shades at times into tension between the constitutionally protected rights of association and privacy on one side and the rights to equal protection of the law on the other. A state may not, for example, directly discriminate in operating a public park, nor may it grant exclusive use to a group that excludes persons because of race. However, if a city were merely to make its parks available to all comers without condition or reservation, it would not violate the Constitution to let segregated groups use the facilities. In fact, "the exclusion of any person or group — all Negro, all oriental, or all white — from public facilities infringes upon the freedom of the individual to associate as he chooses."[160]

The Constitution precludes "government from interfering with private clubs or groups. The associational rights which our system honors permit all white, all black, all brown, and all yellow clubs to be established. Government may not tell a man or a woman who his or her associates must be. The individual may be selective as he desires."[161] Yet, "although the Constitution does not proscribe private bias, it places no value on discrimination. . . . Invidious private discrimination may be characterized as a form of exercising freedom protected by the First Amendment, but it has never been accorded affirmative constitutional protections."[162]

In contrast to private matters, there is no constitutionally protected right to discriminate in public dealings with other persons. Thus, an important question becomes, where is the line to be drawn between private associative behavior, which, however discriminatory, is constitutionally protected and beyond government regulation, and public associative behavior, which can be regulated by the state? As we have noted, the Supreme Court has upheld the application of state public accommodations laws to the Jaycees and Rotarians, because their actions with respect to admitting members fell on the public rather than private side of the line.[163] The same is true of a law partnership with respect to admission of partners.[164] When groups, associations, or businesses open their doors and invite in the public, they may be compelled by the state to stop discriminating.

On the other side are such associations as families, social clubs, and churches. "The freedom to enter into and carry on certain intimate or private relationships is a fundamental element of liberty protected by the Bill of Rights."[165] Public accommodations or other civil rights laws cannot be applied to these intimate relationships. Moreover, as we have noted, the right to engage in activities protected by the First Amendment implies a "corresponding right to associate with others in pursuit of a wide variety of political, social, economic, educational, religious and cultural ends."[166] Thus, as noted on page 164, for certain purposes even political associations have some constitutionally protected right to discriminate for certain expressive purposes.

The national government has not left the protection of civil rights against private discrimination to the states. Today there are federal laws protecting the rights of minorities and women with respect to housing, employment, schools, commerce, and many other activities. Owners of places of public accommodation and businesses affecting interstate commerce — and most businesses do — may not discriminate against persons because of race, religion, or handicap; employers in businesses affecting interstate commerce may not discriminate against persons because of race, sex, national origin, religion, or handicap.

Section 2

Representatives shall be apportioned among the several States according to their respective numbers, counting the whole number of persons in each State, excluding Indians not taxed.

This section supersedes Article I, Section 2, paragraph 3. Originally, three-fifths of the number of slaves was added to the number of free persons to determine representation.

Section 2

[continued] But when the right to vote at any election for the choice of electors for President and Vice President of the United States, Representatives in Congress, the Executive and Judicial officers of a State, or the members of the Legislature thereof, is denied to any of the male inhabitants of such State, being twenty-one years of age, and citizens of the United States, or in any way abridged, except for participation in rebellion, or other crime, the basis of representation therein shall be reduced in the proportion which the number of such male citizens shall bear to the whole number of male citizens twenty-one years of age in such State.

This provision has never been enforced by Congress, and may today be regarded as obsolete through disuse and also, possibly, through obvious disharmony with the Nineteenth and Twenty-sixth Amendments. This provision has been mentioned only twice by the Supreme Court. Once it was cited in support of a decision upholding a state suffrage regulation that denied the vote to felons who had completed their sentences.[167] The other time, a unanimous Court ruled that this section did not exempt a state from complying with the equal protection clause. Thus, Alabama had violated the Constitution, notwithstanding Section 2, in applying a law denying the right to vote to persons convicted of a crime involving moral turpitude. It was clear that this provision had been adopted in 1901 for the express intent of keeping blacks from voting.[168]

Section 3

No person shall be a Senator or Representative in Congress, or elector of President and Vice President, or hold any office, civil or military, under the United States, or under any State, who, having previously taken an oath, as a member of Congress, or as an officer of the United States, or as a member of any State legislature, or as an executive or judicial officer of any State, to support the Constitution of the United States, shall have engaged in insurrection or rebellion against the same, or given aid or comfort to the enemies thereof. But Congress may by a vote of two-thirds of each House, remove such disability.

This section politically disabled those who had led the Southern states into the Confederacy. It was placed in the Fourteenth Amendment by the radical Republicans and was a factor in their struggle with President Johnson. It limited the president's power to pardon the leaders of the Confederacy and thus restore their political and civil rights. Congress removed this disability on June 6, 1898.

Section 4

The validity of the public debt of the United States, authorized by law, including debts incurred for payment of pensions and bounties for services in suppressing insurrection or rebellion, shall not be questioned. But neither the United States nor any State shall assume or pay any debt or obligation incurred in aid of insurrection or rebellion against the United States, or any claim for the loss or emancipation of any slave; but all such debts, obligations and claims shall be held illegal and void.

This section invalidated all the securities and other evidences of debt of the Confederacy and reaffirmed those of the Union.

Section 5

The Congress shall have power to enforce, by appropriate legislation, the provisions of this article.

Until recent decades there were serious constitutional debates about the power of Congress to pass civil rights legislation. In 1883, in the *Civil Rights Cases*, the Supreme Court restricted the power of Congress under this section to the prevention or correction of state (including local) government action that abridged the privileges or immunities of a United States citizen, deprived any persons of life, liberty, or property without due process, or denied them the equal protection of the laws. The Supreme Court held that since the Fourteenth Amendment forbids only state action, Section 5 did not authorize Congress to make it a federal crime for innkeepers and other proprietors of public places to deny accommodations to persons because of race. Congress could adopt legislation under Section 5 only to prevent state discrimination, not abridgement of civil rights by private groups or persons.[169]

In view of the Supreme Court's holdings in the *Civil Rights Cases,* Congress relied on the commerce clause when it adopted the Civil Rights Act of 1964, which forbids discrimination by employers and by operators of places of public accommodation. If Congress had chosen to base the 1964 act more directly on Section 5, the Supreme Court would very likely have sustained it.

In 1966 the Supreme Court gave Section 5 a most interesting new significance. The Court held that Section 5 authorizes Congress to do whatever it thinks is necessary and proper to enforce the rights guaranteed by the Fourteenth Amendment, even to the extent of superseding state regulations that are not themselves an unconstitutional denial of Fourteenth Amendment rights! This ruling came about in a challenge to a section of the Voting Rights Act of 1965 that stipulates that no person who has had a sixth-grade education under the American flag shall be denied the right to vote for not being literate in English. This section was adopted to set aside a literacy requirement of New York that was keeping many citizens who had come to New York from Puerto Rico from voting. Even though the New York law was constitutional, the Court majority held, Congress is empowered by Section 5 to use its own judgment in determining what legislation is needed to keep states from denying persons equal protection of the laws. Justices Harlan and Stewart dissented on the grounds that Congress was exercising judicial power. So long as a state is not denying any person the equal protection of the laws and is operating within its constitutional sphere, according to the dissenting justices, Congress has no power to act under Section 5.[170]

In his separate opinion in *Bakke,* Justice Powell significantly noted that the Court was "not here presented with an occasion to review legislation by Congress pursuant to its powers under Paragraph 2 of the Thirteenth Amendment and Paragraph 5 of the Fourteenth Amendment to remedy the effects of prior discrimination. . . . We have previously recognized the special competence of Congress to make findings with respect to the effects of identified past discrimination and its discretionary authority to take appropriate remedial measures."[171] This language, with the comments in the other *Bakke* opinions, makes it quite clear that when Congress authorizes racial classifications to provide remedial programs for blacks and other ethnic minorities, such programs are on stronger constitutional foundations than are similar programs adopted by trustees of universities or other agencies not empowered by Section 5 of the Fourteenth Amendment "to enforce, by appropriate legislation, the provisions of this article."

Following Reconstruction, the Supreme Court so narrowly interpreted the federal civil rights statutes adopted to protect the recently freed slaves that for decades they were of little use in protecting the civil rights of blacks or anyone else. In recent years, however, those statutes have become an important basis for a variety of suits against state officials. The Civil Rights Act of 1871, now known as 42 U.S.C. 1983, makes personally liable for damages any person acting under color of law or custom of any state who subjects any other person to the deprivation of any rights, privileges, or immunities secured by the Constitution. This statute is being broadly construed by the Court to permit persons to bring actions against public officials, including judges, for any violation of any right protected by the Constitution or federal laws, not just those that stem from the Fourteenth Amendment. Such suits are now an important part of the business of federal courts, creating what Justice Rehnquist has characterized as "staggering effect . . . upon the workload of the federal courts." It should be noted that, independently of any acts of Congress, persons may bring suits directly against federal officials for damages if such officials have willfully deprived them of their constitutional rights. This right to sue to protect constitutional rights flows directly from the Constitution.

AMENDMENT XV: THE RIGHT TO VOTE

Section 1

The right of citizens of the United States to vote shall not be denied or abridged by the United States or by any State on account of race, color, or previous condition of servitude.

This amendment was proposed February 26, 1869, and declared in force by the secretary of state March 30, 1870.

"The Fifteenth Amendment nullifies sophisticated as well as simple-minded modes of discrimination."[1] Yet, for many decades white southerners in charge of registration and voting readily circumvented the Fifteenth Amendment. They had an arsenal of discriminatory schemes. But at the end of World War II, the Supreme Court declared unconstitutional the devices used to keep blacks from registering and voting. The first to go was the white primary. Under the pretense that there was no state action involved, in most Southern states blacks were kept from voting in the Democratic party primaries, in many areas the only elections that really mattered. In *Smith* v *Allwright* (1944) the Supreme Court said, "When primaries become a part of the machinery for choosing officials . . . the same tests to determine the character of discrimination . . . would be applied to the primary as are applied to the general election."[2] The discriminatory use of understanding and good-character tests was also enjoined.[3] The Constitution has been amended to forbid the requirement of a poll tax payment as a condition for voting for presidential electors or for members of Congress, and the Constitution has been construed by the Supreme Court to forbid the requirement of a poll tax payment as a condition for voting in any public election. In lawsuit after lawsuit, the federal courts struck down one discriminatory scheme after another.

A unanimous Court in 1982 reinvigorated an 1875 precedent (*Minor* v *Happersett*)[4] and reaffirmed a 1973 ruling (*San Antonio School District* v *Rodriguez*)[5] to the effect that "the Constitution 'does not confer the right of suffrage upon any one' " and "the right to vote, per se, is not a constitutionally protected right."[6] This holding has little significance for the Fifteenth Amendment, but removes the right to vote from the fundamental rights especially protected by the equal protection clause of the Fourteenth Amendment.

Section 2

The Congress shall have power to enforce this article by appropriate legislation.

Until the Voting Rights Act of 1965, Congress used its powers under Section 2 very little, and when it did use them, it was only to open federal courts for action against discriminatory state practices. This case-by-case litigation was inadequate to combat widespread and persistent discrimination because of the inordinate amount of time and energy required to overcome the obstructionist tactics encountered in those lawsuits. Even after a lawsuit had been won, there was no assurance that blacks would be permitted to vote. So in 1965 Congress, using its authority under this section to do whatever is necessary and proper to ensure that no state shall deprive any person of the right to vote because of race, adopted a new approach.

By the Voting Rights Act of 1965 — three times extended and strengthened by Congress, once in 1970, again in 1975, and most recently in 1982 — Congress set about implementing the Fifteenth Amendment in two ways: first, by securing for blacks the right to vote and second by ensuring that their votes would not be diluted. To accomplish these purposes, the act does several things. First, it prohibits literacy tests everywhere. Second, in Section 2, it forbids governments — any governments anyplace in the United States — from adopting voting or electoral procedures, regardless of intent, that result in the dilution of black voting power. Third, in those states and counties, mostly but not exclusively in the South, that have a persistent history of violating the Fifteenth Amendment, it authorizes the attorney general to send federal officials to observe elections and, if necessary, to enroll voters. If local election officials turn away any voter who federal examiners find entitled to vote, the examiners may secure an order from a federal district court impounding all ballots until all persons entitled to vote have been allowed to do so. The attorney general may also appoint poll watchers to ensure that the votes of all qualified persons are properly counted. Fourth, in Section 5, in the covered areas no new voting law or practice that affects the electoral process is effective unless approved by the attorney general or by the United States District Court for the District of Columbia. For the attorney general or the District Court for the District of Columbia to set aside proposed changes in the electoral practices or procedures of units covered by the act, they do not have to show that the purpose of the change is to discriminate against blacks. It is sufficient to show that the proposed change would result in the dilution of the voting influence of a protected class. Thus, the attorney general refused to allow Rome, Georgia, to alter its system of electing city council members and school boards. They had been elected from wards; in the new system they would have been elected at large. This rather drastic intrusion into local matters was justified by the Court on the grounds that the Fifteenth Amendment was specifically designed as an expansion of federal powers: It gives Congress authority to adopt legislation to enforce its provisions, even if such legislation overrides principles of federalism that might otherwise be an obstacle to congressional authority.[7] A voting district may "bail out" from the prior-clearance requirements for electoral changes only if it proves to the District Court for the District of Columbia that it has had a clean voting rights record for the preceding ten years.

The Voting Rights Act also provides some other protections in areas in which more than 10 percent of voting-age citizens belong to language minorities — persons of Spanish heritage, Asian Americans, American Indians, and Alaskan natives. In such areas bilingual election materials must be provided.

The act also requires that any otherwise qualified persons be allowed to vote for presidential electors even if they fail to meet a state's residency requirements, orders states to keep registration for presidential elections open until thirty days before the election, and lowers from twenty-one to eighteen the voting age in all elections.

The Supreme Court, making it clear that "Congress may use any rational means to effectuate the constitutional prohibition of racial discrimination in voting,"[8] has upheld all provisions of the act except the one lowering the voting age to eighteen in elections for state and local officials (the Twenty-sixth Amendment now governs the age requirement for voting in all elections for all officials).[9]

As a result of the Voting Rights Act of 1965 and its amendments, for the first time in a hundred years, the Fifteenth Amendment became an operating reality throughout the nation. By 1988 there were more than 5,000 blacks holding national, state, and local offices. The act goes considerably beyond protecting the right to vote provided by the Fifteenth Amendment. For one thing, it makes it easier for states to do certain things in response to the promptings of that act than it would be to do those things without such promptings. In *United Jewish Organizations* v *Carey*, the Court ruled that a state acting under provisions of the Voting Rights Act may draw district lines for the state legislature in a way that ensures that blacks will be in a majority in certain voting districts. "Where a plan presents no racial slur or stigma with respect to whites or any other race and does not deprive whites, as a group, of 'fair representation,' " it is constitutional, even though as a consequence of the plan in the case decided, a Hasidic Jewish community was split into two voting districts and thereby had its voting strength diluted.[10]

The Voting Rights Act, especially as amended in 1982, goes beyond the Fifteenth Amendment in another very important way. Electoral arrangements that do not relate directly to voting and are neutral on their face are not violations of the Fifteenth Amendment, even if they dilute the voting power of blacks, unless they are motivated by a discriminatory *purpose.* What does not violate the Fifteenth Amendment, however, may violate the Voting Rights Act. A Supreme Court plurality opinion in *Mobile v Borden* had declared that to establish a violation of either the Voting Rights Act or the Fourteenth or Fifteenth Amendment, minority voters had to prove that a contested electoral mechanism was intentionally adopted or maintained by state officials for a discriminatory purpose.[11] The 1982 amendments set aside this limitation.

Although the 1982 amendments do not guarantee "members of a protected class a right to have members . . . elected in numbers equal to their proportion in the population," they do make it illegal for governments to adopt or maintain procedures, regardless of intent, if such procedures result in the dilution of black voting power. Where blacks make up a substantial proportion of the population, the fact that few or none of them get elected is part of the "totality of circumstances" judges must take into account in determining whether there has been a violation of the act.

What about multimember electoral districts? Does their mere existence violate Section 2 of the Voting Rights Act? Not necessarily. However, if (1) a minority group is sufficiently large and geographically compact to constitute a majority in a single-member district, (2) the minority group is politically cohesive, and (3) the white majority usually votes as enough of a bloc to defeat the minority-preferred candidate, then the multimember district system is a violation of Section 2. To prove this set of facts exists, plaintiffs have to show that a significant number of minority group members usually vote for the same candidate, whatever the candidate's race, and that, in general, a white bloc vote normally has defeated the combined strength of minority support plus white "crossover." It is not necessary to prove that the white voters intend to discriminate against blacks or that blacks vote for blacks only because of race. The mere fact of bloc voting is enough.[12]

TWENTIETH-CENTURY AMENDMENTS

AMENDMENT XVI: INCOME TAXES

The Congress shall have power to lay and collect taxes on incomes, from whatever source derived, without apportionment among the several States, and without regard to any census or enumeration.

This amendment was proposed July 12, 1909, and declared in force by the secretary of state February 25, 1913.

During the Civil War an income tax was levied as part of the war financing program. As was generally expected, the Supreme Court upheld the national government's right to levy such a tax. In 1894 the Wilson-Gorham Tariff levied a 2 percent tax on incomes over $4,000. The year following, after hearing the tax assailed as the opening wedge of populism, communism, and the like, the Supreme Court ruled that a tax on income from property was tantamount to a tax on the property itself and hence a direct tax, which had to be apportioned among the several states according to population (see Article I, Section 2, paragraph 3).[1] The levying of an income tax was thus rendered impracticable until the adoption of the Sixteenth Amendment in 1913.

AMENDMENT XVII: DIRECT ELECTION OF SENATORS

1. The Senate of the United States shall be composed of two Senators from each State, elected by the people thereof for six years; and each Senator shall have one vote. The electors in each State shall have the qualifications requisite for electors of the most numerous branch of the State legislatures.

This amendment was proposed May 13, 1912, and declared in force by the secretary of state May 31, 1913.

The adoption of universal suffrage and the growing strength of the democratic spirit made it inevitable that United States senators should be chosen directly by the people. During the last half of the nineteenth century, dissident labor and farmer parties had called for direct election. The revelation of certain senators' great wealth and of their obligations to various large economic interests reinforced those demands. By the turn of the century, all the major parties supported proposals for direct election; the House of Representatives several times passed resolutions proposing an amendment to make the change. Finally, in 1912 the Senate capitulated. As a matter of fact, by that date the voters in half of the states had obtained the right to indicate their preference for senator in the party primaries; the state legislatures normally followed the wishes of the voters. The adoption of the Seventeenth Amendment merely rounded out a reform that had long been under way.

2. When vacancies happen in the representation of any State in the Senate, the executive authority of such State shall issue writs of election to fill such vacancies: *Provided*, That the legislature of any State may empower the executive thereof to make temporary appointments until the people fill the vacancies by election as the legislature may direct.

Most vacancies are filled by temporary appointments.

3. This amendment shall not be so construed as to affect the election or term of any Senator chosen before it becomes valid as part of the Constitution.

AMENDMENT XVIII: PROHIBITION

Section 1

After one year from the ratification of this article the manufacture, sale, or transportation of intoxicating liquors within, the importation thereof into, or the exportation thereof from the United States and all territory subject to the jurisdiction thereof for beverage purposes is hereby prohibited.

This amendment was proposed December 18, 1917, and declared in force by the acting secretary of state January 29, 1919.

There have always been those who have waged war on demon rum. As long ago as 1842 the state of Maine went dry, and the Prohibition Party has had a candidate on the ballot in at least a few states in every presidential election since 1872. But it was the Anti-Saloon League — a pressure group deluxe, formed in 1895 — that gave the prohibition movement its greatest impetus. During World War I, the necessity of saving grain lent prohibition a guise of patriotism. Although the Eighteenth Amendment was ultimately ratified by all the states except Rhode Island and Connecticut, it always lacked the support of large groups of citizens, especially in the large cities.

Section 2

The Congress and the several States shall have concurrent power to enforce this article by appropriate legislation.

The Volstead Act went into effect January 17, 1920. By 1929 three states had repealed their enforcement acts; most states left it to the national government to implement this amendment.

Section 3

This article shall be inoperative unless it shall have been ratified as an amendment to the Constitution by the legislatures of the several States as provided in the Constitution, within seven years from the date of the submission hereof to the States by the Congress.

AMENDMENT XIX: WOMAN SUFFRAGE

1. The right of citizens of the United States to vote shall not be denied or abridged by the United States or by any State on account of sex.

The Nineteenth Amendment was proposed June 4, 1919, and declared in force by the secretary of state August 26, 1920.

This amendment was the culmination of a struggle that began in the 1840s. In 1890 women were admitted to full suffrage rights in Wyoming; by the time the amendment was adopted, fifteen states and Alaska had given them full suffrage, fourteen states had given them "presidential suffrage," and two states had given them the right to vote in primaries. Many of the arguments advanced against woman suffrage were ludicrous. Much of the opposition came from certain business groups (especially the liquor industry), who feared that women would vote for regulation.

The Nineteenth Amendment did not affect laws dealing with ownership of property, jury service, marriage and divorce, labor regulations, and so forth. Three years after the Amendment had been ratified, the first equal rights amendment was introduced in Congress. Forty-nine years later, Congress finally proposed an Equal Rights Amendment and submitted it to the states. Although it had overwhelming support in both houses of Congress and at first appeared likely to be ratified quickly, it failed to secure the necessary number of votes, even though the time limit for ratification was extended by almost four years. The Supreme Court, as well as the courts in many states, has started to provide more protection for equal rights under existing constitutional language. Although the cases do not arise under the Nineteenth Amendment, that women vote is not unrelated to greater judicial sensitivity to equal rights.

---

2.   Congress shall have power to enforce this article by appropriate legislation.

Congress has had little occasion to use this power. Despite the intensity of the opposition to the proposal of this amendment and the time it took to bring about this constitutional change, once the Nineteenth Amendment was ratified, in contrast to the Fifteenth, there was no attempt to delay or obstruct its implementation.

AMENDMENT XX: THE LAME-DUCK AMENDMENT

Section 1

The terms of the President and Vice President shall end at noon on the 20th day of January, and the terms of Senators and Representatives at noon on the 3d day of January, of the years in which such terms would have ended if this article had not been ratified; and the terms of their successors shall then begin.

This amendment was proposed March 3, 1932, and declared in force by the secretary of state February 6, 1933.

This amendment was eventually ratified by all the states. Senator George W. Norris of Nebraska was the moving force behind the amendment, which is sometimes given his name. Its adoption brought to a close the Progressive Movement's contribution to constitutional reform, a movement that led to the Sixteenth through Twentieth Amendments.

Before the adoption of the Twentieth Amendment, the president and members of Congress elected in November did not take office until the following March, and newly elected members of Congress did not (unless called into special session) actually begin their work until the following December — thirteen months after their election. Meanwhile, members defeated in the November election ("lame ducks") continued to serve until the following March 4 and, although repudiated at the polls, continued to represent their constituencies in the December-to-March session.

Section 2

The Congress shall assemble at least once in every year, and such meeting shall begin at noon on the 3d day of January, unless they shall by law appoint a different day.

This section supersedes Article I, Section 4, paragraph 2, which called for Congress to meet on the first Monday in December and so necessitated every other year a short, ineffective "lame-duck" session. The Twentieth Amendment does away with this session, which was frequently marked in the Senate by filibusters.

Normally Congress meets on the constitutionally designated January 3, but occasionally Congress exercises its option and convenes on the day before or after, especially if January 3 is a Sunday.

Section 3

If, at the time fixed for the beginning of the term of the President, the President elect shall have died, the Vice President elect shall become President. If a President shall not have been chosen before the time fixed for the beginning of his term, or if the President elect shall have failed to qualify, then the Vice President elect shall act as President until a President shall have qualified; and the Congress may by law provide for the case wherein neither a President elect nor a Vice President elect shall have qualified, declaring who shall then act as President, or the manner in which one who is to act shall be selected, and such person shall act accordingly until a President or Vice President shall have qualified.

It should be noted that within the meaning of the Constitution there is no president-elect or vice-president-elect until the electoral votes have been counted by Congress or, in the event that no person has a majority of the electoral votes, until the House of Representatives and the Senate have made their choices.

Congress has now made the same provision for succession in the event of the disability or disqualification of the president-elect and the vice president-elect as in the case of the president and the vice president (see page 264).

Section 4

The Congress may by law provide for the case of the death of any of the persons from whom the House of Representatives may choose a President whenever the right of choice shall have devolved upon them, and for the case of the death of any of the persons from whom the Senate may choose a Vice President whenever the right of choice shall have devolved upon them.

Congress has failed to act under this section.

Section 5

Sections 1 and 2 shall take effect on the 15th day of October following the ratification of this article.

Section 6

This article shall be inoperative unless it shall have been ratified as an amendment to the Constitution by the legislatures of three-fourths of the several States within seven years from the date of its submission.

AMENDMENT XXI: REPEAL OF PROHIBITION

Section 1

The eighteenth article of amendment to the Constitution of the United States is hereby repealed.

This amendment was proposed February 20, 1933, and declared in force by the secretary of state December 5, 1933.

It soon became apparent that the Eighteenth Amendment had failed to diminish the amount of liquor consumed; instead, it diverted taxes and profits from legitimate interests into the hands of bootleggers and criminals and was endangering respect for the Constitution and the laws of the land. The demand for repeal became insistent. In 1928 Alfred Smith, the Democratic candidate for president, advocated repeal; by 1932 the platforms of both major parties were, in the phrase of the day, "dripping wet."

Section 2

The transportation or importation into any State, Territory, or possession of the United States for delivery or use therein of intoxicating liquors, in violation of the laws thereof, is hereby prohibited.

This section turned back to each state the responsibility for deciding whether intoxicating liquors would be allowed to be transported, used, or sold within its boundaries. States may, if they wish, ban completely the transportation or importation of intoxicating liquors.

Although the Twenty-first Amendment gives states greater authority to regulate intoxicating beverages than to regulate other items of interstate commerce, its current construction does not deny the federal government the right to use the commerce clause to interfere with the exercise by the states of their powers under the Twenty-first Amendment. The test is "whether the interests implicated by a state regulation are so closely related to the powers reserved by the Twenty-first Amendment that the regulation may prevail, notwithstanding that its requirements directly conflict with express federal policies." In other words, the states must persuade a majority of the Supreme Court that what they want to do is more important than what conflicting federal law requires. Justices O'Connor and Stevens have charged in separate dissents that "the Court has, over the years, so completely distorted the Twenty-first Amendment 'that [it] now has a barely discernible effect in Commerce Clause cases.' "[1]

In 1964 the Court set aside a Kentucky tax on each gallon of whiskey imported from Scotland as a violation of the export-import clause. Justice Black, in dissent, quipped, "Although I was brought up to believe that Scotch whiskey would need a tax preference to survive in competition with Kentucky bourbon, I never understood the Constitution to require a State to give such preference."[2] Similarly, in 1984 the Court set aside a Hawaii 20 percent tax on wholesale liquor sales, from which tax certain locally produced alcoholic beverages were exempt.[3] And in 1987 the Supreme Court ruled that a price-maintenance arrangement of New York, an arrangement regulating the prices at which alcoholic beverages could be sold, violated the Sherman Antitrust Act and was not within the authority reserved to the states by this section.

That drinking and driving do not mix and that the national government may impose conditions on a state's receipt of federal highway funds — conditions relating both to speed limits and to the the the minimum age of drivers — despite state regulations to the contrary was established in *South Carolina* v *Dole*.[4] The states' powers under the Twenty-first Amendment to regulate the conditions of sale and possession of intoxicating liquors have fared somewhat better in First Amendment contexts. In fact, Justice Stevens has accused his colleagues of "completely distort[ing] the Twenty-first Amendment" and making it "toothless except when freedom of speech is involved."[5] Examples of its application when freedom of speech is involved include the Court's approval of California's prohibition of certain kinds of live and filmed sexual entertainment in places that serve alcohol. The Court recognized that some of the entertainment forbidden could not be deemed obscene but said that just as a state may forbid the sale of liquor where food is not served, where dancing is permitted, where gasoline is sold, and within so many feet of a church or a school, so, because of the Twenty-first Amendment, may it ban entertainment.[6] "The Amendment does not license the States, [however,] to ignore their obligations under other provisions of the Constitution."[7] Thus, as we have noted, a city cannot delegate to a church authority to decide whether a liquor license should be granted to a tavern in the church's neighborhood: that action would violate the establishment-of-religion provisions of the First Amendment. Nor does this amendment exempt states from the supremacy clause. When an Oklahoma law, purportedly authorized by the amendment, that forbade advertisements of wine on cable television came into conflict with an FCC regulation permitting such advertising, the Supreme Court concluded that since Oklahoma permitted circulation of out-of-state newspaper and magazine advertisements of wine, its interest in discouraging consumption by forbidding cable television to advertise wine was not of the same stature as the FCC's interest in ensuring the widespread availability of cable television throughout the United States.[8] (It is doubtful that if Oklahoma had tried to ban all advertising of alcoholic beverages, it would have made any difference.)

Section 3

This article shall be inoperative unless it shall have been ratified as an amendment to the Constitution by conventions in the several States, as provided in the Constitution, within seven years from the date of submission hereof to the States by the Congress.

This is the only amendment Congress submitted to conventions in the several states for ratification rather than to the state legislatures. Congress chose this method because it believed that the "drys" had more influence within some of the rural legislatures than they would have in special ratifying conventions.

Congress left to the judgment of each state legislature how to organize and hold the ratifying conventions. Delegates ran on "dry" and "wet" slates, so, in effect, the voters in each state made the decision, and the conventions merely ratified the decisions of the voters.

AMENDMENT XXII: THE NUMBER OF PRESIDENTIAL TERMS

Section 1

No person shall be elected to the office of the President more than twice, and no person who has held the office of President, or acted as President, for more than two years of a term to which some other person was elected President shall be elected to the office of the President more than once. But this article shall not apply to any person holding the office of President when this Article was proposed by the Congress,

This amendment was proposed March 24, 1947, and certified as adopted by the administrator of general services March 1, 1951.

It is one of the few amendments, perhaps the only amendment, adopted since 1787 that, instead of expanding the power of the electorate, places direct curbs on it. It was adopted in reaction to Franklin D. Roosevelt's election to four terms in office. Decades later, during the early years of President Reagan's second term, many Republicans suggested that this amendment might be repealed. When it became apparent that Reagan would not be a viable candidate for a third term, their interest in its repeal began to wane.

The maximum period that a person can serve is ten years — two years by elevation to the office through the death or disability of the elected president and two elected terms of four years each. In some cases, a person might be limited to six years, since elevation for two years and a day, through death, disability, or resignation of the elected president, would make a person eligible for only one elected term of four years.

Section 1

[continued] and shall not prevent any person who may be holding the office of President, or acting as President, during the term within which this Article becomes operative from holding the office of President or acting as President during the remainder of such term.

The person in office was Harry Truman, and if he had chosen to run again, which he did not, and had been reelected, his term would have extended beyond ten years.

Section 2

This article shall be inoperative unless it shall have been ratified as an amendment to the Constitution by the legislatures of three-fourths of the several States within seven years from the date of its submission to the States by the Congress.

Within four years after submission, forty-one state legislatures ratified this amendment. There was very little discussion of its significance; in some instances, the legislators voted for ratification without debate.

What has been the effect of the Twenty-second Amendment on the influence of the president? When it was possible, even if unlikely, that a president might seek a third term, that president had considerably more influence than presidents who made known their decisions not to run again. Congressional members, governors, and politicians were much less inclined to oppose the person who might be the head of their ticket than the person who was about to retire to the role of elder statesman. The adoption of this amendment has eliminated even the outside possibility of a second-term president's running again.

AMENDMENT XXIII: PRESIDENTIAL ELECTORS FOR THE DISTRICT OF COLUMBIA

Section 1

The District constituting the seat of Government of the United States shall appoint in such manner as the Congress may direct:

A number of electors of President and Vice President equal to the whole number of Senators and Representatives in Congress to which the District would be entitled if it were a State, but in no event more than the least populous State; they shall be in addition to those appointed by the States, but they shall be considered, for the purposes of the election of President and Vice President, to be electors appointed by a State; and they shall meet in the District and perform such duties as provided by the twelfth article of amendment.

This amendment, proposed on June 16, 1960, was ratified March 29, 1961.

On August 22, 1978, Congress proposed an amendment that, if ratified, would have repealed this one. That amendment would have given the District of Columbia the same number of members of Congress that it would have if it were a state, as well as giving the District the same number of electoral votes for president and vice president and the right to participate in the ratification process for constitutional amendments. It did not even come close, however, to being ratified.

Congress set the usual seven-year time limit for ratification when it submitted the Twenty-third Amendment to the state legislatures, but it took only nine months to secure approval of the legislatures in three-fourths of the states. (Tennessee was the only southern state to ratify.)

Since the least populous state, Alaska, has only three electoral votes, that is the number this amendment assigns to the District of Columbia.

Section 2

The Congress shall have power to enforce this article by appropriate legislation.

AMENDMENT XXIV: THE ANTI-POLL-TAX AMENDMENT

Section 1

The right of citizens of the United States to vote in any primary or other election for

President or Vice President, for electors for President or Vice President, or for Senator or Representative in Congress, shall not be denied or abridged by the United States or any State by reason of failure to pay any poll tax or other tax.

Section 2

The Congress shall have power to enforce this article by appropriate legislation.

This amendment, proposed August 27, 1962, was readily ratified within the seven years stipulated by Congress and became part of the Constitution on January 23, 1964. At the time it was submitted, only five states imposed a poll tax as a requirement for voting.

The anti-poll-tax amendment by its own terms forbids payment of a poll tax as a condition for voting for presidential electors and members of Congress. It was rendered superfluous by the Supreme Court in 1966, when, in *Harper* v *Virginia Board of Electors*, it decided that the equal protection clause precludes a state from imposing a poll tax as a requirement to vote in any election.[1]

AMENDMENT XXV: PRESIDENTIAL DISABILITY; VICE PRESIDENTIAL VACANCIES

In the case of the removal of the President from office or of his death or resignation, the Vice President shall become President.

At the time Congress submitted this proposal, on July 6, 1965, it stipulated that ratification would have to take place within seven years to be effective. The amendment was ratified February 10, 1967.

This section merely confirms what has been the consistent practice (see page 90) of the eight vice presidents who have acceded to the presidency on the death of the president. It also deals with an additional situation, the resignation of a president. By making the vice president the president, not merely acting president, after the incumbent resigns, the amendment precludes a person from resigning and then attempting to return to office.

The only incumbent ever to resign was Richard Nixon. The amendment does not deal with the way presidents submit their resignation. Nixon did so by sending a two-line letter to the secretary of state. Thus the precedent has been established.

Section 2

Whenever there is a vacancy in the office of the Vice President, the President shall nominate a Vice President who shall take office upon confirmation by a majority vote of both Houses of Congress.

The vice presidency has been vacant eighteen times. Fortunately, during those periods there has been no need to continue down the line of presidential succession that Congress has provided by law — speaker of the House, president pro tempore of the Senate, and then members of the cabinet in order of the creation of their departments.

The procedure provided by Section 2 has some resemblance to that normally followed in the original selection and election of a vice president. Once a party selects its presidential candidate by a vote of the delegates to its national convention, that candidate normally chooses a vice presidential running mate, who, after confirmation by the national convention and election along with the president, becomes vice president. Section 2 calls on Congress to serve in lieu of the electorate to confirm the presidential choice.

Section 2 received little attention at the time of the adoption of the amendment, since congressional and public attention was focused on the problems of presidential disability dealt with in Section 3. It was generally assumed that Section 2 would be used after the death of a president had elevated into the White House the elected vice president, thereby creating a vacancy in the vice presidency.

But the first time Section 2 was used was in the unanticipated set of circumstances created by the resignation of Vice President Agnew to avoid federal criminal charges at the same time that President Nixon himself was under the cloud of suspicion created by the Watergate affair. President Nixon nominated Gerald Ford, a Republican, then minority leader in the House. The Democratic Party controlled both chambers of Congress, but Congress, in keeping with the spirit of the Constitution, limited its investigation to questions of Ford's fitness and integrity, rather than probing such issues as his policy attitudes, in order that the vice president might be a person reflecting, through the elected president, the wishes of the majority of the voters in the immediately preceding election.

During the interim between Ford's nomination by Nixon and his confirmation by Congress, some wondered what would happen if President Nixon resigned or was removed from office. The speaker of the House would become acting president. Would the Ford nomination for vice president still stand if the speaker were to send to Congress another name? Would Congress have the right to choose between the two nominees? The fact that there are any open questions about presidential succession is, of course, dangerous, for there is nothing more threatening to a constitutional democracy than doubts about who has the legitimate right to govern. But the constitutional crisis passed, and the amendment appeared to be working.

Very soon thereafter, President Nixon resigned to escape being impeached, and Ford became president, once again creating a vacancy in the vice presidency. President Ford nominated Nelson Rockefeller, a former four-term governor of New York and a well-known public figure. After a long examination of Rockefeller's record, Congress finally confirmed the nomination.

Although for the first time in our history we had both a president and a vice president who had not been voted for by the electorate, there was never any question about the rights of President Ford and Vice President Rockefeller to exercise to the full the powers vested in their offices by the Constitution. Nonetheless, some outside and some inside Congress called for a reconsideration of Section 2. President Ford suggested that some time limit should be placed on congressional confirmation. Some in Congress argued that in the event of a vacancy in the presidency with more than two years of a term still to expire, another election should be held. But the consensus seemed to be that if Section 2 worked under the circumstances in which it was first used, it was likely to work under constitutionally less trying conditions.

Section 3

Whenever the President transmits to the President pro tempore of the Senate and the Speaker of the House of Representatives his written declaration that he is unable to discharge the powers and duties of his office, and until he transmits to them a written declaration to the contrary, such powers and duties shall be discharged by the Vice President as Acting President.

Until this amendment, Congress had never established procedures to determine how it should be judged whether or not the president was unable to discharge the duties of office. Six times in our history this question has caused difficulty: when President Garfield suffered a lingering death from an assassin's bullet; when President Wilson had a physical breakdown during the closing years of his second term; when there was concern about President Roosevelt's health just before his fatal attack; when President Eisenhower was temporarily disabled, first by a heart attack and later by a serious operation; and when President Reagan was briefly disabled by a gunshot wound.

In July of 1985, when President Reagan underwent a several hour operation, he made a deliberate decision not to invoke Section 3. "I am mindful," he wrote to Vice President Bush, "of the uncertainties of its application to such brief and temporary periods of incapacity. I do not believe that the drafters of this amendment intended its application to situations such as the instance one." Nevertheless, the president sent a letter to the Speaker and to the president pro tempore of the Senate saying, "consistent with my long-standing arrangement with Vice President George Bush, and not intending to set a precedent binding anyone privileged to hold this Office in the future, I have determined and it is my intention . . . that Vice President George Bush shall discharge those powers and duties in my stead commencing with the administration of anesthesia to me in this instance." After he was once again alert, he sent off a second letter affirming his intention to resume his duties.[1] This following of Section 3 procedures without formally invoking it was the first formal transfer of presidential power in our history.

Section 4

Whenever the Vice President and a majority of either the principal officers of the executive departments or of such other body as Congress may by law provide, transmit to the President pro tempore of the Senate and the Speaker of the House of Representatives their written declaration that the President is unable to discharge the powers and duties of his office, the Vice President shall immediately assume the powers and duties of the office as Acting President.

Section 4 deals with situations in which a president may be unable to declare the inability to discharge the duties of the office. The responsibility then vests in the vice president *and* the cabinet to declare it. Upon such a declaration, the vice president *immediately* becomes acting president.

It is interesting to note that although the Constitution in Article II, Section 2, mentions "the principal officers of the executive departments," in other words the cabinet, this section is the first to assign the cabinet a collective responsibility. The composition of the cabinet has varied from president to president, and there has been no very precise definition of its membership. Vesting this constitutional responsibility in the cabinet as an entity suggests the need for some more formal definition of its composition.

The declaration of presidential disability by a majority of the cabinet is subject to a vice presidential veto. However, whenever the cabinet and the vice president believe the president is unable to discharge the powers and duties of the office, the vice president immediately assumes the powers and duties, but is only the acting president. The disabled president remains president, but, until determined able again (see the remainder of Section 4, which follows the next paragraph), the president is without authority to act.[2]

The only time since the adoption of this provision that it might have been brought into play was when President Reagan was unexpectedly disabled as the result of an attempted assassination in 1982 and for about twenty-four hours was out of commission in the emergency room of George Washington Hospital. His aides did not invoke the Twenty-fifth Amendment, and the cabinet was not asked to consider the matter.

Section 4

[continued] Thereafter, when the President transmits to the President pro tempore of the Senate and the Speaker of the House of Representatives his written declaration that no inability exists, he shall resume the powers and duties of his office unless the Vice President and a majority of either the principal officers of the executive department or of such other body as Congress may by law provide, transmit within four days to the President pro tempore of the Senate and the Speaker of the House of Representatives their written declaration that the President is unable to discharge the powers and duties of his office. Thereupon Congress shall decide the issue, assembling within forty-eight hours for that purpose if not in session. If the Congress, within twenty-one days after receipt of the latter written declaration, or, if Congress is not in session, within twenty-one days after Congress is required to assemble, determines by two-thirds vote of both Houses that the President is unable to discharge the powers and duties of his office, the Vice President shall continue to discharge the same as Acting President; otherwise, the President shall resume the powers and duties of his office.

In case of a conflict between the president, on one side, and the vice president and a majority of the Cabinet, on the other, over the issue of the president's fitness to assume presidential duties, Congress decides. However, the advantage is in favor of the president; a two-thirds vote of both houses is required to retain the vice president as acting president in the face of a declaration by the president of the ability to resume the duties of office.

A contingency still not covered is a method for filling postelection vacancies caused by the death of a winner of an election before there is in a constitutional sense a president-elect or a vice-president-elect.

AMENDMENT XXVI: EIGHTEEN-YEAR-OLD VOTE

Section 1

The right of citizens of the United States, who are eighteen years of age or older, to vote shall not be denied or abridged by the United States or by any State on account of age.

This amendment, proposed on March 23, 1971, was ratified on June 30, 1971, after only five weeks — the fastest ratification of any amendment.

After the Supreme Court ruled that Congress lacked authority to set the voting age for state and local elections but could do so for national elections, Congress proposed this amendment. Ratification was swift, in large part because without the amendment many states would have been faced with the costly and administratively difficult task of operating separate registration books, ballots, and voting apparatuses for election of federal officers and for election of state and local officers.

Section 2

The Congress shall have the power to enforce this article by appropriate legislation.

The Constitution of the United States

We the People of the United States, in Order to form a more perfect Union, establish Justice, insure domestic Tranquility, provide for the common defence, promote the general Welfare, and secure the Blessings of Liberty to ourselves and our Posterity, do ordain and establish this Constitution for the United States of America.

Article I

Section 1. All legislative Powers herein granted shall be vested in a Congress of the United States, which shall consist of a Senate and House of Representatives.

Section 2. The House of Representatives shall be composed of Members chosen every second Year by the People of the several States, and the Electors in each State shall have the Qualifications requisite for Electors of the most numerous Branch of the State Legislature.

No Person shall be a Representative who shall not have attained to the Age of twenty five Years, and been seven Years a Citizen of the United States, and who shall not, when elected, be an Inhabitant of that State in which he shall be chosen.

Representatives and direct Taxes shall be apportioned among the several States which may be included within this Union, according to their respective Numbers, which shall be determined by adding to the whole Number of free Persons, including those bound to Service for a Term of Years, and excluding Indians not taxed, three fifths of all other Persons. The actual Enumeration shall be made within three Years after the first Meeting of the Congress of the United States, and within every subsequent Term of ten Years, in such Manner as they shall by Law direct. The Number of Representatives shall not exceed one for every thirty Thousand, but each State shall have at Least one Representative; and until such enumerations shall be made, the State of New Hampshire shall be entitled to chuse three, Massachusetts eight, Rhode-Island and Providence Plantations one, Connecticut five, New-York six, New Jersey four, Pennsylvania eight, Delaware one, Maryland six, Virginia ten, North Carolina five, South Carolina five, and Georgia three.

When vacancies happen in the Representation from any State, the Executive Authority thereof shall issue Writs of Election to fill such Vacancies.

The House of Representatives shall chuse their speaker and other Officers; and shall have the sole Power of Impeachment.

Section 3. The Senate of the United States shall be composed of two Senators from each State, chosen by the Legislature thereof, for six Years; and each Senator shall have one Vote.

Immediately after they shall be assembled in Consequence of the first Election, they shall be divided as equally as may be into three Classes. The Seats of the Senators of the first Class shall be vacated at the Expiration of the second Year, of the second Class at the Expiration of the fourth Year, and of the third Class at the Expiration of the sixth Year, so that one third may be chosen every second Year; and if Vacancies happen by Resignation, or otherwise, during the Recess of the Legislature of any State, the Executive thereof may make temporary Appointments until the next Meeting of the Legislature, which shall then fill such Vacancies.

No person shall be a Senator who shall not have attained to the Age of thirty Years, and been nine Years a Citizen of the United States, and who shall not, when elected, be an Inhabitant of that State for which he shall be chosen.

The Vice President of the United States shall be President of the Senate, but shall have no Vote, unless they be equally divided.

The Senate shall chuse their other Officers, and also a President pro tempore, in the Absence of the Vice President, or when he shall exercise the Office of President of the United States.

The Senate shall have the sole Power to try all Impeachments. When sitting for that Purpose, they shall be on Oath or Affirmation. When the President of the United States is tried, the Chief Justice shall preside: And no Person shall be convicted without the concurrence of two thirds of the Members present. Judgment in Cases of Impeachment shall not extend further than to removal from Office, and disqualification to hold and enjoy any Office of honor, Trust or Profit under the United States: but the Party convicted shall nevertheless be liable and subject to Indictment, Trial, Judgment and Punishment, according to law.

Section 4. The Times, Places and Manner of holding Elections for Senators and Representatives, shall be prescribed in each State by the Legislature thereof; but the Congress may at any time by Law make or alter such Regulations, except as to the Places of chusing Senators.

The Congress shall assemble at least once in every Year, and such Meeting shall be on the first Monday in December, unless they shall by Law appoint a different Day.

Section 5. Each House shall be the Judge of the Elections, Returns and Qualifications of its own Members, and a Majority of each shall constitute a Quorum to do business; but a smaller Number may adjourn from day to day, and may be authorized to compel the Attendance of absent Members, in such Manner, and under such Penalties as each House may provide.

Each House may determine the Rules of its Proceedings, punish its Members for disorderly Behaviour, and, with the Concurrence of two thirds, expel a Member.

Each House shall keep a journal of its Proceedings, and from time to time publish the same, excepting such Parts as may in their Judgment require Secrecy; and the yeas and Nays of the Members of either House on any question shall, at the Desire of one fifth of those Present, be entered on the Journal.

Neither House, during the Session of Congress, shall, without the Consent of the other, adjourn for more than three days, nor to any other place than that in which the two Houses shall be sitting.

Section 6. The Senators and Representatives shall receive a Compensation for their Services, to be ascertained by Law, and paid out of the Treasury of the United States. They shall in all Cases, except Treason, Felony and Breach of the Peace, be privileged from Arrest during their Attendance at the Session of their respective Houses, and in going to and returning from the same; and for any Speech or Debate in either House, they shall not be questioned in any other Place.

No Senator or Representative shall, during the Time for which he was elected, be appointed to any civil Office under the Authority of the United States, which shall have been created, or the Emoluments whereof shall have been encreased during such time; and no Person holding any Office under the United States, shall be a Member of either House during his Continuance in Office.

Section 7. All Bills for raising Revenue shall originate in the House of Representatives; but the Senate may propose or concur with Amendments as on other Bills.

Every Bill which shall have passed the House of Representatives and the Senate, shall, before it become a Law, be presented to the President of the United States; If he approve he shall sign it, but if not he shall return it, with his Objections to that House in which it shall have originated, who shall enter the Objections at large on their Journal, and proceed to reconsider it. If after such Reconsideration two thirds of that House shall agree to pass the Bill, it shall be sent, together with the Objections, to the other House, by which it shall likewise be reconsidered, and if approved by two thirds of that House, it shall become a Law. But in all such Cases the Votes of both Houses shall be determined by yeas and Nays, and the Names of the Persons voting for and against the Bill shall be entered on the Journal of each House respectively. If any Bill shall not be returned by the President within ten Days (Sundays excepted) after it shall have been presented to him, the Same shall be a Law, in like Manner as if he had signed it, unless the Congress by their Adjournment prevent its Return, in which Case it shall not be a Law.

Every Order, Resolution, or Vote to which the Concurrence of the Senate and House of Representatives may be necessary (except on a question of Adjournment) shall be presented to the President of the United States; and before the Same shall take Effect, shall be approved by him, or being disapproved by him, shall be repassed by two thirds of the Senate and House of Representatives, according to the Rules and Limitations prescribed in the Case of a Bill.

Section 8. The Congress shall have Power To lay and collect Taxes, Duties, Imposts, and Excises, to pay the Debts and provide for the common Defence and general Welfare of the United States; but all duties, Imposts and Excises shall be uniform throughout the United States.

To borrow Money on the Credit of the United States;

To regulate Commerce with foreign Nations, and among the several States, and with the Indian Tribes;

To establish an uniform Rule of Naturalization, and uniform Laws on the subject of Bankruptcies throughout the United States;

To coin Money, regulate the Value thereof, and of foreign Coin, and fix the Standard of Weights and Measures;

To provide for the Punishment of counterfeiting the Securities and current Coin of the United States;

To establish Post Offices and post Roads;

To promote the Progress of Science and useful Arts, by securing for limited Times to Authors and Inventors exclusive Right to their respective Writings and Discoveries;

To constitute Tribunals inferior to the supreme Court;

To define and punish Piracies and Felonies committed on the high Seas, and Offences against the Law of Nations;

To declare War, grant letters of Marque and Reprisal, and make rules concerning Captures on Land and Water;

To raise and support Armies, but no Appropriation of Money to that Use shall be for a longer Term than two Years;

To provide and maintain a Navy;

To make rules for the Government and Regulation of the land and naval Forces;

To provide for calling forth the Militia to execute the Laws of the Union, suppress Insurrections and repel Invasions;

To provide for organizing, arming, and disciplining, the Militia, and for governing such Part of them as may be employed in the Service of the United States, reserving to the States respectively, the Appointment of the Officers, and the Authority of training the Militia according to the discipline prescribed by Congress;

To exercise exclusive Legislation in all Cases whatsoever, over such District (not exceeding ten Miles square), as may, by Cession of particular States, and the Acceptance of Congress, become the Seat of the Government of the United States, and to exercise like Authority over all Places purchased by the Consent of the Legislature of the State in which the Same shall be for the Erection of Forts, Magazines, Arsenals, dock-Yards, and other needful Buildings; — And

To make all Laws which shall be necessary and proper for carrying into Execution the foregoing Powers, and all other Powers vested by this Constitution in the Government of the United States, or in any Department or Officer thereof.

Section 9. The Migration or Importation of such Persons as any of the States now existing shall think proper to admit, shall not be prohibited by the Congress prior to the Year one thousand eight hundred and eight, but a Tax or duty may be imposed on such Importation, not exceeding ten dollars for each Person.

The Privilege of the Writ of Habeas Corpus shall not be suspended, unless when in Cases of Rebellion or Invasion the public Safety may require it.

No Bill of Attainder or ex post facto Law shall be passed.

No Capitation, or other direct, Tax shall be laid, unless in Proportion to the Census or Enumeration herein before directed to be taken.

No Tax or Duty shall be laid on Articles exported from any State.

No Preference shall be given by any Regulation of Commerce or Revenue to the Ports of one State over those of another: nor shall Vessels bound to, or from, one State, be obliged to enter, clear, or pay Duties in another.

No money shall be drawn from the Treasury, but in Consequence of Appropriations made by Law; and a regular Statement and Account of the Receipts and Expenditures of all public Money shall be published from time to time.

No Title of Nobility shall be granted by the United States: And no Person holding any Office of Profit or Trust under them, shall, without the Consent of the Congress, accept of any present, Emolument, Office, or Title, of any kind whatever, from any King, Prince, or foreign State.

Section 10. No State shall enter into any Treaty, Alliance, or Confederation; grant Letters of Marque and Reprisal; coin Money; emit Bills of Credit; make any Thing but gold and silver Coin a Tender in Payment of Debts; pass any Bill of Attainder, ex post facto Law, or Law impairing the Obligation of Contracts, or grant any Title of Nobility.

No State shall, without the Consent of the Congress, lay any Imposts or Duties on Imports or Exports, except what may be absolutely necessary for executing its inspection Laws: and the net Produce of all Duties and Imposts, laid by any State on Imports or Exports, shall be for the Use of the Treasury of the United States; and all such Laws shall be subject to the Revision and Controul of the Congress.

No State shall, without the Consent of Congress, lay any Duty of Tonnage, keep Troops, or Ships of War in time of Peace, enter into any Agreement or Compact with another State, or with a foreign Power, or engage in War, unless actually invaded, or in such imminent Danger as will not admit of delay.

Article II

Section 1. The executive Power shall be vested in a President of the United States of America. He shall hold his Office during the Term of four Years, and, together with the Vice President, chosen for the same term, be elected, as follows

Each state shall appoint, in such Manner as the Legislature thereof may direct, a Number of Electors, equal to the whole Number of Senators and Representatives to which the State may be entitled in the Congress: but no Senator or Representative, or Person holding an Office of Trust or Profit under the United States, shall be appointed an Elector.

The Electors shall meet in their respective States, and vote by Ballot for two Persons, of whom one at least shall not be an inhabitant of the same State with themselves. And they shall make a List of all the Persons voted for, and of the Number of Votes for each; which List they shall sign and certify, and transmit sealed to the Seat of the Government of the United States, directed to the President of the Senate. The President of the Senate shall, in the Presence of the Senate and House of Representatives, open all the Certificates, and the Votes shall then be counted. The Person having the greatest Number of Votes shall be the President, if such Number be a Majority of the whole Number of Electors appointed; and if there be more than one who have such Majority, and have an equal Number of Votes, then the House of Representatives shall immediately chuse by Ballot one of them for President: and if no Person have a Majority, then from the five highest on the List the said House shall in like Manner chuse the President. But in chusing the President, the Votes shall be taken by States, the Representation from each State having one Vote; A quorum for this Purpose shall consist of a Member or Members from two thirds of the States, and a Majority of the States shall be necessary to a Choice. In every Case, after the Choice of the President, the Person having the greatest Number of Votes of the Electors shall be the Vice President. But if there should remain two or more who have equal Votes, the Senate shall chuse from them by Ballot the Vice President.

The Congress may determine the Time of chusing the Electors, and the Day on which they shall give their Votes; which Day shall be the same throughout the United States.

No Person except a natural born Citizen, or a Citizen of the United States, at the time of the Adoption of this Constitution, shall be eligible to the Office of President; neither shall any Person be eligible to that Office who shall not have attained to the Age of thirty five Years, and been fourteen Years a Resident within the United States.

In Case of the Removal of the President from Office, or of his Death, Resignation, or Inability to discharge the Powers and Duties of the said Office, the Same shall devolve on the Vice President, and the Congress may by Law provide for the Case of Removal, Death, Resignation or Inability, both of the President and Vice President, declaring what Officer shall then act as President, and such Officer shall act accordingly, until the Disability be removed, or a President shall be elected.

The President shall, at stated Times, receive for his Services, a Compensation, which shall neither be encreased nor diminished during the Period for which he shall have been elected, and he shall not receive within that Period any other Emolument from the United States, or any of them.

Before he enter on the Execution of his Office, he shall take the following Oath or Affirmation: — "I do solemnly swear (or affirm) that I will faithfully execute the Office of President of the United States, and will to the best of my Ability, preserve, protect and defend the Constitution of the United States."

Section 2. The President shall be Commander in Chief of the Army and Navy of the United States, and of the Militia of the several States, when called into the actual Service of the United States; he may require the Opinion, in writing, of the principal Officer in each of the executive Departments, upon any Subject relating to the Duties of their respective Offices, and he shall have Power to grant Reprieves and Pardons for Offenses against the United States, except in Cases of Impeachment.

He shall have Power, by and with the Advice and Consent of the Senate, to make Treaties, provided two thirds of the Senators present concur; and he shall nominate, and by and with the Advice and Consent of the Senate, shall appoint Ambassadors, other public Ministers and Consuls, Judges of the supreme Court, and all other Officers of the United States, whose Appointments are not herein otherwise provided for, and which shall be established by Law: but the Congress may by Law vest the Appointment of such inferior Officers, as they think proper, in the President alone, in the Courts of Law, or in the Heads of Departments.

The President shall have Power to fill up all Vacancies that may happen during the Recess of the Senate, by granting Commissions which shall expire at the End of their next Session.

Section 3. He shall from time to time give to the Congress Information of the State of the Union, and recommend to their Consideration such Measures as he shall judge necessary and expedient; he may, on extraordinary Occasions, convene both Houses, or either of them, and in Case of Disagreement between them, with Respect to the Time of Adjournment, he may adjourn them to such Time as he shall think proper; he shall receive Ambassadors and other public Ministers; he shall take Care that the Laws be faithfully executed, and shall Commission all the Officers of the United States.

Section 4. The President, Vice President and all civil Officers of the United States, shall be removed from Office on Impeachment for, and Conviction of, Treason, Bribery, or other High Crimes and Misdemeanors.

Article III

Section 1. The judicial Power of the United States, shall be vested in one supreme Court, and in such inferior Courts as the Congress may from time to time ordain and establish. The Judges, both of the supreme and inferior Courts, shall hold their Offices during good Behaviour, and shall, at stated Times, receive for their Services, a Compensation, which shall not be diminished during their Continuance in Office.

Section 2. The judicial Power shall extend to all Cases, in Law and Equity, arising under this Constitution, the Laws of the United States, and Treaties made, or which shall be made, under their Authority; — to all Cases affecting Ambassadors, other public Ministers and Consuls; — to all Cases of admiralty and maritime Jurisdiction; — to Controversies to which the United States shall be a Party; — to Controversies between two or more States; between a State and Citizens of another State; — between Citizens of different States; — between Citizens of the same State claiming Lands under Grants of different States, and between a State, or the Citizens thereof, and foreign States, Citizens or Subjects.

In all Cases affecting Ambassadors, other public Ministers and Consuls, and those in which a State shall be Party, the supreme Court shall have original Jurisdiction. In all the other Cases before mentioned, the supreme Court shall have appellate Jurisdiction, both as to Law and Fact, with such Exceptions, and under such Regulations as the Congress shall make.

The Trial of all Crimes, except in Cases of Impeachment, shall be by Jury; and such Trial shall be held in the State where the said Crimes shall have been committed; but when not committed within any State, the Trial shall be at such Place or Places as the Congress may by Law have directed.

Section 3. Treason against the United States, shall consist only in levying War against them, or in adhering to their Enemies, giving them Aid and Comfort. No Person shall be convicted of Treason unless on the Testimony of two Witnesses to the same overt Act, or on Confession in open Court.

The Congress shall have Power to declare the Punishment of Treason, but no Attainder of Treason shall work Corruption of Blood, or Forfeiture except during the Life of the Person attainted.

Article IV

Section 1. Full Faith and Credit shall be given in each State to the public Acts, Records, and judicial Proceedings of every other State. And the Congress may by general Laws prescribe the Manner in which such Acts, Records and Proceedings shall be proved, and the Effect thereof.

Section 2. The Citizens of each State shall be entitled to all Privileges and Immunities of Citizens in the several States.

A Person charged in any State with Treason, Felony, or other Crime, who shall flee from Justice, and be found in another State, shall on Demand of the executive Authority of the State from which he fled, be delivered up, to be removed to the State having Jurisdiction of the Crime.

No person held to Service or Labour in one State, under the Laws thereof, escaping into another, shall, in Consequence of any Law or Regulation therein, be discharged from such Service or Labour, but shall be delivered up on Claim of the Party to whom such Service or Labour may be due.

Section 3. New States may be admitted by the Congress into this Union; but no new State shall be formed or erected within the Jurisdiction of any other State; nor any State be formed by the Junction of two or more States, or Parts of States, without the Consent of the Legislatures of the States concerned as well as of the Congress.

The Congress shall have Power to dispose of and make all needful Rules and Regulations respecting the Territory or other Property belonging to the United States; and nothing in this Constitution shall be so construed as to Prejudice any Claims of the United States, or of any particular State.

Section 4. The United States shall guarantee to every State in this Union a Republican Form of Government, and shall protect each of them against Invasion; and on Application of the Legislature, or of the Executive (when the Legislature cannot be convened) against domestic Violence.

Article V

The Congress, whenever two thirds of both Houses shall deem it necessary, shall propose Amendments to this Constitution, or, on the Application of the Legislatures of two thirds of the several States, shall call a Convention for proposing Amendments, which, in either Case, shall be valid to all Intents and Purposes, as Part of this Constitution, when ratified by the Legislatures of three fourths of the several States, or by Conventions in three fourths thereof, as the one or the other Mode of Ratification may be proposed by the Congress; Provided that no Amendment which may be made prior to the Year One thousand eight hundred and eight shall in any Manner affect the first and fourth Clauses in the Ninth Section of the first Article; and that no State, without its Consent, shall be deprived of its equal Suffrage in the Senate.

Article VI

All Debts contracted and Engagements entered into, before the Adoption of this Constitution, shall be as valid against the United States under this Constitution, as under the Confederation.

This Constitution, and the Laws of the United States which shall be made in Pursuance thereof; and all Treaties made, or which shall be made, under the Authority of the United States, shall be the supreme Law of the Land; and the Judges in every State shall be bound thereby, any Thing in the Constitution or Laws of any State to the Contrary notwithstanding.

The Senators and Representatives before mentioned, and the Members of the several State Legislatures, and all executive and judicial Officers, both of the United States and of the several States, shall be bound by Oath or Affirmation, to support this Constitution; but no religious Test shall ever be required as a Qualification to any Office or public Trust under the United States.

Article VII

The Ratification of the Conventions of nine States, shall be sufficient for the Establishment of this Constitution between the States so ratifying the Same.

Done in Convention by the Unanimous Consent of the States present the Seventeenth Day of September in the Year of our Lord one thousand seven hundred and Eighty seven and of the Independence of the United States of America the Twelfth *In witness whereof We have hereunto subscribed our Names,*

G° Washington — Presid^t
and deputy from Virginia

New Hampshire	John Langdon Nicholas Gilman
Massachusetts	Nathaniel Gorham Rufus King
Connecticut	Wm Saml Johnson Roger Sherman
New York	Alexander Hamilton
New Jersey	Wil: Livingston David Brearley. Wm Paterson. Jona: Dayton
Pennsylvania	B Franklin Thomas Mifflin Robt Morris Geo Clymer Thos FitzSimons Jared Ingersoll James Wilson Gouv Morris
Delaware	Geo: Read Gunning Bedford Jun John Dickinson Richard Bassett Jaco: Broom
Maryland	James McHenry Dan of St Thos Jenifer Danl Carroll
Virginia	John Blair— James Madison Jr.
North Carolina	Wm Blount Richd Dobbs Spaight. Hu Williamson

| South Carolina | J. Rutledge
Charles Cotesworth Pinckney
Charles Pinckney
Pierce Butler. |
| Georgia | William Few
Abr Baldwin |

Amendments to the Constitution

(The first 10 Amendments were ratified December 15, 1791, and form what is known as the "Bill of Rights")

Amendment 1

Congress shall make no law respecting an establishment of religion, or prohibiting the free exercise thereof; or abridging the freedom of speech, or of the press; or the right of the people peaceably to assemble, and to petition the Government for a redress of grievances.

Amendment 2

A well regulated Militia, being necessary to the security of a free State, the right of the people to keep and bear Arms, shall not be infringed.

Amendment 3

No Soldier shall, in time of peace be quartered in any house, without the consent of the Owner, nor in time of war, but in a manner to be prescribed by law.

Amendment 4

The right of the people to be secure in their persons, houses, papers, and effects, against unreasonable searches and seizures, shall not be violated, and no Warrants shall issue, but upon probable cause, supported by Oath or affirmation, and particularly describing the place to be searched, and the persons or things to be seized.

Amendment 5

No person shall be held to answer for a capital, or otherwise infamous crime, unless on a presentment or indictment of a Grand Jury, except in cases arising in the land or naval forces, or in the Militia, when in actual service in time of War or public danger; nor shall any person be subject for the same offence to be twice put in jeopardy of life or limb; nor shall be compelled in any criminal case to be a witness against himself, nor be deprived of life, liberty, or property, without due process of law; nor shall private property be taken for public use, without just compensation.

Amendment 6

In all criminal prosecutions, the accused shall enjoy the right to a speedy and public trial, by an impartial jury of the State and district wherein the crime shall have been committed, which district shall have been previously ascertained by law, and to be informed of the nature and cause of the accusation; to be confronted with the witnesses against him; to have compulsory process for obtaining witnesses in his favor, and to have the Assistance of Counsel for his defence.

Amendment 7

In Suits of common law, where the value in controversy shall exceed twenty dollars, the right of trial by jury shall be preserved, and no fact tried by a jury, shall be otherwise re-examined in any Court of the United States, than according to the rules of the common law.

Amendment 8

Excessive bail shall not be required, nor excessive fines imposed, nor cruel and unusual punishments inflicted.

Amendment 9

The enumeration in the Constitution, of certain rights, shall not be construed to deny or disparage others retained by the people.

Amendment 10

The powers not delegated to the United States by the Constitution, nor prohibited by it to the States, are reserved to the States respectively, or to the people.

Amendment 11

(Ratified February 7, 1795)

The Judicial power of the United States shall not be construed to extend to any suit in law or equity, commenced or prosecuted against one of the United States by Citizens of another State, or by Citizens or Subjects of any Foreign State.

Amendment 12

(Ratified July 27, 1804)

The Electors shall meet in their respective states and vote by ballot for President and Vice President, one of whom, at least, shall not be an inhabitant of the same state with themselves; they shall name in their ballots the person voted for as President, and in distinct ballots the person voted for as Vice President, and they shall make distinct lists of all persons voted for as President, and of all persons voted for as Vice President, and of the number of votes for each, which lists they shall sign and certify, and transmit sealed to the seat of the government of the United States, directed to the President of the Senate; — The President of the Senate shall, in the presence of the Senate and House of Representatives, open all the certificates and the votes shall then be counted; — The person having the greatest number of votes for President, shall be the President, if such number be a majority of the whole number of Electors appointed; and if no person have such majority, then from the persons having the highest numbers not exceeding three on the list of those voted for as President, the House of Representatives shall choose immediately, by ballot, the President. But in choosing the President, the votes shall be taken by states, the representation from each state having one vote; a quorum for this purpose shall consist of a member or members from two-thirds of the states, and a majority of all the states shall be necessary to a choice. And if the House of Representatives shall not choose a President whenever the right of choice shall devolve upon them, before the fourth day of March next following, then the Vice President shall act as President, as in the case of the death or other constitutional disability of the President. — The person having the greatest number of votes as Vice President, shall be the Vice President, if such number be a majority of the whole number of Electors appointed, and if no person have a majority, then from the two highest numbers on the list, the Senate shall choose the Vice President; a quorum for the purpose shall consist of two-thirds of the whole number of Senators, and a majority of the whole number shall be necessary to a choice. But no person constitutionally ineligible to the office of President shall be eligible to that of Vice President of the United States.

Amendment 13

(Ratified December 6, 1865)

Section 1. Neither slavery nor involuntary servitude, except as a punishment for crime whereof the party shall have been duly convicted, shall exist within the United States, or any place subject to their jurisdiction.

Section 2. Congress shall have power to enforce this article by appropriate legislation.

Amendment 14

(Ratified July 9, 1868)

Section 1. All persons born or naturalized in the United States, and subject to the jurisdiction thereof, are citizens of the United States and of the State wherein they reside. No State shall make or enforce any law which shall abridge the privileges or immunities of citizens of the United States; nor shall any State deprive any person of life, liberty, or property, without due process of law; nor deny to any person within its jurisdiction the equal protection of the laws.

Section 2. Representatives shall be apportioned among the several States according to their respective numbers, counting the whole number of persons in each State, excluding Indians not taxed. But when the right to vote at any election for the choice of electors for President and Vice President of the United States, Representatives in Congress, the Executive and Judicial officers of a State, or the members of the Legislature thereof, is denied to any of the male inhabitants of such State, being twenty-one years of age, and citizens of the United States, or in any way abridged, except for participation in rebellion, or other crime, the basis of representation therein shall be reduced in the proportion which the number of such male citizens shall bear to the whole number of male citizens twenty-one years of age in such State.

Section 3. No person shall be a Senator or Representative in Congress, or elector of President and Vice President, or hold any office, civil or military, under the United States, or under any State, who, having previously taken an oath, as a member of Congress, or as an officer of the United States, or as a member of any State legislature, or as an executive or judicial officer of any State, to support the Constitution of the United States, shall have engaged in insurrection or rebellion against the same, or given aid or comfort to the enemies thereof. But Congress may by a vote of two-thirds of each House, remove such disability.

Section 4. The validity of the public debt of the United States, authorized by law, including debts incurred for payment of pensions and bounties for services in suppressing insurrection or rebellion, shall not be questioned. But neither the United States nor any State shall assume or pay any debt or obligation incurred in aid of insurrection or rebellion against the United States, or any claim for the loss or emancipation of any slave; but all such debts, obligations and claims shall be held illegal and void.

Section 5. The Congress shall have power to enforce, by appropriate legislation, the provisions of this article.

Amendment 15

(Ratified February 3, 1870)

Section 1. The right of citizens of the United States to vote shall not be denied or abridged by the United States or by any State on account of race, color, or previous condition of servitude.

Section 2. The Congress shall have power to enforce this article by appropriate legislation.

Amendment 16

(Ratified February 3, 1913)

The Congress shall have power to lay and collect taxes on incomes, from whatever source derived, without apportionment among the several States, and without regard to any census or enumeration.

Amendment 17

(Ratified April 8, 1913)

The Senate of the United States shall be composed of two Senators from each State, elected by the people thereof for six years; and each Senator shall have one vote. The electors in each State shall have the qualifications requisite for electors of the most numerous branch of the State legislatures.

When vacancies happen in the representation of any State in the Senate, the executive authority of such State shall issue writs of election to fill such vacancies: *Provided*, That the legislature of any State may empower the executive thereof to make temporary appointments until the people fill the vacancies by election as the legislature may direct.

This amendment shall not be so construed as to affect the election or term of any Senator chosen before it becomes valid as part of the Constitution.

Amendment 18

(Ratified January 16, 1919. Repealed December 5, 1933, by Amendment 21)

Section 1. After one year from the ratification of this article the manufacture, sale, or transportation of intoxicating liquors within, the importation thereof into, or the exportation thereof from the United States and all territory subject to the jurisdiction thereof for beverage purposes is hereby prohibited.

Section 2. The Congress and the several States shall have concurrent power to enforce this article by appropriate legislation.

Section 3. This article shall be inoperative unless it shall have been ratified as an amendment to the Constitution by the legislatures of the several States as provided in the Constitution, within seven years from the date of the submission hereof to the States by the Congress.

Amendment 19

(Ratified August 18, 1920)

The right of citizens of the United States to vote shall not be denied or abridged by the United States or by any State on account of sex.

Congress shall have power to enforce this article by appropriate legislation.

Amendment 20

(Ratified January 23, 1933)

Section 1. The terms of the President and Vice President shall end at noon on the 20th day of January, and the terms of Senators and Representatives at noon on the 3d day of January, of the years in which such terms would have ended if this article had not been ratified; and the terms of their successors shall then begin.

Section 2. The Congress shall assemble at least once in every year, and such meeting shall begin at noon on the 3d day of January, unless they shall by law appoint a different day.

Section 3. If, at the time fixed for the beginning of the term of the President, the President elect shall have died, the Vice President elect shall become President. If a President shall not have been chosen before the time fixed for the beginning of his term, or if the President elect shall have failed to qualify, then the Vice President elect shall act as President until a President shall have qualified; and the Congress may by law provide for the case wherein neither a President elect nor a Vice President elect shall have qualified, declaring who shall then act as President, or the manner in which one who is to act shall be selected, and such person shall act accordingly until a President or Vice President shall have qualified.

Section 4. The Congress may by law provide for the case of the death of any of the persons from whom the House of Representatives may choose a President whenever the right of choice shall have devolved upon them, and for the case of the death of any of the persons from whom the Senate may choose a Vice President whenever the right of choice shall have devolved upon them.

Section 5. Sections 1 and 2 shall take effect on the 15th day of October following the ratification of this article.

Section 6. This article shall be inoperative unless it shall have been ratified as an amendment to the Constitution by the legislatures of three-fourths of the several States within seven years from the date of its submission.

Amendment 21

(Ratified December 5, 1933)

Section 1. The eighteenth article of amendment to the Constitution of the United States is hereby repealed.

Section 2. The transportation or importation into any State, Territory, or possession of the United States for delivery or use therein of intoxicating liquors, in violation of the laws thereof, is hereby prohibited.

Section 3. This article shall be inoperative unless it shall have been ratified as an amendment to the Constitution by conventions in the several States, as provided in the Constitution, within seven years from the date of the submission hereof to the States by the Congress.

Amendment 22

(Ratified February 27, 1951)

Section 1. No person shall be elected to the office of the President more than twice, and no person who has held the office of President, or acted as President, for more than two years of a term to which some other person was elected President shall be elected to the office of the President more than once. But this Article shall not apply to any person holding the office of President when this Article was proposed by the Congress, and shall not prevent any person who may be holding the office of President, or acting as President, during the term within which this Article becomes operative from holding the office of President or acting as President during the remainder of such term.

Section 2. This article shall be inoperative unless it shall have been ratified as an amendment to the Constitution by the legislatures of three-fourths of the several States within seven years from the date of its submission to the States by the Congress.

Amendment 23

(Ratified March 29, 1961)

Section 1. The District constituting the seat of Government of the United States shall appoint in such manner as the Congress may direct:

A number of electors of President and Vice President equal to the whole number of Senators and Representatives in Congress to which the District would be entitled if it were a State, but in no event more than the least populous State; they shall be in addition to those appointed by the States, but they shall be considered, for the purposes of the election of President and Vice President, to be electors appointed by a State; and they shall meet in the District and perform such duties as provided by the twelfth article of amendment.

Section 2. The Congress shall have power to enforce this article by appropriate legislation.

Amendment 24

(Ratified January 23, 1964)

Section 1. The right of citizens of the United States to vote in any primary or other election for President or Vice President, for electors for President or Vice President, or for Senator or Representative in Congress, shall not be denied or abridged by the United States or any State by reason of failure to pay any poll tax or other tax.

Section 2. The Congress shall have power to enforce this article by appropriate legislation.

Amendment 25

(Ratified February 10, 1967)

Section 1. In case of the removal of the President from office or of his death or resignation, the Vice President shall become President.

Section 2. Whenever there is a vacancy in the office of the Vice President, the President shall nominate a Vice President who shall take office upon confirmation by a majority vote of both Houses of Congress.

Section 3. Whenever the President transmits to the President pro tempore of the Senate and the Speaker of the House of Representatives his written declaration that he is unable to discharge the powers and duties of his office, and until he transmits to them a written declaration to the contrary, such powers and duties shall be discharged by the Vice President as Acting President.

Section 4. Whenever the Vice President and a majority of either the principal officers of the executive departments or of such other body as Congress may by law provide, transmit to the President pro tempore of the Senate and the Speaker of the House of Representatives their written declaration that the President is unable to discharge the powers and duties of his office, the Vice President shall immediately assume the powers and duties of the office as Acting President.

Thereafter, when the President transmits to the President pro tempore of the Senate and the Speaker of the House of Representatives his written declaration that no inability exists, he shall resume the powers and duties of his office unless the Vice President and a majority of either the principal officers of the executive department or of such other body as Congress may by law provide, transmit within four days to the President pro tempore of the Senate and the Speaker of the House of Representatives their written declaration that the President is unable to discharge the powers and duties of his office. Thereupon Congress shall decide the issue, assembling within forty-eight hours for that purpose if not in session. If the Congress, within twenty-one days after receipt of the latter written declaration, or, if Congress is not in session, within twenty-one days after Congress is required to assemble, determines by two-thirds vote of both Houses that the President is unable to discharge the powers and duties of his office, the Vice President shall continue to discharge the same as Acting President; otherwise, the President shall resume the powers and duties of his office.

Amendment 26

(Ratified July 1, 1971)

Section 1. The right of citizens of the United States, who are eighteen years of age or older, to vote shall not be denied or abridged by the United States or by any State on account of age.

Section 2. The Congress shall have the power to enforce this article by appropriate legislation.

Notes

BACKGROUND OF THE CONSTITUTION

1. Edward Dumbauld, *The Declaration of Independence and What It Means Today* (Norman, OK: University of Oklahoma Press, 1950), p. 27.
2. Letter to Henry Lee, May 8, 1825, *The Writings of Thomas Jefferson*, ed. P.L. Ford, 10 vols. (New York: G.P. Putnam's Sons, 1892 — 1899), 10:343.
3. Letter to John Taylor, 1814, quoted in Adrienne Koch, *The American Enlightenment* (New York: George Braziller, 1965), p. 222.
4. Alpheus Thomas Mason, *Free Government in the Making* (New York: Oxford University Press, 1949), pp. 238 — 241.

BASIC FEATURES OF THE CONSTITUTION

1. National League of Cities v Uscry, 426 US 833 (1976). The decision has been reversed, but this statement from the opinion remains valid.
2. McCulloch v Maryland, 4 Wheaton 316 (1819).
3. Hodel v Virginia Surface Min & Recl Assn , 452 US 264 (1981).
4. Richard E. Neustadt, *Presidential Power* (New York: John Wiley & Sons, Inc., 1980), p. 26.
5. FPC v New England Power Co , 415 US 345 (1974).
6. National Cable Television Assn v United States, 415 US 336 (1974).
7. Schechter Poultry Corp v United States, 295 US 495 (1981).
8. INS v Chadha, 462 US 919 (1983).
9. Commodity Futures Trading Comm'n v Schor, 92 L Ed 2d 675 (1986).
10. Buckley v Valeo, 424 US 1 (1976).
11. Bowsher v Synar, 92 L Ed 2d 583 (1986).
12. Nixon v Administrator of General Services, 433 US 425 (1977).
13. 1 Cranch 137 (1803).
14. Oliver Wendell Holmes, *Collected Legal Papers* (New York: Harcourt, Brace & World, 1920), pp. 295 — 296.
15. Judge Bork quoted by Justice O'Connor, writing for the Court in Allen v Wright, 468 US 737 (1984).
16. Sierra Club v Morton, 405 US 727 (1972).
17. Baker v Carr, 369 US 186 (1962).
18. Justice Powell concurring in United States v Richardson, 418 US 166 (1974).
19. Association of Data Processing Service Organizations, Inc v Camp, 397 US 150 (1970); Barlow v Collins, 397 US 159 (1970).
20. United States v SCRAP, 413 US 669 (1973).
21. Havens Realty Corp v Coleman, 455 US 363 (1982).
22. Secretary of State of Maryland v J H Munson Co., 467 US 947 (1984).
23. Warth v Seldin, 422 US 490 (1975).
24. Los Angeles v Lyons, 461 US 95 (1983).
25. Allen v Wright, 468 US 737 (1984).

26. Allen v Wright, 468 US 737 (1984).

27. Dissenting in United States v SCRAP, 412 US 669 (1973).

28. United States v Richardson, 418 US 166 (1974).

29. Baker v Carr, 369 US 186 (1962); Oneida v Oneida Indian Nation, 470 US 226 (1985).

30. Luther v Borden, 7 Howard 1 (1849); Colegrove v Green, 328 US 549 (1946).

31. Baker v Carr, 369 US 186 (1962).

32. Wesberry v Sanders, 376 US 1 (1964).

33. Gray v Sanders, 372 US 368 (1963).

34. Avery v Midland County, 390 US 474 (1968).

35. Gommilion v Lightfoot, 364 US 339 (1960).

36. Davis v Bandemer, 92 L Ed 2d 85 (1986).

37. Justice Brandeis, concurring, in Ashwander v TVA, 297 US 288 (1936).

38. Myers v United States, 272 US 52 (1926).

39. Powell v McCormack, 395 US 486 (1969).

40. United States v Nixon, 418 US 683 (1974).

41. Rostker v Goldberg, 453 US 57 (1981).

42. J W Peltason, *Federal Courts in the Political Process*, (New York: Random House, 1955).

43. INS v Chadha, 462 US 919 (1983).

44. Stuart Taylor, Jr., "The One-Pronged Test for Federal Judges: Reagan Puts Ideology First," *New York Times*, April 22, 1984, sec. E, p. 5.

THE CONSTITUTION OF THE UNITED STATES

The Preamble; Article I: The Legislative Article

1. Jacobson v Massachusetts, 197 US 11 (1905).

2. McCulloch v Maryland, 4 Wheaton 316 (1819).

3. Constitution of Massachusetts, Part the First, Article XXX.

4. United States v Curtiss-Wright Export Corp , 299 US 304 (1936).

5. Wesberry v Sanders, 376 US 1 (1964).

6. Karcher v Daggett, 462 US 725 (1983).

7. Ibid.

8. Tashjian v Republican Party of Connecticut, 93 L Ed 2d 514 (1986).

9. Ex parte Yarbrough, 110 US 651 (1884).

10. Powell v McCormack, 395 US 486 (1969).

11. Pollock v Farmers' Loan & Trust Co , 157 US 429 (1895).

12. Warren Weaver, Jr., "East and Midwest Expected to Continue Political Lag," *New York Times*, June 28, 1987, sec. Y, p. 13.

13. Eastland v United States Servicemen's Fund, 421 US 491 (1975).

14. Nixon v Fitzgerald, 457 US 731 (1982).

15. Pulliam v Allen, 466 US 522 (1984).

16. Stump v Sparkman, 435 US 349 (1978); Harlow v Fitzgerald, 457 US 800 (1982).

17. Smiley v Holm, 285 US 355 (1932).

18. United States v Classic, 313 US 299 (1941).

19. Oregon v Mitchell, 400 US 112 (1970).

20. Powell v McCormack, 395 US 486 (1969).

21. Roudebush v Hartke, 405 US 15 (1972).

22. Gravel v United States, 408 US 606 (1980).

23. United States v Gillock, 445 US 360 (1980).

24. United States v Helstoski, 442 US 477 (1979).

25. United States v Johnson, 383 US 169 (1966).

26. United States v Helstoski, 442 US 477 (1979); United States v Brewster, 408 US 501 (1972).

27. Gravel v United States, 408 US 606 (1972).

28. Hutchinson v Proxmire, 443 US 111 (1979).

29. Doe v McMillian, 412 US 306 (1973).

30. Ex parte Levitt, 302 US 633 (1937).

31. McClure v Regan, 454 US 1025 (1981); these materials are taken from Stephen L. Wasby, 2nd ed., *The Supreme Court in the Federal Judicial System*, (New York: Holt, Rinehart and Winston, 1984), p. 84.

32. Schlesinger v Reservists to Stop the War, 418 US 206 (1974).

33. Burke v Barnes, 93 L Ed 2d 732 (1987).

34. INS v Chadha, 462 US 919 (1983).

35. Justice White dissenting in INS v Chadha, 462 US 919.

36. Alaska Airlines, Inc v Brock, 94 L Ed 2d 661 (1987).

37. Ibid.

38. From Sibbach v Wilson & Co , 312 US 1 (1941), quoted approvingly by the Court in Alaska Airlines.

39. We have a new Congress every two years. The Congress inaugurates its first session in January of an odd-numbered year. The second session meets the following January, and unless the party lineup in the chamber has changed because of deaths, resignations, or special elections, the organization does not change.

40. McCulloch v Maryland, 4 Wheaton 316 (1819).

41. Dissenting in South Dakota v Dole, 97 L Ed 2d 171 (1987).

42. South Dakota v Dole, 97 L Ed 2d 171 (1987).

43. Pennhurst State School and Hospital v Halderman, 451 US 1 (1981).

44. South Dakota v Dole, 97 L Ed 2d 171 (1987).

45. Massachusetts v Mellon, 262 US 447 (1923); Valley Forge Christian College v Americans United for Separation of Church & State, 454 US 464 (1982).

46. United States v Richardson, 418 US 166 (1974); Valley Forge Christian College v Americans United for Separation of Church & State, 454 US 464 (1982).

47. Flast v Cohen, 392 US 83 (1968).

48. Marchetti v United States, 390 US 39 (1968); Haynes v United States, 390 US 85 (1968); Leary v United States, 395 US 6 (1969).

49. United States v Ptasynski, 462 US 74 (1983).

50. Japan Line, Ltd v County of Los Angeles, 441 US 434 (1979).

51. Ibid.

52. Wardair Canada v Florida Dept of Revenue, 91 L Ed 2d 1 (1986).

53. Gibbons v Ogden, 9 Wheaton 1 (1824).

54. United States v Darby, 312 US 100 (1941).

55. Hodel v Virginia Surface Min & Recl Assn, 452 US 264 (1981).

56. Heart of Atlanta Motel v United States, 379 US 241 (1964).

57. Daniel v Paul, 395 US 298 (1969).

58. Concurring in Hodel v Virginia Surface Min & Recl Assn, 452 US 264 (1981).

59. FERC v Mississippi, 456 US 742 (1982).

60. McLain v Real Estate Board of New Orleans, 444 US 232 (1980); Goldfarb v Virginia State Board, 421 US 733 (1975); Hodel v Virginia Surface Min & Recl Assn, 452 US 264 (1981).

61. United States v Appalachian Electric Power Co, 311 US 377 (1940).

62. Lewis v BT Investment Managers, Inc, 447 US 27 (1980).

63. Northeast Bancorp v Board of Governors, 472 US 159 (1985).

64. Brown-Forman Distillers v NY Liquor Auth, 90 L Ed 2d 552 (1986).

65. Western & Southern LI Co v Board of Equalization of California, 451 US 648 (1981).

66. Minnesota v Clover Leaf Creamery Co, 449 US 456 (1981).

67. Maine v Taylor, 91 L Ed 2d 110 (1986); Hughes v Oklahoma, 441 US 322 (1979).

68. Southern Pacific Co v Arizona, 325 US 761 (1945); Fireman v Chicago, Rock Island and Pacific RR Co, 393 US 129 (1968).

69. Bibb v Navajo Freight Lines, 359 US 520 (1959).

70. Kassel v Consolidated Freightways Corp, 450 US 662 (1981).

71. Ray v Atlantic Richfield Co, 435 US 151 (1978).

72. Philadelphia v New Jersey, 437 US 617 (1978).

73. Ark Elec Coop v Ark Public Ser Commission, 461 US 375 (1983).

74. Maine v Taylor, 461 US 375 (1986).

75. Hughes v Alexandria Scrap Corp, 426 US 794 (1976); Reeves v Stake, 447 US 429 (1980).

76. Complete Auto Transit, Inc v Brady, 430 US 274 (1977); Mobil Oil Corp v Commissioner of Taxes, 445 US 425 (1980); Exxon Corp v Wisconsin Dept of Revenue, 447 US 207 (1980).

77. American Trucking Associations v Scheiner, 97 L Ed 2d 226 (1987).

78. Tyler Pipe Industries, Inc v Washington State Dept of Revenue, 97 L Ed 2d 199 (1987).

79. Container Corporation v Franchise Tax Board, 463 US 159 (1983).

80. The Minnesota Rate Cases, 230 US 537 (1913).

81. Montana v Blackfeet Tribe of Indians, 471 US 759 (1985).

82. Morton v Mancari, 417 US 535 (1974)

83. Ibid.

84. Santa Clara Pueblo v Martinez, 436 US 49 (1978).

85. Ibid.

86. Ramah Navajo Sch Bd v Bureau of Revenue, 458 US 833 (1982).

87. Antoine v Washington, 420 US 194 (1975); Mescalero Apache Tribe v Jones, 411 US 145 (1973); New Mexico v Mescalero Apache Tribe, 462 US 324 (1983).

88. California v Cabazon Band of Indians, 94 L Ed 2d 244 (1987).

89. Montana v United States, 450 US 544 (1981); Oliphant v Suquamis Indian Tribe, 435 US 1911 (1979); Merrion v Jicarilla Apache Tribe, 455 US 130 (1982).

90. Nat Farmers Union Ins Co v Crow Tribe, 471 US 845 (1985).

91. Montana v Blackfeet Tribe of Indians, 471 US 759 (1985).

92. Washington v Confederated Tribes, 447 US 134 (1980).

93. McClanahan v Arizona, 411 US 164 (1973); White Mountain Apache Tribe v Bracker, 448 US 136 (1980); Central Machinery Co v Arizona Tax Comm, 448 US 160 (1980).

94. United States v New Mexico, 455 US 720 (1982).

95. Mescalero Apache Tribe v Jones, 411 US 145 (1973).

96. Fong Yue Ting v United States, 149 US 698 (1893); reaffirmed in Kleindienst v Mandel, 408 US 753 (1972).

97. Kleindienst v Mandel, 408 US 753 (1972).

98. Graham v Richardson, 403 US 356 (1971).

99. Regional Rail Reorganization Act Cases, 419 US 102 (1974).

100. Railroad Labor Executives' Association v Gibbons, 445 US 457 (1982).

101. Regan v Time, Inc, 468 US 641 (1984).

102. Sony Corp v Universal City Studios, 464 US 417 (1984).

103. Diamond v Chakrabarty, 447 US 303 (1980).

104. Graham v John Deere Co, 383 US 1 (1966).

105. Goldstein v California, 421 US 546 (1973).

106. Kewanee Oil Co v Bicron Corp, 416 US 470 (1974).

107. Charles Evans Hughes, "War Powers under the Constitution," Reports of the American Bar Association, September 5, 1971.

108. Rostker v Goldberg, 453 US 57 (1981).

109. Goldman v Weinberger, 475 US 503 (1986).

110. Parker v Levy, 417 US 733 (1974); Secretary of the Navy v Avrech, 418 US 676 (1974).

111. McGrain v Daugherty, 272 US 135 (1927).

112. Watkins v United States, 354 US 178 (1957); Barenblatt v United States, 360 US 109 (1959).

113. Yellin v United States, 374 US 109 (1957).

114. Gojack v United States, 384 US 702 (1966); Russell v United States, 369 US 749 (1962).

115. Wainwright v Sykes, 433 US 72 (1977).

116. Engle v Isaac, 456 US 107 (1982); Wainwright v Sykes, 433 US 72 (1977).

117. Stone v Powell, 428 US 465 (1976); Cardwell v Taylor, 461 US 571 (1983).

118. Kimmelman v Morrison, 91 L Ed 2d 305 (1986).

119. United States v Lovett, 328 US 303 (1946).

120. United States v Brown, 381 US 437 (1965).

121. Nixon v Administrator of General Services, 433 US 425 (1977).

122. Selective Service System et al v Minnesota Public Interest Research Group et al, 468 US 841 (1984).

123. Weaver v Graham, 450 US 24 (1981).

124. Miller v Florida, 96 L Ed 2d 351 (1987).

125. Dobbert v Florida, 432 US 282 (1977).

126. United States v Darusmont, 449 US 292 (1981).

127. Kring v Missouri, 107 US 221 (1883). For due process considerations with respect to retroactive civil laws, see Pension Benefit Guaranty Corp v R A Gray & Co, 467 US 717 (1984).

128. United States v Richardson, 418 US 166 (1974).

129. Zschering v Miller, 389 US 429 (1968).

130. Fletcher v Peck, 6 Cranch 87 (1810); Dartmouth College v Woodward, 4 Wheaton 518 (1819); Sturges v Crowninshield, 4 Wheaton 122 (1819).

131. Charles River Bridge Co v Warren Bridge, 11 Peters 420 (1837); Stone v Mississippi, 101 US 814 (1880).

132. United States Trust Co v New Jersey, 431 US 1 (1977).

133. Allied Structural Steel Company v Spannaus, 438 US 234 (1978).

134. Exxon Corp v Eagerton, 462 US 176 (1983).

135. Energy Reserves v Kansas Power & Light, 459 US 400 (1983).

136. Keystone Coal Association v DeBenedictis, 94 L Ed 2d 472 (1987).

137. Michelin Tire Corp v Wages, 423 US 276 (1976).

138. R J Reynolds Tobacco Co v Durham, 99 L Ed 2d 449 (1986).

139. Washington Revenue Department v Stevedoring Association, 435 US 734 (1978).

140. Northeast Bancorp v Board of Governors, 472 US 159 (1985); US Steel Corp v Multistate Tax Commission, 434 US 452 (1978); New Hampshire v Maine, 426 US 363 (1976); Virginia v Tennessee, 148 US 503 (1893).

141. New Hampshire v Maine, 426 US 363 (1976).

142. US Steel Corp v Multistate Tax Commission, 434 US 452 (1978); Virginia v Tennessee, 148 US 503 (1893).

143. Cuyler v Adams, 449 US 433 (1981).

144. West Virginia ex rel Dyer v Sims, 341 US 22 (1951); Nebraska v Iowa, 406 US 117 (1972).

Article II: The Executive Article

1. John Locke, *Second Treatise of Civil Government*, ed. Charles L. Sherman (New York: D. Appleton-Century Co., (1937), p. 109.

2. Justice Rehnquist for the Court in Dames & Moore v Regan, 453 US 654 (1981), quoting Justice Jackson concurring in Youngstown Sheet & Tube Co v Sawyer, 343 US 579 (1952).

3. Youngstown Sheet & Tube Co v Sawyer, 343 US 579 (1952).

4. New York Times Company v United States, 403 US 713 (1971).

5. United States v United States District Court, 407 US 297 (1972).

6. United States v Nixon, 418 US 683 (1974).

7. Dames & Moore v Regan, 453 US 654 (1981).

8. Williams v Rhodes, 393 US 23 (1968).

9. Moore v Ogilvie, 394 US 814 (1969).

10. Anderson v Celebrezze, 460 US 780 (1983).

11. James Madison, quoted *The Records of the Federal Convention of 1787*, ed Max Farrand (New Haven: Yale University Press, 1937), vol. 2, p. 110.

12. George Mason, quoted ibid, vol. 2, p. 31.

13. Ray v Blair, 343 US 214 (1952).

14. Korematsu v United States, 323 US 214 (1944); Hirabayashi v United States, 320 US 81 (1943); Ex parte Endo, 323 US 283 (1944).

15. Ex parte Milligan, 4 Wallace 2 (1866).

16. Duncan v Kahanamoku, 327 US 304 (1946).

17. Michael Rubner, "Antiterrorism and the Withering of the 1973 War Powers Resolution," *Political Science Quarterly* 102, no. 2 (Summer 1987): 210.

18. Ibid.

19. Schick v Reed, 419 US 256 (1974).

20. David C. Stephenson, acting U.S. pardon attorney, quoted in Pete Earley, "Presidents Set Own Rules Granting Clemency," *Washington Post*, March 19, 1984, sec. A, p. 17.

21. Japan Whaling Assn v Amer Cetacean Soc, 92 L Ed 2d 166 (1986).

22. Goldwater et al v Carter, President of the United States, 444 US 996 (1979).

23. Buckley v Valeo, 424 US 1 (1976).

24. George Lardner, Jr., "A Departmental Aide Says the Independent Counsel System Is Too Much," *Washington Post*, June 29, 1987, National Weekly edition, p. 31.

25. United States v Woodley, 751 F 2d 1009 (9th Cir 1985).

26. Stuart Taylor, Jr., "A New Stand over Contras," *New York Times*, May 25, 1987, p.1.

27. Bowsher v Synar, 91 L Ed 2d 583 (1986).

28. Wiener v United States, 357 US 349 (1958); Myers v United States, 272 US 52 (1926); Humphrey's Executor v United States, 295 US 602 (1935).

Article III: The Judicial Article

1. United States v Raddatz, 447 US 667 (1980).

2. Justice White dissenting in Northern Pipeline Construction Co v Marathon Pipe Line Co, 458 US 50 (1982).

3. Northern Pipeline Construction Co v Marathon Pipe Line Co, 458 US 50 (1982).

4. Commodity Futures Trading Comm'n v Schor, 92 L Ed 2d 675 (1986). See also Thomas v Union Carbide Agric Products Co, 473 US 568 (1985), where the Court struggled inconclusively with these same issues.

5. United States v Will, 449 US 200 (1981).

6. Osborn v Bank of the United States, 9 Wheaton 738 (1824).

7. Verlinden BV v Central Bank of Nigeria, 461 US 480 (1983).

8. Gutierrez v Waterman SS Corp, 373 US 206 (1963).

9. Foremost Insurance Co v Richardson, 452 US 668 (1982).

10. Victory Carriers, Inc v Law, 404 US 249 (1972).

11. California v Arizona, 440 US 59 (1979).

12. Justice Rehnquist dissenting in Maryland et al v Louisiana, 451 US 725 (1981).

13. Illinois v Michigan, 409 US 36 (1972).

14. Maryland et al v Louisiana, 451 US 725 (1981).

15. Vermont v New York, 417 US 270 (1974).

16. Ex parte McCardle, 6 Wallace 318 (1868); Ex parte McCardle, 7 Wallace 506 (1869).

17. Key v Doyle, 434 US 59 (1978).

18. Hicks v Miranda, 422 US 332 (1975).

19. Hopfmann v Connolly, 471 US 459 (1985).

Article IV: States' Relations

1. Williams v North Carolina, 325 US 226 (1945).

2. Johnson v Muelberger, 340 US 581 (1951).

3. Allstate Insurance Co v Hague, 449 US 302 (1981).

4. Nevada v Hall, 400 US 410 (1979).

5. Phillips Petroleum Co v Shutts, 472 US 797 (1985).

6. Supreme Court of New Hampshire v Piper, 470 US 274 (1985).

7. Baldwin v Montana Fish and Game Commission, 436 US 371 (1978).

8. Attorney General of NY v Soto-Lopez, 90 L Ed 2d 899 (1986).

9. United Bldg & Construction Trades v Mayor, 465 US 208 (1984).

10. Supreme Court of New Hampshire v Piper, 470 US 274 (1985).

11. Austin v New Hampshire, 420 US 656 (1975).

12. Supreme Court of New Hampshire v Piper, 470 US 274 (1985).

13. Toomer v Witsell, 334 US 385 (1948).

14. Hicklin v Orbeck, 437 US 518 (1978).

15. White v Massachusetts Council of Construction Employers, 460 US 204 (1983).

16. Baldwin v Montana Fish and Game Commission, 436 US 371 (1978).

17. Hicklin v Orbeck, 437 US 518 (1978).

18. Shapiro v Thompson, 394 US 618 (1969).

19. Dunn v Blumstein, 405 US 331 (1972).

20. Sosna v Iowa, 419 US 393 (1975).

21. Vlandis v Kline, 412 US 441 (1973).

22. Kentucky v Dennison, 24 Howard 66 (1861).

23. Puerto Rico v Branstad, 97 L Ed 2d 187 (1987).

24. Bill Richards, "Governors' Decisions in Extradition Cases Vary All over the Map," *Wall Street Journal*, May 27, 1984, p. l.

25. Michigan v Doran, 439 US 282 (1978); Pacileo v Walker, 449 US 86 (1980); California v Superior Court of California, 96 L Ed 2d 332 (1987).

26. Compare Stearns v Minnesota, 179 US 223 (1900), with Coyle v Smith, 221 US 55 9 (1911).

27. Texas v White, 7 Wallace 700 (1869).

28. Hawaii v Mankichi, 190 US 197 (1903), and Balzac v Puerto Rico, 258 US 298 (1922).

29. Rodriguez v Popular Democratic Party, 407 US 1 (1982).

30. Harris v Rosario, 446 US 651 (1980).

31. C. Gordon Post, review of *The Guarantee Clause of the U.S. Constitution*, by William M. Wiececk, *Annals of the American Academy of Political and Social Science* 402 (July 1972): 169 — 170.

32. Luther v Borden, 7 Howard 1 (1849).

33. Simply stated, the initiative procedure calls for two steps: (1) securing signatures of a required number of voters on a petition calling for submission of the proposed law to the electorate and (2) submission of the proposal to the voters in a general election. If approved by a majority of those voting on the proposition, the proposal becomes a law.

34. Pacific States Tel & Tel v Oregon, 223 US 118 (1912); Colegrove v Green, 328 US 549 (1946). See also Baker v Carr, 369 US 186 (1962).

35. C. Gordon Post, review of *The Guarantee Clause*, by William M. Wiececk.

36. Luther v Borden, 7 Howard 1 (1849).

37. In re Debs, 158 US 464 (1895).

Article V: The Amending Power

1. Larry Green, "Cries Grow for Balanced U.S. Budget," *Los Angeles Times*, February 18, 1984, p. 1.

2. Coleman v Miller, 307 US 433 (1939), concurring opinion.

3. Walter Dellinger, "The Legitimacy of Constitutional Change: Rethinking the Amendment Process," *Harvard Law Review*, 92 (December 1983): 386 — 432.

4. Hammer v Dagenhart, 247 US 251 (1918).

5. United States v Darby, 312 US 11 (1941).

Article VI: The Supremacy Article

1. Pennsylvania v Nelson, 350 US 497 (1956); Uphaus v Wyman, 360 US 72 (1959).

2. Pacific Gas & Electric v Energy Res Commission, 461 US 190 (1983).

3. Hillsborough County v Automated Med Labs, 471 US 707 (1985).

4. Pacific Gas & Electric.

5. Fidelity Federal S & L Assn v De la Cuesta, 458 US 141 (1982).

6. Garcia v San Antonio Metropolitan Transit, 469 US 528 (1985).

7. National League of Cities v Usery, 426 US 833 (1976).

8. Hodel v Virginia Surface Min & Recl Assn, 452 US 264 (1981).

9. United Transportation Union v Long Island Railroad Co, 455 US 678 (1982).

10. EEOC v Wyoming, 460 US 226 (1983).

11. Garcia v San Antonio Metropolitan Transit Authority, 469 US 528 (1985).

12. Ibid.

13. Fitzpatrick v Bitzer, 427 US 445 (1976).

14. Reid v Covert, 354 US 1 (1957).

15. Missouri v Holland, 252 US 416 (1920).

16. Torcaso v Watkins, 367 US 488 (1961).

AMENDMENTS TO THE CONSTITUTION

The Bill of Rights and the States

1. Alexander Hamilton, *The Federalist*, No 84.

2. Barron v Baltimore, 7 Peters 243 (1833).

3. Chicago B & O RR Co v City of Chicago, 166 US 226 (1895).

4. Gitlow v New York, 268 US 652 (1925).

5. Palko v Connecticut, 302 US 319 (1937).

6. Duncan v Louisiana, 391 US 145 (1968).

7. Chapman v California, 386 US 18 (1967).

8. Vasquez v Hillery, 474 US 254 (1986); Gray v Mississippi, 99 L Ed 2d 622 (1987).

9. Chapman v California, 386 US 18 (1967).

10. Schneble v Florida, 405 US 427 (1972).

11. Delaware v Van Arsdall, 475 US 673 (1986).

12. Griffith v Kentucky, 93 L Ed 2d 649 (1987).

13. Gideon v Wainwright, 372 US 335 (1963).

14. *Harvard Civil Rights-Civil Liberties Law Review* 1973, quoted in Robert Welsh and Ronald K. L. Collins, *The Center Magazine*, 14 (September — October 1981): 6.

15. Not only does Justice Stevens outline his views that state courts should strike out on their own more often under their own state constitutions, but he explains why he thinks that whenever a state supreme court has made use of both federal and state cases, the presumption ought to be that it decided under state constitutional law rather than federal constitutional law. The Court majority makes the opposite presumption unless state courts explicitly claim reliance on the state constitution. Michigan v Long, 463 US 1032 (1983); Delaware v Van Arsdall, 475 US 673 (1986).

16. Justice Stanley Mosk of the California Supreme Court, quoted in Fred Barbash, "State Courts Expanding Individual's Rights: Role Reversal in Judicial System," *Washington Post*, April 2, 1984, sec. A, p. 1.

Amendment I: Religion, Speech, Assembly, and Petition

1. Sherbert v Verner, 374 US 398 (1963); Thomas v Review Board, 450 US 707 (1981).
2. Ibid.
3. Justice Jackson concurring in Illinois ex rel McCollum v Board of Education, 333 US 203 (1948).
4. Lynch v Donnelly, 465 US 668 (1984).
5. Jones v Wolf, 443 US 595 (1979).
6. Abington School District v Schempp, 374 US 203 (1963); Engel v Vitale, 370 US 421 (1962).
7. Justice Rehnquist dissenting in Wallace v Jaffree, 472 US 38 (1985), Justice White concurring.
8. Lemon v Kurtzman, 403 US 602 (1971).
9. Edwards v Aguillard, 96 L Ed 2d 510 (1987).
10. Lynch v Donnelly, 465 US 668 (1984).
11. Corporation of Presiding Bishop v Amos, 97 L Ed 2d 273 (1987).
12. Ibid.
13. Abington School District v Schempp, 374 US 203 (1963); Engel v Vitale, 370 US 421 (1962); Stone v Graham, 449 US (1980).
14. Wallace v Jaffree, 472 US 38 (1985).
15. Widmar v Vincent, 454 US 263 (1981).
16. Epperson v Arkansas, 393 US 97 (1968).
17. Edwards v Aguillard, 96 L Ed 2d 510 (1987).
18. Illinois ex rel McCollum v Board of Education, 333 US 203 (1948).
19. Abingdon v Schempp, 377 US 203 (1963).
20. Zorach v Clauson, 343 US 306 (1952).
21. Tilton v Richardson, 403 US 672 (1971); Hunt v McNair, 413 US 734 (1973); Roemer v Board of Public Works of Maryland, 426 US 736 (1976).
22. Witters v Wash Dept of Serv for Blind, 474 US 481 (1986).
23. Edwards v Aguillard, 96 L Ed 2d 510 (1987).
24. Ibid.
25. Norwood v Harrison, 413 US 455 (1973).
26. Board of Education v Allen, 392 US 236 (1968); Wolman v Walter, 433 US 229 (1977).
27. Cochran v Board of Education, 281 US 370 (1930); Everson v Board of Education, 330 US 1 (1947); Board of Education v Allen, 392 US 236 (1968); Meek v Pittenger, 421 US 349 (1975).
28. Wolman v Walter, 433 US 229 (1977); Meek v Pittenger, 421 US 349 (1975).
29. Committee for Public Education v Regan, 444 US 646 (1980).
30. Mueller v Allen, 463 US 388 (1983).
31. Committee for Public Education v Nyquist, 413 US 756 (1973).
32. Wolman v Walter, 433 US 229 (1977).
33. Aguilar v Felton, 473 US 402 (1985).
34. Grand Rapids School District v Ball, 473 US 373 (1985.)
35. Committee for Public Education v Nyquist, 413 US 756 (1973); Sloan v Lemon, 413 US 825 (1973).
36. Levitt v Committee for Public Education, 413 US 472 (1973).
37. Ibid.
38. Wolman v Walter, 433 US 229 (1977); Meek v Pittenger, 421 US 349 (1975).
39. Ibid.

40. McGowan v Maryland, 366 US 420 (1961).

41. Walz v Tax Commission, 397 US 664 (1970); Diffenderfer v Central Baptist Church, 404 US 412 (1972).

42. Larkin v Grendel's Den, 459 US 116 (1982).

43. Lynch v Donnelly, 465 US 668 (1984).

44. Marsh v Chambers, 463 US 783 (1983).

45. Corporation of Presiding Bishop v Amos, 97 L Ed 2d 273 (1987).

46. Walz v Tax Commission, 397 US 664 (1970).

47. Estate of Thornton v Caldor, Inc, 472 US 703 (1985).

48. Sherbert v Verner, 374 US 398 (1963); Thomas v Review Board, 450 US 707 (1981).

49. Welsh v United States, 398 US 333 (1970); Gillette v United States, 401 US 437 (1971).

50. Widmar v Vincent, 454 US 263 (1981).

51. Bender v Williamsport Area School Dist, 475 US 534 (1986).

52. Torcaso v Watkins, 367 US 488 (1961).

53. McDaniel v Paty, 435 US 618 (1978).

54. Wisconsin v Yoder, 406 US 205 (1972).

55. Bowen v Roy, 90 L Ed 2d 735 (1986).

56. Hobbie v Unemployment Appeals Commission, 94 L Ed 2d 190 (1987).

57. Ibid.

58. Braunfeld v Brown, 366 US 599 (1961).

59. Jacobson v Massachusetts, 197 US 11 (1905).

60. Heffron v International Society for Krishna Consciousness, Inc, 452 US 640 (1981).

61. United States v Lee, 455 US 252 (1982).

62. Goldman v Weinberger, 475 US 503 (1986).

63. Bowen v Roy, 90 L Ed 2d 735 (1986).

64. Bob Jones University v United States, 461 US 574 (1983).

65. West Virginia State Board of Education v Barnette, 319 US 624 (1943); Wooley v Maynard, 430 US 705 (1977).

66. Wisconsin v Yoder, 406 US 205 (1972).

67. Pierce v Society of Sisters, 268 US 510 (1925).

68. Hobbie v Unemployment Appeals Commission, 94 L Ed 2d 190 (1987).

69. Sherbert v Verner, 374 US 398 (1963); Thomas v Review Board, 450 US 707 (1981).

70. Bose Corporation v Consumers Union, 466 US 485 (1984).

71. Cohen v California, 403 US 15 (1971); Gooding v Wilson, 405 US 518 (1972).

72. John Hart Ely, "Flag Desecration," *Harvard Law Review* 88 (1975): 1493, quoted in David O'Brien, *The Public's Right to Know: The Supreme Court and the First Amendment*, (New York: Praeger Publishers, 1981), p. 97.

73. Justice Powell, concurring in Lewis v City of New Orleans, 415 US 180 (1974), quoted approvingly by Justice Brennan in the opinion of the Court in Houston v Hill, 97 L Ed 2d 398 (1987).

74. NAACP v Claiborne Hardware Co, 458 US 886 (1982).

75. *New York Times* v Sullivan, 376 US 254 (1964).

76. Herbert v Lando, 441 US 153 (1979).

77. Gertz v Welch, 418 US 323 (1974); Dun & Bradstreet v Greenmoss Builders, 472 US 749 (1985).

78. Philadelphia Newspapers, Inc v Hepps, 89 L Ed 2d 783 (1986).

79. Gertz v Welch, 418 US 323 (1974).
80. Dun & Bradstreet v Greenmoss Builders, 472 US 749 (1985).
81. Calder v Jones, 465 US 783 (1984); Keeton v Hustler Magazine, Inc, 465 US 770 (1984).
82. Bose Corporation v Consumers Union, 466 US 485 (1984).
83. Stanley v Georgia, 394 US 557 (1969).
84. Paris Adult Theatre I v Slaton, 413 US 49 (1973).
85. Miller v California, 415 US 15 (1973).
86. *Memoirs* v Massachusetts, 383 US 413 (1966); Roth v United States, 354 US 476 (1957).
87. Hamling v United States, 418 US 87 (1974).
88. Pinkus v United States, 436 US 293 (1978).
89. Brockett v Spokane Arcades, Inc, 472 US 491 (1985).
90. Pope v Illinois, 95 L Ed 2d 439 (1987).
91. Splawn v California, 431 US 595 (1977).
92. Cooper v Mitchell Brothers, 454 US 90 (1981).
93. Miller v California, 413 US 15 (1973); Paris Adult Theatre I v Slaton, 413 US 49 (1973).
94. Young v American Mini Theatres, 427 US 50 (1976).
95. Ibid.
96. Bethel School District No 403 v Fraser, 92 L Ed 2d 549 (1986).
97. Schad v Mt Ephraim, 452 US 61 (1981).
98. New York v Ferber, 458 US 747 (1982); Ginsberg v New York, 390 US 629 (1968).
99. Dennis v United States, 341 US 494 (1951).
100. Yates v United States, 354 US 298 (1957); Brandenburg v Ohio, 395 US 444 (1969).
101. Organization for a Better Austin v Keefe, 402 US 415 (1971); Nebraska Press Assn v Stuart, 427 US 539 (1976).
102. New York Times Company v United States, 403 US 713 (1971).
103. United States v The Progressive, Inc, 467 F Supp 990 (1979); Moreland v Sprecher, 443 US 709 (1979).
104. Greer v Spock, 424 US 828 (1976); Brown v Glines, 444 US 620 (1980); Secretary of Navy v Huff, 444 US 507 (1980).
105. Snepp v United States, 444 US 507 (1980).
106. Burstyn v Wilson, 343 US 495 (1952); Winters v New York, 333 US 507 (1948).
107. NAACP v Button, 371 US 415 (1963).
108. Los Angeles City Council v Taxpayers for Vincent, 466 US 789 (1984); Secretary of State of Maryland v J H Munson Co, 467 US 947 (1984).
109. Board of Airport Commissioners v Jews for Jesus, 96 L Ed 2d 500 (1987).
110. Houston v Hill, 97 L Ed 2d 398 (1987).
111. Plummer v City of Columbus, 414 US 2 (1973).
112. Schaumburg v Citizens for Better Environment, 444 US 620 (1980).
113. Dun & Bradstreet v Greenmoss Builders, 472 US 749 (1985).
114. Papish v Board of Curators, 410 US 667 (1973).
115. Bond v Floyd, 385 US 116 (1966).
116. Landmark Communications v Virginia, 435 US 829 (1978).
117. Friedman v Rogers, 440 US 1 (1979).
118. Central Hudson Gas & Electric Corporation v Public Service Commission of New York, 447 US 557 (1980).

119. Wooley v Maynard, 430 US 705 (1977); West Virginia State Board of Education v Barnette, 319 US 624 (1943).

120. Zauderer v Office of Disciplinary Counsel, 471 US 626 (1985).

121. Justice Stewart concurring in Virginia Pharmacy Board v Virginia Consumer Council, 425 US 748 (1976).

122. Posadas de Puerto Rico Assoc v Tourism Co, 92 L Ed 2d 266 (1986).

123. San Francisco Arts & Athletics, Inc v Olympic Committee, 97 L Ed 2d 427 (1987).

124. In Re RMJ, 455 US 191 (1982).

125. Friedman v Rogers, 440 US 1 (1979).

126. Pittsburgh Press Co v Human Relations Commission, 413 US 376 (1973).

127. Virginia Pharmacy Board v Virginia Consumer Council, 452 US 746 (1976); Bates v State Bar of Arizona, 433 US 530 (1977); In re RMJ, 455 US 191 (1982).

128. Linmark Associates, Inc v Township of Willingboro, 431 US 85 (1977).

129. Carey v Population Services International, 431 US 678 (1977).

130. First National Bank of Boston v Bellotti, 435 US 765 (1978); Central Hudson Gas v Public Service Commission, 447 US 557 (1980); Consolidated Edison v Public Service Commission, 447 US 530 (1980).

131. Consolidated Edison Company v Public Service Commission of New York, 447 US 530 (1980).

132. Meese v Keene, 95 L Ed 415 (1987).

133. Arcara v Cloud Books, 92 L Ed 2d 568 (1986).

134. Justice Black concurring, Gregory v Chicago, 394 US 111 (1969).

135. United States v O'Brien, 391 US 367 (1968).

136. Paris Adult Theatre I v Slaton, 413 US 49 (1973).

137. Tinker v Des Moines School District, 391 US 367 (1968).

138. United States v O'Brien, 391 US 367 (1968).

139. Buckley v Valeo, 424 US 1 (1976).

140. Citizens Against Rent Control v Berkeley, 454 US 290 (1981).

141. Federal Election Commission v National Conservative Political Action Committee, 470 US 480 (1985).

142. Board of Education v Pic, 457 US 853 (1982).

143. Houchins v KQED, 438 US 1 (1978).

144. First National Bank of Boston v Bellotti, 435 US 765 (1978).

145. Philadelphia Newspapers, Inc v Hepps, 475 US 767 (1986); Dun & Bradstreet v Greenmoss Builders, 472 US 749 (1985).

146. Grosjean v American Press Co, 297 US 233 (1936).

147. *Minneapolis Star* v Minnesota Comm of Rev, 460 US 575 (1983).

148. Arkansas Writers' Project, Inc v Ragland, 95 L Ed 2d 209 (1987).

149. FEC v Massachusetts Citizens for Life, 93 L Ed 2d 539 (1986).

150. Richmond Newspapers, Inc v Virginia, 448 US 555 (1980).

151. Globe Newspaper Co v Superior Court, 457 US 596 (1982).

152. Ibid.

153. Ibid.

154. Press Enterprise Co v Superior Court, 464 US 501 (1984).

155. Press Enterprise Co v Superior Court, 92 L Ed 2d 1 (1986).

156. Branzburg v Hayes, 408 US 665 (1972).

157. Zurcher v *Stanford Daily*, 436 US 547 (1978).

158. Miami Herald Publishing Co v Tornillo, 418 US 241 (1974).

159. CBS, Inc v Federal Communications Commission, 453 US 775 (1978).

160. Metromedia, Inc v San Diego, 453 US 490 (1981).

161. Justice Holmes dissenting in Milwaukee Pub Co v Burleson, 255 US 407 (1921). His views were adopted by the Supreme Court in Lamont v Postmaster General, 381 US 301 (1965).

162. Lamont v Postmaster General, 381 US 301 (1965).

163. Blount v Rizzi, 400 US 410 (1971).

164. Rowan v Post Office Department, 397 US 728 (1970).

165. Ibid.

166. United States Postal Service v Greenburgh Civic Associations, 453 US 114 (1981).

167. United States v Thirty-seven Photographs, 402 US 363 (1971); United States v Twelve 200-Ft Reels of Film, 413 US 123 (1973).

168. Hamling v United States, 418 US 87 (1974); United States v Reidel, 402 US 351 (1971).

169. United States v Orito, 413 US 139 (1973).

170. Federal Communications Commission v Pacifica Foundation, 438 US 726 (1978).

171. Buckley v Valeo, 424 US 1 (1976).

172. Red Lion Broadcasting Co v Federal Communications Commission, 395 US 367 (1969).

173. Federal Communications Commission v Pacifica Foundation, 438 US 726 (1978).

174. FCC v League of Women Voters of California, 468 US 364 (1984).

175. Justice Blackmun concurring in Los Angeles v Preferred Communications, 90 L Ed 2d 480 (1986).

176. Los Angeles v Preferred Communications.

177. Times Film Corp v Chicago, 356 US 43 (1961).

178. Teitel Film Corp v Cusak, 390 US 139 (1968); Freedman v Maryland, 380 US 51 (1965).

179. Burstyn v Wilson, 343 US 495 (1952); Superior Films v Department of Education, 346 US 587 (1954); Kingsley Corp v Regents, 360 US 684 (1959).

180. Southeastern Promotions Ltd v Conrad, 420 US 546 (1975).

181. California v LaRue, 409 US 109 (1972).

182. Amalgamated Food Employees Local 590 v Logan Valley Plaza, Inc, 391 US 308 (1968).

183. Building Serv Employees Union v Gazzam, 339 US 532 (1950).

184. Carey v Brown, 447 US 455 (1980).

185. Ibid.

186. Talley v California, 362 US 60 (1960).

187. Organization for a Better Austin v Keefe, 402 US 415 (1971).

188. United States Postal Service v Greenburgh Civic Assn, 453 US 114 (1981).

189. Kovacs v Cooper, 336 US 77 (1949).

190. Los Angeles City Council v Taxpayers for Vincent, 466 US 789 (1984).

191. Metromedia v San Diego, 453 US 490 (1981).

192. Adderley v Florida, 385 US 39 (1966).

193. Cox v Louisiana, 379 US 536 (1965).

194. Cornelius v NAACP Legal Defense & Ed Fund, 473 US 788 (1986).

195. Hague v CIO, 307 US 496 (1939).

196. Perry Ed Assn v Perry Local Ed Assn, 460 US 37 (1983).

197. Clark v Community for Creative Non-Violence, 468 US 288 (1984).

198. United States v Grace, 461 US 171 (1983).

199. Perry Ed Assn v Perry Local Ed Assn, 460 US 37 (1983).

200. Ibid.

201. United States v Albertini, 472 US 675 (1985).

202. Lloyd Corporation v Tanner, 407 US 551 (1972).

203. Prune Yard Shopping Center v Robins, 407 US 551 (1972).

204. Feiner v New York, 340 US 315 (1951).

205. Edwards v South Carolina, 372 US 229 (1963).

206. Gregory v Chicago, 394 US 111 (1969).

207. Coates v Cincinnati, 402 US 611 (1971).

208. Grayned v Rockford, 408 US 104 (1972).

209. Brown v Louisiana, 383 US 131 (1966).

210. Grayned v Rockford, 408 US 104 (1972).

211. Adderley v Florida, 385 US 39 (1966).

212. Healy v James, 408 US 169 (1972).

213. Roberts v United States Jaycees, 468 US 609 (1984).

214. Healy v James, 408 US 169 (1972).

215. Gibson v Legislative Investigation Commission, 372 US 539 (1963), and cases cited therein.

216. Buckley v Valeo, 424 US 1 (1976).

217. Brown v Socialist Workers, 459 US 87 (1983).

218. Cousins v Wigoda, 419 US 477 (1977). Democratic Party of the United States v La Follette, 450 US 107 (1981).

219. Tashjian v Republican Party of Connecticut, 93 L Ed 2d 514 (1986).

220. Hishon v King & Spalding, 467 US 69 (1984).

221. Roberts v United States Jaycees, 468 US 609 (1984).

222. Board of Directors of Rotary International v Rotary Club of Duarte, 95 L Ed 2d 474 (1987).

223. NAACP v Claiborne Hardware Co, 458 US 886 (1982).

224. International Longshoremen's Association v Allied International, 456 US 212 (1982).

225. Abood v Detroit Board of Education, 431 US 209 (1977): International Association of Machinists v Street, 367 US 74 (1961).

226. Ellis v Railway Clerks, 466 US 435 (1984).

227. Teachers v Hudson, 475 US 292 (1986).

228. Minnesota Board for Community Colleges v Knight, 465 US 271 (1984).

229. Regan v Taxation with Representation, 461 US 540 (1983).

230. Bill Johnson's Restaurants v NLRB, 461 US 731 (1983).

231. McAuliffe v Mayor of New Bedford, 155 Mass 216 (1892).

232. Rankin v McPherson, 97 L Ed 2d 315 (1987).

233. Elfbrandt v Russell, 384 US 11 (1966); Connell v Higginbotham, 403 US 207 (1971).

234. Connick v Myers, 461 US 138 (1983).

235. Ibid.

236. Connick v Myers; Pickering v Board of Education, 391 US 563 (1968).

237. Rankin v McPherson, 97 L Ed 2d 315 (1987).

238. United Public Workers v Mitchell, 330 US 75 (1947); Civil Service Commission v Letter Carriers, 413 US 548 (1973); Broadrick v Oklahoma, 413 US 601 (1973).

239. Clements v Fashing, 457 US 957 (1982).

240. Branti v Finkel, 445 US 507 (1980); Elrod v Burns, 427 US 347 (1976).

Amendment II: Militia and the Right to Bear Arms

1. *State* refers to a generic state rather than a state of the Union.

2. Lewis v United States, 445 US 55 (1980).

3. United States v Miller, 307 US 174 (1939).

4. Adams v Williams, 407 US 143 (1972).

Amendment III: Quartering of Soldiers

1. Samuel F. Miller, *The Constitution*, (1893), p. 646, quoted in *The Constitution Annotated*, 1964 ed., p. 923.

Amendment IV: Searches and Seizures

1. Schneckloth v Bustamonte, 412 US 218 (1973), and quoting Justice Harlan in Ker v California, 374 US 23 (1963).

2. Chimel v California, 395 US 752 (1969); United States v Harris, 403 US 573 (1971).

3. United States v Edwards, 415 US 800 (1974).

4. Winston v Lee, 470 US 753 (1985).

5. Kolender v Larson, 461 US 352 (1983).

6. Florida v Royer, 460 US 491 (1983).

7. INS v Delgado, 466 US 210 (1984); United States v Mendenhall, 446 US 544 (1980).

8. INS v Delgado.

9. Terry v Ohio, 392 US 1 (1968).

10. United States v Cortez, 449 US 411 (1981).

11. Hayes v Florida, 470 US 811 (1985).

12. Payton v New York, 445 US 573 (1980).

13. Welsh v Wisconsin, 466 US 740 (1984).

14. Michigan v Summers, 452 US 693 (1981).

15. Tennessee v Garner, 471 US 1 (1985).

16. Mincey v Arizona, 437 US 385 (1970). Thompson v Louisiana, 469 US 17 (1985).

17. Arizona v Hicks, 94 L Ed 2d 347 (1987).

18. Ibid.

19. Justice Powell concurring in Robbins v California, 453 US 420 (1981).

20. United States v Ross, 456 US 798 (1982).

21. Michigan v Thomas, 458 US 259 (1982); United States v Johns, 469 US 478 (1985).

22. United States v Ross, 456 US 798 (1982).

23. California v Carney, 471 US 386 (1985).

24. Terry v Ohio, 392 US 1 (1968); United States v Sharpe, 470 US 675 (1985); Hayes v Florida, 470 US 811 (1985).

25. United States v Hensley, 469 US 221 (1985).

26. Adams v Williams, 407 US 143 (1972).

27. Chimel v California, 395 US 752 (1969); United States v Edwards, 415 US 800 (1974); Illinois v Lafayette, 462 US 640 (1983).

28. Colorado v Bertine, 93 L Ed 2d 739 (1987).

29. Cupp v Murphy, 412 US 291 (1973).

30. Schneckloth v Bustamonte, 412 US 218 (1973); United States v Matlock, 415 US 164 (1974).

31. Almeida-Sanchez v United States, 413 US 266 (1973); United States v Ortiz, 422 US 891 (1975).

32. United States v Ramsey, 431 US 606 (1977).

33. Torres v Puerto Rico, 442 US 465 (1979).

34. Coolidge v New Hampshire, 403 US 443 (1971); Texas v Brown, 460 US 730 (1983).

35. Arizona v Hicks, 94 L Ed 2d 347 (1987).

36. Michigan v Taylor, 436 US 499 (1978); Mincey v Arizona, 437 US 385 (1978).

37. Thompson v Louisiana, 469 US 17 (1984).

38. Oliver v United States, 466 US 170 (1984).

39. California v Ciraolo, 90 L Ed 2d 210 (1986).

40. United States v Salvucci, 448 US 83 (1980).

41. Hudson v Palmer, 468 US 517 (1984).

42. Maryland v Macon, 472 US 463 (1985).

43. United States v Payner, 447 US 727 (1980).

44. Oliver v United States, 466 US 170 (1984).

45. United States v Dunn, 94 L Ed 2d 326 (1987).

46. Ibid.

47. California v Ciraolo, 90 L Ed 2d 210 (1986).

48. Dow Chemical Co v United States, 90 L Ed 2d 226 (1986).

49. From footnote to California v Ciraolo, reserving this question.

50. Griffin v Wisconsin, 97 L Ed 2d 709 (1987).

51. O'Connor v Ortega, 94 L Ed 2d 714 (1987).

52. Ibid.

53. Marshall v Barlow's 436 US 307 (1978); See v City of Seattle, 387 US 541 (1967); Camara v Municipal Court, 387 US 523 (1967).

54. Colonnade Catering Corp v United States, 397 US 72 (1970); United States v Biswell, 406 US 311 (1972).

55. Donovan v Dewey, 452 US 594 (1981); New York v Burger, 96 L Ed 2d 601 (1987).

56. T. Taylor, *Two Studies on Constitutional Interpretation*, (Columbus: Ohio State University Press, 1969), quoted by Justice Stevens, dissenting in Marshall v Barlow's, 436 US 307 (1978).

57. Marshall v Barlow's, 436 US 307 (1978).

58. Franks v Delaware, 438 US 154 (1978).

59. Shadwick v Tampa, 407 US 345 (1972); Coolidge v New Hampshire, 403 US 433 (1971); Connally v Georgia, 429 US 245 (1977).

60. Aguilar v Texas, 378 US 108 (1964).

61. Lo-Ji Sales, Inc v New York, 442 US 319 (1979).

62. Illinois v Gates, 462 US 213 (1983).

63. Illinois v Gates. New York v P J Video, Inc, 475 US 868 (1986).

64. Ybarra v Illinois, 444 US 85 (1979).

65. Zurcher v Stanford Daily, 436 US 547 (1978).

66. Schmerber v California, 384 US 757 (1966).
67. Winston v Lee, 470 US 753 (1985).
68. Olmstead v United States, 277 US 438 (1928).
69. Katz v United States, 389 US 347 (1967).
70. United States v Giordano, 416 US 505 (1974).
71. United States v United States District Court, 407 US 297 (1972).
72. United States v Place, 462 US 696 (1983).
73. On Lee v United States, 343 US 747 (1952); Hoffa v United States, 385 US 293 (1966); United States v White, 401 US 745 (1971).
74. United States v Knotts, 460 US 276 (1983).
75. United States v Karo, 468 US 705 (1984).
76. Bivens v Six Unknown Named Agents of the Bureau of Narcotics, 403 US 388 (1971).
77. Weeks v United States, 232 US 383 (1914); Mapp v Ohio, 367 US 643 (1961).
78. People v Defore, 242 NY 13 (1926).
79. Justice Brennan dissenting in United States v Leon, 468 US 897 (1984).
80. Harris v New York, 401 US 222 (1971); United States v Havens, 446 US 620 (1976).
81. Stone v Powell, 428 US 465 (1976).
82. Illinois v Gates, 462 US 213 (1983).
83. United States v Leon, 468 US 897 (1984).
84. Massachusetts v Sheppard, 468 US 981 (1984).
85. Dissenting in United States v Leon.
86. Dissenting, along with Justices Brennan and Marshall, in New Jersey v TLO, 469 US 325 (1984).
87. Illinois v Krull, 94 L Ed 2d 364 (1987).
88. United States v Calandra, 414 US 338 (1974).
89. INS v Lopez-Mendoza, 468 US 1032 (1984).

Amendment V: Grand Juries, Double Jeopardy, Self-Incrimination, Due Process, and Eminent Domain

1. Hobby v United States, 468 US 339 (1984).
2. United States v Miller, 471 US 130 (1985).
3. Marvin E Frankel and G P Naftalis, *The Grand Jury: An Institution on Trial* (New York: Shill & Way, 1977), pp. 18 — 19.
4. Gerstein v Pugh, 420 US 103 (1975).
5. Solorio v United States, 97 L Ed 2d 364 (1987), reversing O'Callahan v Parker, 359 US 258 (1969).
6. Kinsella v Singleton, 361 US 234 (1960), and companion cases.
7. Toth v Quarles, 350 US 11 (1955).
8. McLucas v De Champlain, 421 US 21 (1975).
9. Benton v Maryland, 359 US 784 (1969).
10. Breed v Jones, 421 US 519 (1975).
11. North Carolina v Pearce, 395 US 711 (1969).
12. Whalen v United States, 445 US 684 (1980).
13. Ibid.
14. Crist v Bretz, 437 US 28 (1979).

15. Albernaz v United States, 450 US 333 (1981).
16. Justices of Boston Municipal Court v Lydon, 466 US 294 (1984).
17. Tibbs v Florida, 457 US 31 (1982).
18. Ibid.
19. Hudson v Louisiana, 450 US 40 (1981); Burks v United States, 437 US 1 (1978).
20. Oregon v Kennedy, 456 US 667 (1982).
21. Oregon v Kennedy; United States v Scott, 437 US 82 (1978); Arizona v Washington, 434 US 497 (1978); United States v Martin Linen, 430 US 564 (1977).
22. United States v DiFrancesco, 449 US 117 (1980).
23. Blockburger v United States, 284 US 299 (1932).
24. Brown v Ohio, 432 US 161 (1977).
25. Diaz v United States, 223 US 442 (1912); Garrett v United States, 471 US 773 (1985).
26. Ashe v Swenson, 397 US 436 (1970).
27. Ohio v Johnson, 467 US 493 (1984).
28. Ianelli v United States, 420 US 770 (1975).
29. United States v One Assortment of Firearms, 465 US 354 (1984).
30. One Lot Emerald Cut Stones and One Right v United States, 409 US 232 (1972).
31. United States v One Assortment of Firearms.
32. Breed v Jones, 421 US 519 (1975).
33. Bartkus v Illinois, 359 US 121 (1972).
34. Rinaldi v United States, 434 US 22 (1977); Petite v United States, 361 US 529 (1960).
35. United States v Wheeler, 435 US 313 (1978).
36. Heath v Alabama, 474 US 82 (1986).
37. Waller v Florida, 397 US 387 (1970).
38. Texas v McCullough, 475 US 134 (1986); Bullington v Missouri, 451 US 430 (1981); North Carolina v Pearce, 395 US 711 (1969).
39. Bullington v Missouri, 451 US 430 (1981); Arizona v Rumsey, 467 US 203 (1984).
40. Missouri v Hunter, 459 US 359 (1983).
41. Malloy v Hogan, 378 US 1 (1964).
42. Murphy v Waterfront Commission, 378 US 52 (1964).
43. Nix v Whiteside, 475 US 157 (1986).
44. Allen v Illinois, 92 L Ed 2d 296 (1986).
45. United States v Apfelbaum, 445 US 115 (1980).
46. Pillsbury v Conboy, 459 US 248 (1983).
47. Marchetti v United States, 390 US 39 (1968); Haynes v United States, 390 US 85 (1968); Leary v United States, 395 US 6 (1969).
48. California v Byers, 402 US 424 (1971).
49. United States v Freed, 401 US 601 (1971).
50. United States v Ward, 448 US 242 (1980).
51. Allen v Illinois, 92 L Ed 2d 296 (1986).
52. Garrity v New Jersey, 385 US 493 (1967); Spevack v Klein, 385 US 511 (1967); Gardner v Broderick, 392 US 273 (1968); Sanitation Men v Sanitation Comm, 392 US 281 (1968); Lefkowitz v Turley, 414 US 70 (1973).
53. Selective Service System v Minnesota Public Service Research Group, 468 US 841 (1984).

54. Ibid.
55. Schmerber v California, 384 US 757 (1966); South Dakota v Neville, 459 US 553 (1983).
56. Couch v United States, 409 US 322 (1973).
57. Concurring in United States v Doe, 465 US 605 (1984).
58. Griffin v Illinois, 351 US 12 (1956).
59. Griffin v California, 380 US 609 (1965); Bruno v United States, 308 US 287 (1939); Carter v Kentucky, 450 US 288 (1981); James v Kentucky, 466 US 341 (1984).
60. Haynes v Washington, 373 US 503 (1963); Lego v Twomey, 404 US 477 (1972).
61. Mincey v Arizona, 437 US 385 (1978).
62. Miranda v Arizona, 384 US 436 (1966).
63. Moran v Burbine, 475 US 412 (1986).
64. Berkemer v McCarty, 468 US 420 (1984); Mathis v United States, 391 US 1 (1968); Orozco v Texas, 394 US 324 (1969).
65. California v Beheler, 463 US 1121 (1983).
66. Oregon v Mathiason, 429 US 492 (1977); California v Beheler, 463 US 1121 (1983).
67. Berkemer v McCarty, 468 US 420 (1984).
68. Minnesota v Murphy, 465 US 420 (1984).
69. New York v Quarles, 467 US 649 (1984).
70. Edwards v Arizona, 451 US 477 (1981); Rhode Island v Innis, 446 US 291 (1980); Michigan v Jackson, 475 US 625 (1986).
71. Solem v Stumes, 465 US 638 (1984).
72. Estelle v Smith, 451 US 454 (1981).
73. Harris v New York, 401 US 222 (1971).
74. Quoted in Blackledge v Allison, 431 US 63 (1977); Bordenkircher v Hayes, 434 US 357 (1978).
75. Brady v United States, 397 US 742 (1970).
76. Mabry v Johnson, 467 US 504 (1984).
77. Davidson v New Orleans, 96 US 97 (1878).
78. Bolling v Sharpe, 347 US 497 (1954).
79. Blum v Yaretsky, 457 US 991 (1982).
80. Lugar v Edmonson Oil Co, 457 US 922 (1983).
81. Meyer v Nebraska, 262 US 390 (1923).
82. Lochner v New York, 198 US 45 (1905); Muller v Oregon, 208 US 424 (1908); West Coast Hotel v Parrish, 300 US 379 (1937).
83. Bounds v Smith, 430 US 817 (1978).
84. Leis v Flynt, 439 US 438 (1979).
85. Meachum v Fano, 427 US 215 (1976); Jago v Van Curen, 445 US 14 (1981).
86. Board of Regents v Roth, 408 US 564 (1972).
87. Cleveland Board of Education v Loudermill, 470 US 532 (1985).
88. Givhan v Western Line Consolidated School District, 439 US 410 (1979); Rankin v McPherson, 97 L Ed 2d 315 (1987).
89. Bishop v Wood, 426 US 341 (1976).
90. Greenholtz v Nebraska Penal Inmates, 442 US 1 (1979); Connecticut Board of Pardons v Dumschat, 452 US 458 (1981).
91. Meachum v Fano, 427 US 215 (1976); Olim v Wakinekona, 461 US 238 (1983).
92. Block v Rutherford, 468 US 576 (1984).

93. Morrissey v Brewer, 408 US 471 (1972).

94. Mathews v Eldridge, 424 US 371 (1971).

95. Connally v General Construction Co, 269 US 385 (1926).

96. Grayned v Rockford, 408 US 104 (1972).

97. Papachristou v City of Jacksonville, 405 US 156 (1972), quoting Thornhill v Alabama, 310 US 88 (1940).

98. Lewis v City of New Orleans, 415 US 130 (1974).

99. Smith v Goguen, 415 US 566 (1974).

100. Palmer v City of Euclid, Ohio, 402 US 544 (1972).

101. Kolender v Lawson, 461 US 352 (1983).

102. Papachristou v City of Jacksonville, 405 US 156 (1972).

103. Colautti v Franklin, 439 US 379 (1979).

104. Hoffman Estates v Flipside Hoffman Estates, 455 US 489 (1982).

105. City of Mesquite v Aladdin's Castle, 455 US 283 (1983).

106. Rivera v Minnich, 97 L Ed 2d 473 (1987).

107. In re Winship, 397 US 358 (1970); Estelle v Williams, 425 US 501 (1976); Taylor v Kentucky, 436 US 478 (1978); Kentucky v Whorton, 441 US 786 (1979); Francis v Franklin, 471 US 307 (1985).

108. Ulster County Court v Allen, 442 US 140 (1979).

109. Leary v United States, 395 US 6 (1969).

110. Turner v United States, 396 US 398 (1970).

111. Bell v Burson, 402 US 535 (1971).

112. Wisconsin v Constantineau, 400 US 433 (1971).

113. Stanley v Illinois, 405 US 645 (1972).

114. Ward v Village of Monroeville, 409 US 57 (1972).

115. Drope v Missouri, 420 US 162 (1975).

116. Schall v Martin, 467 US 253 (1984).

117. Groppi v Leslie, 404 US 496 (1972); Goldberg v Kelly, 397 US 254 (1970); In re Gault, 387 US 1 (1967); Thorpe v Housing Authority, 393 US 268 (1969).

118. Mathews v Eldridge, 424 US 319 (1976).

119. Hodel v Virginia Surface Min & Recl Assn, 452 US 264 (1981); Haig v Agee, 453 US 280 (1981).

120. United States v Eight Thousand Eight Hundred and Fifty Dollars, 461 US 555 (1983).

121. Goss v Lopez, 419 US 565 (1975).

122. Board of Curators, University of Missouri v Horowitz, 435 US 78 (1978).

123. Memphis Light, Gas & Water Division v Craft, 436 US 1 (1978).

124. Schweiker v McClure, 456 US 188 (1982).

125. Santosky v Kramer, 455 US 745 (1982).

126. Lassiter v Department of Social Services, 452 US 18 (1981).

127. Parham v JR, 442 US 584 (1979).

128. Vitek v Jones, 445 US 480 (1980).

129. Sniadach v Family Finance Corp, 395 US 337 (1969).

130. Fuentes v Shevin, 407 US 67 (1972).

131. Mitchell v W T Grant, 416 US 600 (1975).

132. North Georgia Finish, Inc v Di-Chem, Inc, 419 US 601 (1975).

133. Brock v Roadway Express Co, 95 L Ed 2d 239 (1987).

134. West Coast Hotel v Parrish, 300 US 379 (1937).

135. Hodel v Virginia Surface Min & Recl Assn, 452 US 264 (1981); Exxon v Maryland, 437 US 117 (1978); National Road Passenger Corporation v AT & SFR 470 US 451 (1985).

136. US Dept of Agriculture v Murry, 413 US 508 (1973).

137. US Dept of Agriculture v Moreno, 413 US 528 (1973).

138. Cleveland Board of Education v LaFleur, 414 US 632 (1974).

139. Regents of University of Michigan v Ewing, 474 US 214 (1986).

140. Moore v East Cleveland, 431 US 494 (1977).

141. Roe v Wade, 410 US 113 (1973).

142. Maher v Roe, 412 US 464 (1977).

143. Akron v Akron Center for Reproductive Health, 462 US 416 (1983).

144. Thornburgh v American Coll of Obst & Gyn, 90 L Ed 2d 779 (1986).

145. Bowers v Hardwick, 92 L Ed 2d 140 (1986).

146. Kelley v Johnson, 425 US 238 (1976); Harrah Independent School District v Martin, 440 US 194 (1979).

147. Chicago, Milwaukee & St Paul Ry v Minnesota, 134 US 418 (1890).

148. Williamson Planning Comm v Hamilton Bank, 473 US (1985) quoting from Justice Holmes's opinion for the Court in Pennsylvania Coal v Mahon, 260 US 393 (1922).

149. Thompson v Consolidated Gas Corp, 300 US 55 (1937).

150. Hawaii Housing Authority et al v Midkiff, 467 US 229 (1984).

151. Pittsburgh v Alco Parking Corp, 417 US 369 (1974).

152. Agins v City of Tiburon, 447 US 255 (1980).

153. FCC v Florida Power Corp , 94 L Ed 2d 282 (1987).

154. YMCA v United States, 395 US 841 (1962).

155. Penn Central Transportation Co v City of New York, 438 US 104 (1978).

156. United States v Causby, 328 US 256 (1946).

157. Regional Rail Reorganization Act Cases, 419 US 102 (1974).

158. Kaiser Aetna v United States, 44 US 164 (1979).

159. Pennsylvania Coal Co v Mahon, 260 US 393 (1922).

160. Keystone Coal Association v DeBenedictis, 94 L Ed 2d 472 (1987).

161. Nollan v California Coastal Comm'n, 97 L Ed 2d 677 (1987).

162. United States v 564.54 Acres of Land, 441 US 506 (1979).

163. United States v 50 Acres of Land, 469 US 24 (1984).

164. First Lutheran Church v LA County, 96 L Ed 2d 250 (1987).

165. United States v Sioux Nation of Indians, 448 US 371 (1980).

Amendment VI: Criminal Court Procedures

1. United States v Ewell, 383 US 116 (1966).

2. Strunk v United States, 412 US 434 (1973).

3. United States v Ewell

4. Smith v Hooey, 393 US 374 (1969).

5. United States v Marion, 404 US 307 (1971).

6. United States v Lovasco, 431 US 783 (1977).

7. Barker v Wingo, 407 US 514 (1972).

8. In re Oliver, 333 US 257 (1948).

9. Nixon v Warner Communications, 435 US 589 (1978).

10. Gannett Co v de Pasquale, 443 US 368 (1979).

11. Press-Enterprise Co v Superior Court of California, 464 US 501 (1984); Waller v Georgia, 467 US 39 (1984).

12. Chandler v Florida, 449 US 560 (1981).

13. Sheppard v Maxwell, 384 US 333 (1966).

14. Duncan v Louisiana, 391 US 145 (1968).

15. Dyke v Taylor Implement Manufacturing Co, 391 US 216 (1968).

16. Bloom v Illinois, 391 US 194 (1968); Frank v United States, 395 US 147 (1969).

17. Williams v Florida, 399 US 78 (1970).

18. Ballew v Georgia, 435 US 223 (1978).

19. Apodaca v Oregon, 406 US 404 (1972); Johnson v Louisiana, 406 US 356 (1972).

20. Burch v Louisiana, 419 US 522 (1975).

21. Singer v United States, 380 US 24 (1965).

22. Lockhart v McCree, 90 L Ed 2d 137 (1986); Buchanan v Kentucky, 97 L Ed 2d 336 (1987).

23. Peters v Kiff, 407 US 493 (1972); Taylor v Louisiana, 419 US 522 (1975).

24. Duren v Missouri, 439 US 357 (1979).

25. Turner v Murray, 90 L Ed 2d 27 (1986).

26. Ham v South Carolina, 409 US 524 (1973).

27. Witherspoon v Illinois, 391 US 510 (1968); Adams v Texas, 448 US 38 (1980).

28. Wainwright v Witt, 469 US 412 (1985).

29. Wainwright v Witt; Lockhart v McGree, 90 L Ed 2d 137 (1986).

30. Batson v Kentucky, 90 L Ed 2d 69 (1986).

31. Ibid.

32. Pennsylvania v Ritchie, 90 L Ed 2d 40 (1987); Kentucky v Stincer, 96 L Ed 2d 631 (1987).

33. Dutton v Evans, 400 US 74 (1970).

34. Ohio v Roberts, 448 US 56 (1980).

35. Mancusi v Stubbs, 408 US 204 (1972).

36. Kentucky v Stincer, 96 L Ed 2d 631 (1987).

37. Illinois v Allen, 397 US 337 (1970); Taylor v United States, 414 US 17 (1973).

38. Davis v Alaska, 415 US 308 (1974).

39. Bruton v United States, 391 US 123 (1968); Richardson v Marsh, 95 L Ed 2d 176 (1987).

40. United States v Inadi, 475 US 387 (1986).

41. Burber v Page, 390 US 719 (1968).

42. Pennsylvania v Ritchie, 94 L Ed 2d 40 (1987).

43. Burber v Page, 390 US 719 (1968).

44. Washington v Texas, 388 US 14 (1967).

45. United States v Valenzuela-Bernal, 458 US 866 (1982).

46. Johnson v Zerbst, 304 US 458 (1938); Miranda v Arizona, 384 US 436 (1966).

47. Gideon v Wainwright, 372 US 335 (1963); Faretta v California, 422 US 806 (1975).

48. McKaskle v Wiggins, 465 US 168 (1984).

49. Moran v Burbine, 475 US 412 (1986); United States v Gouveia, 467 US 180 (1984).

50. Herring v New York, 422 US 853 (1975); Kirby v Illinois, 406 US 682 (1972); United States v Wade, 388 US 218 (1967); Moore v Illinois, 434 US 220 (1977).

51. Massiah v United States, 377 US 201 (1964); United States v Henry, 447 US 264 (1980); Maine v Moulton, 474 US 159 (1986).

52. Brewer v Williams, 430 US 387 (1977).

53. Nix v Williams, 467 US 431 (1984).

54. Evitts v Lucey, 469 US 387 (1985).

55. Ross v Moffit, 417 US 600 (1974); Pennsylvania v Finley, 95 L Ed 2d 539 (1987).

56. Morris v Slappy, 461 US 1 (1983).

57. United States v Cronic, 466 US 648 (1984); Strickland v Washington, 466 US 668 (1984).

58. Argersinger v Hamlin, 407 US 25 (1972).

59. Scott v Illinois, 440 US 367 (1979).

60. Ake v Oklahoma, 470 US 68 (1985).

Amendment VII: Trial by Jury in Common-Law Cases

1. Lorillard v Pons, 434 US 575 (1978); Curtis v Loether, 415 US 189 (1974).

2. Tull v United States, 95 L Ed 2d 365 (1987).

3. Colegrove v Battin, 413 US 149 (1973).

Amendment VIII: Bail and Cruel and Unusual Punishments

1. Stack v Boyle, 342 US 1 (1951); Schlib v Kuebel, 404 US 357 (1971).

2. United States v Salerno, 95 L Ed 2d (1987).

3. Ford v Wainwright, 91 L Ed 2d 335 (1986).

4. Rhodes v Gamble, 429 US 97 (1972).

5. Whitley v Albers, 475 US 312 (1986).

6. Estelle v Gamble, 429 US 97 (1972).

7. Coker v Georgia, 433 US 588 (1977); Hutto v Finney, 437 US 678 (1978).

8. Rummel v Estelle, 445 US 263 (1980).

9. Hutto v Davis, 454 US 370 (1982).

10. Solem v Helm, 463 US 277 (1983).

11. Robinson v California, 370 US 660 (1962).

12. Powell v Texas, 392 US 514 (1968).

13. Ingraham v Wright, 430 US 651 (1977).

14. Gardner v Florida, 430 US 349 (1977); Woodson v North Carolina, 428 US 280 (1976).

15. Chief Justice Burger in Coker v Georgia, 433 US 584 (1977).

16. Godfrey v Georgia, 446 US 420 (1980); Enmund v Florida, 458 US 782 (1982).

17. Tison v Arizona, 95 L Ed 127 (1987).

18. Justice Brennan concurring in Adams v Texas, 448 US 38 (1980).

19. Godfrey v Georgia, 446 US 420 (1980)

20. Roberts v Louisiana, 431 US 663 (1977); Summer v Shuman, 97 L Ed 2d 56 (1987).

21. Skipper v South Carolina, 90 L Ed 2d 1 (1986); Hitchcock v Dugger, 95 L Ed 2d 347 (1987).

22. Booth v Maryland, 96 L Ed 2d 440 (1987).

23. Spaziano v Florida, 468 US 447 (1984).

24. McCleskey v Kemp, 95 L Ed 2d 262 (1987).

25. Ford v Wainwright, 91 L Ed 2d 339 (1986).

Amendment IX: Rights Retained by the People

1. United Public Workers v Mitchell, 330 US 75 (1947).

2. Griswold v Connecticut, 381 US 479 (1965).

Amendment X: Reserved Powers of the States

1. United States v Butler, 297 US 1 (1936).

2. Ibid.

3. Hammer v Dagenhart, 247 US 251 (1918); Child Labor Tax Cases, 259 US 20 (1922).

4. United States v Darby Lumber Co, 312 US 100 (1941); Wickard v Filburn, 317 US 111 (1942).

5. Fry v United States, 421 US 542 (1975).

6. Garcia v San Antonio Metropolitan Transit Authority, 469 US 528 (1985).

7. United States v Tax Commission of Mississippi, 421 US 599 (1975).

8. Massachusetts v United States, 435 US 444 (1978); New York Gaslight Club v Carey, 447 US 54 (1980).

Amendment XI: Suits Against States

1. Chisholm v Georgia, 2 Dallas 419 (1793).

2. Hans v Louisiana, 134 US 1 (1890).

3. Green v Mansour, 474 US 64 (1986); Welch v Department of Highways, 97 L Ed 2d 389 (1987).

4. Lake Country Estates v Tahoe Regional Planning Agency, 440 US 391 (1979); Mt Healthy City Board of Education v Doyle, 429 US 274 (1977).

5. Nevada v Hall, 440 US 410 (1979).

6. Edelman v Jordan, 415 US 651 (1974); Florida Department of Health v Florida Nursing Home Association, 450 US 147 (1980).

7. Employees v Missouri Health Department, 411 US 279 (1973); Atascadero State Hospital v Scanlon, 473 US 234 (1985).

8. Welch v Department of Highways, 97 L Ed 2d 389 (1987).

9. Ex parte Young, 209 US 123 (1908).

10. Papasan v Allain, 92 L Ed 2d 209 (1986); Pennhurst State School & Hospital v Halderman, 465 US 89 (1984).

11. Green v Mansour, 474 US 64 (1985).

12. Ex parte Young, 209 US 123 (1908).

13. Kentucky v Graham, 473 US 159 (1985).

14. Scheuer v Rhodes, 416 US 233 (1974); Wood v Strickland, 420 US 308 (1975); Monroe v Pape, 365 US 167 (1961); Kentucky v Graham, 473 US 159 (1985).

15. Stump v Sparkman, 435 US 349 (1978).

16. Pulliam v Allen, 466 US 522 (1984).

17. Imbler v Pachtman, 424 US 409 (1976).

Amendment XIII: Slavery

1. The Slaughter House Cases, 16 Wallace 36 (1873).
2. Pollock v Williams, 322 US 4 (1944).
3. General Building Contractors v Pennsylvania, 458 US 375 (1982).
4. Jones v Alfred H Mayer Co, 392 US 409 (1968); Memphis v Greene, 451 US 100 (1981).
5. The Civil Rights Cases, 109 US 3 (1883).
6. Jones v Alfred H Mayer Co, 392 US 409 (1968).
7. McDonald v Santa Fe Trail Transportation Co, 427 US 273 (1976); Runyon v McCrary, 427 US 160 (1976); Tillman v Wheaton-Haven Recreation Association, 410 US 431 (1973); Sullivan v Little Hunt Park, 376 US 226 (1969).
8. Saint Francis College v Al-Khazraji, 95 L Ed 2d 582 (1987); Shaare Tefila Congregation v Cobb, 95 L Ed 2d 594 (1987).

Amendment XIV: Citizenship, Privileges and Immunities of United States Citizenship, Due Process, and Equal Protection of the Laws

1. Scott v Sandford, 19 Howard 393 (1857).
2. Vance v Terrazas, 444 US 252 (1980); Trop v Dulles, 356 US 86 (1958); Kennedy v Mendoza-Martinez, 372 US 144 (1963); Schneider v Rusk, 377 US 163 (1964); Afroyim v Rusk, 387 US 253 (1967).
3. Vance v Terrazas.
4. Rogers v Bellei, 401 US 815 (1971).
5. The Slaughter House Cases, 16 Wallace 36 (1873).
6. Twining v New Jersey, 211 US 78 (1908).
7. Bolling v Sharpe, 347 US 497 (1976); Washington v Legrant, 394 US 618 (1969); Richardson v Belcher, 404 US 78 (1971).
8. Dandridge v Williams, 397 US 471 (1970); Jefferson v Hackney, 406 US 535 (1972).
9. Ibid.
10. Hodel v Virginia Surface Min & Recl Assn, 452 US 264 (1981).
11. Califano v Jobst, 434 US 47 (1977)
12. Justice Marshall dissenting in Bowen v Owens, 90 L Ed 2d 316 (1986).
13. Justice Powell concurring in Schweiker v Wilson, 450 US 221 (1981).
14. United States Railroad Retirement Board v Fritz, 449 US 166 (1980).
15. Metropolitan Life Insurance Co v Ward, 470 US 869 (1985).
16. Dunn v Blumstein, 405 US 330 (1972).
17. Craig v Borden, 429 US 190 (1976).
18. Justice White for the Court quoting from Justice Cardozo in Palko v Connecticut, 302 US 319 (1937), and from Justice Powell in Moore v East Cleveland, 431 US 494 (1977), in Bowers v Hardwick, 92 L Ed 2d 140 (1986).
19. San Antonio School District v Rodriguez, 411 US 1 (1973); Roe v Wade, 410 US 113 (1973); Beal v Doe, 432 US 464 (1965); Jones v Helms, 452 US 412 (1981); Haig v Agee, 453 US 280 (1981); Califano v Aznarorian, 439 US 179 (1978); Illinois Elections Board v Socialist Workers Party, 440 US 173 (1979); Attorney General of New York v Edwardo Soto-Lopez, 90 L Ed 2d 899 (1986).
20. Papasan v Allain, 92 L Ed 2d 209 (1986).
21. Bowers v Hardwick, 92 L Ed 2d 140 (1986).
22. United States v Carolene Products Co, 304 US 144 (1938).
23. San Antonio School District v Rodriguez, 411 US 1 (1973).

24. Nyquist v Mauclet, 432 US 1 (1977); Graham v Richardson, 403 US 365 (1971); Fiallo v Bell, 430 US 787 (1977).

25. Trimble v Gordon, 430 US 762 (1977); Matthews v Lucas, 427 US 495 (1976).

26. Ibid.

27. Trimble v Gordon.

28. Beal v Doe, 432 US 438 (1977).

29. Lenhausen v Lake Shore Auto Parts Co, 410 US 356 (1973).

30. San Antonio School District v Rodriguez, 411 US 1 (1973).

31. Village of Belle Terre v Boraas, 416 US 1 (1974).

32. Idaho Employment v Smith, 434 US 100 (1977).

33. Barry v Barchi, 443 US 55 (1979).

34. Minnesota v Clover Leaf Creamery Co, 449 US 456 (1981).

35. United States Railroad Retirement Board v Fritz, 449 US 166 (1980).

36. California v Boles, 443 US 282 (1980).

37. Bown v Owens, 90 L Ed 2d 316 (1986).

38. Regan v Taxation with Representation, 461 US 540 (1983).

39. Zobel v Williams, 457 US 55 (1982).

40. Williams v Vermont, 472 US 14 (1985).

41. Cleburne v Cleburne Living Center, 473 US 432 (1985).

42. Metropolitan Life Insurance Co v Ward, 470 US 869 (1985).

43. Northeast Bancorp v Board of Governors FRS, 472 US 159 (1985).

44. Chief Justice Burger dissenting in Plyler v Doe, 457 US 202 (1982).

45. Plyler v Doe, 457 US 202 (1982).

46. Califano v Torres, 435 US 1 (1978).

47. Jones v Helms, 452 US 412 (1981).

48. Turner v Fouche, 396 US 346 (1970).

49. Hill v Stone, 421 US 289 (1975).

50. Kramer v Union Free School District, 395 US 621 (1969).

51. Eisenstadt v Baird, 405 US 438 (1972).

52. Stanley v Illinois, 405 US 645 (1972).

53. Cruz v Beto, 405 US 319 (1972).

54. Bullock v Carter, 405 US 134 (1972).

55. Palmore v Sidoti, 466 US 429 (1984).

56. San Antonio School District v Rodriguez, 411 US 1 (1973).

57. Plessy v Ferguson, 163 US 537 (1896).

58. Brown v Board of Education, 347 US 483 (1954).

59. Bazemore v Friday, 92 L Ed 2d 315 (1986).

60. Brown v Board of Education, 349 US 294 (1955).

61. Alexander v Board of Education, 396 US 19 (1969).

62. Swann v Charlotte-Mecklenburg Board of Education, 402 US 1 (1971). See also Chief Justice Burger's further elaboration in Winston-Salem/Forsythe Board of Education v Scott, 404 US 122 (1971).

63. Columbus Board of Education v Penick, 443 US 449 (1979).

64. Milliken v Bradley, 433 US 267 (1977).

65. Swann v Charlotte-Mecklenburg Board of Education, 402 US 1 (1971); Milliken v Bradley, 433 US 267 (1977).

66. Milliken v Bradley, 418 US 717 (1974).
67. Washington v Seattle School District No 1, 458 US 457 (1982).
68. Crawford v Los Angeles Board of Education, 458 US 527 (1982).
69. Mayor v Dawson, 350 US 877 (1956); Gayle v Browder, 352 US 903 (1956).
70. Loving v Virginia, 388 US 1 (1967).
71. Palmore v Sidoti, 466 US 429 (1984).
72. Justice Powell for the Court in a footnote in Wayte v United States, 470 US 598 (1985).
73. Washington v Davis, 426 US 229 (1976); Mobile v Bloden, 446 US 55 (1979); Arlington Heights v Metro Housing Corp, 429 US 252 (1977).
74. Hunter v Underwood, 471 US 222 (1985).
75. Ibid.
76. Dothard v Rawlingson, 433 US 321 (1977).
77. McCleskey v Kemp, 95 L Ed 2d 262 (1987).
78. Mobile v Bolden, 446 US 55 (1980); Rogers v Lodge, 458 US 613 (1982).
79. Board of Education of New York v Harris, 444 US 130 (1979); Texas Department of Community Affairs v Burdine, 450 US 248 (1981); Griggs v Duke Power Co, 401 US 424 (1971).
80. General Building Contractors v Pennsylvania, 458 US 375 (1983).
81. Fullilove v Klutznick, 448 US 448 (1980).
82. Regents of the University of California v Bakke, 438 US 265 (1978); Wygant v Jackson Board of Education, 89 L Ed 2d 260 (1986).
83. Regents of the University of California v Bakke, 438 US 265 (1978); Johnson v Transportation Agency, 94 L Ed 2d 615 (1987).
84. Fullilove v Klutznick, 448 US 448 (1980).
85. Johnson v Transportation Agency, 94 L 2d 615 (1987).
86. Steelworkers v Weber, 443 US 193 (1979).
87. Justice Brennan in Sheet Metal Workers v EEOC, 92 L Ed 2d 344 (1986).
88. Justice Powell in Wygant v Jackson Board of Education, 90 L Ed 2d 260 (1986).
89. Firefighters v Cleveland, 92 L Ed 2d 405 (1986); United States v Paradise, 94 L Ed 2d 203 (1987).
90. Wygant v Jackson Board of Education, 90 L Ed 2d 260 (1986).
91. Justice Marshall in Fullilove v Klutznick, 448 US 448 (1980).
92. Ambach v Norwich, 441 US 68 (1979).
93. Cabell v Chavez-Salido, 454 US 432 (1982).
94. Bernal v Fainter, 467 US 216 (1984); Graham v Richardson, 403 US 365 (1971); Nyquist v Mauclet, 432 US 1 (1977).
95. Foley v Connelie, 435 US 291 (1978); Ambach v Norwich, 441 US 68 (1979).
96. Toll v Moreno, 441 US 458 (1979), quoting DeCana v Bica, 424 US 351 (1976)
97. Toll v Moreno.
98. Bernal v Fainter, 467 US 216 (1987).
99. Pickett v Brown, 462 US 1 (1983); Mills v Habluetzel, 456 US 96 (1982), and cases cited therein.
100. San Antonio School District v Rodriguez, 411 US 1 (1973).
101. United States v Kras, 409 US 434 (1973); Boddie v Connecticut, 401 US 371 (1971).
102. Justice Rehnquist for a plurality in Clements v Fashing, 457 US 957 (1982).
103. Griffin v Illinois, 351 US 12 (1956); Douglas v California, 372 US 353 (1963); Meyer v City of Chicago, 404 US 189 (1971).
104. Ross v Moffit, 417 US 600 (1974).

105. Bearden v Georgia, 461 US 660 (1983).

106. Boddie v Connecticut, 401 US 371 (1971).

107. United States v Kras, 409 US 434 (1973).

108. Ortwein v Schwab, 410 US 656 (1973).

109. Little v Streater, 452 US 1 (1981).

110. Harper v Board of Elections, 338 US 663 (1966).

111. Massachusetts Board of Retirement v Murgia, 427 US 307 (1976); Vance v Bradley, 440 US 93 (1979).

112. Schweiker v Wilson, 450 US 221 (1981).

113. Goesaert v Cleary, 335 US 464 (1948).

114. Phillips v Martin Marietta Corp, 400 US 542 (1971).

115. Reed v Reed, 404 US 71 (1971).

116. Frontiero v Richardson, 411 US 677 (1973).

117. Stanton v Stanton, 421 US 7 (1976).

118. Craig v Borden, 429 US 190 (1976).

119. Orr v Orr, 440 US 268 (1979).

120. Caban v Mohammed, 441 US 380 (1979).

121. Califano v Westcott, 443 US 76 (1979).

122. Mississippi University for Women v Hogan, 458 US 718 (1982).

123. Davis v Passman, 442 US 228 (1979).

124. Kahan v Shevin, 416 US 351 (1974).

125. Schlesinger v Ballard, 419 US 498 (1975).

126. Califano v Webster, 430 US 313 (1977).

127. Fiallo v Bell, 430 US 787 (1977).

128. Lehr v Robertson, 463 US 248 (1983).

129. Michael M v Superior Court of Sonoma County, 450 US 464 (1981).

130. Personnel Administrator of Massachusetts v Feeney, 442 US 256 (1979).

131. Rostker v Goldberg, 453 US 57 (1981).

132. Califano v Webster, 430 US 313 (1977), and cases cited therein.

133. Dothard v Rawlinson, 433 US 321 (1977).

134. Los Angeles Department of Water and Power v Manhart, 435 US 702 (1978); General Electric Co v Gilbert, 429 US 125 (1976).

135. Ibid.

136. Regents of the University of California v Bakke, 438 US 265 (1978).

137. Johnson v Transportation Agency, 94 L Ed 2d 615 (1987).

138. Gray v Sanders, 372 US 368 (1963).

139. Moore v Ogilvie, 394 US 814 (1969).

140. Sayler Land Co v Tulare Lake Basin Water Storage District, 410 US 719 (1973); Associated Enterprises, Inc v Toltec District, 410 US 743 (1973); Ball v James, 455 US 355 (1981).

141. Wells v Edwards, 409 US 1095 (1973).

142. Reynolds v Simms, 377 US (1964), and companion cases.

143. Wells v Rockefeller, 394 US 542 (1969); Kirkpatrick v Preisler, 394 US 526 (1969).

144. Avery v Midland County, 390 US 474 (1968).

145. Hadley v Junior College District of Kansas City, 397 US 50 (1972).

146. Abate v Mundt, 403 US 182 (1971); Connor v Williams, 404 US 549 (1970); Mahan v Howell, 410 US 315 (1973).

147. Chapman v Meier, 420 US 1 (1975); Connor v Finch, 431 US 407 (1977).

148. Dean Alfange Jr, "Gerrymandering and the Constitution: Into the Thorns of the Ticket at Last," *Supreme Court Review,* 1986, p. 220.

149. Davis v Bandemer, 92 L Ed 2d 85 (1986).

150. Terry v Adams, 345 US 461 (1953).

151. Marsh v Alabama, 326 US 501 (1946).

152. Flagg Brothers, Inc v Brooks, 436 US 14 (1978), and cases cited therein.

153. Rendell-Baker v Kohn, 457 US 830 (1982).

154. Shelley v Kraemer, 344 US 1 (1948); Barrows v Jackson, 346 US 249 (1953).

155. Moose Lodge No 107 v Irvis, 407 US 163 (1972).

156. Burton v Wilmington Parking Authority, 365 US 715 (1961).

157. Reitman v Mulkey et al, 387 US 369 (1967).

158. Crawford v Los Angeles Board of Education, 458 US 527 (1982).

159. Jackson v Metropolitan Edison Co, 419 US 345 (1974).

160. Gilmore v City of Montgomery, 417 US 556 (1974).

161. Moose Lodge No 107 v Irvis, 407 US 163 (1972).

162. Norwood v Harrison, 413 US 455 (1973); Hishon v King & Spaulding, 467 US 69 (1984).

163. Roberts v Jaycees, 468 US 609 (1984); Bd of Dirs of Rotary Int'l v Rotary Club, 95 L Ed 2d 474 (1987).

164. Hishon v King & Spaulding, 467 US 69 (1984).

165. Bd of Dirs of Rotary Int'l v Rotary Club, 95 L Ed 2d 474 (1987).

166. Ibid.

167. Richardson v Ramirez, 418 US 24 (1974).

168. Hunter v Underwood, 471 US 222 (1985).

169. Civil Rights Cases, 109 US 3 (1883).

170. Katzenbach v Morgan, 384 US 641 (1966).

171. Regents of the University of California v Bakke, 438 US 256 (1978).

Amendment XV: The Right to Vote

1. Lane v Wilson, 307 US 368 (1939).

2. Smith v Allwright, 321 US 649 (1944); Terry v Adams, 345 US 461 (1953).

3. United States v Mississippi, 380 US 128 (1965); Louisiana v United States, 380 US 145 (1965).

4. Minor v Happersett, 21 Wallace 162 (1875).

5. San Antonio School District v Rodriguez, 411 US 1 (1973).

6. Rodriguez v Popular Democratic Party, 457 US 1 (1982).

7. Rome v United States, 446 US 156 (1980).

8. South Carolina v Katzenbach, 383 US 301 (1966).

9. Oregon v Mitchel, 400 US 112 (1970)

10. United Jewish Organizations v Carey, 430 US 144 (1977).

11. Mobile v Bolden, 446 US 64 (1980).

12. Thornburg v Gingles, 92 L Ed 2d 25 (1986).

Amendment XVI: Income Taxes

1. Pollock v Farmers Loan & Trust Co, 158 US 601 (1895).

Amendment XXI: Repeal of Prohibition

1. Justice O'Connor dissenting in 324 Liquor Corp v Duffy, 93 L Ed 2d 667 (1987), quoting from Justice Stevens's dissent (he did not dissent in this case) in Newport v Iacobucci, 93 L Ed 2d 334 (1986).
2. Dept of Revenue v James Beam Co, 377 US 341 (1964).
3. Bacchus Imports, Ltd v Dias, 468 US 263 (1984).
4. South Carolina v Dole, 97 L Ed 2d 171 (1987).
5. City of Newport v Iacobucci, 93 L Ed 2d 334 (1986).
6. California v LaRue, 409 US 109 (1972); New York State Liquor Authority v Bellanca, 452 US 714 (1981), City of Newport v Iacobucci, 93 L Ed 2d 334 (1986).
7. Capital Cities Cable, Inc v Crisp, 467 US 691 (1984).
8. Ibid.

Amendment XXIV: The Anti-Poll-Tax Amendment

1. Harper v Virginia Board of Elections, 383 US 663 (1966).

Amendment XXV: Presidential Disability; Vice Presidential Vacancies

1. *Time,* July 22, 1985, p. 24.
2. See William Safire, *Full Disclosure* (Garden City, N.Y.: Doubleday & Company, 1977), for a political novel dealing with the ramifications of the Twenty-fifth Amendment.

Index